THE PRACTICAL BOOK
OF
AMERICAN ANTIQUES

The
PRACTICAL BOOK
of
AMERICAN ANTIQUES

Exclusive of Furniture

REVISED AND WITH A NEW SUPPLEMENT BY

HAROLD DONALDSON EBERLEIN

and

ABBOT McCLURE

The Chapter On Early Lace By
MABEL FOSTER BAINBRIDGE

The Chapter On Sandwich Glass By
LENORE WHEELER WILLIAMS

WITH 257 ILLUSTRATIONS
THE DRAWINGS BY ABBOT McCLURE

GARDEN CITY PUBLISHING CO., INC.
GARDEN CITY, NEW YORK

FOREWORD

THE quest for American antiques is more than a temporary craze. It is the awakening of a permanent interest in the beautiful and the curious household arts of our own forebears; things which, therefore, have for us an intimate charm that no foreign products, however lovely, can ever quite replace.

For our beds to-day we are only too delighted if we can get an old American " pieced " quilt or handwoven coverlet. Favoured, indeed, are those of us who boast an handmade rug, dyed with the imperishable brews of our resourceful foremothers, or a specimen of their realistically embroidered pictures. An old slip-ware jar or an engraved bit of Stiegel glass is sufficient to give a modern drawing-room distinction and, if you want to be truly envied, search the attic for a pewter teapot, a slip-decorated plate, or a quaintly painted clock or dower-chest. In a word, whether it be the recent craze for the peasant art of Russia and Czecho-Slovakia that has led to it or not, we have wakened to the beauty of early American craftsmanship.

It is a tried and sturdy beauty, beaten out of copper and lustrous silver by honest Colonial smiths, or stitched bit by bit by the skilful fingers of Colonial maids and matrons. It is easy to learn, easy to recognise, once you know it. Every Ghiselin beaker, every Paul Revere tankard, every scalloped tin sconce and every wafer iron leads you straight into the humours of social life in those early days. American antiques afford a fascinating study that rewards us all alike—

i

collectors, amateurs and searchers for fine old things—
with the precious knowledge of our artistic heritage.

In these pages the collector will find assistance in
pursuing the objects of his quest; the average person,
who does not aspire to collect extensively, but appreci-
ates the varied work of early American artificers and
wishes to know fully and definitely about the many
antiques that are exerting an ever widening appeal,
will find set forth in detail the facts he seeks.

The record of early American achievement in the
several fields considered is one of which all Americans
may justly feel proud. Untiring search, along with
careful tabulation and comparison of data, daily adds
to our fund of knowledge regarding the work and personality of those craftsmen who left behind them such a
rich legacy of beauty and inspiration, an heritage
long forgotten and neglected but now rated at its true
worth and eagerly employed in the beautifying of our
homes, an heritage all-inclusive from the hooked rugs
under our feet or the hand-woven coverlets on our beds
to the glass in our cabinets and the silver on our tables.
In the matter of silver alone, our records of silversmiths
and their marks have been considerably augmented
within the past two or three years.

In this new and enlarged edition, therefore, the list
of silversmiths and their marks has been brought down
to date, additions have been made to the list of pewterers, supplementary material on hooked rugs has
been included in an addendum, and Sandwich glass,
previously omitted because not a little of it belonged to
the mid-nineteenth century, has now been treated in
view of the changed attitude as to what is to be considered " early American."

The general reader will find the record of early

American achievement in the decorative arts so intimately interwoven, from the outset, with the story of the nation's social and economic growth that it may not be disregarded if any value be attached to an intelligent and comprehensive knowledge of American history.

Those who seek to revive the old fireside crafts and decorative household arts—some of them have already been and others are being successfully revived in both their industrial and artistic phases—will find the following pages pregnant with suggestion.

The authors desire to express their cordial appreciation of the assistance and co-operation of the following: The Honourable A. T. Clearwater; R. T. Haines Halsey, Esq.; the officials and staff of the Metropolitan Museum for unfailing courtesy and helpfulness, especially Mr. Kent, Mr. d'Hervilly, Miss Robinson and Mr. Plimpton; Dr. Edwin AtLee Barber and the staff of the Pennsylvania Museum and School of Industrial Art; Miss Florence V. Paull of the Boston Museum of Fine Arts; the Librarian and staff of the Library Company of Philadelphia; the Librarian and staff of the Pennsylvania Historical Society; the Free Library of Philadelphia; the Library of the University of Pennsylvania; the Rector and Vestry of Christ Church, Philadelphia; the Rector and Vestry of St. Peter's Church, Philadelphia; the Essex Institute of Salem, Massachusetts; Miss Anne S. Van Cortlandt; Henry Chapman Mercer, Esq.; Dr. Frederick Tuckerman; James M. Townsend, Esq.; Charles Brendon, Esq.; John C. Nippes, Esq.; James de Wolfe Cookman, Esq.; Alfred C. Prime, Esq.; Wilfred Jordan, Esq., Curator of the State House, Philadelphia; Mr. Richard W. Lehne; Mr. James Curran; to M.

Maurice Brix, of Philadelphia, for his gracious permission to supplement the list of Philadelphia silversmiths from his own list; to *The Antiquarian* for permission to incorporate the list of pewterers in its past publications; and, finally, all those who have so faithfully assisted in the preparation of a volume requiring unusual exactitude of mechanical details.

HAROLD DONALDSON EBERLEIN
ABBOT MCCLURE

PHILADELPHIA,
NOVEMBER, 1926

CONTENTS

ILLUSTRATIONS

DOUBLETONES

3

ILLUSTRATIONS IN THE TEXT

CHRONOLOGICAL KEY OF SILVER

*The illustrations of the Chronological Key of Silver Contours appear by Courtesy of the
following:*

FIRST CHRONOLOGICAL DIVISION:

1–7.	Honourable A. T. Clearwater.
8.	J. deWolfe Cookman, Esqr.
9.	Boston Museum of Fine Arts

SECOND CHRONOLOGICAL DIVISION:

1–15.	Honourable A. T. Clearwater.

THIRD CHRONOLOGICAL DIVISION:

1–16.	Honourable A. T. Clearwater.

FOURTH CHRONOLOGICAL DIVISION:

1–4; 10–15.	Honourable A. T. Clearwater.
5 and 6.	In possession of H. D. Eberlein, Esqr.
7 and 8.	Pennsylvania Museum and School of Industrial Art.
9.	C. Hartman Kuhn Collection, Pennsylvania Museum and School of Industrial Art.

CHRONOLOGICAL SEQUENCES:

1–21.	Honourable A. T. Clearwater.

The Pieces shown in the Chronological Key of Silver are by the following makers:

FIRST CHRONOLOGICAL DIVISION:

1 and 2.	Edward Winslow	E W (in rectangle)
3.	John Cony	I C (crowned, in shaped shield, coney below)
4.	Unmarked	
5.	Garrett Onclebagh	G O B (monogram in trefoil)
6.	John Cony	Mark as above
7.	Unknown	I R
8.	Unmarked	
9.	Jeremiah Dummer	v. p. 173

SECOND CHRONOLOGICAL DIVISION:

1.	Unknown	I. W (in rectangle)
2.	Daniel Henchman	D. H (in rectangle)
3 and 4.	Daniel Henchman	Henchman (in rectangle)
5.	Paul Revere	REVERE (in rectangle)
6.	J. Clarke	J. Clarke (script, in long oval)
7.	Unknown	D. R (in shaped oval)
8.	Joseph Edwards	I. Edwards (italics, in rectangle)
9.	Nicholas Roosevelt	N R-V (monogram, in oval)
10.	David Tyler	D T (in rectangle)
11.	Unmarked	
12.	Benjamin Burt	B. Burt (italics, in rectangle)
13.	E. Davis (?)	Lion passant to right. E. D (in rectangle)
14.	John Dixwell	I.D. (in oval)
15.	Margueriette Hastier	M. H. (in rectangle)

THIRD CHRONOLOGICAL DIVISION:

1 and 2.	Unknown	I. L (in rectangle)
3 and 4.	John Burger	Burger (script, in shaped rectangle)
5.	Paul Revere	Mark as before
6.	Unknown	J & M (script, in rectangle)
7 and 8.	Paul Revere	Mark as before
9.	Unknown	R. C. (script, in shaped oval)
10	Paul Revere	Mark as before
11.	Andrew Underhill	A. Underhill (in rectangle) / A. U. (in oval)

12.	Jacob G. Lansing	I. g L (in oval)
13.	Unknown	S. R. (in rectangle)
14.	Isaac Hutton	{ HUTTON (in rectangle) ALBANY (in rectangle)
15.	Daniel van Voorhis	D. V. VOORHIS (in rectangle, twice, with eagle displayed in lozenge, between)
16.	Paul Revere	No mark

FOURTH CHRONOLOGICAL DIVISION:

1 and 2.	W. Roe	W. ROE (in rectangle)
3 and 4.	T. Keeler	T. KEELER (in rectangle)
5 and 6.	P. Gordon	P. GORDON (in rectangle)
7 and 8.	Nicholas Coleman	
9.	————	
10.	Unknown	Leopard's head in oval, I. T. (in rectangle)
11.	Unknown	Anchor, L. H. M (in rectangle)
12.	Lewis & Smith	Same, in shaped rectangle
13.	G. Forbes	G. FORBES (in rectangle)
14.	Fellows	FELLOWS (in rectangle)
15.	Dunn	DUNN (in rectangle)

CHRONOLOGICAL SEQUENCES:

1.	Benjamin Wynkoop	BWK (in heart)
2.	Hendrik Boelen	HB (in oval)
3.	John Dixwell	Mark as before
4.	Margueriette Hastier	Mark as before
5.	Samuel Drowne	S x D (in rectangle)
6.	Joseph Moulton II.	MOULTON (in rectangle)
7.	Samuel Minott	{ M (script, in rectangle) Minott (script, in rectangle)
8.	John Cony	Mark as before
9.	Joseph Edwards	Mark as before
10.	Daniel van Voorhis	Mark as before
11.	G. Forbes	Mark as before
12.	(?)	
13 and 14.	Unmarked	
15.	Paul Revere	Unmarked
16.	Daniel van Voorhis	Mark as before
17.	Benjamin Burt	Mark as before
18.	E. Davis (?)	Mark as before
19.	Joseph Moulton II	Mark as before
20.	Unknown	Mark as before
21.	Lewis & Smith	Mark as before

BIBLIOGRAPHY

Maiolica of Mexico; Edwin AtLee Barber. Printed for the Pennsylvania
    Museum and School of Industrial Art.
Stiegel Glass; Frederick William Hunter. Privately Published.
Tulipware of the Pennsylvania German Potters; Edwin AtLee Barber.
    Printed for the Pennsylvania Museum and School of Industrial Art.
Catalogue of an Exhibition of Silver, Used in New York, New Jersey and
    the South with a Note on Early New York Silversmiths by R. T.
    Haines Halsey. Published by Metropolitan Museum of Art, 1911.
American Silver; The Work of 17th and 18th Century Silversmiths. Ex-
    hibited at the Boston Museum of Fine Arts, 1906. Introduction by
    R. T. Haines Halsey; Technical Description by J. H. Buck. Pub-
    lished by Boston Museum of Fine Arts, 1906.
Old Silver Plate; J. H. Buck. Published by Gorham Co.
American Church Silver of the 17th and 18th Centuries. Exhibited at
    the Boston Museum of Fine Arts, 1911. Introduction by George
    Munson Curtis. Published by Boston Museum of Fine Arts, 1911.
Hudson-Fulton Catalogue; Silver Section. Published by the Metropolitan
    Museum of Art, 1909.
The Old Silver of American Churches; E. Alfred Jones.
Old Pewter; Malcolm Bell.
Pewter and the Amateur Collector; Edward J. Gale (exceptionally good
    for American Pewter).
Pewter Plate; an Historical and Descriptive Handbook; H. J. L. J. Massé.
Samplers and Tapestry Embroidery; Marcus B. Huish.
Quilts, Their Story and How to Make Them; Marie D. Webster.
Hand Woven Coverlets; Eliza Calvert Hall.
The Bible in Iron; Henry Chapman Mercer.
The Survival of the Mediæval Art of Illuminative Writing among Penn-
    sylvania Germans; Henry Chapman Mercer.
Early American Craftsmen; Walter A. Dyer.
Colonial Furniture in America; Luke Vincent Lockwood.
The Practical Book of Period Furniture; Eberlein and McClure.
The Architecture of Colonial America; H. D. Eberlein.
Colonial Homes of Philadelphia and Its Neighbourhood; Eberlein and
    Lippincott.
Besides these, Sundry Bulletins Published by the Metropolitan Museum,
    the Boston Museum and the Pennsylvania Museum and School of
    Industrial Art.

THE PRACTICAL BOOK OF EARLY AMERICAN ARTS AND CRAFTS

CHAPTER I

INTRODUCTORY

PRODUCTS of the decorative arts afford the visible evidence of man's progress in civilisation. This is true of the world's history considered as a whole. It is equally true of the history of each individual people. It is essentially true of our own history in both its Colonial and national phases. If we would fully know what manner of men and women laid the foundations of our country and builded thereon the first courses of a structure now grown to imposing size, if we would have a true and lively picture of their daily circumstances, we must know somewhat of the arts they practised, arts which, simple and homely as some of them were, none the less played a significant part in the lives of our forebears.

In our school and college days the political and military aspects of our Colonial past were chiefly impressed upon us and their dramatic appeal to the imagination was often emphasised at the expense of the less obviously insistent factors of social existence. In our subsequent study, the homely, quiet forces have all too often been overshadowed and put in abeyance by national affairs that loomed larger upon our mental horizon than did the products of unobtrusive craftsmanship. In consequence, comparatively little attention has been paid the less conspicuous but nevertheless

11

highly important manifestations of a deeply implanted
instinct, common to the human race in all ages and in
every land, to contrive adornment and add the perennial
interest of colour and design to everyday surroundings.
Indeed, we have sometimes been in ''danger of wholly
forgetting much that was worthy and memorable in
the lives of our forefathers.'' Furthermore, we have
been altogether too ready, in many instances, to attribute specimens of worthy craftsmanship to an imported
origin without sufficient warrant for the assumption.
This has been notably the case with regard to silver, for
how many know that there were more than four hundred
silversmiths working in the American Colonies? Thus,
through our careless ignorance, has the American
craftsman of past generations often been robbed of the
recognition that is in justice due him.

From the rude bone scratchings wrought by the
primeval cave-dwellers to the delicately finished lacquer
or the gracefully moulded and chastely decorated porce-
lains made in China in the seventeenth and eighteenth
centuries, or the wondrous fabrics and beautiful furniture produced by the artisans and craftsmen of Europe
at the same epoch, the achievements in the several
decorative arts furnish us with an eloquent commentary
upon the men and manners of each succeeding generation, and give us an insight into their social condition
and ideals more intimate than we can get in any other
way. If we remember Mr. Lethaby's dictum that ''art
is the well doing of what needs doing,'' we shall better
understand and more truly appreciate the spirit that
actuated and inspired the artificers of the past who put
into so much of their handiwork a vital quality and
livening touch of personality that shame the products

ɔf sordid industrialism to which we of to-day have become too much accustomed. If work was primitive, and it often was, it was, however, honest and possessed of strong individuality, and generally showed a striving to realise, albeit blindly and imperfectly at times, the inherently sound principle of ubiquitous grace, so dear to and so consistently practised by the Greeks, who deemed the meanest pots and pans not unworthy of comely shape and fitting ornament. Many of the articles were the product of *home manufacture,* and so it would not be fair to contrast them with the work of skilled artisans. And yet, if we do contrast them with much of the cheaper present-day merchandise it would often be to the advantage of the home-made; for, while frankly amateurish and primitive, few examples of this home-made work were downright *ugly,* as are the hideous carpets, pieces of furniture, and the like, sold by some of the cheaper establishments of to-day. Few things are more to be lamented than the lost art of "making things" formerly practised in families; in this respect American homes are far below the peasant families of Russia and Scandinavia, upon whom we look down for their ignorance, but who could, we suspect, teach us many things in the art of living. If we look for a trustworthy commentary upon the intimate social history of past nations and races in the varied record of the arts and crafts they practised and are well rewarded, we may look, with equal propriety and with equally confident expectation of fruitful results, for an insight of the greatest value into the everyday social conditions of our own land in the past from a study of the work achieved by early American craftsmanship. Incidentally, we shall both establish for ourselves a truer standard of "apprecia-

tion of our historic and artistic heritage'' and create a
''more vivid and human background'' for the events of
our national history. The industrial arts ''touch life at
many points and intimately; and the students and collectors of Americana have been, unconsciously perhaps,
reconstructing for us a more living picture of the men
and manners of a former time, and history is made
thereby a more vital thing. The collector has ceased to
be absorbed entirely by the quest for a bargain and has
become a delver after human facts.''

The story of the pursuit and development of the
decorative arts in Colonial America is replete with
varied and, needless to say, engrossing interest. From
the beginnings of European colonisation in the new
lands of the Western World to the end of the first
quarter of the nineteenth century, while the afterglow
of the Colonial period still shed its waning light and the
exercise of the decorative handicrafts had not been
wholly blotted out by the fast falling night of industrial
banality and machine-made ornament of ugly, sordid
character, we find a wide diversity in the products put
forth by the workers in the decorative crafts and an
equally wide geographical distribution of localities
where they wrought. From the lofty table land of
Mexico to the forests of Canada and Nova Scotia,
craftsmen and craftswomen plied their skill, partly in a
continuous commercial manner, partly in the occasional
creation of some homely embellishment or the adornment of some object of domestic utility.

While several of the arts considered in the following
chapters were carried on almost everywhere throughout the Colonies, others were purely local in their
practice. Still others were applied in sundry different

places where conditions favoured their pursuit. Of the arts or crafts practised more or less universally throughout the Colonies may be mentioned, besides the spinning and weaving of linen and the making of other homespun textiles, the weaving of woollen coverlets, now eagerly sought after in all parts of the country and regarded with admiration both for their colour and the beauty of their pattern; the piecing, patching and quilting of bedspreads; the working of samplers and the more ambitious embroidering of allegorical, scriptural or pastoral pictures, both forms of stitchery held in high esteem as satisfactory evidences of proper and indispensable feminine accomplishment; the embroidering of wearing apparel and lesser objects and, finally, among the activities pursued by women, the making of dyes and the dyeing of the threads or fabrics to be used in the sorts of handiwork just enumerated. These activities did more than satisfy the promptings of the world-old creative instinct; they were a source of companionship and a boon to the woman who had to endure the inevitable hours of frontier loneliness. They provided wholesome occupation for the brain as well as for the hands. If more of these household crafts were practised at the present day, contributing their quota of colour and constructive interest to humdrum and pathetically colourless lives, we should probably not hear of such appalling statistics of insanity among the wives and daughters of farmers. Many a city woman, too, might profitably take pattern from her grandmother's manual skill and industry in womanly crafts. While not a few are busied in a manner beyond criticism, there are, nevertheless, far too many whose preoccupation with bridge, and kindred devices for killing

time, could well give place to employments better calculated to increase feminine capability, charm and
dignity.

Among the decorative crafts practised by men in
practically all the Colonies, one naturally expects to
find metal work and carving in wood and stone. The
metal work includes the simpler decorative forms for
domestic or architectural use in iron, copper, brass,
lead and tin. Nor must we forget furniture making and
decorative painting on furniture, glass, tin, and other
substances—both arts pursued in distinctively local
forms, at one time or another, along the whole Atlantic
seaboard.

The arts that were purely local began, in point of
time, with the making of glass and maiolica at Puebla
in Mexico towards the end of the sixteenth century.
The next essay at making glass on the continent of
North America took place at Jamestown shortly after
the arrival of the colonists. Almost wholly local, too,
were the later attempts at making glass until nearly the
end of the eighteenth century. As will be seen in the
chapter devoted to early American glass, whether the
establishment of eighteenth century glass houses was
undertaken by Caspar Wistar, the picturesque Baron
Stiegel or their energetic New England contemporaries,
the manufacture of this brittle commodity was virtually
confined to Pennsylvania, South Jersey and Eastern
Massachusetts until the time of the Revolutionary War,
or slightly later. The making of slip-decorated pottery
was confined altogether to Pennsylvania with the exception of sporadic attempts at a similar process in
Connecticut and in West Virginia. The art of "fractur" painting also was essentially local and was prac-

tised only among the German population in certain counties in Pennsylvania.

The making of silverware, on the other hand, was practised wherever conditions were favourable to the craft of the silversmith, that is to say, in the cities and large towns or wherever there was a recognised centre of wealth. Hence Boston, Philadelphia, New York, Baltimore, Richmond, Charleston, Newport, Newburyport, Albany and various other places could boast the production of silverware of the most admirable workmanship at a very early date. Pewter was as widely made, and in much larger quantities, and the pewterers, not content with merely copying British models, originated several interesting local forms which are noted in their proper place. Allegorical painting, sign painting and very early portraiture, which is scarcely to be judged by the same standards as we are accustomed to apply under ordinary circumstances, were, like silversmithing, practised chiefly in the cities or in centres of local wealth.

Without entering into a full catalogue of all the Colonial craft activities, it is plain to be seen that every part of our country settled before the third decade of the nineteenth century has some share in early craft development, some point of interest, some cause for proper local pride. It is also to be noted that, in most cases, early American art was truly folk art. That is, it was of and by the people. Therefore it was vital. The truest and most vigorous art has generally come from the people *upward* and not from one or two individuals *downward*. Great masters in craftsmanship have been those that did the folk things pre-eminently better than their fellows. The vitality and vigour of

2

early American decorative craftsmanship are two of its greatest charms and it is gratifying to note that several traditional forms of craft expression have persisted to our own day in the Southern mountains while other forms are being revived in many different places and under widely different auspices. The industries of the Southern mountaineers have been placed on a basis pecuniarily remunerative to the workers, and their wares are marketed in the cities of the North by philanthropists whose laudable philanthropy consists largely in helping others to help themselves. The excellent and growing collections of Americana in our museums are doing much to stimulate interest in the old and to encourage the effort at revivals. If the following chapters shall contribute to an increased and patriotic appreciation of the decorative craftsmanship of our forefathers or yield encouragement to the more vigorously constructive task of reviving for our own use what was best in the practice of bygone generations, the authors will feel the most sincere gratification.

CHAPTER II

EARLY MEXICAN MAIOLICA AND GLASS

MEXICO is a land of surprises. This is true, at least so far as most of us in America are concerned. Although Mexico is our next neighbour, we really know but little of the country or her history as compared with the knowledge of European countries deemed essential for every educated person. The majority of people, and well-informed people at that, do not know that the making of maiolica was a craft, important both artistically and commercially, as early as the last quarter of the sixteenth century, and that it so continued until near the middle of the nineteenth, when it fell into a debased condition, from which in recent years attempts have been made, and not altogether without success, to restore it to its former dignified estate.

There was a tradition that pottery like the Spanish Talavera earthenware had anciently been made somewhere in Mexico, but nothing was surely known about it until, within very recent years, the thorough investigations of Dr. E. A. Barber, of the Pennsylvania Museum and School of Industrial Art, disclosed the fact that tin-enamelled pottery was being produced soon after the Conquest. This ware students of ceramics had previously either ignored or attributed to a Spanish origin. We know, however, that from the sixteenth century onward the fabrication of this ware has gone on without interruption, and that it dropped into obscurity only in the nineteenth century, when its character declined.

19

Puebla, or Puebla de los Angeles, to give the town its full name, a city founded by the Spanish conquerors in 1531, one hundred and fifteen miles south-east of the city of Mexico, at the foot of Popocatepetl and Ixtaccihuatl, was the first seat of various manufactures introduced into the New World by European craftsmen, and here, among other enterprises, glass factories and potteries were established. For nearly three centuries Puebla was the only place where maiolica was made in the western hemisphere. The art of glazing, brought hither by Spanish maiolists—the Aztecs had made only unglazed pottery—prospered, and there is little doubt that by 1575 or 1580 Mexican-made tiles of excellent quality were produced in sufficient quantity to render the new land almost independent of Spanish importations. Tiles were not the only objects made, for the craftsmen turned out all the various articles usually fashioned by potters.

By 1653 the industry had assumed sufficient importance in Puebla to warrant the incorporation of a potters' guild with stringent regulations and penalties attached for their infraction. The manufacture and sale of pottery were regulated by law, and no one might practise the trade of a potter without examination by the inspectors of the guild. A certain standard of quality in the wares was rigorously enjoined and jealously guarded.

PROCESSES. From the rules of the guild we learn that there were three grades of pottery: the fine, the common, and the yellow. The difference lay in the workmanship and the glaze employed. Two clays were used, white and red, being combined in equal parts. The variations in colour to be found in the body in different pieces are due to the amount of firing and not to the varying proportions of the clay ingredients. After the various pieces were shaped and allowed to dry they were put in the first kiln. When taken out of the kiln they were dipped in a liquid glaze or enamel and then allowed to dry. The decorations were next painted on in vitrifiable colours made from metallic oxides, and the pieces were then subjected to a second firing, during which the colours became incorporated with the glaze and took on the appearance of underglaze painting. The glaze for the finer ware was made of twenty-five parts of lead to six of tin; the glaze for the common and yellow ware had twenty-five parts of lead to two of tin. These lead and tin oxides were carefully baked, ground, and mixed together, and water and fine sand were added. A little molasses was also put into the mixture to make it adhesive.

COLOURS. It was permissible to use five colours in decorating the finer ware, and for the common ware three colours were permissible. This did not mean that the use of so many colours was in any sense prescribed, and many of the finest pieces have monochrome decoration. If vases and other ornamental pieces had polychrome decorations before the beginning of the eighteenth century, they have disappeared. Tiles, however, which were classed as common ware, have been found in three colours and undoubtedly date from the seventeenth century, as they were built into the walls of churches and convents erected at that period. Blue, green, and yellow were favourite hues for tile decoration. It was also enjoined in the directions for making the fine pottery that the ware was to be first painted with black "in order that its beauty might shine out."

This evidently meant that the pattern was to be outlined with black or dark brown and then filled with blue or whatever colour was to be used, for some of the early pieces were treated in this way, especially some of the pieces done in the Chinese style.

VARIETIES. The manufacture of Mexican maiolica may be divided into four well-defined phases, which began at successive dates, but several of which continued concurrently. The first was the Hispano-Moresque phase, which lasted till the end of the seventeenth century and shows a strong Moorish influence, which is characterised by the strapwork and interlacing scrolls. The second phase was the Spanish or Talavera, so called because the style of design peculiar to the maiolica made at Talavera, in Spain, furnished the inspiration for a type of decoration developed by the potters of Puebla and practised by them from about the beginning of the seventeenth century to almost the end of the eighteenth. The third phase was called the Chinese, in which the *motifs* and style were derived from the Chinese pottery and porcelain imported into Mexico in the early seventeenth century. This style made its appearance about 1650, and endured to the end of the eighteenth century. The last phase was the Hispano-Mexican or Pueblan, which began about 1800 and lasted till slightly past the middle of the century, when it sank into a totally debased commercial style. By comparing dates, therefore, we see that the Spanish or Talavera and the Chinese phases apparently possessed the greatest vitality and enjoyed the longest vogue, lasting concurrently through the greater part of two centuries.

HISPANO-MORESQUE. While it is quite true that a

good deal of pottery and a good many tiles were imported into Mexico from Spain, from which patterns
were copied or adapted, it is also quite true that the
native potteries in Puebla were flourishing vigorously
and the decorators there employed were fully capable
of developing designs that displayed not a little
originality, and this truly Mexican quality often helps
to identify them as of Pueblan origin.   The work-

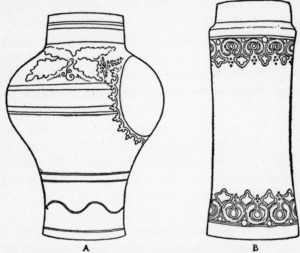

A   B

Fig. 1. A, inverted Pear-shaped Jar, blue decorations outlined with black, Talavera
period, c. 1650–1750. **B,** Albarello or Drug Jar, same period.

Courtesy of Pennsylvania Museum and School of Industrial Art, Philadelphia.

manship, too, differs somewhat from Spanish methods,
and a noticeable characteristic and almost infallible
proof of Mexican authorship is the way in which thick,
blue glaze stands out in visible relief from the surface.

TALAVERA. One of the characteristics of the Spanish
Talavera maiolica was the introduction of animal, bird,
and human forms along with flowers and foliage (Fig. 1,
A), oftentimes crowded together without the least feel-

ing of restraint in composition. Blue figure-work on a white enamel ground was also characteristic. These features the Talavera phase of Mexican maiolica incorporated, and another distinctive peculiarity is found in it besides—the tattooed ornamentation "rudely painted in dots and dashes in dark blue," which appears on many of the pieces of this period. It is distinctly impressionistic in suggestion, and must be regarded at a distance to get its real artistic value and see the coherence of its design. Another highly characteristic type of decoration found upon the Mexican Talavera maiolica consists of flowers, birds, or heavy conventional patterns, boldly silhouetted in raised dark blue, nearly covering the white surface.

CHINESE. So early as the fore part of the seventeenth century trade relations of some magnitude existed between Mexico and the Orient, and, naturally enough, a good deal of excellent porcelain and pottery from Cathay found their way through this channel to the shores of New Spain. Naturally enough, also, their presence produced an appreciable effect upon the colour, design, and shape of Mexican pottery. The Chinese influence, once introduced, lent a new refinement to the ware made at Puebla, and continued a powerful factor in the maiolica industry until quite the end of the eighteenth century. This influence is easily detected in colour, a full rich blue; in shape, in the contour of jars, which closely followed the lines of ginger jars, and, also, in the contour of vases, of which not a few were potted in the inverted pear form; finally, in types of design and methods of decoration we find not only Chinese figures and decorative *motifs* freely employed, but also a noticeable following of Chinese forms of combination.

MEXICAN MAIOLICA LAVABO: DECORATIONS IN BLUE OUTLINED
WITH BLACK, HISPANO-MORESQUE PHASE, c. 1650
Courtesy of Pennsylvania Museum and School of Industrial Art

MEXICAN MAIOLICA BARREL-SHAPED FLOWER JARS. BLUE DECORATION,
CHINESE INFLUENCE, c. 1750
Courtesy of Pennsylvania Museum and School of Industrial Art

MEXICAN MAIOLICA BATH (24" HIGH, 40" LONG). DECORA-
TIONS BLUE AND BROWN. c. 1650–1680.
TALAVERA AND CHINESE PHASES
Courtesy of Pennsylvania Museum and School of Industrial Art

MEXICAN MAIOLICA VASE, BLUE DECORA-
TION. CHINESE PHASE, c. 1700
Courtesy of Pennsylvania Museum and School of
Industrial Art

Four varieties of Chinese decoration are found in the Mexican maiolica. In the first, designs in white are reserved in a blue ground; in the second, Chinese figures appear in the scheme; in the third, the important figures are of European character, but there is a perceptible addition of Chinese *motifs,* while in the fourth variety there are white medallions upon which are conventionalised floral designs.

HISPANO-MEXICAN OR PUEBLAN. The fourth phase of Mexican maiolica, the Hispano-Mexican or Pueblan

Fig. 2. Polychrome Tile, Hispano-Mexican phase, c. 1780.
Courtesy of Pennsylvania Museum and School of Industrial Art, Philadelphia.

phase, was really ushered in during the latter part of the eighteenth century by the introduction of a greater range of colours, in which greens, purples, yellows, and browns were of frequent occurrence. By the beginning of the nineteenth century the Chinese influence was a negligible quantity and the Mexican maiolists were developing a style in which crudely drawn figures (Fig. 2) appeared. There was also greater chromatic latitude, and red, black, and other hues, in addition to those already mentioned, came into popular use. Much of the more delicate colouring, such as rose and mauve (Fig. 3), were introduced at a later date. Some of this fourth-period work was exceedingly *gauche* and clumsy, while some of it, on the contrary, was delicate in conception and beautiful in execution and colour. The period of decay had set in and, by 1850 or 1860, nearly all the ware of Puebla had sunk to a state of commercial vulgarity, with very little to redeem it.

In very recent years efforts have been made to restore the craft to its old level, and much creditable work is being produced. The movers in this renais-

Fig. 3. Bowl in green and mauve, Hispano-Mexican phase, c. 1800.
Courtesy of Pennsylvania Museum and School of Industrial Art, Philadelphia

sance of Mexican maiolica, while adhering to the old processes, are not copying the old designs nor trying to deceive purchasers. Since interest has been manifested in the old ware, fakers have sprung up and achieved a certain degree of success in counterfeiting the original pottery, so that a collector must be keen-eyed in examining specimens. By close observation, however, and comparison with authenticated pieces it is possible to detect forgeries. The objects usually found in Mexican maiolica, besides the tiles with which the façades and interiors of churches and convents were often encrusted, are albarelli or drug jars, jars for chocolate or cocoa, vases, barrel-shaped flower jars, bowls, circular dishes, salt-cellars (Fig. 4), inkstands, dishes, cup-holders, and basons.

GLASS. There is record of glass being made in Puebla at an early date, and much glass of beautiful quality and workmanship has been collected in Mexico. For a long time some of this was thought to be of Mexican origin and was so labelled in museum collec-

A   B

Fig. 4. A, Inkstand. B, Albarello. Both polychrome. Hispano-Mexican phase, c. 1800–1830.
Courtesy of Pennsylvania Museum and Schoool of Industrial Art, Philadelphia

tions. On more recent investigation, however, it turns out to have been of Spanish manufacture, made for the Mexican market. There are also simpler pieces of doubtful origin. It is impossible to say definitely whether they were made in Mexico or not.

The best collections of Mexican maiolica are in the Pennsylvania Museum of Industrial Art, Philadelphia, and the Metropolitan Museum of Art, New York City.

CHAPTER III

EARLY AMERICAN GLASS

ONCE broken, never mended. The frailty of glass is proverbial, and doubtless it is chiefly because of this unfortunate quality that the search for specimens of the glass-blowers' art, an art of absorbing interest and variety, has afforded less encouragement to collectors than some other less brittle products of the craftsman's skill. Its fragility is certainly to blame for our not having more of it left from bygone days. Even with care, accidents will befall from time to time and treasured heirlooms meet a tragic end beyond all hope of salvation from rivets or glue. And this, too, though one sedulously averts the ravages committed by well-intentioned but heavy-fingered housemaids, whose feather-dusters occasionally become veritable besoms of destruction.

Nevertheless, despite all ruin and breakage, we still have a good deal of old American glass remaining—quite enough to whet the appetite of the collector and add zest to the studies of the antiquary or historian.

In the magazines that pay more or less attention at intervals to subjects of special interest to the collector or connoisseur, old American glass has received less notice than anything else. Indeed, such scant consideration has it been accorded that not seldom do people say in an incredulous tone, on hearing it mentioned, "Old American glass—what is that?" It is only since the recently awakened wave of appreciation for the smaller antiques of American origin has swept

28

over the land that people have gone a-searching in musty, dusty, and long-neglected corners and brought to light many a vitreous treasure whose existence they had entirely forgotten or to whose charms they had hitherto been blind or indifferent.

High honour is due to glass by right of seniority among American crafts or manufacturers. Glass-making was the first manufacture engaged in by our English forefathers in North America. It was first made in Jamestown, Virginia, in 1608, and this initial essay at what is now a vast and immensely profitable industry was undertaken under the supervision of Captain Christopher Newport, while the second, a few years subsequently, was carried out under the eye of that most picturesque and redoubtable old hero, Captain John Smith.

Glass, too, if we may believe the records, formed a part of the first cargo exported from the infant colony to the Mother Country to show what could be produced on this side of the Atlantic and excite an interest among men of substance and adventurous investors at home that might redound to the profit of the settlers.

After the first manufacturing venture, we hear little or nothing of glass-making until, in 1621, a second glass-house was built in Jamestown, which continued in operation till 1625. Of the product of this old Virginia glass-house we have but a few shattered fragments and a few coloured beads that seem to have been made for trade with the Indians. In a way, therefore, the first American glass factory was also the first American mint. Eight Poles and Germans had been brought over to work at the first attempt at glass-making in 1608, and, for the second attempt, the London

Company sent out four Italians. Some of the beads produced in the second Jamestown glass-house are to be seen at Memorial Hall (a part of the Pennsylvania Museum and School of Industrial Arts), in Fairmount Park, Philadelphia. Some are round, of the bigness of a pea, some elliptical, and a few square. In colour they are "light transparent green with longitudinal white markings, opaque white and translucent turquoise." The workmanship of the beads attests a high order of skill on the part of the workers, as does also a fragment of a bowl top and a few broken bits of window glass—the only remaining evidence of the output of this short-lived undertaking.

Then glass-making was abandoned at Jamestown, and we hear no more of it till fourteen or fifteen years later, when different conditions attended the enterprise. Rude bottles, window glass, bulls' eyes or roundels, and sundry other glass articles, much needed by the colonists, began to be manufactured at Salem, Massachusetts, in 1638 or 1639, and some of the quaint specimens preserved to us, and still occasionally to be found in out-of-the-way places, date very probably from the inception of this first New England attempt. This venture was abandoned after three or four years.

The next essay at glass manufacture was made in New York. There, in 1654, we find one Jan Smeedes operating a glass-house. In 1655, a rival, Evert Duyckingk, ventured into the field. What they made we can only conjecture, for no authenticated specimens of their handiwork have come to light.

By 1683 a glass-house was in operation in Philadelphia, one Joshua Tittery, a glass-maker from Newcastle-on-Tyne, being employed in that capacity by the

"Society of Traders." In 1707, at Schwenksville, on the Perkiomen Creek, Pennsylvania, a member of the Pennypacker family founded a glass-house, which continued in operation for four or five years and produced bottles and other articles much needed by the colonists of the neighbourhood. New York followed with two factories in operation by 1732; then came Caspar Wistar's New Jersey factory in 1739, an enterprise of great importance in the annals of American glass; while Connecticut came next, in 1747; Boston records a venture in 1749, and in 1754 still another glass establishment was set up in Brooklyn by Loderwick Bamper. Between 1750 and 1760 a glass-house was operated at Quincy, Massachusetts, which seems to have turned out little else than the coarsest green bottles. Between 1753 and 1785 a glass establishment of some consequence was conducted at New Windsor, Orange County, New York, and, between 1754 and 1757, the Glass House Company in New York made "all sorts of Bottles from 1 Qt. to 3 Gallons and upwards as also a variety of other Glass Ware too tedious to mention, all at reasonable rates," and sold them, along with "Chymical Glasses" at their "Store on the late Sir Peter Warren's dock at the North River," a spot on part of the Glass House Farm.

Between 1763 and 1765, that extraordinary man, "Baron" Heinrich Wilhelm Stiegel, was starting his glass-works in Lancaster County, Pennsylvania, which, along with Caspar Wistar's earlier establishment at Wistarberg, near Allowaystown in West Jersey, may be regarded as the two Colonial enterprises of paramount distinction and significance in the manufacture of glass, both from the great variety of the products turned out and the excellence of their quality, and like-wise for the interest attaching to the personality of the founders. Both of these are treated more fully later in this chapter.

In the latter part of the eighteenth and early part of the nineteenth centuries we hear of a number of glass factories springing up and being successfully operated for various periods of time. Some were quite meteoric in their careers and disappeared as suddenly as they arose; others continued until varying local or personal conditions dictated their abandonment; while still others, with singular stability, have continued in active progress to our own day.

These factories were found scattered over different parts of the country. One was at Temple, New Hampshire (1779), another at Keene, in the same State. Boston (1787), Albany (1792), and, in Connecticut, Coventry (1813), also had important works. Besides the Caspar Wistar glass-house, founded in 1739, near Allowaystown, in Salem County, New Jersey boasted flourishing factories at Columbia (1812) and Glassboro (1775), the last named of which must be classed with some of the glass works in Kensington (Dyottville, 1771), Philadelphia, and the Baltimore glass works (1790), all of them founded in the eighteenth century and enjoying the distinction of being the "oldest glass establishments in the United States that are still in operation." It is interesting to note that glass-making was begun in Pittsburgh in 1795.

As we have noted, the chief product of the Jamestown adventure seems to have been a quantity of coloured beads for Indian trade. Not many years later, the works started at Salem, Massachusetts, engaged in

the making of bottles, and from thence onward, as one
might expect, bottles and window glass were the staple
products of the American glass factories, along with
the other articles they turned out as demand required.

The flasks and bottles blown and pressed in moulds
were a later development and enjoyed tremendous
vogue during the first half of the nineteenth century.
They were made in many colours, in a wide variety of
shapes, and the devices moulded on their sides represented every conceivable phase of American life, social,
political, or what not. There were Henry Clay bottles
and Jenny Lind bottles, Robert Fulton bottles and
Lafayette bottles, Washington bottles and Thomas Jef-
ferson bottles—in short, if any American or distinguished foreigner had attained either fame or notoriety,
it was deemed sufficient cause to make his or her likeness an outer decoration for the whiskey or rum bottles
whose contents assisted the patriotism or pride of
the possessor. The pressed glass ''cup plates,'' several
of which are shown in one of the plate illustrations,
also belonged to the first half of the nineteenth century
and were a concession to the objectionable table manners of the period which condoned the sloppy practice
of pouring tea or coffee out of cups into saucers and
drinking it therefrom. The glass ''cup plates,'' decorated with a variety of designs, as accessories to this
habit were meant to stand the dripping cups in and
keep them from soiling the table-cloth while the saucers
were perverted to an unnatural use.

After the beginning of the nineteenth century the
design of glass-ware seems to have experienced a period
of pronounced decadence, and, although a ''dyed-in-the-
wool'' collector, inspired by collecting instincts only,

3

may find much to interest him in the later productions, it is chiefly to the glass of Colonial and immediately post-Colonial days that we must turn for grace of form to delight the eye. Even the old milk bowls, pitchers, jam pots, sugar bowls, and tumblers for common use possessed a refinement of shape and a grace that captivate us. The decorative value of the old glass is very great. One needs only to glance at some of the specimens to be seen in museums and antique shops to be convinced of this. Furthermore, this decorative value is susceptible of profitable application to our own domestic needs.

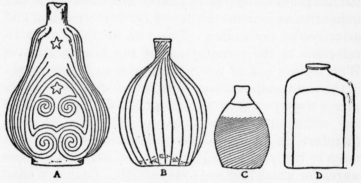

A   B   C   D

Fig. 1. Old American Bottles: A, fiddle-shaped, raised design of stars and scrolls; B, ribbed or corrugated sides; C, spiral ribbed or corrugated sides, from Pitkin Glass Works, Manchester, Conn., between 1783 and 1830, blown in patterned moulds; D, square-shouldered snuff bottle, made at Coventry, Conn., c. 1825.

Courtesy of Pennsylvania Museum and School of Industrial Art, Philadelphia.

One cannot help wondering what may have been the sources of the shapes in which many pieces of early glass were blown, for forms quite as much as anything else experience a process of evolution or, at least, are traceable to some germ of suggestion. It is not at all impossible that some of our early flask forms were patterned after Chinese prototypes brought out by East India merchants whose importations caused the Oriental note in so much of the Colonial household gear in New England and other parts of the country (Fig. 1).

Personality, in every imaginable connexion, counts for more than we ordinarily realise. Its intrinsic force and the interest it compels now and again come plainly into evidence above the surface of the prosaic, every-day affairs and lay bare the romance attaching even to business dealings and enterprises that we are apt to regard as altogether commonplace. The inherent romance attending business venture and the glamour of picturesque personality are present quite as much in the inception and pursuit of early American crafts and industries as in undertakings of far greater extent and more recent upbuilding. This was notably true with reference to the manufacture of the Wistar glass in West Jersey and of the Stiegel glass in Pennsylvania in the eighteenth century. The founders of both enterprises were men who would have made their mark in any community. Some biographical notice of each, therefore, is desirable and will doubtless contribute much to the interest and appreciation pertaining to the wares for which they were responsible. Caspar Wistar is one of those sterling figures that stand forth with refreshing piquancy in the sturdy pioneer age of our country. Baron Stiegel of Manheim presents one of the most picturesque as well as one of the least understood personalities in our Colonial history.

CASPAR WISTAR AND HIS GLASS WORKS IN WEST JERSEY

Caspar Wistar, who, in 1739, established the glass works in Salem County, in West Jersey, near what is now Allowaystown, came from Wald-Hilspach, in the Electorate of Heidelberg, and settled in Philadelphia in

1717. He engaged in mercantile pursuits and soon won recognition as a merchant of substance and active public spirit. To his merchandising he soon added manufacturing, and was highly successful as the maker of brass buttons "warranted for seven years." In 1726 he married Catherine Jansen, of Wyck, in Germantown (see "The Colonial Homes of Philadelphia and Its Neighbourhood," page 236; Eberlein and Lippincott), and in the following year was born his son Richard, who eventually succeeded him in the making of glass and in the other industries in which he was interested.

Like many another of the strenuous pioneers who aided in laying the foundations of our national prosperity, Caspar Wistar was resourceful, always had his eyes open to opportunities to be grasped, and, what was more to the point, knew how to make the best use of them when they came. He had been keenly alive to the need of glass works to supply the constant and growing demand in the Province and the adjacent Colonies, for all the previous attempts at manufacturing glass had either been abandoned as failures shortly after their inception or else had dragged out a weak and insignificant existence. Accordingly, in 1738 and the early part of the following year, he acquired several tracts of land in Salem County, in West Jersey, a site that commended itself as uniting the advantages of an abundant supply of both wood for fuel and sand and also, by no means the least important, easy access by water, as shallops and sloops could come up Alloways Creek to a wharf on the property. Here he built his glass-house and other necessary buildings, including a store for the sale of general merchandise.

Late in 1739 the factory was put into operation with

the assistance of expert artisans fetched hither from Holland. In a document dated December 7, 1738, Caspar Wistar agreed to pay Captain James Marshall for the transportation from Rotterdam of John William Wentzell, Casper Halter, John Martin Halton, and Simon Kreismeier. By the further terms of the agreement these men were to teach Caspar Wistar and his son Richard, and no one else, the mysteries of the craft of making glass. He, in return, was to "provide land, fuel, servants, food and materials," and "to advance money for all expenses, including their support, and to give them one-third of the net profits" of the undertaking.

At the period when Wistar set his glass factory in operation wealth was rapidly increasing in the Colonies, and one result of the prosperity was a corresponding increase in building. Houses were becoming larger and architecturally more imposing, and a great deal more glass was needed for glazing them than in previous years. That Wistar clearly foresaw a growing market for window glass, a market that was bound to expand rapidly under favourable conditions of supply, and that he also recognised the rich opportunity awaiting any one who could adequately meet the American demand for indispensable bottles of various types, we may be sure, knowing, as we do from his earlier history, his characteristic business acumen. The importance of the conditions just alluded to, and the improving facilities for water traffic with the other Colonies from Philadelphia as a shipping centre, doubtless influenced him in reaching a well-matured determination to engage in the enterprise under discussion. The soundness of his calculations was fully borne out by the result of the undertaking, for the factory at Wistarberg was the first important, enduring, and commercially successful venture in the manufacture of glass in the Colonies.

Under the conditions just pointed out, it was but natural that the chief output of the Wistarberg glass works should consist of window glass and bottles. But, though these two staple products insured the financial success of the new industry, sundry articles of household ware were made as the demand for them became evident or as the initiative of the workers prompted their design and manufacture from time to time. These articles included dishes, the several sorts of drinking vessels, bowls, pitchers, pickle jars, snuff canisters, scent bottles, drug bottles, lamp glasses, vases, measures, mustard pots, pitchers, and like objects of utility or decoration. Globes, tubes, and other laboratory accessories also formed a part of the output of the factory.

The technical skill displayed in the making of these miscellaneous wares was of no mean order, and, in colour and design, the pieces possessed a marked individuality and genuine refinement. Inasmuch as the skilled workmen employed at Wistarberg came from Holland, at least at the beginning of operations, it is easy to understand the characteristically Dutch forms exhibited by many of the pieces produced in the factory.

Wistar was the first American glass manufacturer to make flint glass. This he used for the white and coloured table and household ware, sometimes employing a single colour, sometimes combining several colours in the same piece or fashioning a pitcher or jar partly of transparent flint, partly of coloured glass. A rich green flint glass was evidently much favoured by the makers. Numerous pieces were also made in a rich brown with a lively amber light in it. While dark blue

was not employed to any great extent, as it was afterwards at the Stiegel works, such as was made was of
exceptionally fine quality. Interesting and varied decorative effects were obtained by superimposing coatings
of glass, in sundry patterns such as waves and spirals,
upon portions of partly finished pieces, the imposed
coating and the original body then being welded together. This method of variegation was in addition
to the combination, before mentioned, of several colours,
where one finds clear flint or emerald green with opaque
white; clear flint or emerald green with brown; blue,
green, and opaque white or blue, amber and flint. Then
there were turquoise blue glass, both opaque and transparent, and a "bluish, golden opalescent" glass, peculiar
to the factory at Wistarberg. Some of the early "bottle"
or "green" glass bowls, pitchers, and dishes showed
agreeable green, bluish-green, or brown colourings.

Caspar Wistar died in 1752, and the business was
then carried on by his son Richard, who had been associated with his father since the inception of the enterprise. In September, 1769, when the Stiegel glass works
at Manheim were flourishing vigorously, the following
advertisement appeared in the *Pennsylvania Gazette:*

> "Made at the subscriber's Glass Works between 300 and
> 400 boxes of Window glass consisting of common sizes
> 10 × 12, 9 × 11, 8 × 10, 7 × 9, 6 × 8. Lamp glasses
> or any uncommon sizes under 16 × 18 are cut on short
> notice. Most sort of bottles, gallon, ½ gallon, and
> quart, full measure ½ gallon cafe bottles, snuff and
> mustard bottles also electrofying globes and tubes &c.
> All glass American Manufacture and America ought
> also encourage her own manufacture. N.B. He also
> continues to make the Philadelphia brass buttons noted
> for their strength and such as were made by his de-
> ceased father and warranted for 7 years.
>
> RICHARD WISTAR."

There seems to be good reason to believe that the glass works continued in uninterrupted and prosperous operation until the early part of 1780. At that time the business stagnation that had undermined or seriously affected so many other American industries made it advisable to discontinue work at Wistarberg, and the factory was offered for sale in the pages of the *Pennsylvania Journal,* in October of that year, with the accompanying description of the plant:

> "Two furnaces with the necessary ovens for casting glass, drying wood &c. Near by are two flattening ovens in separate houses, a store house, a pot house, a house with tables for cutting glass, stamping mill, rolling mill for preparing glass for working pots. Dwellings for workmen. Mansion House, 6 rooms to a floor. Bake house and wash house. Store house. Retail shop kept for 30 years being a good stand 1½ miles from the Creek where shallops land from Philadelphia, 8 miles from Salem, ½ mile from good mill. 250 acres of cleared land in fence, 100 acres of mowable meadow for large stock of horses and cattle. Stalling for 60 head of cattle, a barn, granary, wood house and wood lot."

Richard Wistar died in 1781, and, by the terms of his will, his executors had authority to lease or sell the glass-house. Thus ended an exceedingly interesting chapter in the history of American glass manufacture. To Caspar Wistar and his son Richard must be accorded the credit of having founded and conducted for nearly half a century the first successful glass-making enterprise in the Colonies, and likewise the credit of producing the first flint glass. At the same time, the Wistarberg glass factory must be credited with putting forth at an early date in Colonial history decorative

MEXICAN MAIOLICA JAR (18 INCHES
HIGH). POLYCHROME DECORATION
PUEBLA PHASE. c. 1800
Courtesy of Pennsylvania Museum and
School of Industrial Art

MEXICAN MAIOLICA BASON (20¼ INCHES IN DIAMETER).
BLUE TATTOO DECORATION; TALAVERA PHASE. c. 1680
Courtesy of Albert Pepper, Esq.

1. Mexican Maiolica Salt, Polychrome Decoration. Mexican Phase, c. 1830
Courtesy of Pennsylvania Museum and School of Industrial Art
2, 3 and 4, Mexican Maiolica Drug Jars or Flower Vases. Blue Decoration.
Talavera Phase, c. 1700–1740
Courtesy of Dr. Edwin AtLee Barber

MEXICAN MAIOLICA TILES
1, 2 and 3, Chinese Phase, Dark Blue Ground, Figures Reserved in White, c. 1650–
1700; 4, Painted in Blue, Talavera and Chinese Phases, c. 1656–1680
Courtesy of Pennsylvania Museum and School of Industrial Art

glass-ware of a high order of technical merit and artistic beauty that compares most favourably with, and often far surpasses, the finished products of a much later day.

"BARON" STIEGEL OF MANHEIM

The good ship *Nancy*, Thomas Coatam, master, sailed up the Delaware in August, 1750, and on the 31st came to anchor in the port of Philadelphia, then the metropolis and most important shipping centre of the Colonies. Among her passengers was one Heinrich Wilhelm Stiegel—or Henry William Stiegel, as he later signed his name—a young German of twenty-one, hailing from the Rhine country near Cologne. His personal history prior to his coming to America and for a short period thereafter is obscure. Unfortunately, we can give but little credence to most of what has been printed about him in past years, but a considerable bulk of manuscript material relating to him and his enterprises may be found in the collection of the Pennsylvania Historical Society. Aided by these documents, and as a result of careful search in other quarters, F. W. Hunter, Esq., of New York, an enthusiastic collector and investigator, published, in 1914, a volume that has thrown much fresh light on the story of Stiegel and his ill-starred ventures.

Whatever else may be uncertain, we do know that he was a person of substance, for he soon assumed a prominent position as a landowner and iron-master in Lancaster County, whither the business associations he formed, soon after his arrival, led him. It is said of him that, dissatisfied with conditions in his native land and fired with enthusiasm by the reputed opportunities to be found in the American Colonies, he migrated hither with a fortune of forty thousand pounds to invest in the upbuilding of a new country where he might shape his future without let or hindrance from Old-World tradition or prejudice. We know, also, that in November, 1752, he married Elizabeth Huber, the daughter of Jacob Huber, of Brickerville, in Lancaster County, who owned one of the oldest iron furnaces in the Province. Not long after, he built a house near the Falls of Schuylkill, now a part of Philadelphia, and seems to have kept up an active connexion both with city concerns and his affairs in Lancaster County.

In 1757 he bought a large interest in the Brickerville establishment, tore down the old building, and replaced it by a larger and more efficient plant, which he named Elizabeth Furnace, in honour of his wife. As an independent iron-master he prospered and won wide reputation, largely augmenting, no doubt, whatever fortune he may have possessed at his arrival in America. He specialised in stoves with great success, constantly improving on early models until he finally put forth the famous "Baron Stiegel" ten-plate wood stove. He likewise introduced an improved stove form of Benjamin Franklin's open hearth. Later still he made all kinds of castings for sundry purposes, and a considerable item of his business was the supplying of sugar planters' and refiners' castings for the West India trade.

His stoves are still occasionally to be found and are sometimes ornamented with the much-favoured tulip device cast in one of the plates. Others bear the legend:

"Baron Stiegel ist der Mann
Der die Ofen Machen Kann"

also cast in one of the plates.

Whether Stiegel had or had not a right to the title of "baron" has long been a subject of dispute, but the foregoing inscription certainly lends colour to the contention of those who believe he had. His manner of life and the state he always maintained about him in his prosperous days were probably suggested by early recollections of some such ceremonious surroundings rather than the result of mere fantastic vagary and love of ostentation. The varied accomplishments of which he gave evidence from time to time also bespeak an education and training beyond the ordinary that would have ill assorted with the charlatanry of an arrant impostor.

In 1762 Stiegel associated himself with Charles and Alexander Stedman, merchants, of Philadelphia, who had bought a tract of land in Lancaster County which included the small settlement of Manheim. In this enterprise Stiegel at first had a third interest, but increased his holdings, the partnership took the name of "The Stiegel Company," and acquired more and more ground, and, eventually, gained control of more than eleven thousand acres of the most valuable mineral land in Pennsylvania. In the end Stiegel bought the interests of the Stedman brothers from Isaac Cox, of Philadelphia, and became sole owner and master of a truly baronial estate. This large investment in undeveloped lands with borrowed capital, along with disturbed economic conditions between Great Britain and her American Colonies and a too lavish expenditure for the upkeep of his personal establishment, was ultimately the cause of Stiegel's undoing. Before the blows of misfortune fell, however, he was to make his name famous, both as a manufacturer of exquisite

glass-ware that rivalled some of the choicest products
of the Old World, and as an eccentric character about
whom the generations that followed loved to relate
picturesque stories.

Soon after his association with the Stedmans,
Stiegel began to turn his attention seriously to the
making of glass, and, with his wonted energy, in a
short time put the industry on a paying basis. His
interest in this undertaking was so great that he seems
to have preferred to be known as a glass manufacturer
rather than as an iron-master. Between 1763 and 1765
he conducted the experimental steps of his new venture
at Brickerville while the larger glass works at Manheim
were a-building. The output of the Brickerville works,
of course, never rivalled the products of Manheim,
being purely commercial and consisting chiefly of
bottles and window glass. In 1763–1764, while in England, he engaged skilled English and German glass-
blowers at Bristol to come to America, and it was
doubtless to the presence of these trained workmen at
Manheim that the Stiegel glass produced there owed
much of its excellence and its well-deserved fame.

Although Stiegel had a comfortable home at Elizabeth Furnace, or Brickerville, his chief place of abode
was now at Manheim, where he had built himself a
spacious and costly house, in which he maintained a ret-
inue of servants and altogether kept up a style of life
quite in accord with the baronial title. It is said, when he
drove abroad or went from one estate to another, that
he rode in a great coach drawn by eight white horses
with outriders. A pack of hounds was wont to precede
this imposing equipage, and when the "baron" either
went out from or came back in state to his hall his de-

GLASS BEADS MADE IN JAMESTOWN, VIRGINIA, EARLY IN SEVENTEENTH
CENTURY. NINETEENTH CENTURY GLASS CUP PLATES
Courtesy of Pennsylvania Museum and School of Industrial Art

STIEGEL GLASS OF CHARACTERISTIC PATTERN: COLOURED
AND MOULDED
Courtesy of Metropolitan Museum of Art, New York City

GREEN GLASS FLOWER JAR OF NEW JERSEY   SPIRAL MOULDED PITCHER, PROBABLY
MAKE, PROBABLY FROM WISTARBERG   FROM WISTARBERG
Courtesy of John C. Nippes, Esq., Haddonfield, New Jersey

parture or return was announced by the firing of a small cannon. He is also said to have maintained a band of musicians to accompany him and play for his delectation at meals and other times, but if the truth were fully known, it would probably turn out that there were certain skilled performers among his workmen who voluntarily associated themselves for ensemble playing and occasionally gave recitals for the pleasure of their patron, who is reputed to have been no mean musician himself. In the same way it is highly probable that a thorough sifting of tradition and weighing of evidence would show the state coach with its eight horses to have been a coach-and-four, such as many people of substance kept at the time and used frequently. They were huge, lumbering concerns, high swung on springs, with folding steps to let down when the doors were opened. The coachman was perched on a high box in front, while behind, on the post-board, stood the liveried footmen. On the door panels were blasoned the arms of the owner, and there was usually some additional painted or gilt decoration. Several of these old coaches are still to be found in Philadelphia and its neighbourhood, and doubtless in other places as well, carefully treasured as curiosities by the descendants of the original possessors.

Besides the lordly house at Manheim, with its tapestried walls and the quaint chapel in which the master was accustomed to expound the Scriptures to his retainers, Stiegel built himself a commodious office and the glass works already referred to. The latter were constructed of bricks hauled from Philadelphia in Conestoga waggons to Lancaster and thence to Manheim. It is said that the bricks were imported from

England, which may or may not have been the case, as Colonial bricks are frequently termed ''English'' or ''Dutch,'' to distinguish the traditional differences in size and shape which were perpetuated among the Colonists of English or Dutch extraction.

The glass-house of these works, built in the form of a dome, was large enough, we are told, for a six-horse team to drive in, turn about, and drive out again. Here, in 1765, with thirty-five blowers in his employ, Stiegel began to produce the beautiful glass that is now so deservedly and so highly prized by all collectors and connoisseurs. The improved product won quick recognition, and the new venture proved a lucrative success, bringing the ''baron'' an income of £5000 per annum. A ready market was found for all the output of Manheim glass in Philadelphia, New York, Boston, Baltimore, Lancaster, and York. In Boston, especially, the Stiegel glass was highly esteemed and much sought for, but in all the places named large quantities were disposed of, and, even now, pieces may be found from time to time in the neighbourhoods of its greatest distribution.

In the immediate vicinity of its manufacture the field has been pretty thoroughly scoured, and most of the possessors of such pieces as remain are fully aware of its value and hold it at an almost prohibitive figure. Nevertheless, the patient and persistent collector is occasionally rewarded by a find, and the search is always well worth the effort put forth. If one is interested in collecting this now precious product of Colonial craftsmanship, which is constantly becoming more and more valuable, it is a wise thing to scrutinise carefully the recesses of every junk-shop and the shelves of every antique dealer, especially in the places where this glass once enjoyed wide favour.

In addition to the glass for personal, decorative, and table use, the Manheim factory produced an excellent quality of window glass, sheet glass, and all manner of bottles and flasks. Likewise all sorts of glass tubes and retorts for chemists and the general requisites for laboratories and scientific purposes were

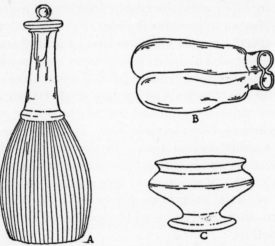

FIG. 2. A, Cologne Bottle blown in patterned mould, early nineteenth century; B, Double Bottle, early nineteenth century; C, Salt Cellar, early nineteenth Century.
Courtesy of Pennsylvania Museum and School of Industrial Art.

manufactured in large quantities. It is to the articles for domestic use, however, that Stiegel glass chiefly owes its fame (Fig. 2).

The list of these articles is exceedingly varied and includes every kind of drinking glass—goblets, tumblers, rummers, flip and toddy glasses, wine-glasses of many patterns, steins and mugs. To accompany them there were high-shouldered cordial bottles, decanters, and pitchers of sundry shapes and sizes. Besides these, there were all the necessaries for table equipment—salt cellars, pepper boxes, cruets, sugar bowls, creamers, finger bowls, vases and dishes, big and little, deep and shallow. For personal use there were ink wells, scent bottles, snuff bottles, and even small toys and ornaments.

All these objects were made in flint glass—the colourless or "white" glass—and a great number of them were also produced in glass of different colours. A rich, deep blue was the favourite colour employed, but wine, amethyst, olive, light green, and deep emerald green were also largely used. Some of the articles, too, were bi-coloured, presenting combinations of flint and blue, flint and amethyst, and blue with opaque white. The quality of the flint glass is exceptionally pure and beautiful, while the coloured pieces possess an evenness and opulence of hue of peculiar excellence. A distinguishing feature of the Stiegel glass is its "high structural tension and resultant, bell-like resonance and brittleness characteristic of all early flint glass." Its texture is universally satisfying and beautiful.

For decorative effects, besides those obtained by the use of a coloured body, Stiegel employed the processes of engraving, painting with enamel colours, and, for some of the wine glasses, the blowing of "cotton stems." A good many of the articles, too, depended for their embellishment upon their tastefully moulded surfaces of "quilted" or other designs, the condensed pattern being impressed upon them in a small pattern mould prior to being blown by hand in the open air. The "cotton stems" were so-called because of the opaque, white spirals contained in the transparent flint stems.

The engraved glass is particularly pleasing in its lightness and remarkable brilliancy, the latter quality being seemingly enhanced by the presence of the engraved design. The patterns of the engravings, while occasionally crude, are always graceful and instinct with vitality. A primitive quality of design, however, is by no means universal, and some of the patterns are of the most charming delicacy.

Much of the glass painted in enamel colours quite rivals the Bavarian glass of the same sort, both in design and execution. The favourite colours used in the decoration of the Stiegel glass were brilliant reds, yellows, blues, and white, and, under the direct personal inspiration of the "baron," his workmen achieved most remarkable results. Besides the bandings and little decorative *motifs,* the subjects chosen for representation included bold, vigorous leafage, flowers, birds, animals, and, occasionally, houses and human figures were attempted. The mug in one of the illustrations shows a castle with its turrets. Many of the conventionalised flowers and decorative bands are extremely graceful, and the lively representations of parrots and tulips, always favourite *motifs* among the Germans, are highly commendable.

Stiegel's career as a glass manufacturer came to an end when, in 1774, as the culmination of his misfortunes, which had latterly fallen upon him in close succession, he was imprisoned for debt. But, although the making of Stiegel glass ceased in an untimely manner, the impetus had been given and a high standard set, and many years were not to elapse before other attempts were made in other places to improve the average output of American glass works. None of the other

4

manufacturers, however, since Stiegel's day has ever achieved such charming and artistic results, full of the vitality of true and intelligent craftsmanship.

Stiegel's subsequent history is rather obscure, and what we do know of it is sad. He eked out a precarious existence by first one shift and then another, sometimes teaching school or giving music lessons, until his death in broken-hearted poverty.

KINDS OF GLASS

In studying the history of early American glass manufacture, there are two varieties of glass that must be considered—glass with lead as a second base, and glass with lime as a second base. The former is commonly known as "flint" glass, while the second is designated as "bottle" glass, "green" glass, or, after it has been made colourless by the use of manganese and careful processes of manufacture, as "crown" glass.

Glass is a vitreous fusion or compound of silica (usually in the shape of sand) and at least two alkaline bases, one of them being some form of either soda or potash and the other either lime or else an oxide of lead, according to whether "bottle," "green," or "crown" glass, on the one hand, is desired, or "flint" glass, on the other. The quality of the resulting glass depends upon the purity of the ingredients entering into the composition. The coarse, dark glass produced by some of the early makers, known as "black metal," was composed of ingredients with many impurities in them.

"Green" glass of a light sea-green colour, but of good quality, was the first product of American makers before Caspar Wistar entered the field. Early window glass and many of the old milk pans, bowls, pitchers, mugs, and bottles are made of this "green" glass and are beautiful in colour, texture, and shape. The small air-bubbles or "tears" very often seen in this old "green" glass are caused by insufficient "cooking." It takes from sixteen to thirty-six hours for the molten glass to cook before it is manipulated and either blown or moulded into its destined form. During the cooking process, impurities rise to the surface and are skimmed off, and the air-bubbles are thrown off at the same time. Lead glass or "flint" glass is softer than glass with a lime base, and is therefore better adapted to cutting, engraving, etching, and other processes of decorative manipulation.

ARTICLES MADE

Besides the staples of window glass and bottles, the following articles are to be found in early American glass: beads, milk pans, bowls, mugs, tumblers, goblets, wine-glasses, cordial glasses, decanters, cordial bottles, pitchers, large and small, finger bowls, sugar bowls, vases with and without covers, snuff bottles, drug bottles, scent bottles, laboratory equipments, such as tubes, globes, beakers, and flasks, of sundry shapes, pocket flasks and flasks for the cabinet, mustard jars, flip glasses, rummers, funnels, carafes, sweetmeat jars, creamers, egg glasses, salt cellars, cruets, toys, jugs, compotes, and cup plates—everything, in short, that we are nowadays accustomed to having made in glass and some things, besides, for which we generally employ some other material.

PATTERN AND METHODS OF DECORATION

Up to a certain point the names of the articles indicate the shapes that may be expected, but in certain

of the pitcher, bottle, decanter, and vase forms, especially, the nationality of the craftsman counted for much.
For instance, we find many of the articles produced at
the Wistarberg factory, where expert workmen from
Holland were first employed, showing characteristically
Dutch square and squat shapes, with bulbous lines in
the curves. On the other hand, at Manheim, where
many skilled workmen from Bristol were employed, we
find shapes that have a close affinity with contemporary
English forms.

While speaking of form, a word must be said, in

Fig. 3. A, Deep Milk Bowl of green glass made at Clark's Glass Factory, Washington,
D. C. c. 1837; B, Snuff or Drug Bottle.
Courtesy of Pennsylvania Museum and School of Industrial Art.

passing, about one article that is frequently met with of
such an unusual shape that its original purpose is often
a puzzle. This is the milk pan, a bowl-like vessel with
flaring sides and a rim with a flat lip or spout. Milk
was set away in these for the cream to rise. They are
found of varying sizes and of different depths. Fig. 3
shows one of these milk pans or bowls.

The decorative processes employed were cutting,
etching, superimposing partial coatings over a partly
finished body, enamelling in colours, and pressing in
moulds. Gilding was employed to a very slight extent
and only in the latter years of the Manheim factory.

1 and 2, "Green" Glass Saucer and Milk Bowl, New Jersey, Early Eighteenth Century
3-7, Tumblers, Wine Glasses and Milk Bowl, Eighteenth and Early Nineteenth Centuries
Courtesy of Pennsylvania Museum and School of Industrial Art
8 and 9, Bottle Mould and Moulded Bottle, Early Nineteenth Century
Courtesy of Pennsylvania Museum and School of Industrial Art

STIEGEL GLASS, COLOURED AND WHITE
Courtesy of Pennsylvania Museum and School of Industrial Art

1. Stiegel Glass Tumbler with Cover. Courtesy of Metropolitan Museum of Art, New York City. 2. Pear-shaped Bottle with Tree Device. In possession of H. D. Eberlein, Esq. 3. Stiegel Glass Multi-Coloured Enamelled Tumbler. In possession of Abbot McClure, Esq.

COLOUR

Besides the "black metal" and the light sea-green "green" glass, we commonly find transparent colourless glass, emerald green, deep green, turquoise blue, both opaque and transparent, amber, brown, amethyst, reddish purple, and opaque white. The special colours to which the Wistarberg and Manheim factories were addicted are noticed in the sections devoted to those establishments.

DECORATIVE DEVICES

The decorative devices employed for the ornamentation of glass include the following that are most usually met with: Waves and spirals where a coating has been superimposed upon another body; diamond lattices, depressed ovals and circles, parallel spiral mouldings, applied mouldings, flutings and reedings in moulded forms; lettering, foliated and floriated scrolls, flowers, especially tulips and fuchsias, birds, especially doves, in etched or engraved glass, and likewise geometrical hatchings; scrolls of leafage and sprays of flowers, human figures, animals, birds, ships, houses, trees, castles, and steeples, along with lettered scrolls or ribbon and mottoes in the enamel painted glass; in the glass pressed in moulds, such as the later bottles and the cup plates, geometrical patterns, trees, medallions with heads and representations of historical scenes or objects.

The study of early American glass is a subject that may well whet the curiosity of the historical student and the appetite of the collector. Specimens of it, and excellent specimens at that, are to be found throughout the older parts of the country. While it is a matter of historical record that great quantities of the Wistar and Stiegel glass were sold in certain localities, and while there is an especially strong likelihood of finding bits of it in those favoured neighbourhoods, the glass produced by the various other concerns is widely distributed, and any one who searches for it is almost sure to be rewarded with a find worth possessing. Stiegel and Wistar glass, too, had a habit of wandering, and one can never tell where a choice piece of it may turn up. In obscure parts of South and West Jersey excellent pieces of glass now and again come to light which it seems reasonable to ascribe to the works at Wistarberg.

Apart from all antiquarian interest attaching to the subject, there is a deal of inspiration to be derived by those who would revive traditions of national craftsmanship. While the manufacture of glass on a large scale necessitates a large plant and adequate financial backing, there are some craftsmen who have essayed in a small way to produce glass possessing exceptional artistic merit, and, in their own way, they have admirably succeeded. It would be well worth their while, however, to study past American achievements, and there can be little doubt that a return to some of the old forms and methods of decoration would meet with an enthusiastic acceptance. The best collections of early American glass are to be found in Memorial Hall (Pennsylvania Museum and School of Industrial Art), Philadelphia, and the Metropolitan Museum of Art, New York City.

CHAPTER IV

DECORATIVE METAL-WORK: IRON, BRASS, COPPER, LEAD, AND TIN

A JUNK-HEAP is a pile of possibilities. One never can tell what a little poking and grubbing in one of them may reveal. Ordinarily we do not associate the ideas of art or antiquarian research with heaps of scrap iron or other old metal, and yet it is from such scrap heaps, or from places of equal lowliness or obscurity, that many of the specimens have come that have brought to our acquaintance several crafts of no mean merit practised in Colonial America, crafts that had all but passed into utter oblivion. So little, indeed, do people in general know or realise of the deftly or curiously cast and wrought metal objects that chance occasionally brings to light, or of the circumstances of their making, that a foreign origin is more often than not attributed to them, when, in reality, they were fashioned by our own American craftsmen.

The subject of early American decorative metal work may be divided into classifications covering what was achieved with the following metals: *iron, brass, copper, lead,* and *tin.* Silver and pewter are each so important that they require separate chapters.

IRON

Iron was both cast and wrought by the Colonial craftsmen in decorative devices and patterns of greater or less elaboration as the occasion might demand. These two methods of iron working must be kept in mind in considering the work of the moulder or the

55

smith. Both methods were practised throughout the
extent of the Colonies almost from the time of their
first settlement. Cast iron, owing to the process by
which it was produced, is inflexible and brittle. It
cannot be bent, but breaks. The surface of old cast
iron is granular or smooth, according to the exposure
to which it has been subjected or the wear it has had.
Wrought iron is pliable, will bend easily, and is apt to
show slight irregularities on the surface caused by
the marks of the smith's hammer. Iron was so indispensable that furnaces were among the earliest establishments of industry, and the smith was an invaluable
member of every community. Consequently, the interest attaching to the achievements of the blacksmith
or moulder are in no sense local, but extend to every
portion of the older States.

Most of us are so accustomed to taking the ironwork we see as a matter of course that comparatively
few stop to contemplate the niceties of craftsmanship
unless something occurs to draw our attention especially to them in individual instances. The Colonial
blacksmith, therefore, generally suffers at our hands
the same lack of appreciation as does his modern suc-
cessor, and yet, in nine cases out of ten, the Colonial
smith was a far more capable and versatile artisan.
The skill that some of them showed in their work was
truly admirable, and a few of the inheritors of their
tradition of thoroughness have remained in out-of-the-
way places till recent times. The writers well remember one blacksmith who could take a ten-cent piece and
make from it an absolutely perfect miniature horse-
shoe, using only the same tools he worked with, day in
and day out, in shoeing the horses brought to him by

1 and 2. Stiegel Glass Snuff Bottle and Mug, Multi-Coloured and Enamelled.   3 and 4,
Stiegel Glass Tumbler and Mug, Etched
Courtesy of Metropolitan Museum of Art, New York City

MOULDED BOTTLES, EARLY NINETEENTH CENTURY
Courtesy of Pennsylvania Museum and School of Industrial Art.

the neighbouring farmers. With the fresh recollection
of such a feat of smithing dexterity on the part of one
of the old-school country smiths, it becomes easier to
understand and appreciate the excellence of much of
the architectural and domestic ironwork of the Colonial
and post-Colonial periods and feel a proper pride in
it as an American production.

For the sake of convenience we shall discuss the
decorative products of the early American iron worker
under the heads of *Architectural Ironwork, Domestic
Utility Ironwork,* and *Stoves and Firebacks.*

FIG. 1. Eighteenth century wrought iron Lock.
Collection of the Pennsylvania Historical Society.

ARCHITECTURAL IRONWORK. Under the head of
architectural ironwork must be included hinges of all
kinds, knobs, latches, latch grasps, handles, keys, key
plates, locks (Fig. 1), bolts, knockers, gates, railings,
foot-scrapers, weather-vanes (Fig. 2), and tie irons.

Hinges were of four types—strap, angle, T, and H.
All of them were wrought. Strap hinges were both
short and long. Sometimes they were carried across
the full breadth of a door or shutter. The expanse of
ironwork offered an invitation for decorative treatment.
At the large end, strap hinges were bent round into an
eye to fit over a thumb or upright pin fastened to the
door or window frame. Sometimes, at the thumb-end,

a strap hinge was divided into three sections and the two side pieces were turned outward in the manner of tendrils. While fulfilling a decorative purpose, this arrangement also supplied a reinforcement. In most cases, however, the strap hinge was a single strip of metal whose small end was peculiarly susceptible of ornamentation, and the smiths usually took advantage of it. The commonest form of termination was spear or cusp-shaped, single or triple, but numerous other patterns were evolved, according to the fancy of the worker. The spear-shaped ending was common to all the English Colonies. Besides this, there was another shape much favoured by the Dutch smiths of New York, North Jersey, and Long Island. Near the eye end the hinge was hammered out into a circle. The angle, the H and the T hinges are so called because of their shape. Their names sufficiently identify them, and the illustration shows their general characteristics, which remained distinct, notwithstanding numerous minor and local variations.

Knobs, latches, latch grasps, and handles followed a few well-defined types, but exhibited minor variations attributable to the fancy of the individual worker. All of them, however, had grace of proportion and evidenced a feeling for refinement of line on the part of the craftsman. While speaking of handles, attention should be directed to the combined handle and knocker to be found on many of the divided doors of Dutch New York and New Jersey.

Key plates, keys, bolts, and locks (Fig. 1) also furnished inspiration for interesting design. They were generally simple in pattern, but very often bore some little grace of adornment where a surface or contour admitted of its legitimate employment. Many of the locks and keys were of enormous size and complex mechanism, and the expanse of metal really demanded amenity of design and workmanship.

Knockers, while occasionally of unique pattern, were ordinarily wrought in simple but graceful shapes, many of which were afterwards reproduced in brass.

The opportunity afforded for decorative treatment by gates and railings was so rich and varied that a whole chapter might readily be devoted to this subject alone. Both cast and wrought iron entered into the composition of the more elaborate creations of this sort. Such ironwork is scarcely to be considered an object of the collector's quest, but it is a proper object for admiration and for emulation on the part of modern iron workers. The designs employed were characterised by refinement and ingenuity. Inasmuch as this subdivision of the subject covers such a wide field territorially and in point of varied treatment, we can only bid the reader examine carefully all the old gates and railings that chance presents to view. An abundant reward of interest awaits the quest. While it is manifestly impossible to discuss individual instances of railing ironwork at length, it would be an inexcusable oversight to pass on without calling especial attention to the several specimens illustrated. The railing from the balcony on the front of an old warehouse belonging to Stephen Girard, on Delaware Avenue, in Philadelphia, is of wrought iron. The other example is partly wrought and partly cast.

Foot-scrapers, fastened into blocks of stone or marble beside doorsteps, also lent themselves to interesting manipulation. They were both simple and ornate, but always well proportioned. The illustrations show how elaborately all these articles might be treated upon occasion.

Weather-vanes as an object of embellishment were not neglected by the Colonial architects and the smiths who wrought for them. In addition to the scrolls,

Fig. 2. Weather-vane, wrought iron, from the mill built by William Penn, Samuel Carpenter, and Caleb Pusey, at Chester, Pennsylvania, 1699.

Collection of Pennsylvania Historical Society.

tendrils, or other ornaments that graced the stock, it was not unusual for the peak to bear an appropriate device—such, for instance, as the mitre on the vane of Christ Church, Philadelphia, or the heraldic birds sur-mounting the vanes on the turrets of Mulberry Castle, in South Carolina. In the vane itself the initials of the master of the house or the date of its building were often pierced: witness the vane at Graeme Park, Horsham, Pennsylvania (see "Colonial Homes of Philadelphia and Its Neighbourhood," Eberlein and Lippincott), or the vane from Samuel Carpenter's mill shown in the illustration (Fig. 2). Then, again, the vane was not infrequently so cut that the pattern of some beast, bird, or fish would be silhouetted against the sky. Oftentimes the vanes and the stocks supporting them, as well as any accompanying metal embellishments, were gilded or painted.

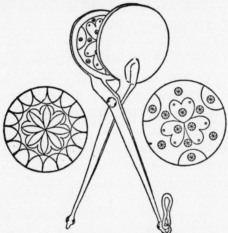

FIG. 3. Wafer Irons. Frishmuth collection, Pennsylvania Museum and School of Industrial Art.

Tie irons, used to brace the ends of beams and pull the masonry of walls in toward them, were the subjects of decorative effort in many cases. Occasionally they were shaped to form figures indicating the date of a building's erection or the initials of the owner. Then, again, they were sometimes made in fanciful devices.

DOMESTIC UTILITY IRONWORK. Among the articles included under the above category were numbered wafer irons (Fig. 3), waffle irons, trivets, gridirons, lamps, tongs, shovels, andirons, and other cooking utensils or fireplace paraphernalia.

The wafer irons are exceptionally rich in interesting design. The flat inner surfaces which came in contact with the wafer were fashioned with a great variety of designs, often exceedingly elaborate in character (Fig. 3). These designs were reproduced in relief on the baked wafer.

Trivets of more or less intricate pattern, with pierced foliation, were made in different parts of the Colonies and lent their little additional note of charm to the fireside.

Gridirons and other cooking utensils, though structurally of the utmost simplicity, were often given a decorative value and grace by making the handles or some of the bars with a spiral twist and turning the ends over in a curve.

Tongs and the handles of hearth shovels were nearly always wrought with an eye to pleasing contour, but the andirons were the articles of fireplace equipment upon which the smith spent his best efforts, both as regards general outline and the shaping of such details as feet, stocks, and finials. Many of the early andirons, wrought by obscure local smiths, possess a degree of grace that some of their more pretentious successors in brass have failed to retain.

Little iron lard-oil lamps and the so-called "betty" lamps, intended to hang on the end of a mantel or hook over the back of a chair, occasionally bore some small ornament on the handle by which the lid was lifted, or on the shank of the hook by which the lamp itself was suspended.

Then, again, very graceful hanging lamps or lanthorns with glass sides, were fashioned of wrought iron. The old lamp or lanthorn, shown in the illustration (Fig. 4), made for the Philadelphia Library in 1731 and now hanging just inside the entrance of the present building, is an excellent example of this type of lighting equipment made at an early date.

STOVE PLATES AND FIREBACKS. Many of the curious cast-iron plates that come to light now and again were,

FIG. 4. Wrought iron Lanthorn.
Courtesy of the Library Company of Philadelphia.

for a long time, regarded as firebacks, when, in truth, they are something quite different. The patient investigations and assiduous collecting of Henry Chapman Mercer, Esq., to whose painstaking antiquarian research we owe much in other fields also, have identified them as parts of the old five-plate and six-plate stoves made in the middle of the eighteenth century.

It does not, at first, sound very promising to speak about fragments of old stoves, and yet these Colonial stove plates have in them a "leaven of art" that invests them with unusual interest. Primitive they are, to be sure, but their wide variety of quaint design, the naïve conception and choice of subjects thereon depicted, and their dramatic elemental vigour of execution render them fascinating as an ingenuous expression of folk-art.

Before passing to a discussion of the individual examples illustrated, it is necessary to tell exactly how these "iron heirlooms" of Colonial life were used and in what condition they were latterly discovered. Those that had not found their way to the scrap heap of the junk dealer—thousands of them, doubtless, have gone thence to be melted and recast in some other form—had been "abandoned to rust and weather, as pavings for fireplaces, smoke-houses, and bake-ovens, as the sluices of dams and the bridges of gutters," or a score of other purposes for which they were not originally intended. The vicissitudes through which they have passed will explain their frequently battered and corroded condition, which is occasionally so bad that the device and its accompanying inscription are well-nigh indecipherable.

These plates are all approximately two feet square —some are slightly more and some are less—and five of them, clamped together, formed what has been called a "jamb stove." It consisted of a simple box, made of these plates, built into a chimney jamb or the back of a fireplace and protruding into the room it was intended to warm on the other side of the wall into which the fireplace was built. Hot, glowing embers were shovelled into this box from the fireplace and allowed to smoulder there so long as there was any heat in them. Then they were scraped out and others put in their place. The only opening from this five-plated box was in the fireplace, whence the embers were shovelled in. There was no aperture of any kind in the room to be warmed where this box-like contrivance, projecting from the wall back of the fireplace in the adjoining room, was fully visible. It became so hot from its smouldering contents that it must have proved a fairly effectual radiator. The top and bottom plates were plain, while the two side plates and the end plate were embellished with elaborate and varied cast devices. The broad bevel at one side of many of these shows where they were built into the masonry of the wall, and it is therefore an easy matter to tell whether they were made for the right or left side of the stove. The end plate, which was clamped on to the two side plates, had only a rim and no broad bevel. Sometimes the end farthest from the wall had the additional support of two stout legs. Such was the structure of the five-plate or "jamb" stove. The six-plate stove, which was introduced slightly later, stood out in the room, had a stovepipe and a fuel door and draught opening at one end, but was intended solely for heating and not for baking or cooking purposes.

From about 1740 to 1760 these stove plates were cast in great number, and this was the period of the best design. After that time there was a distinct deterioration in the character of ornamentation employed until, with the introduction and growing popularity of the "ten-plate" stove, all decorative inspiration withered and the cast embellishments descended to a low stage of commercial conventionality utterly devoid of any suggestion of craftsmanship or individual feeling.

The decorated stove plates were cast at the old furnaces in Pennsylvania and possibly also in New Jersey and other Colonies, but of the Pennsylvania

5

plates we have the fullest and most certain knowledge. They were made chiefly at Durham, Warwick, and Elizabeth furnaces, the last-named establishment being operated by "Baron" Stiegel, whose glass-making at Manheim forms the subject of a part of the chapter on "Early American Glass." The best plates, however, came from Durham and Warwick, for "Baron" Stiegel did not begin their manufacture until the period of decadence had set in. The casting was done in open sand and the moulds were made of wood, or, perhaps, in some instances, of stucco or glued clay.

Quite apart, however, from all antiquarian interest attaching to the structure and manufacture of these early five-plate or "jamb" stoves, the decorative craft brought to bear in their making was a most important consideration, and it is just there that our present concern chiefly lies. The designs chosen for their adornment were scriptural, legendary, or symbolic, and were expressed with a striking degree of vigour or a refreshingly quaint decorative sense, as the illustrations show.

The patterns of the earliest plates were executed with bold, incisive drawing and a clear-cut, free simplicity that is exceedingly impressive and well calculated to drive home the dramatic force or moral import of the incident pourtrayed, the legendary significance of the folk-lore allusion, or the mystic symbolism of the conventionalised *motifs*. In lieu of reading matter, which was not abundant, these cast designs, conspicuously and frequently presented to the eye, performed a valuable service in the way of both education for the young and diversion for their elders. One of these plates, dated 1741, depicts the death of Abel at the hands of his insanely jealous and envious brother.

Beneath a classic, festooned arcade, with the trees and vines of Eden in the background, like the setting of a stage, are the figures of the brothers in low but clear relief, costumed, curiously enough, in a garb that strongly resembles the dress of the Scottish highlanders. Burly, brawny, bare-armed Cain stands with bludgeon uplifted and just about to bring it down on the pate of pudgy little Abel, who stands before his infuriated relative with hands deprecatingly outspread. Underneath is the legend, *"Cain Seinen Bruter Awel tot Schlug,"* which might be rather literally and forcefully, though somewhat colloquially, translated, "Cain *slugged* his brother Abel dead," for the unmistakably violent action conveyed in the spirited drawing of this scene of fraternal infelicity seems to require the use of the word "slugged" rather than "struck." It will be noticed in these Pennsylvania stove plates that the inscriptions are often either partly or wholly in the peculiar local dialect form of the "Pennsylvania Dutch," and that abbreviations and phonetic spelling are also indulged in. The Cain and Abel plate is in an excellent state of preservation, as it was discovered unharmed in its original position.

Another early plate, dated 1749, sets forth the encounter between Joseph and Potiphar's wife. Mrs. Potiphar, with an air of grim and vixenish determination, has seized the mantle of chubby-cheeked Joseph, who, to judge from the direction in which his feet are turned, is making a bee-line to escape from the clutches of his resolute temptress. Were it not for the attitude of his feet, it would be hard to say whether the expression on his flabby visage is indicative of amusement or extreme sadness. The rough-and-ready and, withal, tremendously direct conception and pourtrayal of scriptural scenes and personages on these plates are quite comparable in point of unconscious humour with the treatment of some of the figures in medieval painted glass.

Still another plate, undated but of unquestionably early manufacture, shows a wedding scene and affords an insight into the manners and costume of the time in which it was cast. Under draped arches springing from fluted columns, a portly, bewigged, and begowned parson stands in a high, canopied wine-glass pulpit, about to join in matrimony the bride and groom, who approach from open doors at opposite sides of the church. The groom, also rejoicing in a curled wig, cuts an impressive figure in his long coat. The bride, a dumpy little creature, tightly grasping a nosegay in her fist, looks much like a veritable Mother Bunch or a pen-wiper in her full-tucked double cloak. It is worth noting that all the figures in these early plates present a singularly comfortable, well-fed appearance. Beneath the wedding scene is an inscription in Pennsylvania German which, being done into English, says, "Let him who will only laugh at this, make it better; many can find fault, but the real fun is to do better."

A fourth plate of the early period, dated 1747, is rather cryptic at first glance. Close inspection, however, shows that it is not one of the dramatic, descriptive, or symbolic pieces, but is purely admonitory in character. The whole treatment is just about as archaic as it could possibly be. The entire base of the plate is taken up with the legend, *"Jesus aber Sprach zu Ihm wer seine Hand an den Pflug legd und seht zurück der ist nicht geschickt zum Reich Gottes, Lc. A. 9"* (And

Jesus said unto him, no man having put his hand to the plough, and looking back, is fit for the Kingdom of God. Luke, ch. 9). This scriptural quotation supplies us with a clew to the meaning of the picture. At the left, beneath the cactus-like trees with the fluted trunk, is a plough which the ploughman, unfit for the Kingdom of Heaven, has incontinently deserted. The presence of the field to be ploughed is indicated by the gigantic weeds—or, perhaps, they are stalks of rye to be turned under—and the sun is radiantly shining at the left, in close proximity to the conventional frilled curtain that seems to have been introduced at the north-east corner for the sake of architectural amenity. What the large circular device, like an aureoled star-fish or an old-fashioned pink-iced gingerbread disc, may be, it is impossible to say.

The plate dated 1751 and bearing the cross and tulip design immediately beneath the crown of each arch is one of the symbolic sort upon which some religious sentiment was often inscribed, and is very similar in the general character of the composition to the Stiegel plate dated 1758. Tulips and hearts were always favourite *motifs,* and it is not impossible that the same craftsman may have made the moulds from which both these plates were cast. In all of them, whether of early or late date, there is a strong leaning towards the employment of architectural forms of ornament.

These stove plates, made and used in the middle of the eighteenth century by the Pennsylvania Germans, are amusing for their very primitive tone and child-like simplicity, but they are more than that, and any one who sees nought but the humorous side of them misses their true significance. Along with the art of *fractur*

and the making of slip-decorated pottery, they form one
more link in the chain that bound the peasant craftsmanship of the Rhine countries with the craftsmanship
of the immigrants in the New World. All of these crafts
were direct survivals on American soil of institutions
that were deeply rooted in mediæval German character,
and all of the articles made by the Pennsylvania
German colonists had their prototypes and precedents
in similar articles made in the Old World.

BRASS

The casting of brass was an industry or craft that
American artisans did not engage in, to any appreciable
extent, until a comparatively late date; that is to say,
till towards the latter part of the eighteenth century.
Prior to that time it had been customary to depend upon
England for such brass articles as were required.

American cast pieces having a decorative value included knockers, candlesticks, door knobs, furniture
mounts, warming pan lids, and buttons, the last named
being in great demand. The making of brass buttons,
warranted to last seven years, was, as we have seen in
the foregoing chapter, a source of very considerable
revenue to Caspar Wistar and his son Richard, of
glass fame.

In pattern the American-made knockers closely followed patterns that had previously been made in iron
or the patterns of brass knockers brought out from
England, so that it can scarcely be said that there were
any distinctively American brass knocker designs. It
is interesting to know, however, that American workmanship as exhibited in the making of knockers was in
no respect inferior to that of the imported articles. The

same is true in a general way of candlesticks, door knobs, and furniture mounts. The more elaborate work seems not to have been attempted.

Warming pan lids furnished the greatest opportunity for the brass worker to display his skill and inventive powers in decoration. Scrolls, conventional designs, oliage and flowers of all sorts were chased on the top surface of the lids. The illustration (Fig. 5) indicates the usual style followed

COPPER

The coppersmith, like the brasier, found his chief

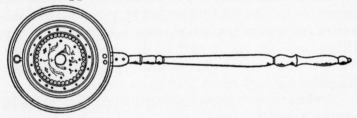

FIG. 5. Warming Pan with copper lid, chased decoration. Eighteenth century.
Collection of the Pennsylvania Historical Society.

field for decorative expression in the lids of warming pans, which were made in copper as well as in brass. The same style of chased work was employed for their ornamentation.

Sometimes figures were cut out of copper in silhouette and used to embellish tin sconces and similar objects (see Fig. 8, *A*).

LEAD

Lead has never been as popular a medium for decorative moulding in America as it has in England. Nevertheless, examples of good lead work by American artisans are not wanting. As in England, rain-water heads for down pipes gave an opportunity for the display of good craftsmanship in lead. Eagles, foliage, dates, and other devices were cast in the outer surface of the box-like head. The rain-water head bearing an open book, shown in the illustration (Fig. 6), was cast for the old building of the Philadelphia Library, at Fifth and Library Streets, Philadelphia, in 1790.

The clasped hands (Fig. 7, *B*) and the tree (Fig. 7, *A*),

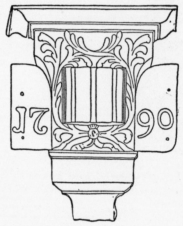

FIG. 6. Leaden Rain-water Head made for the old building of the Philadelphia Library in Library Street.
Collection of Pennsylvania Historical Society.

mounted on wooden shields and attached as badges to the fronts of eighteenth-century Philadelphia houses (the custom was continued well into the nineteenth century) by the two old fire insurance companies, the Contributionship and the Mutual Assurance (see "The Colonial Homes of Philadelphia and Its Neighbourhood," Eberlein and Lippincott, pages 33–35), were cast in lead and then painted.

Lead was also occasionally used for casting the fine

EIGHTEENTH AND EARLY NINETEENTH CENTURY PHILADELPHIA CAST AND WROUGHT IRON STEP RAILS

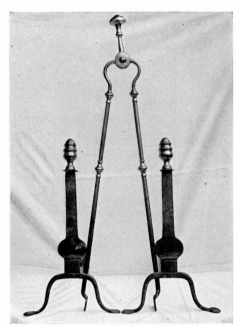

IRON ANDIRONS WITH BRASS FINIALS,
EARLY EIGHTEENTH CENTURY; STEEL TONGS.
In possession of Harold D. Eberlein, Esq.

WROUGHT IRON BALCONY RAILING FROM WAREHOUSE OF
STEPHEN GIRARD, PHILADELPHIA

detail—swags and drops or urns and similar forms—to be applied to the frieze of cornices on houses designed in the Adam style of late Georgian work.

TIN

Not a few well-fashioned articles of household utility were made of tin and decorated in various ways.   The

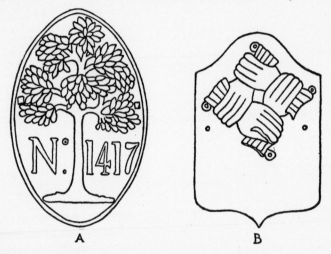

A   B

FIG. 7. A, Leaden Insurance Badge of the Mutual Assurance Company, Philadelphia; B, Leaden Insurance Badge of the Contributionship, Philadelphia, the first fire insurance company in America.

Collection of the Pennsylvania Historical Society.

tin articles of most frequent occurrence are sconces (Fig. 8, *A* and *B*), candle boxes, candlesticks, lanthorns, sand shakers, candle moulds, foot-warmers, tea-caddies, bread trays, and small tin boxes for sundry purposes.

Sconces of the simplest decorative form were made with their edges pressed into scallops (Fig. 8, *B*). Sometimes a species of simple embossing or *repoussé* work was effected by hammering. Again, decorative devices were achieved by punch-work, the punch either piercing all the way through the metal or else merely indenting it. One example illustrated (Fig. 8, A) shows the application of a silhouetted copper device to enhance the effect of the tin by contrast in colour. Yet other tin sconces with a painted decoration were japanned.

Candle boxes, made to hang in farm-house kitchens,

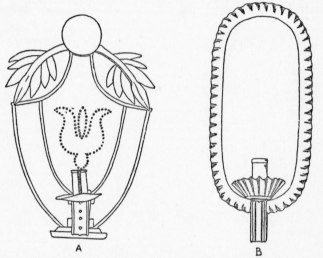

Fig. 8. A, Tin Sconce with copper circle at top, central tulip device punched. From an old church in Pennsylvania; B, Tin Sconce with scalloped edge.
Frishmuth Collection, Pennsylvania Museum and School of Industrial Art.

were often made cylindrical in shape and decorated with perforated or punched work designs.

Lanthorns, both circular and square, with conical top and a ring handle to carry them by, were decorated with a punched design, the numerous small holes permitting the light from the candle to stream through. The more holes there were, the more light the lanthorn gave. The makers made a virtue of necessity and disposed the many punctures in ingeniously ornamental patterns. The illustration (Fig. 9) will give some idea of the character of the method pursued.

Sand shakers, if decorated, were painted in the manner referred to in the chapter on "Decorative Painting."

Foot-warmers were intended to hold hot coals or heated bricks and stones, which radiated sufficient

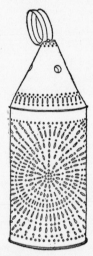

FIG. 9. Punched work Tin Lanthorn with conical top. Eighteenth century. Frishmuth Collection, Pennsylvania Museum and School of Industrial Art.

warmth to comfort those using them on long, cold rides or during the services in icy churches and meeting-houses. Like lanthorns, the more holes they had, the the better they were and the freer the radiation of heat. The holes were punched in decorative patterns. The tin box body of the foot-warmer was contained in a wooden framework with turned spindles at the corners, and there was usually a wire handle to carry it by.

The tea-caddies, bread trays, and little boxes of divers shapes and sizes were ordinarily adorned with painted designs. The style of this painted decoration is discussed in the chapter on "Decorative Painting."

In parts of Pennsylvania, tin tea and coffee pots and some other pieces of hollow-ware were occasionally decorated with engraved or scratched patterns that suggest, in their design, the "wriggled" decorations on pewter.

There is not a single phase of the early American metal work, whether it be in iron, brass, copper, lead, or tin, that is not pregnant with meaning for both the collector and the craftsman with a desire to revive what is good in the work of the eighteenth- and early nineteenth-century artisans.

The collector finds before him a field that has not been depleted by diligent search as have some others, and the field is co-extensive with all the older settled parts of the country. The increasing interest in Americana has added materially to the scope and volume of the collections in our different museums, and even such cities as Milwaukee—where there is a particularly excellent collection—far removed from the habitat of the early colonists, have creditable showings of the products of eighteenth-century American craftsmanship. All of these collections are worthy of close study and have stimulated an intelligent and widespread interest. Many of the smaller objects, which it is possible to turn up with a little search, are still as suitable for household employment as they ever were and thus possess a genuine decorative value quite apart from their rôle as curiosities of a bygone generation.

The study of the early ironwork, in particular, has a

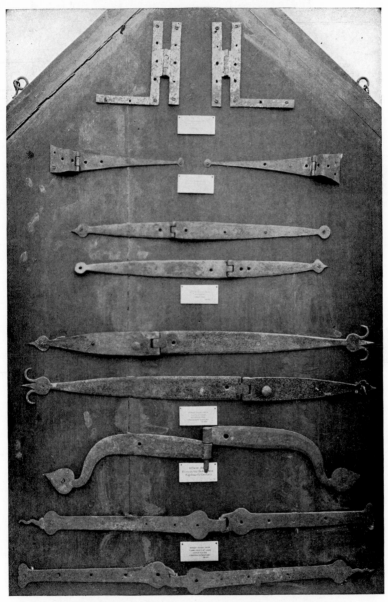

EIGHTEENTH CENTURY HINGES, WROUGHT IRON
Frishmuth Collection, Pennsylvania Museum and School of Industrial Art

PENNSYLVANIA GERMAN CAST IRON STOVEPLATE;
CAIN AND ABEL
Courtesy of Henry Chapman Mercer, Esq., Font Hill, Doyles-
town, Bucks, Pennsylvania

PENNSYLVANIA GERMAN CAST IRON STOVEPLATE BY
JOHN POTTS
Courtesy of Henry Chapman Mercer, Esq., Font Hill, Doylestown,
Bucks, Pennsylvania

very practical and applicable value over and above whatever the individual craftsman may be inspired by it to do, for it is furnishing patterns to architects for reproduction in buildings of our own day, both in the matter of hardware and exterior ornamentation.

The possibilities of an intelligent revival of lead-work are also beginning to awaken consideration. As to the smaller objects made of tin, decorators have found them so useful in filling a long-felt want that they are being reproduced, and the old style of painted decoration, also, is being attempted with varying degrees of success. It may be said in this connexion that the most successful tin decorators are those that are most familiar with the old methods and patterns. This does not imply the desirability of *copying,* but it does imply the necessity of understanding the old spirit, which had the merit of being consistent and appropriate in its manifestations with regard to both style and medium.

Metal-work has occupied a humble place in the collector's purview, but it is rich in worth, and the appreciation now awakened will go far to improve design in the making of modern objects in those same materials. Perhaps the banal, commercialised, and often positively ugly forms of the articles usually made nowadays in the metals discussed in this chapter have been largely responsible for our past attitude of indifference or contempt.

Excellent collections of Colonial metal-work are to be found in the Pennsylvania Museum of Industrial Art, Philadelphia; the Metropolitan Museum of Art, New York City; the Boston Museum of Art, Boston, and the Milwaukee Museum, Milwaukee.

CHAPTER V

EARLY AMERICAN DECORATIVE NEEDLE-CRAFT

OUR Colonial foremothers were paragons of competency. One of the most important particulars wherein this manifold capability was everywhere noticeable was their marvellous proficiency in needlecraft. For any woman, rich or poor, to lack skill with her needle or neatness in her work was held to be cause for shame and rebuke.

Admirable, however, as were the utilitarian performances in Colonial needlework, essays in the field of embroidery and ornamental lettering were quite as remarkable in their way, and are of immediate interest to us from considerations of decorative craftsmanship. Thanks to their universal skill with the needle, the women of the Colonial and post-Colonial periods were able to derive from an accomplishment that is apt to be more stressed in its homely utilitarian aspect a valuable decorative resource, and to supply thereby, with their own handiwork, a general deficiency in mural adornment and small household embellishments.

From the point of view of the collector, the social historian, and the reviver of domestic crafts alike, the achievements of decorative needlework make an appeal for consideration not local but universal in scope and affecting every part of the country with equal force. Wherever fresh settlements were planted by the newly come immigrants, thither the women of the colony brought with them the common heritage of stitchery lore that had formed an essential part of feminine education in the Old-World lands of their birth. It

78

was as much a matter of course for them to engage in the decorative manifestations of needlecraft, so far as the arduous duties of life in an untamed wilderness allowed them leisure, as it was for them to make clothing for themselves and their families Besides that, the practice of decorative stitchery, however simple or limited in extent, afforded a legitimate channel for the necessary and natural expression of creative instinct, a subject to which allusion was made in the introductory chapter, and added a wholesome and cherished object of interest in narrow lives.

The heritage of stitchery lore brought overseas by the first women colonists was perpetuated by their daughters and granddaughters, and, as leisure and affluence increased with easier conditions of existence, more extensive and more elaborate application was made of it. Just as the colonists, directly the first rigours of settlement were past and a little wealth began to accumulate, were punctilious that their attire should correspond in pattern with the modes in vogue in the Mother Country, so also were the women careful to learn and keep pace with current European fashions in the art of needlework. What were the range and variety of the seventeenth-century English needle-workers' repertoire of stitches may, to some extent, be gathered from the following lines of the poet John Taylor, written in 1640:

For tent worke, raised worke, first worke, laid worke, net worke,
Most curious purl, or rare Italian cut worke,
Fire, ferne stich, finny stitch, new stitch, chain stitch,
Brave bred stitch, fisher stitch, Irish stitch, and Queen stitch,
The Spanish stitch, Rosemary stitch, and mowle stitch,
The smarting whip stitch, back stitch, and cross stitch;
All these are good, and this we must allow,
And they are everywhere in practice now.

Add to this brave array of stitches *petit point, gros point,* and a few more that "were everywhere in practice," and one will have a fair idea of the diversity of resources open to the proficient needlewoman. That some of the women who crossed the Atlantic to the American wilderness to make their homes were highly skilled in the art of needlecraft is a matter of historical record, and the samplers they brought with them are still in existence to attest the fact. Thus we may see that, from the very first, the practice of fine stitchery had a good start upon American soil.

So indispensable was skill in the finer branches of needlework considered, all during the eighteenth and the early part of the nineteenth century, that, in a great number of cases, girls were not left to pick up at home what proficiency they could, but were sent to instructresses who conducted schools for the express purpose. Advertisements in the newspapers of the period bear witness to the prevalence of professional instruction in the niceties of embroidery and kindred subjects, and in some of the "young ladies' finishing schools" advanced needlework was the chief item of the curriculum. The following incident will serve to show the importance attached to aptitude with the needle as a dominant feature in feminine education. One illustration shows an embroidered picture, worked by a maiden of Salem, in West Jersey, in 17—. She had been sent to Philadelphia to receive the "finishing touches" and spent a year in the metropolis. As the result of her year's training she brought back the embroidered picture. It was a diploma that spoke for itself and by visible evidence substantially attested the reason for giving it.

When referring to early American decorative

needlecraft, one is too apt to have in mind only the
samplers that our grandmothers and great-grand-
mothers worked as children, and to forget the embroidered pictures, the sprays of flowers and leaves with
perching birds, wrought on a white satin background,
the mirror tops, the fire-screens and chair seats, the
purses, bags and needlecases, and, finally, the sundry
articles of clothing, for both women and men, embellished with fine embroidery. All of these articles were
duly appreciated and cherished by the generations that
made them, and bequeathed as valued possessions, deserving of specific mention in wills and inventories.
Many an embroidered skirt or waistcoat was handed
down from one possessor to another and treasured by
each owner in turn. When the frock or other piece of
apparel, for which the embroidery was an embellishment, wore out, as often as not the embroidery was
removed and put to some new decorative use. Thus
the panels of the white altar frontal in St. Peter's
Church, Philadelphia, are made from the embroidered
satin wedding gown of one of the former members of
the parish. The embroidery was exquisitely wrought,
but the gown, a treasured heirloom, was falling to
pieces, and it was deemed that no better or more pious
use could be made of the embroidery than by converting
it into part of an altar antependium.

Inasmuch as the phases of early American decorative needlecraft were so many and so varied, it will
conduce to a clear and orderly understanding of the
subject if we observe certain classifications rather than
attempt an unclassified discussion. The most natural
divisions will be as follows: *Samplers, Pictorial Embroidery, Patchwork, Quilting* and *Embroidery for the*

6

Enrichment of Personal Attire and Domestic Articles
of utility or adornment. The last class covers a wide
field of needlework activity, embracing even the marking of household linen and clothing. All of these sorts
of needlework were universally and concurrently practised throughout the extent of the land.

SAMPLERS

A sampler, as its name denotes, was an example
both of the repertoire of stitches to be used and of the
worker's mastery of them. It was also, to some extent,
an example of the worker's command of design and
lettering, the latter an important item of stitchery as
well as the former, since personal and household
linen had to be appropriately marked with initials
and numbers.

The well-spring of English tradition, whence came
the immediate inspiration and precedent for early
American needlecraft, is in itself of singular interest.
As early as Tudor times, embroidered pictures were
executed, wrought at first in emulation of tapestry, and
in the Stuart period they appeared in considerable
number and with a degree of variety that adds appre-
ciably to the fascination of their study. These tapestry
pictures, in point of date, precede the earliest samplers
of which there are any remaining specimens.

The sampler did not spring into being as a fully
developed creation. Like most other things, it under-
went a course of evolution, and the steps of this evolutionary process it is necessary for us to trace briefly.
The sampler is unquestionably of great antiquity, and
numerous allusions in contemporary literature show
that it occupied a well-recognised position in the realm

of needlework for centuries before the date to which the oldest existing specimens can be ascribed. But, although there can be no doubt of the sampler's existence and popularity prior to that period, there seems to be, curiously enough, an absolute lack of examples before the end of the first quarter of the seventeenth century. In nearly every case the seventeenth-century sampler was a marvel of needle dexterity and was worked in sundry decorative patterns and in the various stitches that were habitually employed in the embroidered pictures, settee and chair covers, bed hangings, or any of the divers other pieces of stitched household or clothing embellishment. In most cases it contained excellent specimens of drawn work, also. Being intended for drawn-work patterns as well as for the display of embroidery designs, its body or groundwork was of stout linen, and this fact partly accounts for the good state of preservation of the specimens that have escaped loss or absolute destruction.

The seventeenth-century sampler was long and narrow, as compared with the shape common at a later period, being about a quarter of a yard wide and over a yard in length. It could be rolled up as it was worked, to suit the convenience of the worker, and could also be put away in that form, for reference, if desired. Its purpose seems to have been primarily utilitarian and not ornamental, "consisting originally of odds and ends of decorative design, both for embroidery and lace-work, scattered without any order over the surface" or else worked across the breadth in horizontal courses, so that it was evidently intended as a collection of patterns and stitches that could be adapted and applied to the decoration of specific objects of apparel or household equipment as occasion might require. It was, in the strictest sense, a sampler or example to be referred to, and was presumably worked by women who had reached a point of discrimination and skill at which they needed and could use intelligently such a set of fragmentary suggestions in elaborating a finished scheme of embroidery design.

The samplers of this description known to have been brought from England to America by the early colonists, alluded to in the fore part of this chapter, were three in number. No doubt there were others, too, but it will suffice to mention three, because their record is so clear. The earliest is that of Anne Gower, first wife of Governour Endicott, and is now preserved in the Essex Institute, at Salem, Massachusetts. Governour Endicott's wife went to Salem in 1628 and died the next year, so that the sampler must have been worked somewhat prior to that time. The second is in the collection in Pilgrim Hall, Plymouth, and was worked by Lora Standish, daughter of Miles Standish. The third is dated 1654 and bears the names of Miles and Abigail Fleetwood. Judging from the appearance of the names of both husband and wife, it was presumably worked at some time subsequent to their marriage.

Towards the latter part of the seventeenth century, texts and verses began to occupy an increasingly prominent place in the composition of the sampler until, in the course of general decadence, the decorative devices —they were, be it remembered, detached and unrelated specimens of *motifs* to be employed on such pieces of work as chair and settee covers, bed hangings, window draperies, or articles of clothing and personal use— were gradually supplanted and the sampler became

JOSEPH AND POTIPHAR'S WIFE

WEDDING SCENE

PENNSYLVANIA GERMAN CAST IRON STOVEPLATES

Courtesy of Henry Chapman Mercer, Esq., Font Hill, Doylestown, Bucks, Pennsylvania

PENNSYLVANIA GERMAN CAST IRON STOVEPLATE BY
"BARON" STIEGEL

Courtesy of Henry Chapman Mercer, Esq., Font Hill, Doylestown,
Bucks, Pennsylvania

PENNSYLVANIA GERMAN CAST IRON STOVEPLATE BY "BARON"
STIEGEL

Courtesy of Henry Chapman Mercer, Esq., Font Hill, Doylestown, Bucks,
Pennsylvania

virtually a vehicle for the display of lettering and numerals, usually done in cross-stitch. Nearly all the old variety and deftness of stitchery disappeared, as did also the drawn-work patterns. With this prefatory explanation of the seventeenth-century sampler in mind and its position as an antecedent to the more familiar form numerously represented by eighteenth-century American specimens, we may address ourselves to a more particular discussion of the sampler's development in the Colonies. Seventeenth-century samplers are rare and precious in England, but ten times more so in America.

We have said that the sampler was both a study of designs and stitches for extended reproduction and, at the same time, a specimen of the worker's command of design and skill in lettering. It was, indeed, both of these, but the first aspect was the really important and essential one during the seventeenth century, while the second was emphasised during the eighteenth century and subsequently—so much so, in fact, that the original intention was ultimately lost sight of altogether. The transition from one phase to the other, though gradual and evolutionary, was none the less complete and significant. At one end of the scale we see the sampler a potential example of what could be done; at the other we see it a specimen of what the individual worker could do. In the former instance it stood in the place of a pattern book for reference, to be used by the skilled worker in applying her prowess with the needle to mature creative work; in the latter it was, for the most part, merely a record of comparatively jejune achievement in lettering or indifferent, and sometimes perfunctory, application of design, often wrought by a child of tender years.

Close akin to samplers in general form, decorative aspect, and method of stitchery were the towel covers of the eighteenth century and fore part of the nineteenth, wrought chiefly by Pennsylvania German women to hang over the common towel on the back of the kitchen door when the kitchen was put to rights or arrayed in holiday attire against the expected arrival of "company." These towel covers, two of which are shown in the illustration, were usually made by sewing two or more small linen towels together, all of which were duly worked in cross-stitch and sampler-like devices.

PURPOSE. In its lowest condition, the sampler occupied a position analogous to that of a child's copy-book at school. The only difference was that letters were written in one with pen and ink and worked on the other with needle and silk or yarn. It was duly recorded thereon that Ann, Jane, or Maria had done these alphabets of large and small letters and these numerals at the age of eight, nine or ten years. If Ann, Jane, or Maria were ambitious or their preceptresses urgent, they might dignify their work with a stiff little border in cross-stitch or with some unrelated devices scattered here and there where space permitted. The *chef d'œuvre* was then framed and hung up as an exhibition trophy of the state of proficiency to which Ann, Jane, or Maria had advanced, just like a good report gained at school or a graduation certificate. Under such circumstances, although the colour might be pleasing and to some extent diverting, the sampler could scarcely be regarded as a valuable decorative adjunct.

In their better form, quite as numerously represented, fortunately, as the glorified alphabets and

numerals, samplers showed a degree of both pictorial
and decorative sense on the part of their makers. The
decadence in both pictorial and strictly decorative
needlework at the end of the seventeenth century in
England may, in part, be accounted for by the increasing abundance of domestic and imported fabrics of
brilliant colour and elaborate pattern. But the creative
instinct in both these directions could not be wholly
quenched, despite supplanting elements that ministered
to much the same needs. As it was in England, so also
was it in America. The women continued to work pictorial and decorative devices on samplers, and, in consequence, we have all grades of elaboration, from the
unpretentious alphabet sampler to the sampler devoted
chiefly to pictorial or decorative *motifs,* or both in combination. Samplers of this description formed the
connecting link with the eighteenth-century embroidered pictures and maps and the little silk or satin panels
adorned with birds and sprays of leaves, flowers, and
fruit. Indeed, in the Colonies, where the brilliant-hued
and intricately patterned woven fabrics were comparatively rare, there was even more occasion for the
decorative sampler and more incentive to work it than
there was in England. Framed and hung on the wall,
it both served its utilitarian end as a stitch pattern
and also fulfilled a useful decorative purpose, making
up, to some extent, for the scarcity of pictures or other
suitable wall adornment. Our present concern is chiefly
with the decorative sampler, and the ensuing para-
graphs deal with its several characteristics.

MATERIALS. The eighteenth- and nineteenth-century
samplers were ordinarily worked on rough canvas,
coarse linen, or coarse linen crash. The letters and

devices were wrought sometimes in silk, sometimes in woollen yarn.   Cross-stitch was always popular, although many other stitches also were employed. Usually, the shape was approximately square or else oblong, with the length slightly greater than the width. In size there was considerable variation.   Some of the samplers, especially those devoted to lettering and numerals, were very small, being only about eight inches by ten.   Others were as much as twenty inches square or even larger.

COLOUR.   In colouring, the seventeenth-century samplers were rich without being garish, and, although bright hues were used, there was a general preference for less aggressive tones, with a strong tendency toward greens, pinks, and blues of tender shades.

The eighteenth century saw a changed colour fashion, which the sampler workers manifested in their predilection for vigorous, insistent, and even raw reds, greens, yellows, and blues of tones that were frequently conflicting.   The kaleidoscopic effect was carried into the lettering as well as the borders, and the divers coloured letters in one short word often gave it the appearance of a veritable Joseph's coat.

About the middle of the eighteenth century, strong reds waned in popularity and quieter schemes, in which blacks, greens, yellows, and blues predominated, became the fashion.

DESIGN.   While the element of deliberate composition was largely lacking in the seventeenth-century samplers, because they were primarily of utilitarian intent as a record of designs and stitches to be used in other work, the altered conception of the sampler in the eighteenth century made the question of composition

PICTORIAL SAMPLER WROUGHT BY ANNA TOWNSEND OF
NEW HAVEN, 17.

Courtesy of James M. Townsend, Esq., New York City

EMBROIDERED PICTURE; A TESTIMONIAL OF ACCOMPLISH-
MENT IN STITCHERY

Courtesy of Mr. James Curran, Philadelphia

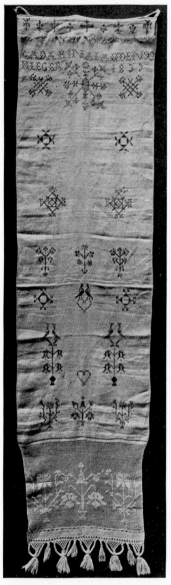

EMBROIDERED AND LACE-
TRIMMED PENNSYLVANIA
GERMAN TOWEL COVER, EARLY
NINETEENTH CENTURY

Courtesy of Metropolitan Museum
of Art, New York City

EMBROIDERED PENNSYL-
VANIA GERMAN TOWEL
COVER, NINETEENTH
CENTURY

Courtesy of John C. Nippes, Esq.,
Haddonfield, New Jersey

a matter of more moment. Even the samplers devoted almost entirely to lettering and numerals were arranged with a view to symmetrical effect, which was generally increased by some sort of border, however insignificant. In the samplers where lettering, whether in the form of alphabets or inscriptions, occupied only a part of the space and there was ample opportunity for the display of decorative features, composition became a more obvious factor, involving the choice of *motifs* and the marshalling of design. The sampler worker employed a wide range of subjects for the embellishment of her handiwork, including mottoes, texts, the human figure, architectural features, beasts, birds, flowers, fruits, leaves, tendrils, and divers miscellaneous subjects of only occasional introduction.

INSCRIPTIONS. So conspicuous a part did inscriptions play in the samplers of the eighteenth and early nineteenth centuries that they must be regarded as an essential element in the scheme of sampler design. They began to appear, in scattered instances, as early as the middle of the seventeenth century, but, in the first years of the eighteenth century, the fashion had become universal and was firmly established. The inscription was used in addition to the almost invariably present alphabet and numerals. Sometimes it was merely the name of the worker, with her age and the date of the sampler's completion. Again, at the other extreme, it might be the Creed or the Ten Commandments or even a whole chapter from Scripture. More usually, however, it took the form of a motto, a proverb, or a Scripture text intended to inculcate in the mind of the youthful sampler worker obedience to parents, the fear of God, duty to neighbours, sobriety of conduct, diligence or some other religious precept or maxim of prudent behaviour. Occasionally a set of verses, with halting metre and a plenitude of distressing morbid religiosity, emphasised graphically the shortness and uncertainty of human life, an affected longing for death, the fickleness of friends, the falsity and vanity of human nature, or similar reflections of equally gruesome or misanthropic tone, betraying a close relationship with the melancholic sentiments so commonly carved on the gravestones of the period. Imagine the utter incongruity of a child of only eight or nine spending weary hours in working with her needle the following lugubrious lines:

> Our days, alas! our mortal days
> Are short and wretched, too.
> Evil and few the patriarch says,
> And well the patriarch knew.

In his admirable book on samplers, from which the foregoing inscription is quoted, Mr. Huish gives a number of other examples of a like gloomy tenour from which all trace or suggestion of the blithesomeness or the joy of living is conspicuously and remotely absent. Less depressing, by far, are the verses containing moral reflections upon virtue, happiness, and other abstract qualities, or the verses commemorative of some church festival, some historical event, or cast into the form of prayers.

While sampler inscriptions, almost without exception, were distinctly "moral and improving" in tone, those that were replete with unhealthy and dismal self-introspection are to be explained by the spirit of the age—an age in which evangelicalism was rampant and Methodism took its rise; an age that produced Dr. Isaac Watts's "Divine and Moral Songs for Children," Wesley's hymns, and the effusions of Dr. Philip Doddridge; an age when it pleased those that considered themselves serious-minded to speak pessimistically and despitefully of themselves and their fellows as "vile earth and miserably clay" or as "very worms and no men," rather than to contemplate the nobility of the "human form divine."

THE HUMAN FIGURE. It is a relief to turn from the subject-matter of the sampler inscriptions, with their often uncomfortable and distorted moral attitude, to the examination of the human figure as pourtrayed by the samplerist. In the borders, and occasionally elsewhere, in samplers of the first half of the eighteenth century, stiff little figures now and then appear which seem to be *amorini* or *erotes* that have persisted from a seventeenth-century *motif*. Adam and Eve are seen again and again, while figures clothed in contemporary costume are commonest of all. Owing to the limitations of a square stitch and the executant's deficiencies as a limner, the figures are ordinarily shown from a front view, with heels together and toes pointed in opposite directions, or else in profile, with the quaint angularity observable in Egyptian frescoes or the warriors of the Bayeux Tapestry. One rarely finds any approximation to accurate drawing or perspective such as were to be seen in the seventeenth-century English tapestry pictures and a few of the samplers of the same date.

ARCHITECTURAL FEATURES. Houses, buildings that are to be reckoned as houses by implication and courtesy of imagination rather than by completeness of visible characteristics, urns, fountains, vases, and other *motifs* of an architectural or semi-architectural nature were chosen for sampler embellishment with great frequency.

They formed one item in the progress towards the conception of the embroidered picture as developed in the eighteenth century. These sampler houses reflect the architecture of the period and are ordinarily accompanied by a bit of landscape—a tree and a patch of grass, if nothing more—and human figures or animals. One example illustrated both shows an architectural *motif* and is a good instance of the sampler that occupies a middle ground between the type, on the one hand, that was merely lettered and figured, with perhaps the amenity of a floral border, and the wholly pictorial representation, on the other. It was wrought by Anna Townsend, of New Haven, "aged 12," in 1771, and is representative of a fairly numerous class of departures from the lettered and bordered talk in needlework, and marks an illuminating evolutionary step as well as a rebellion against mere utility. Its dual character satisfied both the New England sense of duty and the yearning to create a work of purely decorative value. The laws of perspective troubled the youthful artist not at all, and neither did any principles of comparative proportions. What she saw in her mind's eye was a stately New England house of Georgian type, with the door flanked by two windows on each side, and that she very graphically pourtrayed with considerable dexterity of stitchery of a sort not usually met with in samplers of the merely lettered and figured type. The people in the picture doubtless belong in some way to the house, but Anna, "aged 12," was not sufficiently adroit in a dramatic way to give them something to do and prevent them from being a bit pokerish. All things considered, the sampler is pleasing and surely does credit to a little girl of twelve—where is one to-day could do the like?—

but it is a sampler and, as such, marks for us, with its long and short stitch and its pictorial aspect, a transitional influence toward work of purely decorative intent.

BEASTS AND BIRDS. Many of the animals and birds that figure in sampler ornamentation can be described only as ''just animals and birds.'' It would require a broader knowledge of natural history than the average person possesses, coupled with a vivid imagination, to assign definite names and species to them. On the other hand, the identity of not a few of them is quite unmistakable. Stags, horses, dogs, rabbits, sheep, and cows appear, and now and then some of the wilder beasts of the forest or jungle may be distinguished.

Among the birds we may readily recognise peacocks, doves, swans, parrots, birds of Paradise, jays, and robins, and occasionally the characteristics of others.

FLOWERS, FRUITS, AND LEAVES. What was said of the possibility of recognising animals and birds in the samplers applies with equal force to flowers and fruits. Some of them are conventionalised in such a peculiarly original manner by the worker that they defy classification. The decorative effect, however, is usually good. Among the flowers whose names can be definitely assigned are roses, single and double, conventionalised and natural; pinks or carnations, tulips, asters, thistles, fuchsias, forget-me-nots, harebells, and morning glories.

The fruits that can be named are the strawberry, apple, currant, pineapple, and grape.

Of trees, we can readily distinguish the pine, the oak, the elm, the cedar of triangular variety, reminiscent of the painted trees in the Noah's Ark sets of our childhood, and the willow, the forerunner of the Washington memorial *motifs* that became so popular early in the nineteenth century.

Leaves, among which the clover or trefoil may be distinguished, and conventionalised tendrils played a prominent part in borders.

MISCELLANEOUS MOTIFS.   Among these, sundry geometrical patterns were of frequent occurrence. Maps, also, now and again supplied a theme for the whole surface of a sampler.   They also formed the *motif* for some of the embroideries on silk and satin which belong under the head of "Pictorial Embroideries." Besides these, divers other subjects appear in isolated instances, according to the inspiration of the individual worker.

PICTORIAL EMBROIDERY

We come now to the embroidered picture, an important and conscious effort in decorative art that flourished in the latter part of the eighteenth century and continued over into the nineteenth, until it was displaced from favour by the enormities of Victorian "fancy work" which it would be depressing and unprofitable to discuss.

Some of the embroidered pictures are really objects of beauty as well as eloquent testimonials to consummate skill in needlecraft, and their authors took a just and proper pride in them, if we may judge from the careful and substantial way in which they were framed. For the better exhibition of their charms they were usually surrounded by a broad margin of black glass with a narrow, gold-lined edge.

The pictures—landscapes, portraits, maps, pastoral scenes, architectural subjects; almost anything, in fact, that a painter would essay on canvas—were worked in a great variety of stitches, and with careful gradations of shading and colour, on bolting cloth or silk, canvas, crash, or satin. Nor did their makers disdain the aid of paint. Faces, hands, feet, legs, arms, and distant parts of the landscape, as well as skies, were often painted on the silk or satin.

In "Ruth and Boaz," wrought in Long Island, in 17—, by Ann Valentine, the background is of bolting cloth originally white, but now a brownish cream from age. Ruth's face, arms, hands, and feet are daintily painted, while her hair and gorgeous blue robe are ingeniously embroidered. Boaz's face, arms, and legs are painted, and his turban, whiskers, and garment are stitched. The trees and vegetation in the foreground are embroidered, but the sky and distant figures are painted. This picture well exemplifies the combination of paint and embroidery, a combination not at all unusual in about equal parts, although many pictures were wholly embroidered, without depending upon the agency of paint. In "Ruth and Boaz" the colouring, drawing, and execution are all creditable, and it has a real decorative value that is not to be despised.

Such pictorial embroidery was the sort taught in the finishing schools for young ladies, and great store was set by it as not only a desirable but an almost indispensable accomplishment.

PURPOSE. These embroidered pictures were frankly decorative in their purpose. Allusion has previously been made to the comparative scarcity of pictures in the majority of houses of the Colonial and early post-Colonial periods, and these pieces of elaborate needlework somewhat supplied the want for chromatic adornment. Furthermore, they may be regarded as diplomas stitchery, testifying in a very real way to the skill and taste of the executants, who, with the members of their fond families, looked upon them with pardonable pride.

MATERIALS. White bolting cloth—a very thin silk—or white satin usually formed the groundwork on which these pictures were wrought, although canvas or crash was sometimes used instead. The Pennsylvania Pastoral Scene is thus worked on a coarse, loose-woven canvas and, where the sky is painted in, the meshes of the weave are ill-concealed. Satin or bolting cloth made a far better ground for paint.

The work was done both with floss silk and twisted silk, and a close examination of the illustrations will serve to show what a diversity of stitches was employed.

COLOUR. The workers of embroidered pictures ran the full scale of colours in their work. While their colour knowledge was not always profound, and while some of the combinations they produced can hardly be considered happy in point of harmony or restfulness, in the long run their management of tones was agreeable and, in some cases, showed great refinement and charm. There was a general preference for lively colours, and this fondness, now and then, betrayed a worker into crudities, but, in the main, the colour balance was good, and heavy, garish tones in harsh, revolting combinations were not common until the inroads of Berlin wool had gone far to deprave public colour sense.

DESIGN. The subjects treated in the embroidered pictures of the late eighteenth and early nineteenth centuries were varied in scope, as were the subjects chosen by painters for pourtrayal on canvas. It is to be noted, however, that there was a strong bias in favour of pastoral themes. When the subject was not actually pastoral, it was apt, nevertheless, to have a pastoral flavour about it, and the manners of the English eighteenth-century school of painting were plainly reflected in the general tone of the embroidered pictures. Tamed rusticity with a bit of architecture introduced as a foil was much esteemed. Tall, languishing ladies with Gainsborough hats and baskets of flowers or shepherdesses with beribboned crooks, seated on the banks of purling brooks, were highly approved *motifs.*

After the death of Washington, there was a veritable epidemic of embroidered pictures whose central feature was a monument surmounted by a cinerary urn or else by a bust of the Father of his Country. The name "Washington" was duly inscribed on the shaft, that there might be no mistaking the intent. A willowy lady in short-waisted white Empire frock was either placing a laurel wreath on the bust or shedding tears upon the urn. Weeping willows were the conspicuous features at the sides or in the background.

The drawing was usually creditable, and this is to be explained by the fact that, in many instances, ready prepared designs, kept in stock by the purveyors of embroidery materials, were traced or pounced upon the satin, silk, or bolting cloth, all ready to be filled in with stitch-work. Even the shading was indicated. Many of the cruder pictures, such as the Pennsylvania Pastoral Scene, were evidently altogether designed and executed by the worker, a fact that will explain the peculiarities of perspective and scale in this particular instance.

The pictures were done both with and without

7

borders. When borders were used, floral devices were commonly employed.

PATCHWORK AND QUILTING

Samplers and embroidered pictures are to be reckoned as belonging to the ornamental rather than the utilitarian province of decorative needlecraft. There *was* a thoroughly utilitarian province of decorative needlework, and it included quilting and the making of pieced and patchwork bed coverings. The working of samplers and embroidered pictures was more or less of a polite accomplishment, and, however desirable it was considered and however commonly practised, it was not absolutely essential to the creature comfort of the colonists. The making of bed coverings, on the other hand, was a stern necessity and universally engaged in. And just because the women accepted the necessity and added a genuine touch of artistry to it, the stitching of quilted and patchwork bed covers is even more thoroughly and democratically representative of folk-art than the execution of the purely decorative samplers and silken pictures.

A distinction is to be drawn between "piecing" and "patching." A "pieced" quilt is one whose whole surface is composed of contiguous pieces of material, of the same colour or of various colours, stitched together in geometrical or random patterns and then quilted down. A "patched" or "patchwork" quilt is one whose surface is decorated with pieces or patches of another coloured material applied or *appliqué* at intervals so that its pattern is silhouetted on the background. These pieces are then quilted down to the body of the quilt and the lines of the quilting are made to enhance the design created by the *appliqué*. Patch-work gave more play for originality and diversity of decorative treatment than did piecing, and it can readily be seen how wide a field of opportunity such a method of needlework opened to the worker. Historically speaking, quilted patchwork had a long and honourable past and abundant precedents in many of the gorgeous hangings of the Middle Ages and the Renaissance which come under this definition.

Quilting denotes the fastening together of several layers of material by stitching through them. The lines of the stitching may be as numerous as desired, and may be made to form any pattern, according to the inclination of the quilter. Many of the old quilts, of various materials, coarse or fine, without the agency of *appliqué* patches, are marvels of beauty and dexterity. Table covers, frocks, petticoats, tester valances, and other articles were subjects for intricate quilted embellishment as well as bed coverings.

The patterns were passed from one woman to another and were known by name, just as were the patterns for the hand-woven coverlets treated in a later chapter. The practice of making quilts was universal and continues to our own day in rural districts and old-fashioned places, so that the manifestation of this phase of folk-art, with all its traditions, has always been kept alive. It offers untold possibilities for further decorative development.

The colour and pattern of the old patchwork quilts were often admirable and evidenced a widespread native intuition of fitness, even among the humblest, that is deserving of all honour and appreciative study.

EMBROIDERY FOR THE ENRICHMENT OF PERSONAL
ATTIRE AND DOMESTIC ARTICLES

The last class of decorative stitchery to be considered deserves more attention than it usually receives. Under personal attire are to be counted the skirts, the bodices, the caps, the waistcoats, and the coats in which our forefathers and foremothers arrayed themselves so bravely. Besides these larger and more conspicuous articles, there were the many little objects of a more or less personal nature and use that they were wont to ornament with embroidery. Such are the handkerchief holders, portemonnaies, reticules, needlebooks, and sundry other small articles of a similar nature upon the embellishment of which our grandmothers often lavished considerable time and pains. A little search with open eyes will reveal many a piece of such deftly wrought work, sometimes even lying forgotten and neglected in trunks or chests in our own attic because we did not know what they were or what they stood for in old American decorative needlecraft. The nightcap case or handkerchief holder—tradition says it was the former—shown in the illustration will serve to show the kind of work one may expect to find in such small articles of elegance. The object in question is closely worked in one of the old tapestry picture stitches and is brilliant in colour, as one might infer from the character of the design. It folds over three or four times and is lined with red silk. When closed, it is about the size of a man's bank-note case.

The articles of domestic utility were such things as fire-screens, chair seats, book-covers, and numerous other odds and ends of similar character. Besides these must be counted the less ambitious flights of pictorial embroidery, such as the floral sprays, birds, and butter-flies worked on panels of white satin and framed. Fruits, flowers, leaves, birds with gay plumage, and butterflies with dazzling markings are all depicted with painstaking verisimilitude and a good deal of stiffness. Both the accuracy and the stiffness are the same one sees in the old coloured plates in ornithological books or within the leaves of press albums. Notwithstanding their rigidity, however, many of them possess great merit as pieces of embroidery, and they have a distinct decorative value which we are becoming more disposed to recognise. Tufting or knotting and the execution of drawn-work as well as simple beaded embroidery are likewise to be reckoned in the tale of accomplishments in which many needlewomen of the Colonies were ex-pert. Other white work in great variety was wrought with cotton on linen and muslin, and metal stamps in-serted in wood blocks, with floral and other designs, were used for stamping the outlines to be filled in with stitchery.

In the realm of decorative needlecraft in all its branches the collector will find a rich field for explora-tion, a field that is co-extensive with the whole eastern portion of the country, the South, and some of the middle West. The craftsworker may find therein abundant inspiration for fresh development and adaptation to modern needs that will make a minute study of the subject well worth while.

CHAPTER VI

SILVER; DOMESTIC AND ECCLESIASTICAL

OLD silver plate is the most fascinating, perhaps, of all the products of early American craftsmanship. Quite apart from the intrinsic beauty and grace of the various objects themselves and their value as treasured heirlooms, as most of them are, there is attached to them a wealth of historic association on account of the silversmiths who made them and the part these worthy craftsmen played in the affairs of their day and generation. Thus, indeed, our early plate not only represents the cunning handiwork of skillful artists of whom any age and country might well be proud—there is nothing primitive about the character of old American silver as there was about some of our first essays in other fields—but it also represents the "personalities of men who gave to the country the best they possessed in the form of service to Church and State and thereby assisted in the gradual moulding and welding together of the various integral units of Colonial life into the great republic of which we are so proud and whose traditions we hold so dear."

As silversmithing was one of the finest crafts practised in Colonial America, so was it also one of the earliest. There was a silversmith in Jamestown, Thomas Howard by name, whose presence there in 1620 is recorded in the register of the Virginia Company. Unfortunately no authenticated pieces of his workmanship are known. In the other Colonies, too, the craft of the silversmith received substantial encouragement

102

at an early date. It was not long after the period of settlement of Boston and Philadelphia before there was a demand for silverware by colonists whose affairs had prospered, and, in response to the demand, silversmiths, or goldsmiths, as they were often termed, began to ply their craft and proved themselves skillful masters by the quality and design of their handiwork. As early as 1634, John Mansfield, a silversmith, seems to have been working in Charlestown, Massachusetts, but no pieces of his work have been identified.

In Boston silversmithing began before the close of the first half of the seventeenth century, and a mint, of which John Hull of pine-tree shilling fame was chosen master, was set up there in 1652. The profitable trade driven by New England with the English and Spanish colonies to the south resulted in a rich influx of coin into the coffers of New England merchants and provided abundant material for the silversmiths of Boston and other prosperous communities to work upon.

In Philadelphia we find one smith, Cesar Ghiselin by name, a Huguenot who early cast in his lot with William Penn's "Holy Experiment" by the banks of the Delaware. The said Cesar Ghiselin* made spoons and other articles of plate almost at the very outset of the city's history, and examples of his workmanship are shown in the illustrations. Thus was begun a worthy tradition that was worthily and widely sustained throughout the city's subsequent history, as abundant examples of her silversmiths' work bear eloquent witness. Boston and Philadelphia being essentially English, their smiths naturally followed English patterns

---

*This name is frequently given as Griselm, which is incorrect. The name is Ghiselin as here printed and was so spelled by the testator in his will.

and precedents in their silverware, even though they might, as they frequently did, make modifications and adaptations and display originality that was quite distinct in some of its manifestations from contemporary English forms.

In New York, on the contrary, where some of the smiths, especially the earlier smiths, were Dutch and some were English, plate was made after both Dutch and English designs. While the earlier conditions under Dutch domination were scarcely favourable to silversmithing and trade was carried on chiefly by barter, affluence and luxury increased considerably after the English occupation, and, despite the small size of New York as compared with Philadelphia or Boston at that time, some exquisitely beautiful pieces of plate were produced during the eighteenth century and even during the latter part of the seventeenth.

There is record of so many seventeenth- and eighteenth-century American silversmiths in what are now our large cities, and also in a number of old towns whose growth has remained comparatively stationary, although they were once important centres, and most of them seem to have prospered, that the inference is natural that a great quantity of silver plate—far more than is generally supposed—must have been made. Much of it still remains, and the fact that a yet larger amount has disappeared is easily explained by the habit our forebears had of melting their silver and converting it into specie in times of stress and necessity. In this way a vast proportion of it, doubtless, vanished during the War for Independence. Having one's silver in the form of plate was, in the eyes of the colonists, tantamount to having it in the bank. Indeed, during the

EMBROIDERED AND PAINTED PICTURE, EIGHTEENTH CENTURY
Courtesy of Colonel William J. Youngs, Garden City, Long Island

EARLY NINETEENTH CENTURY EMBROIDERED PICTURE WITH
FLOWERED BORDER
Courtesy of Mr. James Curran, Philadelphia

MULTI-COLOURED EMBROIDERED NIGHT CAP HOLDER,
EIGHTEENTH CENTURY
Courtesy of Colonel William J. Youngs, Garden City, Long Island

EMBROIDERED POCKET-BOOK, BOOK COVER AND RETICULE, EIGHTEENTH
AND EARLY NINETEENTH CENTURIES
Frishmuth Collection, Pennsylvania Museum and School of Industrial Art

WHITE ALTAR ANTEPENDIUM OF ST. PETER'S CHURCH, PHILADELPHIA:
MADE FROM THE EMBROIDERED WEDDING GOWN OF A FORMER
PARISHIONER
Courtesy of the Rector and Vestry of St. Peter's Church, Philadelphia

seventeenth century and most of the eighteenth, in the absence of banks where they might deposit such surplus funds as were not needed for immediate expenditure, the conversion of coin into household plate afforded a convenient way of keeping it intact and also, incidentally, added not a little to the gratification of ownership and the luxury of living. Wills and inventories of the period bear witness to the quantity and variety of silver plate possessed by well-to-do colonists and by those whose estate was not reckoned of any great consequence.

The specimens of early American silver, of unquestionably authentic Colonial make, are usually so excellent in design and workmanship, regardless of the particular locality in which they were produced, that we may conclude, not unreasonably, that the majority of American craftsmen were quite the equals of their British cousins in manual skill and mastery of design. The high quality of the American silver has been responsible for a good deal of it, in time past, being attributed to an English origin by people who have not taken the pains to examine the marks and properly identify its source. A thorough examination and inventory of the old silver plate in America, both domestic and ecclesiastical, would probably show that much of it that popular tradition has ascribed to a British source is really of American fabrication. It is even not impossible that many a proudly treasured piece, which time-honoured tradition and a fine fancy for romance have invested with the glamour of an English origin, supplying circumstantial details of its being fetched overseas to the new land among the effects of a revered ancestor, might turn out, upon close inspection, to have been made in New York, Philadelphia, or Boston. Tradition is a most valuable handmaid to history, but she is only a handmaid and must not be regarded as the ultimate mistress. That tradition, especially tradition fondly flattering to family pride, cannot always be accepted with implicit confidence one may judge from the following instance. Plenty of similar instances might readily be adduced. The writers were invited, upon one occasion, by an acquaintance, to come and see an exceptionally fine sideboard which, so the informant positively averred, had been in his wife's family for two hundred years to his certain knowledge and perhaps longer. Upon examination, the two-hundred-year-old sideboard, instead of being a Stuart buffet or a Queen Anne dresser, as one might reasonably have expected it would be from the date assigned, turned out to be a particularly good Hepplewhite piece of American manufacture that could not possibly have been made before 1780 and was probably not made until some years later.

This little incident serves to show how wary one must be in accepting tradition. The proud possessor of the two-hundred-year-old sideboard had no desire to deceive. He honestly believed the mass of inaccurate tradition that had gradually accumulated in his wife's family anent the piece in question. Absolute, incontrovertible facts are the only sure things to rely upon, and absolute facts we fortunately have in old silver to a greater degree than is the case with any other sort of antiques. English pieces are distinctly marked and bear exact evidence of their place of origin and date of manufacture. American pieces, while usually bearing the maker's mark or name, have no date letter, such as appears on English silver. Their age, therefore, can be fixed only approximately, either by knowing the

years between which the silversmith worked or else, in
default of such specific knowledge or in the total absence
of maker's name or mark—a circumstance by no means
uncommon—by the contour, which affords a fairly
accurate index to date, for there was a regular evolution and development of silver styles that can be traced
throughout the whole period under consideration.
While we have a trustworthy record of the names of
many seventeenth-, eighteenth-, and early nineteenth-
century silversmiths, the dates of their manufacturing
activity, the marks they used, and the places where they
worked, it also happens that the list is unfortunately
by no means complete; that their dates are not definitely
fixed, there being often only a single year with which
it is possible to connect a smith's name; that the places
in which they worked are not always surely known;
finally, that not a few of the well-known smiths, and
doubtless those less known as well, varied their marks
from time to time as the fancy struck them, and that
there is no fully exhaustive table so far compiled for
the identification of all the marks employed. It still remains for some enterprising and enthusiastic collector
or antiquary to bring the various lists to perfection.
The lists given in this chapter are as full as the authors
have been able to make them, and embody the sum of
the results attained by R. T. Haines Halsey, Esq., Miss
Florence V. Paull, of the Boston Museum of Art, J. H.
Buck, Esq., of the Metropolitan Museum of Art, New
York; Dr. Edwin AtLee Barber, of the Pennsylvania
Museum and School of Industrial Art; the Honourable
A. T. Clearwater, and others who have contributed such
valuable results to the elucidation of all matters per-
taining to early American silver and have done so much

to further appreciation of the labours of the Colonial and post-Colonial silversmiths.

What manner of men the American silversmiths of the seventeenth and eighteenth centuries were, how they pursued their calling and how their personalities counted in the life of the Colonies during the formative stage of our country's growth, we may gather from a brief review of the careers of a representative few who followed the mystery of St. Dunstan. Among the first to occur to mind in such connexion is the first American mint-master, John Hull. Born in England in 1624, he was brought to Boston in 1635, and his diary tells us that "after a little keeping at school, I was taken to help my father plant corn, which I attended to for several years together, and then, by God's good hand, I fell to learning (by the help of my brother) and to practise the trade of Goldsmith." When the General Court of Massachusetts, in 1652, set up the first American mint in Boston to coin shillings and their fractions, Hull was made mint master, as previously noted, and compensated for his services by being allowed to retain for himself one shilling out of every twenty.

In this public work Hull associated with himself his friend Robert Sanderson, probably his senior and master in craftsmanship and whom he seems also to have made his partner in his silversmithing business, and together, for thirty years, they supplied Massachusetts with shillings and smaller coinage from the little mint-house, sixteen feet square by ten feet high. After Hull's death, Sanderson continued the silversmith's business alone, and his pieces are stamped with his own individual mark in distinction to the earlier work which bears the joint imprint of both Hull and Sanderson.

Hull soon amassed a most substantial fortune which was further increased by successful trading ventures to the West Indies. He was Town Treasurer in 1660 and Treasurer of the Colony in 1676, financing the Ship of State in stringent periods and acting in the general capacity of a banker. His daughter became the wife of Judge Sewall, whose diary is such a storehouse of information regarding early New England life. Hull's own diary, "Penned down that I may be the more mindful of, and thankful for all God's Dispensation towards me," has been published by the Massachusetts Historical Society and is highly interesting reading. In addition to filling the posts of Town Treasurer and Treasurer of the Colony, as just mentioned, Hull represented the Town of Wenham in 1668, and was for a long time actively associated with Boston's Artillery Company—now the Ancient and Honourable Artillery Company—serving as ensign in that early organisation for preparedness in 1663, lieutenant in 1664, and captain in 1671 and 1678. He was no less active in the affairs of the Church militant than in the affairs of the State militant, and was one of the prime movers in establishing the Old South Church. He was a man of broad education and, though not possessed of a college training, was a student of the classics. His advice and counsel were sought and valued alike in matters of civic moment and personal concern. In short, he filled so important a place both in private life and in the public affairs of the community that he is unquestionably to be regarded as one of early Boston's most representative citizens. He is buried in the Granary Burial Ground, in the midst of the pulsing life of the city whose infancy he served so faithfully.

In speaking of Boston's early silversmiths, another name that immediately suggests itself is that of Paul Revere, who, besides being a most skillful silver crafts-man, was an engraver, a painter, a cartoonist, a founder of brass, a manufacturer in several fields, an ardent patriot, and, to sum it all up briefly, Boston's general handy man who seemed able to do almost anything and, what was more, to do it well. Incidentally, he usually contrived to be well paid for what he did. It would be hard, indeed, to find any sort of activity into which Paul Revere did not enter at one time or another, but so much has been well written about him elsewhere, with due reference also to his father, who was a silversmith of no mean ability, that it is unnecessary to engage here in further details of a biographical nature. Suffice it for our present purpose to remind the reader of Revere's prominence in the doings of Boston in his day.

Among Boston's other early and notable silver-smiths mention must be made of Jeremiah Dummer (1645–1718), who learned his craft from Hull, to whom he was apprenticed as a lad, and, besides producing highly creditable work, "became an important person-age in the Colony, serving as non-commissioned officer in the Artillery, as Selectman, Justice of the Peace, Treasurer of the County, Judge of one of the Inferior Courts, and as one of the Council of Safety in 1689, at the time of the trouble with France." None of these honours was bestowed lightly nor without sufficient reason, and that Dummer filled them is conclusive evi-dence of his personal worth and of the esteem in which he was held by his fellow-citizens. He was weighty enough in ecclesiastical matters for Increase Mather to dedicate one of his discourses to him, and the following obituary notice in the *Boston News Letter* of June 2, 1718, plainly attests the public regard entertained for his qualities: "On the 25th past, Departed this **life** *Jeremiah Dummer*, Esq., in the 73rd year of his Age, after a long retirement, under great infirmities of Age and Sickness, having served his country faithfully in several Publick Stations, and obtained of all that knew him the Character of a Just, Virtuous, and Pious Man, and was Honourably Interr'd on Thursday last; He was Son to Richard Dummer, Esq.; who was one of the first and principal settlers of the Massachusetts colony, and died at Newbury." Of Jeremiah Dummer's two sons, William, the elder, became Lieutenant Governour and discharged the duties of Governour, in the absence of Governour Shute, from 1716 to 1728, and also in 1729, following the death of Governour Burnett, while the younger son, Jeremiah Dummer junior, likewise distinguished himself in public life for a considerable period. John Cony (1655–1722), the brother-in-law of Jeremiah Dummer, from whom it is likely he received his training in craftsmanship, was another silversmith well known for his excellent work and prominent in the civic life of his day. He it was who, almost beyond all question, engraved the plates for the first American paper money.

John Dixwell (1680–1725), a son of the regicide Colonel John Dixwell, not only made excellent silverware, but was active in the life of his day and a deacon in the New North Church, which enjoyed the distinction of being "erected in 1714 by seventeen mechanics, 'unassisted by the more wealthy part of the community, except by their prayers and good wishes.'" John Edwards (1687–1743), represented by numerous admirable pieces, was a man of education above the average, conspicuous in public affairs, and of sufficiently prominent social position to be granted, by the Selectmen, the use of the tomb built by Governour Endicott as being the nearest of living kin to that worthy. He was a member of the Artillery Company and was, therefore, one of the fifteen or more early Boston silversmiths whose names appear on the rolls of that time-honoured organisation. Edward Winslow (1669–1753), at one time captain of the Artillery Company, was a notable figure both from the position of his family and also from the influence he exercised in civil and military affairs, serving at one time or another as Tithingman, Constable, Overseer of the Poor, Sheriff of the Town, Colonel of the Boston Regiment, and Judge of the Inferior Court of Common Pleas. Andrew Tyler (1691–1741) had influential family connexions, married a sister of Sir William Pepperrell, and was a conspicuous figure in political affairs.

An advertisement inserted by James Turner in the *Boston Evening Post* of June 24, 1745, gives some idea of the manifold activities pursued by the silversmiths of the period:

> "James Turner, Silversmith & Engraver, Near the Town House in Cornhill, Boston, Engraves all sorts of Copper Plates for the Rolling Press, all sorts of Stamps in Brass or Pewter for the common Printing Press, Coats of Arms, Crests, Cyphers, &c., on Gold, Silver, Steel, Copper, Brass or Pewter. He likewise makes Watch Faces, makes and cuts Seals in Gold, Silver, or Steel; or makes Steel Faces for Seals, and sets them handsomely in Gold or Silver. He cuts all sorts of Steel Stamps, Brass Rolls and Stamps for Sadlers and Bookbinders and does all other sorts of work in Gold and Silver. All after the best and neatest manner, and at the most Reasonable Rates."

CHRONOLOGICAL KEY OF SILVER CONTOURS

This Key shows characteristic pieces of silver in the distinctive styles of each successive period.

In using the Key, note carefully the shape and prominent characteristics of the *piece to be identified* and then look for those characteristics in the Key illustrations.

Then refer to the text of Chapter VI, under the subhead of the piece in question, for full details.

CHARACTERISTIC CONTOURS OF FIRST CHRONOLOGICAL DIVISION, c. 1650–c. 1730

1 and 2, Trifid Handled Spoons; 3 and 4, Domed and Globular Teapots; 5, Tankard with Flat Drum Cover and without Midband; 6, Tankard with Midband and Domed Cover with Finial; 7, Beaker, Flat Bottom and Moulded Base; 8, Salt; 9, Cup with Gadrooned Bottom and Moulded Base.

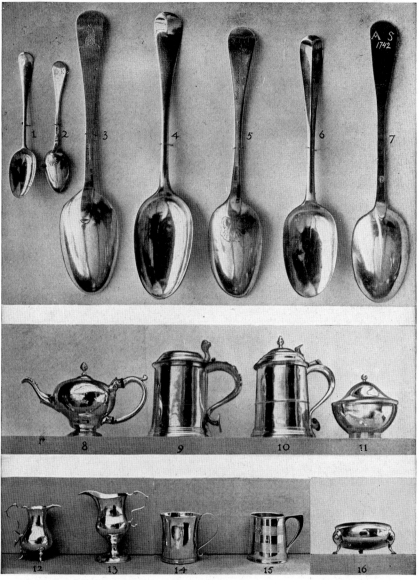

CHARACTERISTIC CONTOURS OF SECOND CHRONOLOGICAL DIVISION, c. 1730–c. 1765

1–7, Tea-spoons and Dessert-spoons with Handle Turned *Up*, Moulded Drop on Bowl, with or without additional Ornament, Engraving and Monograms on *Back* of Head; 8, Pear-shaped Tea-pot; 9 and 10, Tankards; 11, Covered Bowl; 12 and 13, Cream Pitchers; 14 and 15, Mugs; 16, Three-legged Salt.

CHARACTERISTIC CONTOURS OF THIRD CHRONOLOGICAL DIVISION,
c. 1765–c. 1800

1–8, Tea-spoons and Table-spoons with Handle End Turned *Down*, "Bright-cut"
Engraving, Moulded Drops on Bowl, with or without additional Ornament; 9, Boat-
shaped Salt; 10, 11 and 12, Tankards; 13, Cream Pitcher; 14, Straight-sided Teapot,
"Bright-cut" Engraving; 15, Urn-shaped Sugar Bowl; 16, Oval Sugar Bowl or Basket

CHARACTERISTIC CONTOURS OF FOURTH CHRONOLOGICAL DIVISION
c. 1800–c.1830

1–6, Table-spoons and Tea-spoons, "Coffin-headed" and "Fiddle-headed; 7 and 8,
Cream Pitcher and Hot Water Jug; 9, Cup or Can; 10, Moulded Teapot; 11, Gadrooned
Oblong Sugar Bowl; 12, Moulded Cream Pitcher; 13, Moulded Oblong Sugar Bowl;
14 and 15, Mugs or Cups

CHRONOLOGICAL SEQUENCE OF CHARACTERISTIC CONTOURS
1–4, Mugs; 5, Beaker; 6 and 7, Cans; 8–11, Teapots; 12–16, Porringer, Bowls and Sugar Bowls; 17–21,
Cream Pitchers

Beaker with characteristic Dutch Strapwork and Foliage
Ornament. New York, Latter Part of Seventeenth Century. Mark indistinct so that Maker cannot be identified

Cup or Small Bowl of Oval Shape. Late Seventeenth
Century. New York. Maker unidentified; Mark T. T.
crowned in Shield

Clearwater Collection, Metropolitan Museum of Art,
New York City

Courtesy of the Honourable A. T. Clearwater, Kingston-
on-Hudson

Pair of Forks by John Noyes (1674–1749). Mugs: 1, Formerly attributed to Cesar Ghiselin and so ascribed in the text. Since the book has gone to press investigation has proved attribution incorrect. Maker (G. G.) unidentified; 2, by John Dixwell (1680–1728); 3, Maker unknown; 4, Maker unknown (possibly Spanish)

Forks, 1 and 2, Clearwater Collection, Boston Museum of Art and Metropolitan Museum of Art, New York City

Courtesy of the Honourable A. T. Clearwater, Kingston-on-Hudson

3 and 4, Courtesy of Metropolitan Museum of Art

Turner was a silversmith of much repute, but, as the advertisement clearly indicates, he did not hesitate to engage in sundry other activities germane to his craft, and most of the seventeenth- and eighteenth-century silversmiths doubtless did precisely the same thing. Not a few of them made jewellery as well as fashioning spoons and porringers, tankards and cans, and it seems to have been not an unusual thing for them to turn their hands to engraving. This was a natural line of expansion, inasmuch as they made such frequent use of engraving for the embellishment of their finer pieces of silverware. Jeremiah Dummer printed the first paper money for Connecticut, "and presumably engraved the plate" from which it was made.

One might go on almost indefinitely recounting biographical data of Boston's early silversmiths who occupied prominent places in civic life, but the foregoing notice is sufficient for our purpose. In the post-Colonial period silversmithing in Boston was largely concentrated among members of the Burt, Hurd. and Revere families.

While Boston led in the number and personal consequence of her silversmiths, there were other places in Massachusetts where excellent silverware was wrought at an early period. Among them may be mentioned Salem, Hingham, Marblehead, Newburyport, Hull, Concord, Stockbridge, Milton, Plymouth, New Bedford, Braintree, Deerfield, Taunton, Dedham, Ashby, Natick, Ipswich, Medford, and Bolton. Charlestown and Roxbury, though at that time separate from Boston, were geographically so close that the several smiths who lived there may be counted in the Boston list.

Elsewhere in New England, too, but especially in

8

Connecticut and Rhode Island, silversmiths were fairly numerous and seem to have produced a good deal of highly creditable ware. In Newport we find them at work in the neighbourhood of 1700—Samuel Vernon (1683–1737) appears to have been the first; in Providence, at a somewhat later date, Jabez Gorham worked at the craft, and his descendants carried the name on to its present connexion with a great modern business; in Milford, Connecticut, Job Prince, who died in 1703, was the first known to have worked in that colony. New Haven, Norwich, and Hartford could boast an honourable list of silversmiths, but, besides these, there were others of their craft who worked at Killingworth, Norwalk, Guilford, Waterbury, Preston, Goshen, Litchfield, Bridgeport, Stratford, Colchester, Canterbury, Middletown, Farmington, Mansfield, Stonington, East Hartford, New London, Danbury, Windham, East Haddam, Hebron, Hampton, Cheshire, Durham, Enfield, Lyme, and several other small towns.

Some of the Rhode Island and Connecticut silversmiths, as, for instance, Major Jonathan Otis, of Newport, who died in 1791—a skilful jeweller, too—or Captain Robert Fairchild (1703–1794), of New Haven, were men of eminence and filled conspicuous rôles in public affairs. Not a few of them volunteered for military service, especially in the War for Independence, and acquitted themselves so creditably that we hear of Captain Phineas Bradley, Colonel Aner Bradley, Colonel Miles Beach, Captain Samuel Parmelee, and many more of official rank. It must be remembered, however, that there was not the same opulence in agricultural Connecticut and Rhode Island as there was in the area of commercial concentration about Boston and the towns

nearby, and consequently there was not a sufficient demand for the silversmiths' services to keep them all
continuously busy at their craft. It is not surprising,
therefore, to find that not a few of them were obliged
to carry on other trades as well to eke out a living. This
one made clocks, that one did cabinet work, another kept
a tavern and still another was a blacksmith, so that it
is no uncommon thing to discover the members of a
semi-rural community calling upon the same sturdy
yeoman to shoe their horses and fashion their teapots.
These local silversmiths, despite their intermittent
diversion to other pursuits, "did most creditable work
when occasion demanded, although," owing to the wont
of persons of means to patronise, then as now, the
craftsmen of Boston or New York for "articles of exceptional quality and worth," "their products seem
to have been distributed almost wholly in their own
localities—one might indeed say among their fellow-
townsmen. One never finds in Hartford the work of a
New Haven smith, nor in New Haven the product of a
man who was working in New London, except when
recent migration carried the ware from home."

The early silversmiths of New York, like their contemporaries in New England, were often in the public
eye and appear to have enjoyed the confidence and
esteem of their fellow-citizens, if we may judge from
the records of their activities in the service of the com-
monweal. There was worthy old Ahasuerus Hendricks
or Hendrickse, who came from Holland in the seventeenth century and made "jewellery, rings, funeral
spoons, and beakers, and, as well, fashioned the silver
spears, pikes, and sword hilts affected by the militant burghers" of New York. His name appears on

the list of those swearing allegiance to the King in
1675; in 1686 he was commissioned to assist in better-
ing the city supply of drinking water; in 1687 he
became constable for the North ward; between 1675
and 1693 his name is often entered in the records of
the Dutch Reformed Church "as a witness to the
baptisms of the children of many well-known families";
in 1689 the city settled his voucher, along with the
vouchers of Johannes Kip and Teunis DeKay, for
"Sundry to ye poore & Acc^tt," so that, besides fulfilling various other benevolent functions, he was evidently charged with a share in the oversight of the
needy inhabitants of the city. Carol van Brugh was
likewise a personage of weight and also a picturesque
character in seventeenth-century Manhattan. He it was
who "made the gold cup presented to Governour
Fletcher in 1693, the bullion for which was purchased
for one hundred and six pounds sterling and turned
over to Vanderburgh [van Brugh] to fashion," the
Council providing "that the revenue from the ferry be
used for no other purpose until the bill for this was
paid." The Huguenot Bartholomew LeRoux, first of
the noted New York silversmiths of that name, was
actively concerned in behalf of the people's cause at
the time of the Leisler Rebellion in 1689. Of the two
Boelens, Jacob and Hendrik, father and son, who came
from Holland soon after 1680, and did a thriving business, the elder figured conspicuously in matters of the
city's concerns, as may be seen by glancing at a list of
some of the positions of responsibility entrusted to him:
he was nine years assessor for the North ward; he was
sometime brant master, by appointment of the Council,
which also ordered that "five Ladders be made to serve

upon occasion of Fyre, with sufficient hooks thereto";
in 1693 he was one of the special assessors detailed "to
assess & rate the inhabitants Residence & Freeholders
(the) 1725 proportion for the City for Raising £6000
for payment 300 volunteers to reinforce the Frontiers
at Albany May 1693–4"; he was made alderman for the
North ward in 1695 and 1697; he served on the com-
mittee for choosing a site and finding ways and means
for erecting the new City Hall; he was among the peti-
tioners for the restoration of the bolting monopoly, and
in other ways, also, bore his share of the city's corporate
responsibilities—a record surely ample to attest the
public confidence reposed in his integrity and judgment.
Jacobus Van der Spiegel, of American birth and of a
family "long prominent in social life," was an ensign
in Captain Walter's company, sent to Albany in 1689
"to protect the northern frontier against the impending
French invasion," later held a captain's commission
and, in 1698, "was elected to the highly honourable
position of constable." Garrett Onclebagh, who served
several successive aldermanic terms, and Cornelius
Kierstede or Kierstead, who wrought first in New York
and afterwards in New Haven, whither he removed
about 1722, having some interest in a copper mining
project in the Blue Hills district, were both men of local
note and of influential family connexions and may be
regarded as representative of the New York silversmiths of the seventeenth and eighteenth centuries. To
the list of silversmiths already given one might add the
names of various members of the Van Dyck, LeRoux,
and other families of Dutch or Huguenot extraction,
besides many more of English blood, who became increasingly numerous as the eighteenth century wore on,

all of whom were eminently substantial citizens and time and again appointed or elected to posts of influence and trust. Albany, too, may claim a respectable list of silversmiths who worked during the latter part of the eighteenth century and the fore part of the nineteenth, while Utica, Kingston-on-Hudson, and other places must be remembered also.

In the Middle Colonies, that is to say, in Pennsylvania and New Jersey, we find admirable traditions of silversmithing established almost at the very beginnings of colonisation and that the silversmiths were men of repute amongst their neighbours. At the head of the list are Cesar Ghiselin, the Huguenot, and Philip Syng the elder, both of whom plied their craft while Penn's Colony was still in swaddling clothes and both of whom left enduring witnesses to their skillful craftsmanship in a part of the silver belonging to Christ Church, witnesses that would entitle them to high rank in their calling even if there were no other extant evidences of their handiwork to attest their prowess. Ghiselin's beaker and plate, the gift to Christ Church of "Margaret Tresse, spinstor," are shown in one of the illustrations as also are the flagon and the great baptismal bowl made by Philip Syng the elder and presented to Christ Church, in 1712, by that excellent but tempestuous gentleman, Colonel Robert Quarry. Ghiselin occupied a respected position in the community, and numerous descendants, in the female line, are to be found among those bearing honoured names in the city annals.

Philip Syng was more conspicuous in the life of the infant city than was Ghiselin, had influential connexions by blood and marriage and left issue whose widespread ramifications may easily be traced to-day in the "genealogical centre of the universe." He was succeeded in business by his son, Philip Syng the younger, who, in 1752, made for the Assembly of Pennsylvania the tray, ink-pot, quill holder and sand shaker (shown in one of the illustrations), afterwards used in signing both the Declaration of Independence and, eleven years later, the Constitution of the United States, and still carefully preserved among the treasures of the State House.

To name but one more, although there are many others no less deserving of extended biographical mention, there was Joseph Anthony (1762–1814) of prominent connexions and cousin to Gilbert Stuart, who owed his training abroad and his successful start in life as a portrait painter to the generosity of Anthony's father, a Philadelphia merchant. While mentioning Anthony's excellent silverwork, one would willingly go on and speak at length of William Vilant and Elias Boudinot, of Lownes and Richardson, of Shoemaker and Williamson, of Anthony Rasch and Nicholas Coleman and a long list of other Philadelphia and New Jersey silversmiths who adorned their craft and served their several communities and country; one would also gladly chronicle somewhat of the smiths who, though fewer in number, wrought in Virginia and also in Annapolis and, late in the eighteenth century, in Baltimore, but our purpose has been sufficiently fulfilled in calling attention to two things—first, what manner of men the Colonial silversmiths were and, second, how goodly a company of them, during the Colonial period and the immediately post-Colonial period, plied their calling.

In his admirable volume, "The Old Silver of

American Churches," E. Alfred Jones notes the fact that, "of the 2000 odd pieces of ecclesiastical silver," therein described by him, "of manufacture anterior to 1825," about 1640 were made by American silversmiths. He also notes that "in the late seventeenth century and down to the year 1800, over one hundred and seventy silversmiths were at work in the city of New York." If this was true of a relatively small place, it is plain to be seen how great must have been the aggregate when the larger, wealthier and altogether more important centres like Philadelphia and Boston were taken into account. A conservative estimate of the smiths coming within our purview might readily give their number as 500 or even more. It is manifestly evident, therefore, that it is well worth while for the collector and the connoisseur to be keenly on the lookout for the many specimens of their work that still remain.

PROCESSES

American silver of the Colonial and post-Colonial periods was a product in whose making the cunning of the artificer's hand and his conception of form were the factors of paramount importance, while the hard, perfunctory element of mechanical exactitude figured scarcely at all. To this intimate manual connexion between the craftsman and the wares he fashioned are to be in great measure attributed the flexibility, vigour, and freshness of design and also the subtly individual diversities of form characteristic of the early silver, hardly any two pieces ever being exactly the same.

Tradition, too, was a powerful agent for the goodness of both pattern and workmanship. The appren-

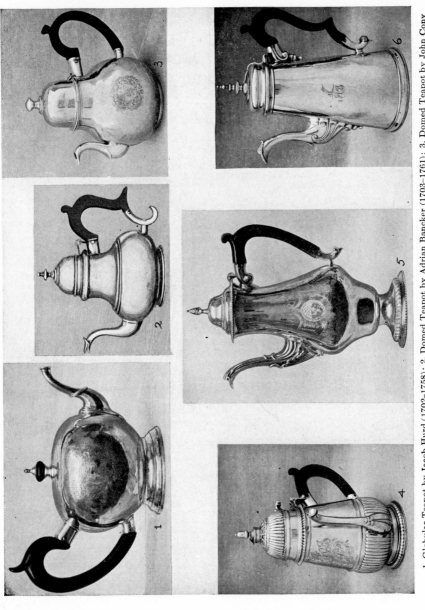

1, Globular Teapot by Jacob Hurd (1702–1758); 2, Domed Teapot by Adrian Bancker (1703–1761); 3, Domed Teapot by John Cony (1655–1722); 4, Chocolate Pot by Edward Winslow (1669–1753); 5, Coffee Pot by Paul Revere (1735–1818); 6, Coffee Pot by Pygan Adams (1712–1776)
1 and 5, Courtesy of Boston Museum of Fine Arts; 2, Courtesy of R. T. Haines Halsey, Esq., New York City; 3, 4 and 6, Clearwater Collection, Metropolitan Museum.   Courtesy of the Honourable A. T. Clearwater, Kingston-on-Hudson

1, Sugar Tongs, unmarked, c. 1730; 2, Porringer by Samuel Vernon (1683–1737); 3, Porringer by William Cowell (1682–1736); 4, Porringer by John Cony (1655–1722); 5, Candlestick, Baluster Stem and Moulded Base; Marked B. M. (unidentified) c. 1745; 6, Porringer by Adrian Bancker (1703-1761). Clearwater Collection, Metropolitan Museum of Art, New York City
Courtesy of the Honourable A. T. Clearwater, Kingston-on-Hudson

tice system was in full force, and a lad, whose parents were minded that he should follow the silversmith's craft, left the parental roof at the age of twelve or thereabouts and went to live with his master. The mysteries of silver working thenceforward became a part of his daily life, a part of the very atmosphere in which he had his being. A feeling for the metal, the forms into which it was meet to be worked and the methods of decoration to be employed thereon, became ingrained in his very nature. Small wonder, then, when he had faithfully fulfilled the years of his apprenticeship, that he should be well able to practise worthily the sound tradition of craftsmanship he had imbibed. In this respect the old smiths had a vast advantage over their modern successors, who must, perforce, learn all they know in a brief space of training, and that after their most impressionable years are past.

The texture of the metal is another reason for the great beauty of old silver, and this texture was due to the method of working it wholly by hand. Compare a piece of modern silver, no matter how excellent its make, with a good piece of the old work, and the superior beauty of the metal surface in the latter is at once apparent. The modern metal, rolled out before working under heavy mechanical pressure, has all the life crushed out of it, and no amount of subsequent working by hand can take away its hardness of aspect and impart to it the soft, lustrous, mellow appearance of the old metal that was discretely alloyed, annealed, and wrought by hand from the moment the molten coin was run into ingots from the melting-pot. Even the conscientious modern craftsworker can do no more to produce texture than dent the surface with hammer marks, unless he resorts wholly to the methods of the seventeenth- and eighteenth-century smiths. This will necessarily increase the cost of his product, and there are few who are willing to pay the price. The texture of old silver is comparable in a way to the patina of old furniture, at least so far as its charm is concerned; but patina on wood is largely a surface matter and may be cleverly simulated if the "antiquer" is expert enough and willing to take the pains. The texture of silver, on the contrary, is more than skin deep, and can be arrived at only by fundamental processes.

The workshops, in which many of the early silversmiths produced their rarely beautiful wares, were insignificant little structures, oftentimes not as large as the country roadside smithies where one may still see a farrier shoeing horses from the neighbouring farms. When John Hull and Robert Sanderson wrought drinking vessels, church silver services and domestic tableware and supplied the Commonwealth of Massachusetts with "pine tree" shillings and smaller coinage in a little mint house "sixteen feet square by ten feet high," one can readily understand the entry in Judge Sewall's diary, under date of June 21, 1707, anent the silversmith William Cowell, that "Billy Cowell's shop is entered by the chimney and a considerable quantity of plate was stolen."

Some knowledge of how the metal was manipulated from its ingot stage to its finished shape will contribute to our appreciation of a precious heritage of handiwork fit for modern emulation. Such knowledge we may gather from an inventory of the tools belonging to John Burt of Boston, who died in 1745, and from the lucid explanatory comment thereon by R. T. Haines

Halsey, Esq., to whom we are indebted for so much valuable work for the preservation, study and appreciation of early American silver.

INVENTORY OF JOHN BURT

316 oz 4 pwt of Silver @ 36/ p oz £560.3/ Gold 18 oz 12 pwt @ £27 p oz £500.17/	1070		
Cash £100—33 oz of Correll @ 20 pr oz. £33	133		
5 pair of stone earings & 3 sett of stone buttons £30 a parcell of old stones £7	37		
a parcell of Christalls for Buttons & Earings	32		
a parcell of old stone work	5		
2 Show Glasses .£5.0/53 pair of Chapes & tongs £10 .2/ ..,.................................	15	2	
11 Files, 33/ a pair of large and small bellows 40/	3	13	
a large Forgin Anvil 120 ld @ 2/ 6 p £15—1 small do £9	24		
9 raising Anvils 217 ld @ 3/ 6 p ld £37 .19 .6 .2 planishing Teaster 39 ld @ 3/6 £6 16 .6	44	16	
2 Spoon Teaster £26—2 planishing ditto 25/3 bench vises £12	39	5	
9 small vises 45/ 2 beak irons 20/ 40 hammers @ 8/ pr hammer 18 .16 .10	22	1	
2 Melting Skillets £5 . 37 bottom stakes & punches 155 @ 4/ £31	36		
a Drawing bench & tongs 40/ 11 Drawing Irons £11 10 pair of shears £6	19		
2 brass Hollowin stamps £5 . a pair of brass Salt punches 30/	6	10	
1 Thimble stamp £4 . 10/ 6 pr of flasks for casting £4 .10	9		
15 pair of tongs & plyers @ 5/ a pr. 75/ a pair of large scales and weights £8	11	15	
4 pair of small scales & weights 40/ pewter and lead moulds 85 ld @ 1/6 £6 .7 .6	8	7	6
36 old files, 18/ 12 strainers 12/ 1 Oyl Stove 25, 3 small saws 25	4		
4 boreax boxes 5/ 3 burnishers 20/ 1 Triblet 10 2/ boiling pans 60/	4	15	
a parcell of punches £5, 1 Touch Stone 5/	5	5	

Mr. Halsey says: "The inventory of the tools, which belonged to John Burt, gives between its lines the method of fashioning employed by the Colonial silversmith. First, the bullion was melted and refined in the *boiling-pans*, the fineness of the alloy tested by rubbing on a *touch-stone*, and the resultant streak compared with a streak obtained from silver of known quality. The metal was then remelted and run into a *skillet* and came out in a rectangular form, thinner than an ingot. In the making of hollow-ware the form thus obtained was rolled out, or hammered on the *Forgin Anvil* into a sheet of the requisite thickness. In the fashioning of a cup, a circle was cut with *saws* or *shears* from this sheet of silver; the diameter of this is somewhat larger than the contour of the vessel desired. This circular sheet was gently hammered with frequent annealings, over a *teaster*, until it took the form of a bowl, which was then gradually hammered over the various *raising anvils* and bellying anvils into the form finally desired. For work on the interior of the vessel, the *beak irons* (anvils with long beaks or horns, adapted to reach the interior surface of hollow-ware) were used. In shaping the vessel much use was made of *stakes* (small movable anvils of various sizes and shapes, which stood upon small iron feet on the work-bench). The brilliant facets, which covered the surface of all of our early silver, were obtained by lightly and skilfully beating the surface of the shaped vessel with *hammers* over the *planishing anvil*, both hammer-head and anvil being highly polished. The strips employed for rims, handles, and bases were made on the *drawing bench*—an apparatus in which the strip of metal is brought to an exact thickness and width by being drawn through a gaged opening made by two cylinders fastened at the required distance apart and prevented from rotating. Handles, finials, thumb-pieces, tips and in some cases spouts, were often cast in *pewter* or *lead moulds*, or more frequently by the old wax process in which the forms sought were first cast in wax, and then were embedded in moistened casting-sand contained in *casting-flasks*. This sand was then pounded into an almost solid mass and the *flasks* were put into the fire, the melted wax run off and replaced by molten silver; the rough castings thus obtained were then finished up with *saws, punches* and *files*. The casting was then placed on a pitch-block and the surface finished with *punches*. Defects in the casting were made good by soldering in and annealing solid pieces of metal, and chasing the surface. The *spoons*, as a rule, were cut or stamped out of thin sheets of metal, and bowls shaped over a *teaster* and planished over a *planishing spoon-teaster*. *Salts* and *thimbles* were *punched* out or *stamped* from thin sheets of metal. The *vises, boreax-boxes*, and *oyl stove* were used in the process of soldering on the bases, handles, rims, etc."

From this minute description of the purpose and manner of using each of the sundry tools in the silversmith's outfit one may form an accurate idea of the processes followed in manufacturing the silverware of Colonial days. Briefly epitomised, one may say that the processes engaged in included rolling the metal into thin sheets and beating it into the required shapes upon anvils; mounting these articles, when shaped, upon pitch or cement and applying decorative patterns with punches or else chasing the surface; casting in moulds and finishing by filing or chasing or, in the case of circular objects, on a lathe; at a later period "spinning" hollow-ware over a rapidly revolving mould; soldering or riveting the several pieces together when finished; the impressing of ornaments with a roller or striking them from dies and then applying them to the part to be decorated.

ARTICLES MADE

Articles of silverware made by early American silversmiths may be broadly classified as *Domestic* and *Ecclesiastical*. *Domestic* silver may be subdivided, according to its uses, as follows: (1) Silver for Eating and Small Table Accessories; (2) Silver for Drinking Purposes; (3) Silver for Containing or Pouring; and, finally, (4) Silver for Miscellaneous Table, Household, and Personal Uses.

SILVER FOR EATING AND SMALL TABLE ACCESSORIES. Spoons, marrow spoons, forks, knives (the handles), porringers, plates, platters, salt cellars, muffineers, pepper shakers, nutmeg graters, chafing dishes or brasiers, saucepans, sauce-boats, sugar tongs, trays, apple corers, casters, cruet stands, and coasters.

SILVER FOR DRINKING PURPOSES. Cans, cups, standing cups, goblets, caudle cups, loving cups with two and three handles, mugs, tankards, beakers, flip straws, tumblers, wine tasters.

SILVER FOR CONTAINING OR POURING. Bowls, baskets, boxes, coffee-pots, pitchers, creamers or cream jugs, chocolate pots, sugar bowls, tea-caddies, spout cups, strainers, flagons, teapots, urns, cruets, syphons, funnels, and punch ladles.

SILVER FOR MISCELLANEOUS TABLE, HOUSEHOLD, AND PERSONAL USES. Buckles, thimbles, sconces, candle snuffers, candlesticks, snuff-boxes, patch boxes, sword hilts, whistles, wine labels, trays.

Besides the above, other special pieces for sundry purposes occasionally come to light.

ECCLESIASTICAL Silver included chalices, patens, flagons, beakers, cups, alms basons, collection plates, and baptismal bowls and basons.

CONTOUR

It has been found expedient to make a somewhat arbitrary division of American silver of the Colonial and post-Colonial periods into four chronological classifications. This division, nevertheless, seems warranted by certain general groups of characteristic contours that coincide pretty nearly with the classifications, so that the method resorted to is justified by actual facts. The chief reason for making such a division, besides the convenience thus gained for classification and reference, was to direct attention to the striking parallelisms of contour and type of decorative design observable between the silver, furniture,[1] and architecture [2] of any

---

[1] v. "Practical Book of Period Furniture"; Eberlein and McClure.
[2] v. "The Architecture of Colonial America"; Eberlein: Little, Brown & Co.

given period. These noteworthy instances of similarity, while doubtless partly attributable to fashion, seem to have been mainly due to a widely diffused and dominant conception of line prevalent among artists and craftsmen of contemporary date.

For the sake of example, attention may be directed to the rotund, swelling curves and much-shaped contours in evidence during the latter part of the seventeenth century and the early years of the eighteenth, in the reigns of William and Mary and of Queen Anne. In architecture the profiles of mouldings displayed lines swelling into impressive rotundity; the panel heads of doors were shaped and curved; the bases of balusters on the stair had rotund curving contours closely resembling the forms of contemporary globular or globular and cupolaed teapots; hoods above house-doors were arched and coved, sometimes enriched with carving in the cockle-shell *motif*, and supported on shaped brackets; pediments over doorways were often curved in arcs, and, in a dozen other ways, a tendency toward well-rounded lines was abundantly manifest.

In furniture we see the prevalence of the cabriole leg; chair seats were rounded at the corners and in front; backs were spooned; the double-hooded *motif* was common both in cabinet work and settee backs, while panels and mirror frames echoed the same swelling curves.

In silver of the period there is visible a striking correspondence to the foregoing contour characteristics, especially in teapots, tankards, porringers, and cups, which the reader may easily discern by looking at the illustrations, particularly those in the chronological key at the beginning of the chapter. The shapes are instinct with elegance, but it is a rotund, Dutch elegance.

Again, in the Adam period of the latter part of the eighteenth century, the oval and the parabolic curve were in high favour and fashion. In architecture we see the oval in the shape of rooms and in various forms of applied decoration. Close akin to the oval is the oft-recurring urn *motif,* either as a flat decoration or as a modelled form.

In furniture we see half-oval-topped side tables and consoles, oval chair backs and a numerous display of kindred ovals and of urn-shaped finials. One point, however, should be remembered in this connexion, respecting both architecture and furniture—although curved lines appeared in structural work as an occasional variant to the dominant rectilinear features, they were *not* lines of structural support, save in the case of chair backs, but were purely decorative in function. Barring this occasional exception and the fashioning of urns and vases, lines in a per-pendicular plane were not curved or shaped, and the shaped lines occurred in a horizontal plane. The types of decorative detail common to architecture and furni-ture included the familiar swags and drops, pendent husks, round and oval pateræ, oval and spandrel fans, sundry vase and urn shapes and similar *motifs* which it is not necessary to enumerate in full.

Turning to the silver of the period, we find precisely the same principles of design in fashion, with only occasional and insignificant modifications. To verify this statement, the reader is again referred to the illus-trations, and especially to the Revere teapot, which is a silver embodiment of the contemporary Adam spirit both in its contour and in point of engraved surface ornamentation. No end will be served by multiplying instances of parallelisms; they are sufficiently obvious to be readily discerned in the other periods also.

This series of correspondences between silver, furniture, and architecture cannot be regarded as the result of purely fortuitous happening. It has a definite meaning for us, and, if it shows anything at all, it proves the close kinship existing between architecture and the decorative arts and it emphasises the necessity of becoming reasonably familiar with all the art and craft manifestations of a period if we would fully understand any one of them, for none of them stood alone, but each bore some relation to the others and was, in turn, influenced by them.

Inasmuch as the majority of early American silversmiths were of either British birth and training or of British descent, we naturally expect to find in their handiwork a perpetuation of British methods and a loyal adherence to English types of design, progressing almost contemporaneously—new styles were generally just a few years later in making their appearance in America than in England—with the march of fashions in the Mother-Country. The close adherence to English design was not only a matter of tradition, but also a matter of preference, "for the Colonials gloried in the name of Englishmen, and loved the customs of the old country," which they followed with punctilious and affectionate exactitude, a point of view that persisted even after the Revolution, for Washington and his fellow-founders of our government, fully realising the oneness of our blood with that of the parent stock, regarded themselves as Englishmen—*American* Eng-

9

lishmen, to be sure—till their dying day, and would have repelled indignantly any insinuation to the contrary. American silver, it is true, was, as a rule, simpler than much of contemporary English make, and, in a few cases, minor modifications, some of which were of purely local occurrence, were made by the Colonial smiths, but in the main the resemblance was so strong as to amount to virtual identity.

Only one other influence, beside the English, in the design of American silver has to be seriously considered, and that is the Dutch, which was, of course, strongest in New York and was never more than local, being confined to the sections of the country adjacent to, and in close and constant contact with, Manhattan.

The design of both English and American silver was subject in certain respects to an influence exerted by contemporary porcelain and pottery, which seem to have suggested contours to the silver craftsmen, who were no more averse to taking a cue, now and then, from Oriental sources than were the designers of furniture or the weavers of textiles. This ceramic influence may be especially traced in some of the teapots and bowls. One can easily see the resemblance to porcelain contours in such silver objects as the little covered bowl (Key II, 11), very like a china bouillon cup, or the globular teapot (Key I, 4).

The divisions adopted for the chronological key which seem best to exemplify and bear out the correspondences to which attention has been called are as follows: (I) Late Seventeenth and Early Eighteenth Century (synchronous with the late Stuart, William and Mary and Queen Anne forms in furniture and architecture); (II) Middle Eighteenth Century (synchron-

ous with Early Georgian forms); (III) Late Eighteenth
Century (synchronous with late Georgian, especially
Adam forms); (IV) Early Nineteenth Century (syn-
chronous with Empire forms in furniture and Classic
Revival forms in architecture).

SILVER FOR EATING AND SMALL TABLE ACCESSORIES

Spoons typical of the 1st division (Key I, 1), the
latter part of the seventeenth century, had oval or
elliptical bowls, instead of fig-shaped bowls, as did the
English spoons of an earlier date. The stem was flat,
instead of round or hexagonal, as previously; the end
of the handle was flattened, broad, and notched by two
clefts to make three points or projections, somewhat in
the manner of a trefoil; the end of this trifid handle was
also turned up. The junction of the handle or stem with
the bowl was continued and reinforced by a tongue or
grooved "rat-tail" on the back or convex surface of
the bowl (Key I, 2). This trifid form of spoon is sometimes known as the "hind's foot and rat-tail" pattern,
and continued to be made into the early years of the
eighteenth century (till about 1730).

In the forms typical of the 2d division we find, from
about 1725 to 1750, the rat-tail extending down the back
of the bowl, well defined, but without grooves (Key II,
7). It is an extension of the drop which reinforces the
junction of the handle and bowl and is now more pronounced than formerly. The bowl itself is more egg-
shaped and tapering towards the end. The end of the
handle, instead of being notched or trifid, is rounded
and turned up. The stem is no longer flat, but rounded,
at least in front, near the bowl (Key II, 6), and the
rounded and turned-up end is marked by a prominent

mid-rib (Key II, 6). From about 1750 to 1770, while the moulded drop at junction of handle and bowl was the essential method of reinforcement, and often more pronounced and longer than in earlier spoons (Key II, 3), a decorative device was sometimes added on the bottom of the bowl, such as the cockle-shell on the Revere spoon (Key II, 5) and the small spoon (Key II, 2). The end of the handle is still turned up (Key II, 1 and 4), and the mid-rib on the front is much less conspicuous, almost disappearing in some cases (Key II, 1).

In spoons of the 3d division, from about 1760 to 1800, one significant change is that the rounded ends of the handles are turned down (Key III, 1–8). The moulded drop at junction of bowl and handle, while distinctly in evidence, does not usually extend so far down the bowl as in previous examples. Scroll embellishments, as on the Revere spoon (Key III, 8), cockle-shells (Key III, 6), birds, or floral subjects were sometimes added at the termination of the drop. The front of the handle and stem often became a subject for elaborate ornamentation in "bright-cut" engraving from the end to the bowl (Key III, 7) in a pattern of essentially Adam provenance (Key III, 7 and 3). From about 1780 to 1800 the handles became lighter and the ends were more pointed (Key III, 1, 2, 3, and 4) than at an earlier date. Throughout this division bowls tended to become more tapering toward the end.

In spoons of the 4th division, from about 1800 to 1815, the ends continue turned down and are frequently of the shape known as "coffin-headed" (Key IV, 1, 2, 3, and 4). The bowls are distinctly more pointed than previously. The pattern of the engraving on these spoon-handles is still plainly reminiscent of Adam design. The drop at the junction of handle and bowl is much flattened and less pronounced (Key IV, 1 and 3). From about 1810 onward, spoons of the "fiddleheaded" pattern (Key IV, 5 and 6) came into vogue with a sharp, angular shoulder on each side of the stem just above the bowl (Key IV, 5 and 6). In some of these later spoons, all of which show a deterioration in design after 1815 or 1820, when the Adam influence had ceased to be an appreciable factor, the head of the handle is turned up (Key IV, 6), thus showing a reversion to an earlier custom, while in others it is turned down. Likewise, in numerous instances, the moulded drop at the junction of bowl and handle is omitted (Key IV, 5), but in others it persists.

A comparison of the chronological key-plates will show that both types and individual characteristics persisted from one period to another, and that fashions overlapped to some extent, just as they did in furniture and architecture, so that it is impossible to say that this or that style began at such a date and ended at such another; but the stages of evolution are sufficiently defined to justify the assignment of the several distinctive types to approximate periods of time, periods of which one type was representative and numerically in the ascendant.

Most of the spoons illustrated are of large size, about the size of our dessert-spoons or slightly larger, and many are the size of the largest modern table-spoons. This average is representative of the relative numbers in the Colonial period. Tea-spoons followed the styles of the larger spoons, but were not found in any considerable number before the middle of the eighteenth century. Some notion of the disparity in sizes of both large and small spoons may be obtained by looking at Fig. 1. Tea-spoons were not of a standard size any more than were the large spoons. Many of the old tea-spoons are of smaller bowl and shorter

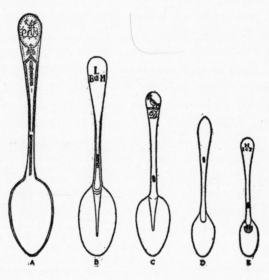

FIG. 1. A, Table-spoon with "Bright Cut" engraving, by Underhill & Vernon, New York, c. 1796.
B, Spoon of Second Period, with "Rat Tail" and initials in back.
C, Spoon of Second Period with Crest and initial engraved on back of handle.
D, Small Tea-spoon of Third Period.
E, Small Tea-spoon of Third Period with shell ornament on bowl.

Courtesy Pennsylvania Museum and School of Industrial Art.

handle than the modern tea-spoon (Fig. 1, D and E), and we can well understand, in looking at their dimensions, how they could easily and without any suggestion of clumsiness be laid across the tops of the small, handleless tea-cups as an indication that one desired no more tea.[3]

SALT-SPOONS were fashioned like the larger spoons, except for their circular or wide bowls.

MARROW-SPOONS began to be used about the beginning of the eighteenth century. The early forms had the ordinary bowl, while the handle was made into a long, narrow scoop. The later spoons of this sort had scoops at both ends, one of which was usually longer and narrower than the other.

FORKS, although common enough in the eighteenth century, have rarely survived the vicissitudes of time and usage. They became worn and damaged much more quickly and easily than spoons, and most of them, therefore, found their way back to the melting-pot. Some were wholly of silver, such as the pair by John Noyes (Boston, 1674–1749), now in the Boston Museum, while others had only silver handles, the prongs or tines being of steel or other metal. The handles usually followed the handles of contemporary spoons in shape and manner of decoration. While the forks by Noyes had only two prongs, we find three-pronged forks be-

---

[3] "An amusing incident, illustrative of the customs of the time, occurred at the house of Mrs. Robert Morris upon the occasion of the Chevalier de la Luzerne taking the Prince de Broglie into that hospitable household. The Prince writes: 'Monsieur de la Luzerne conducted me to the house of Mrs. Morris to tea. I partook of most excellent tea, and I should be even now drinking it, I believe, if the Ambassador had not charitably notified me at the twelfth cup that I must put my spoon across it when I wished to finish with this sort of warm water. He said to me: "It is almost as ill-bred to refuse a cup of tea when it is offered to you as it would be for the mistress of the house to propose a fresh one when the ceremony of the spoon has notified her that we no longer wish to partake of it."'"—"Colonial Homes of Philadelphia and Its Neighbourhood," Eberlein and Lippincott.

fore the middle of the eighteenth century for Peter Faneuil with some ostentation ordered from England about 1738, ''one dozen silver forks with three prongs, with my arms cut upon them, made very neat and handsome.''

KNIVES were occasionally made with silver handles, but they were rare, the majority having bone grasps. Butter knives were made, toward the end of the eighteenth century, with both handle and blade of silver.

PORRINGERS, big and little, were much used during the seventeenth and eighteenth centuries, but particularly during the early and middle portion of the latter, and so commonly performed the office of general utility vessels that it is well-nigh impossible to fix upon any one specific use for which they were intended. They are also known as ''wine tasters'' and ''bleeding cups,'' the latter in allusion to the leech's habitual practice of profuse bloodletting upon every possible occasion. Necessity has always been the mother of invention, and our Colonial forebears were much too inventive, resourceful, and practical to devote numerous silver and pewter vessels of this type solely to the requirements of the physician. If porringers were used in the operation of bloodletting, it was because they were the handiest article that chance presented, and probably only a small proportion of them were ever so employed. Their customary use was, doubtless, on the table to hold jam, honey, or even vegetables, and the complete absence of sugar bowls of a very early date justifies one in supposing that they were also used to contain sugar. Upon this strong probability, a porringer (Key V, 12) has been placed as the first in a line of

BOWL BY UNKNOWN MAKER, MARKED G. B. (IN OVAL), LION (IN OVAL) BELOW, c. 1740. PLATE BY SAMUEL
MINOTT (1732–1803). COVERED BOWL, UNMARKED, c. 1730
Metropolitan Museum of Art, New York City; Boston Museum of Fine Arts, Clearwater Collection,
Courtesy of the Honourable A. T. Clearwater, Kingston-on-Hudson

TOP AND BOTTOM OF PATCH BOX, EARLY EIGHTEENTH CENTURY, UN-
MARKED. TOP OF PATCH BOX BY JOHN WINDOVER, 1694–1726, MARKED
I W (IN OVAL). TEAPOT AND STAND BY PAUL REVERE

Clearwater Collection, Metropolitan Museum of Art, New York City
Courtesy of the Honourable A. T. Clearwater, Kingston-on-Hudson

chronologically arranged representative sugar bowls of
early American make and use.

The handles were of flat open-work in geometrical
or tracery designs (Fig. 2, A) or else of the later "key-
hole" type, convenient for hanging from a hook on the
dresser. The bowls were of various dimensions and
depths. Sometimes the sides were flaring (Fig. 2, B),
sometimes they swelled out and returned inward near

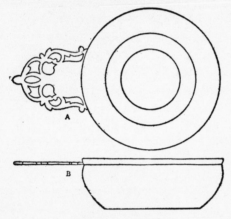

FIG. 2. A, Porringer, top view, by Richard Humphreys, Philadelphia, c. 1775;
B, side view of same.
C. Hartman Kuhn Collection. Pennsylvania Museum and School of Industrial Art.

the top. Both of these contour types are well shown in
one of the accompanying plates.

PLATES AND PLATTERS, while usually made of pewter,
were sometimes found of silver, in very limited numbers, in the houses of the most wealthy. Although the
Thomas Hancock plate, shown in one of the illustrations, was a piece of church silver, the same form was
followed when no ecclesiastical use was intended. In
other words, save for the difference in metal, silver

plates and platters were very like their fellows in pewter. Several reasons may be assigned for the comparative scarcity of silver plates and platters. In the first place, a large percentage of them, where they did exist, were no doubt melted down during the financial stress of the Revolutionary era. A much commoner reason was that, by the time a large class of the colonists had reached sufficient affluence to be able to afford silver plates and platters, attention was directed rather to the importation of fine Oriental services for the equipment of the table. A third and last reason is that a very considerable number of the gentle-born and wealthier colonists, who were likely to possess such articles, were Loyalists, and their silver was either confiscated or else taken with them when they fled to Halifax or returned to England.

SALTS, like spoons, teapots, and several other articles, were strongly characteristic in design of the period of their manufacture. In the 1st division we have the circular salt with a broad flaring base to obviate the danger of upsetting, possibly a willing concession to the old superstition. The particular salt with the gadrooned base and gadrooned rim at the top, around the edge of the shallow well, shown in the illustration (Key I, 8), is one of a pair made in 1665, presumably in New York, for Helena Willet, the daughter of Thomas Willet, the first English-speaking Mayor of New York. There is no maker's name nor mark. It is substantially the same as some of the better designed trencher salts, and may be considered as a link in the evolution from the "standing salt," by whose place on the table the station of those sitting at the board was indicated, to the individual salt or the pairs of salts for the common benefit of family and guests. Salts of a similar pattern in pewter are not unusual. This type doubtless continued to be made till well into the first quarter of the eighteenth century.

In the 2d division, salts of the pattern shown in Key II, 16 may be regarded as typical from about 1730 onward. The round bowl is supported on three cabriole legs with hoofs or hind's feet—an item of resemblance to certain chair legs of a not much earlier date.

In the 3d division,—that is, during the latter part of the eighteenth century,—the prevailing taste for ovals and urn contours is evidenced in the characteristic example shown in Key III, 9. The contrast between this type, with its flaring top rising from a pedestal, a type beautiful but easily upset, and the staunch seventeenth-century type of Key I, 8, possibly indicates some weakening of the superstition anent spilling salt.

In the 4th division, the early nineteenth century, heavy glass salts were largely used, but those made of silver followed, in general, the oblong, swelling contours to be seen in so many of the tea-pots and sugar bowls of the period.

Pepper Boxes appeared in the first half of the eighteenth century. A common form was between three and four inches high, had octagonal or round barrel, straight sides, a moulded base, encircling moulded bands near the top and bottom, a thin scrolled handle and a perforated drum-like cover either with or without a finial. In exhibitions they are sometimes catalogued as sugar sifters. As a matter of fact they would answer either purpose and were doubtless so used as inclination dictated.

CASTERS appeared about the middle of the eighteenth century and may be regarded as the ultimate development of the pepper box. If one preferred to use them as sugar sifters, they were practically analogous to the English muffineers. They were usually between five and six inches high, had a splayed moulded foot, a shaped cylindrical body, tapering slightly toward the top and bellied prominently outward in bulbous fashion at the bottom, and a high domed cover or lid, perforated and surmounted by a finial. A slightly earlier form was not quite so tall; had a larger pear-shaped moulded body and a low, convex perforated cap or cover without finial.

NUTMEG GRATERS, APPLE CORERS, and various other similar pieces of small silver table accessories rarely appeared before the middle or latter part of the eighteenth century, and, in general, followed the more important pieces in the matter of contour and decoration.

CRUET STANDS AND GALLERIED COASTERS likewise were comparatively late pieces of table service refinement for which it is useless to look much before the end of the eighteenth century.

CHAFING DISHES or BRASIERS were made at an early date and continued to be made throughout the eighteenth century and the early part of the nineteenth. They displayed great elegance of pattern and beauty of workmanship. There was little significant change in details of contour or decoration, and the example shown in Fig. 3 will convey an adequate idea of the class. The handles were of wood.

SAUCEPANS with lids and spouts (Fig. 4), sides tapering outwards towards the top, and wooden handles were made in considerable numbers during the eighteenth century. They were of elegant shape, but usually without decoration. Occasionally the sides were straight, at other times they swelled outward toward the bottom.

SAUCE-BOATS, dating from the latter part of the eighteenth century, were somewhat similar to cream

FIG. 3. Small Chafing Dish or Brasier by Philip Syng, the younger, Philadelphia, c. 1780.
C. Hartman Kuhn Collection. Pennsylvania Museum and School of Industrial Art.

pitchers in general contour, but had a longer body and wider spout.

TRAYS of sundry shapes came into use about the third quarter of the eighteenth century, sometimes rest-

FIG. 4. Saucepan by Joseph Richardson, Philadelphia, c. 1796.
C. Hartman Kuhn Collection. Pennsylvania Museum and School of Industrial Art.

ing flat on the table and sometimes supported on legs (v. illustration of Revere tea-pot). The legs also frequently resembled those of salts or cream pitchers (Key II, 12 and 16). They had raised rims, flaring edges or galleries, as the case might be, and were often ornately engraved.

Sugar Tongs came into use fairly early in the eighteenth century. The pair shown in the illustration dates from about 1730. This "scissors" type, with its graceful scrolls, was cast and then filed, and the plates covering the pivot were sometimes beautifully engraved. The later types, belonging to the latter part of the eighteenth century and the early part of the nineteenth, were generally in the form of tongs and made from a single piece of metal, bent into proper shape, with nipper ends for grasping the lump of sugar. In contour and decoration they resembled the other characteristic pieces of contemporary date.

Cake Baskets were made late in the eighteenth century and continued in favour during the succeeding period. They corresponded with the general style of the other contemporary silver and were usually fretted and also elaborately chased or engraved. In shape they were usually round or oval with a handle in the manner of a basket and ordinarily stood on a slightly raised base. In some cases they were designed with a raised base or pedestal but lacked the handle.

SILVER FOR DRINKING PURPOSES

All the sundry drinking vessels of early American manufacture, by their great number and variety, bear eloquent witness to the universally prevalent bibulous habits of our forebears. They are found in every section of the country, and the contours of the several members of the group show an evolution comparable to that in other articles, but no appreciable diminution in numbers during the period with which we are concerned.

CANS OR CUPS WITH HANDLES were virtually the same thing, and, if any distinction is to be drawn, it is that the term *can* is of early use and seems preferably to be applied to vessels of more generous capacity than the other appellation. Both varieties seem to have been evolved from the bowl with handles, a vessel seemingly used to drink from upon some occasions. Akin to the two- or even three-handled bowls were the large two-handled loving-cups with covers, belonging to the latter part of the seventeenth century and the early part of the eighteenth. The great loving-cup with cover and two handles, made by John Cony and presented to Harvard in 1701 by the Honourable William Stoughton, is an admirable example of this type, apparently the nearest relative of the *can* or *cup*.

Cans or cups of the 1st chronological division, embracing the latter years of the seventeenth century and the fore part of the eighteenth, were of various heights and diameters, with either one or two thin, ear-shaped handles, moulded bases, and straight or nearly straight perpendicular sides with an outward flare at the top. This type (Key V, 3, and Key II, 14) continued to be made during the first half of the eighteenth century. It was especially in favour in New England. The two-handled type went out of fashion before its one-handled brother. A heavier handle, of the same pattern as the tankard handle or the handle of contemporary mugs (*v.* mug by Cesar Ghiselin in one of the plate illustrations), was also used at the same time.

Cans or cups of the 2d division included both the type just described and also a barrel-shaped variety, encircled with hoops or bands (*v.* plate illustration of the can immediately beneath the mug by Ghiselin).

An exact technical distinction may be drawn between *cups* or *cans* and *mugs* by saying that the *cup* or *can* had a *rounded* bottom, stood upon a splayed, moulded or reeded base and had sides shaped either much or little —either a slight, beaker-like flare (Key II, 14) or a pronounced contour with pear-like bellying (Key V, 6 and 7). A *mug,* in the other hand, was derived from a tankard and its essential points of difference from its *cup* or *can* relative consisted in its having, beaker-like and tankard-like, a *flat* bottom with moulded base and

Fig. 5.   Can or Cup by Joseph Richardson, Philadelphia, 1796.
C. Hartman Kuhn Collection.   Pennsylvania Museum and School of Industrial Art.

straight sides, either tapering tankard-like toward the top or perpendicular (Key V, 1, 2 and 4).

Mugs, to all *practical* intent, however, were identical with cans or cups, except in point of their immediate tankard ancestry—they were really small, lidless tankards—whose straight sides, tapering inward toward the top, and scroll handles they closely followed. They were made both with bands (Key V, 1 and 2, and Ghiselin mug, plate illustration) and without bands. These were of the earliest type. A later banded type may be seen in Key II, 15.

HOLYOKE ARMS; EXAMPLE OF HERALDIC ENGRAVING
CUP OR BEAKER BY SAMUEL DROWNE, 1749–1815
REPOUSSÉ AND CHASED

Clearwater Collection, Metropolitan Museum of Art, New York
Courtesy of the Honourable A. T. Clearwater, Kingston-on-Hudson

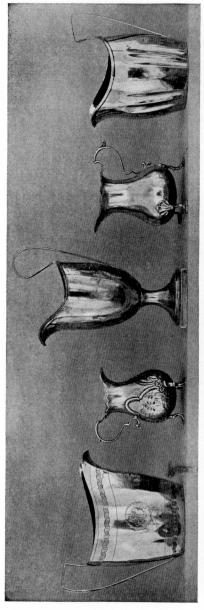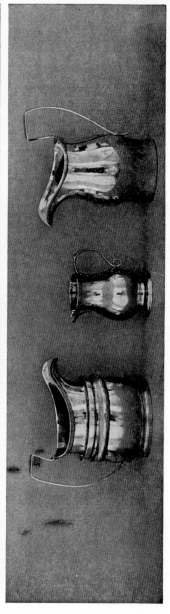

Cream Pitchers: 1, by Joel Sayre, 1778–1818; 2, by Jacob Hurd, 1702–1758; 3, by Ephraim Brasher, 1786–1805; 4, by John Windover, 1694–1726; 5, by William Moulton III, c. 1805; 6, by Lewis & Smith, c. 1811; 7, by J. Coburn, 1725–1803; 8, by Paul Revere, 1735–1818 1–5, Courtesy of H. T. Haines Halsey, Esq.; 6, Courtesy of the Honourable A. T. Clearwater, Kingston-on-Hudson; 7, Courtesy of Hollis French, Esq., Boston; 8, Courtesy of George S. Palmer, Esq.

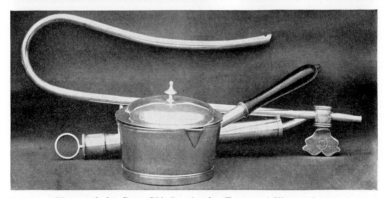

Bottom of Plate made by Cesar Ghiselin, showing Texture of Silver and Maker's Mark
Courtesy of the Rector and Vestry of Christ Church, Philadelphia
Tray, Quill Holder, Ink Pot and Sand Shaker, made by Philip Syng, the Younger, in 1752,
for the Pennsylvania Assembly.   Used in Signing the Declaration of Independence.
Courtesy of the Curator of the State House, Philadelphia
Pear-shaped Sugar Bowl by George Dowig, 1765; Saucepan, by Joseph Richardson, c. 1796;
Wine Syphon
C. Hartman Kuhn Collection, Pennsylvania Museum and School of Industrial Art

ONE OF PAIR OF SMALL TANKARDS OR COVERED
MUGS BY JOHN MYERS, c. 1796
C. Hartman Kuhn Collection, Pennsylvania Museum and School
of Industrial Art

TANKARD BY JOHN CONY (1655–1722)
Clearwater Collection, Metropolitan Museum of Art, New York City.
Courtesy of the Honourable A. T. Clearwater, Kingston-on-Hudson

From the middle of the eightenth century onward, mug and can types become so closely identified that a separate classification would only cause confusion. We find a variety with splayed and moulded base, a swelling, bulbous lower part, a shaped and outward curving upper part, and shaped scroll handle (Key V, 6 and 7) or a plain S handle (Fig. 5), while later on, in the early nineteenth century, along with this type, which seems to have maintained its popularity, there is to be seen much the same form, though with less pronouncedly shaped sides, on a pedestal or baluster base (Key IV, 9) and, besides this, there was likewise a frequent reversion or approximation to a much earlier model, such as the examples shown in Key IV, 14 and 15.

BEAKERS were tall, tumbler-shaped vessels whose form seems to have been derived from Holland. They were never as popular as cans or mugs, and the examples, therefore, are not so numerous as in the case of many other domestic articles. The simplest type was plain, with sides tapering towards the bottom, which was *flat*. Frequently the upper part flared outwards. A moulding (*v.* plate illustration of Dutch beaker by unknown maker and Key I, 7) was next added, or a splayed moulded foot. There was also a form (according to the foregoing strict definition, a *cup*) with moulded foot and the lower part of the body gadrooned (Key I, 9). Occasionally an example is found with ornate embellishment, such as the beaker with acanthus base in high relief (*v.* plate illustration) and decorated band a little below the mouth. The Dutch beakers (*v.* plate illustration and Figs. 8 and 9) were much more apt to be ornately engraved than beakers by smiths of English descent and tradition. In contour, beakers re-

10

mained much the same, and some of the slightly differing forms were made contemporaneously, so that it is not advisable to attempt to classify them in a chronological contour sequence. The beaker may have a handle.

STANDING CUPS AND GOBLETS on baluster stems, with moulded foot, while sometimes made at an early date for domestic use, belonged rather to the very end of the eighteenth century and the first part of the nineteenth as articles of domestic appointment. The great majority of early examples belonged to church sets and are, therefore, treated under ECCLESIASTICAL SILVER.

WINE TASTERS were very small, flat cups of porringer shape, sometimes with a scroll handle, at others with a flat handle like that of a porringer. The sides were either plain or gadrooned. They were not numerous.

TUMBLERS were the same as small beakers.

CAUDLE CUPS were two-handled mugs or cups, of low stature and of swelling pear-like contour in the lower part. They belong especially to the last of the seventeenth century and the first half of the eighteenth. Their characteristics closely resemble those of contemporary mugs and cups.

FLIP STRAWS were long-stemmed tubes with enlarged ends for stirring flip, and were pieces of drinking paraphernalia found only in houses of wealthy Colonials who could afford to have all the small occasional appointments made of precious metal.

TANKARDS were made and used from the beginning of the Colonial period to the early part of the nineteenth century, and display varying characteristics, according to the date of their manufacture. The tankards of the seventeenth century and the fore part of the eighteenth, corresponding to the 1st chronological division, show a broad, flat base, straight, tapering sides, a flat top or lid, scroll purchase and S handle with plain whistle, shield-shaped end or tip. Sometimes the handle was reinforced by a rib down the side. The base had a moulding, and there was a moulded lip. This early type was often embellished with a line of acanthus leaves or crockets above the base moulding and with moulded ornaments on the back of the handle, but such examples were usually pieces of a fairly late date in which the early contour had been retained (Key I, 5).

A little later, a mid-band was added, or occasionally several bands; the covers assumed the form of a swelling drum surmounted by a finial; the whistle tip, instead of being plain, was frequently adorned with a decorated plate bearing a moulded cherub's head or some such device, and the back of the handle oftentimes became a subject for moulded decoration. This form, also, dates from the 1st chronological division, as attested by specimens made by John Cony (Key I, 6) and some contemporary smiths. It continued in fashion through the 2d chronological division and well into the 3d, as evidenced by the tankards produced by Paul Revere (Key III, 10). In the 3d division we also meet with tankards of shaped body (Key III, 12), a form that seems to have been carried over into the early part of the nineteenth century. Latterly we find a smaller tankard, belonging to the end of the eighteenth century and the first years of the nineteenth, with straight, barrel-hooped sides and flat lid without finial (v. Hamilton tankard in plate illustration).

It may be noted that the type with mid-band, drum

top, and finial seems to have enjoyed special popularity in New England, while a form with plain sides (without mid-band) and top without finial apparently found general preference in New York, Connecticut, Philadelphia, and the country within their sphere of influence.

SILVER FOR CONTAINING OR POURING

Of all the silver belonging to this category, no articles show a clearer and more characteristic chronological progression of contour types than tea-pots. In considering them it is to be borne in mind that they show a disposition to increase in size as the eighteenth century advances. In the seventeenth century and during the early part of the eighteenth tea was an expensive luxury, and this fact will account for the small dimensions of the earlier tea-pots.

TEA-POTS of the 1st chronological division are of bulbous or bell shape, with a high, domed lid surmounted by a moulded finial, making the general contour somewhat similar to that of a pear with the big end down, as in the example by John Cony (Key I, 3), or else they are globular, with a flat, rimless lid, surmounted by a finial, as in another example of nearly the same date (Key I, 4). The bulbous or bell-shaped tea-pots with domed lid had no foot, but stood flat, with merely a narrow and inconspicuous base mould to terminate the inward curve of the sides; a short S-curved spout and a hooped or C-shaped wooden handle let into sockets soldered to the back. The globular tea-pots had a splayed moulded foot, an S-shaped or curved spout, but not turned so sharply upward; and a curved or C-shaped wooden handle, usually with a thumb-piece or purchase at the top. A contemporary Dutch type (*v.* tea-pot by Adrian Bancker in the plate illustration), made only in New York and the vicinity, was also bulbous or bell-shaped, had a squat splayed foot, curved spout, and shaped wooden handle. The lower handle socket was more ornate, the lower part of the body was flatter and turnip-shaped, the narrow neck was longer and more sharply defined in contour than in the related tea-pots of English type, and the high, domed lid, as well as the body, was marked with moulded bands. In the plate illustration, the three types in the upper row afford interesting grounds of comparison and also suggest certain points of ceramic relationship.

In the 2d division, towards the middle of the eighteenth century, we find a pear-shaped tea-pot (the large end up) in fashion (Key II, 8 and Key V, 9). The base or foot is splayed and moulded; the spout slightly S-curved and projecting well forward from the body; the small lid without rim, slightly drummed and surmounted by a pineapple or other finial, and a hooped or C-shaped wooden handle.

In the 3d division, the epoch of Adam influence in design, tea-pots have oval-shaped bodies with straight or slightly curved sides, flat bottoms without moulding, straight spouts, C-shaped wooden handles and lids either flat or slightly drummed and surmounted by a pineapple or moulded silver finial, or, sometimes, an ivory, bone, or wooden finial (Key V, 10 and Key III, 14). Such tea-pots often stood on oval trays with feet, made especially for them. The oval body contour of these tea-pots was frequently broken into a succession of small, concave, parabolic curves (Key III, 14, and also plate illustration of Revere tea-pot), and there were no mouldings at either base or top. Occasionally

these oval tea-pots had dished or concave tops, the ends
high and the middle low (*cf.* top line of sugar bowl,
Key III, 16). A variation from the perpendicular-
sided, oval tea-pots of this period, retained the oval
shape but had sides slightly swelling outward toward
the middle. Still another variety of tea-pot that belonged to this period was urn-shaped, stood on a pedestal and had a curved spout.

In the 4th division, under Empire influence, swelling
curves again became fashionable. The tea-pots often
stand on four ball feet (Key V, 11), and, while the sides
are broken into curves, the general shape is either round
or oblong (Key V, 11), the spout is curved and projecting, the lid flat with a pineapple or moulded finial, and
the handle C-shaped or scrolled (Key V, 11). The top
is often dished or concave in contour with the ends
higher than the middle (Key V, 11).

Spout Cups, with covers and S-curved spouts, were
made during the 1st and 2d divisions, and, in general
contour, resembled the bell-shaped tea-pots, except that
the spouts were at the side.

Sugar Bowls, as vessels specifically made for holding sugar, do not belong to our 1st chronological
division. As it is highly probable that the porringer,
the general utility vessel at that period, did duty for a
sugar bowl, a porringer has been placed first in the
chronological sequence of sugar bowls shown in Key V,
12, 13, 14, 15 and 16. Vessels such as the engraved bowl,
by an early but unknown maker, shown in the plate illustration below the engraved Dutch beaker, may also
have served as sugar bowls. At this period there was
no effort made to have complete tea sets of uniform
pattern, such as those that came into use later in the
eighteenth century.

In the 2d division, bowls of varied pattern, such as those shown in Key V, 13 and 14, were doubtless used for sugar and may, upon occasion, have served for other purposes, too. There were also standing, covered, pear-shaped bowls, similar to the contemporary pear-shaped tea-pots, made for sugar (v. sugar bowl by George Dowig in plate illustration).

In the 3d division, when the elegancies of the late eighteenth century tea-table had become more highly organised, sugar bowls were made of a pattern to correspond closely with the tea-pot and its accompanying paraphernalia. Favourite types were in the form of urns with rising, shaped covers (Key V, 16), or of oval baskets with handles (Key V, 15). Dished or concave contours were common (Key V, 15).

In the 4th division the sugar bowl closely corresponded with its neighbour, the tea-pot. Common shapes were oblong, with ear-like handles at each end (Key IV, 11 and 13), round, and pear-shaped, rising from a moulded pedestal and surmounted with a rising shaped cover with a pineapple or moulded knob (v. plate illustration of sugar bowl with gadrooned base by George Dowig). The oblong sugar bowls with ear handles stood on four ball or knob feet (Key V, 11 and 13), and the tops, as were also the tops of many of the contemporary tea-pots, were dished or concaved in contour, with the ends high and the middle low (Key V, 13). Gadrooning (Key IV, 11) was a favourite method of ornamentation for sugar bowls, tea-pots, and other large pieces of hollow-ware.

CREAM PITCHERS, as well-defined articles of specific purpose, make their appearance before the middle of the eighteenth century. There are obviously numerous

points of similarity and contour correspondence between the little, round-bellied cream pitchers with
moulded and cast scroll handles, three cabriole legs with
hoof or web feet, and shaped rims and spouts, on the
one hand, and the contemporary three-legged salts, the
brasiers, the pear-shaped tea-pots, and the cast sugar
scissors, on the other. These cream pitchers had usually a plain body, but occasionally (as in the left-hand
example of the plate illustration of eight cream
pitchers) engraving and chasing were added. These
three-legged cream pitchers of the 2d chronological
division (Key II, 12; Key V, 17, and Fig. 6, A) were
supplemented by a second, nearly contemporary
variety, supported on a stem or stand rising from a
broad, circular foot (Key II, 13, and Key V, 18) with a
cast scrolled handle.

In cream pitchers of the 3d division we find more
restraint and less rotundity of contour. Even where
the shape of the contour has not been obviously inspired
by classic models, refinement of line (Key V, 19, and
the left- and right-hand specimens on the top row of the
full-page plate of cream pitchers) was a dominant characteristic. The general form, in a horizontal plane, was
oval or oval with concaved shapings (Key V, 19), and
the contour line of the top was usually concaved. In a
vertical plane we find elliptically curved lines. Some
of the cream pitchers were polygonal, following a general oval outline. Another favourite form, besides the
flat-bottomed types just mentioned, rose on a pedestal
from a square base and continued upward in the manner of an urn (Key V, 20; Key III, 13, and Fig. 6, B).
The handles of these cream pitchers were scrolled (Key
III, 13), ear-shaped (Key V, 19), or straight-topped
with descending curve (Fig. 6, B).

1 and 3, Front and Side Views of Tankard by Paul Revere (1735–1818)
Courtesy of Dr. Frederick Tuckerman, Amherst, Massachusetts
2, Flagon by Nathaniel Morse (1685–1748)
Courtesy of Boston Museum of Fine Art and the Church in Brattle Square, Boston

BAPTISMAL BOWL (14¾ INCHES IN DIAMETER) AND FLAGON, BY PHILIP SYNG,
THE ELDER, 1712
BEAKER AND PLATE BY CESAR GHISELIN, c. 1710
Courtesy of the Rector and Vestry of Christ Church, Philadelphia

Cream pitchers of the 4th division coincided with the prevalent pompous and imposing contours of companion pieces. They were flat bottomed (Key IV, 12) and also had base mouldings (Key V, 21). The bodies displayed swelling lines and were sometimes oblong or elongated to correspond with the tea-pots and sugar bowls. The sides were either shaped with many curves (Key V, 21) or followed one graceful outward curving

Fig. 6.   A, Three-legged Cream Pitcher, by Joseph Richardson, Philadelphia, c. 1790; B, Cream Pitcher, by Joseph Shoemaker, Philadelphia, 1797–1817.

C. Hartman Kuhn Collection. Pennsylvania Museum and School of Industrial Art.

and returning line (Key IV, 7). There was also a type, with S scroll handle and contour approximating, but not equalling in grace, that of the earlier three-legged pattern (v. full-page plate of cream pitchers, in middle of bottom row).

PITCHERS of a larger size but generally similar contour were to be found, particularly in the early nineteenth century, when they often assumed an approximately barrel or jug shape.

EWERS, of an urn shape, with short spout or mouth and a cover came into use in the latter part of the eighteenth century. They were not numerous, however. They were used for wine, water or cyder.

URNS, as their name denotes, were of urn shape and became popular in the latter part of the eighteenth century, when the Adam influence was still strong and determined their design, as hot-water receptacles for the tea service. They stood on square bases, with or without feet; had two ear-shaped handles; a rising lid with finial atop and a spigot or tap in front, at the base of the urn, the thumb piece being of wood or ivory. The body of the urn, of tall, slender, pointed oval, classic shape—similar to that of the tall covered sugar bowl (Key V, 16) of the same period—might present either a continuously curved surface in circumference, or a surface fluted with a succession of shallow, concave, parabolic curves, like the surface of the sugar bowl or basket (Key V, 15) or the Revere tea-pot, or, finally, the polygonal circumference might be broken into a number of vertical facets.

In the ensuing period of Empire influence the urns, though retaining their name and use, and the base and pedestal stock or support, developed either a round or oblong base (with or without feet) and a round body, sometimes of globular contour, sometimes of approximately pear form; a surface broken horizontally into many swelling and returning moulded curves, like that of the tea-pot (Key IV, 10); otherwise a body of oblong contour, similar to that of the tea-pot (Key V, 11), the transverse swellings and moulded curves still appearing. The tops corresponded in style to the tops of contemporary tea-pots and sugar bowls. The handles were either of ear type or scroll shaped and placed vertically; rings hanging from lions' mouths; or else of shaped contour and fixed horizontally.

COFFEE POTS were not often to be met with till towards the middle of the eighteenth century. The earliest were of a cylindrical form tapering towards the top, had a curved spout, shaped scroll wooden handle let into sockets (Fig. 11, H) soldered to the back, and a drum lid with finial (*v.* plate illustration of coffee pot by Pygan Adams). Coffee pots were always built on tall, cylindrical lines as opposed to the low and often globular contour of tea-pots. The later coffee pots, however, while maintaining and even increasing their height and relative circumference, shared somewhat in the characteristics of contemporary tea-pots. They had shaped sides, swelling out noticeably, like inverted pears, in the lower portion of the body and then sharply receding to the stock or pedestal which rose from an ornate moulded or gadrooned and splayed base or foot. The curved spouts and handle sockets were often elaborately decorated and the drum lids—more swelling than in the earlier type—were moulded and capped with pineapple or other finials (*v.* plate illustration of coffee pot by Paul Revere).

There was still another form, slightly later than the preceding, of shaped contour, swelling out in the lower part. It closely resembled the late, shaped tankards (Key III, 12) and had neither stock nor receding curve of the lower body (such as that noted in the type just discussed) but rested directly upon a splayed moulded foot. Otherwise it did not differ widely. While coffee pots of the two types just described continued to be made through the eighteenth century, yet another type as was to be expected, came into fashion as well towards the end of that period. This last mentioned style was urn shaped, in accord with the strong Adam influence, stood upon a slender pedestal or stock and differed from the previously described urns of classic lines only in having a spout and scrolled wooden handle instead of two ear-shaped handles of silver. During the period of Empire influence, while usually retaining their traditional height, coffee pots were made closely resembling, both in general contour and detail, the urns and tea-pots of contemporary vogue. They commonly stood upon buxom stocks. In the early nineteenth century also occurred melon-shaped coffee pots, standing upon legs, and elaborately decorated.

CHOCOLATE POTS were cylindrical in form, swelling at the base and tapering towards the top, with a domed cover (v. plate illustration). The curved spout was at the side and both base and cover were especially subject to ornamentation. This same general contour seems always to have been preserved, despite the mutations of fashion that affected the shapes of other articles, and is to be seen also in Oriental porcelain chocolate pots.

PUNCH LADLES had bowls flaring sidewise or bowls with lips or spouts at the sides to facilitate pouring; the handles were long and oftentimes were made of wood capped at the end with silver.

STRAINERS were fashioned with great elegance and care, for punch brewing was an highly important social function requiring the best of accessory appointments. Rims and handles were chastely moulded and the handles were scrolled (Fig. 7, B). Some strainers had two long handles, projecting on each side, which stretched across the diameter of the punch bowl, resting upon the opposite rims; others had but one handle, in which case there was apt to be a catch projecting downward (Fig. 7, A) to hold the strainer in place at the side of the bowl. The perforations (Fig. 7, B) were in decorative, and usually geometrical, patterns.

SYPHONS AND FUNNELS were made in silver (*v.* plate illustration) for the convenience of householders in a

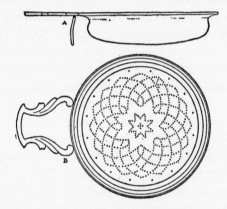

FIG. 7. Side view of Strainer by Benjamin Halstead, Philadelphia, 1783, showing catch; B, Top view of same Strainer.

C. Hartman Kuhn Collection. Pennsylvania Museum and School of Industrial Art.

day when heads of families had regard enough for their port and Madeira to be punctilious about handling it themselves and before the appreciation of those potables had been lessened by cocktails, highballs and their plebeian congeners.

BOWLS, such as those shown in Key II, 11; Key V, 13 and 14, and in the plate illustrations, besides being used for sugar or for tea slops, fulfilled a variety of other uses. Their contour affinities have already been noted.

TEA-CADDIES OR CANISTERS, towards the latter part of the eighteenth century, were made to accompany the silver tea services. Their shape was derived from the porcelain tea-caddies of the period while the details of form and decoration corresponded with the other articles they were intended to accompany. They were not numerous, as Oriental lacquer boxes or wooden caddies, made in Hepplewhite or Sheraton designs to accord with the knife boxes and sideboards of the time, and containing two or more pewter compartments, were in far more general use.

FLAGONS were much the same as tankards in point of contour, only taller and narrower in proportion, and, while sometimes probably employed domestically for filling tankards, were more commonly of ecclesiastical use and always retained their early form. They are further discussed under ECCLESIASTICAL SILVER.

BUCKLES for shoes and knee breeches were made from an early date, were both plain and ornate, and, in general, corresponded with the dominant characteristic details of ornament of the period of their manufacture. Line engraving, "bright cutting" and chasing were sometimes used for their embellishment. Unfortunately a very large number of knee and shoe buckles found their way to the melting pot, when they were no longer in demand as items of personal apparel, and emerged in the form of tea spoons.

THIMBLES, needlecases, bodkins and other small sewing accessories of silver were numerous during the eighteenth century.

PATCH BOXES AND SNUFF BOXES during the eighteenth century were made in a variety of shapes, as fanciful conceit dictated, and were often objects of great elegance and elaborate workmanship. Even relatively plain patch and snuff boxes were not seldom beautifully engraved or chased with decorative designs on the top and sometimes on the bottom as well (*v.* plate illustration).

SWORD HILTS, WHISTLES and other of the less common elegancies were determined more by personal fancy than by any prevailing period influences.

WINE LABELS appeared late in the eighteenth century and both at that time and afterwards accorded with current silver styles. They were both oblong and shaped and were concaved to lie close to the rounded contour of the decanter. They occasionally display "bright cut" edge bands or other decorative engraving or chasing as well as the lettering to indicate the contents of the decanter.

CANDLESTICKS of the first chronological division had square or round bases, a *bobèche*-like projection low down on the stock for convenience in carrying, and plain stocks with mid-bands or else fluted stocks, tapering toward the top. In the second chronological division, or from about the second quarter of the eighteenth century, candlesticks had baluster stems with octagonal, round or shaped bases (*v.* plate illustration). Branching candelabra belong to the latter part of this era. In the third chronological division, the shafts or stems were of a more pronouncedly architectural pattern with square bases, the sides of the stem frequently being fluted and the socket moulded like a pillar capital. The architectural candlestick maintained its popularity in the early nineteenth century.

SCONCES occur now and again but are not numerous and are generally of a plain pattern with S-shaped stems.

CANDLE SNUFFERS AND TRAYS, made of a design suitable to accompany candlesticks, occur from about the middle of the eighteenth century onward.

JEWELLERY. It has been pointed out that many of the silversmiths, as was quite natural, were goldsmiths as well. In this capacity they fabricated not a little jewellery, including bracelets, necklaces, chains, settings for brooches and seals, rings, earrings and the like. In this phase of their business, they wrought in both gold and silver and displayed no less taste and deftness of touch than in the manufacture of church plate and domestic tableware. Attention has also been called to the fact that a large proportion of the silversmiths were proficient in the art of engraving and it is, therefore, not surprising to find them cutting numerous seals.

The subject of Colonial Jewellery is too large to treat in the chapter on Silver. Many excellent pieces of Colonial workmanship remain and a little investigation would readily yield sufficient material for a valuable monograph.

NOTE: It is manifestly impossible that all discoverable forms of early American silver could be included in the descriptions set forth in the foregoing sections. Variations from these representative types must inevitably occur but, notwithstanding the points of difference they exhibit, they are plainly and unmistakably derivations from the more usual and representative types and a reader familiar with the general type characteristics, as noted in this chapter, will find no difficulty in classifying them according to their stylstic affinities.

ECCLESIASTICAL SILVER

In church silver, owing to the strong conservatism that always prevails in matters ecclesiastical, there is to be found less change of style than in the domestic silver of the same periods and early forms persisted with great pertinacity.

CHALICES may be defined as standing cups or goblets on baluster stems rising from a broad, round foot or base. The lower part of the cup, immediately above the baluster stem, might be either plain or gadrooned. It was usually plain, however, and the sides of the cup might be either straight or flared slightly outward, while the rim might or might not be flared. In some instances the bowl of the cup was of great depth and the stem comparatively short. Stem and base might be plain or elaborately moulded and gadrooned. Chalices were often made with flanged covers to fit tightly over the top and these covers were frequently made in the form of patens (v. Patens) with a base, the paten being inverted when used as a chalice cover.

Owing to the strong Puritan element in New England and the general desire to eliminate, as far as possible, all points of resemblance to the usages of the Church of England, it was a common thing to substitute beakers, cans, mugs or other drinking vessels instead of chalices for sacramental purposes, and consequently chalices, though not unknown, were comparatively rare wherever the Puritan influence was paramount. In Dutch New York and the Dutch parts of Long Island and North Jersey we find the same prevalence of beakers and the same scarcity of chalices for a similar reason. In Pennsylvania, however, in South, West and Eastern Jersey, and in Delaware and the Southern Colonies, where the Church of England was far stronger numerically, exactly the opposite condition obtained and chalices were the rule while beakers were the exception. All the same, beakers did occur once in a while and that, too, in unquestionably orthodox and conservative parishes, as, for example, the Ghiselin

11

beaker (*v.* plate illustration) among the collection of plate at Christ Church, Philadelphia, or a beaker of Dutch workmanship at St. Mary's, Burlington. In the Swedish parishes of Pennsylvania, West Jersey and Delaware the chalice was used.

PATENS were discs or plates, either with or without rims, and were made of a pattern to correspond with the chalice. The two odinarily went together in the case of an individual's gift to a church. The paten was usually flat bottomed, like a plate (*v.* plate illustration of Ghiselin plate or paten), but was sometimes raised on a low base or stock. Both chalice and paten were commonly plain save, perhaps, for an engraved inscription or the arms of the donor.

FLAGONS were virtually of tankard shape but much taller and narrower in proportion. The straight sides of their cylindrical bodies or barrels were either perpendicular or tapered toward the top and there was no moulded mid-band, as in some of the tankards. Whatever moulded bands encircled the body or barrel of the flagon were near either the top or the bottom. When inscriptions or heraldic engraving were used, they were ordinarily placed on the body about the middle of the front. The projecting base was moulded and the lid or cover was drummed (*v.* plate illustration of Quarry flagon at Christ Church, Philadelphia, by Philip Syng, the elder) and might be either flat on top or finished with a finial (*v.* plate illustration of the flagon of Brattle Street Church, Boston). The lid or cover was raised by pressing down a purchase (*v.* Fig. 11 (*b*), K) or thumb piece. The handles were "S" scrolled and there were no spouts at the lip whose circumference was unbroken by any shape to facilitate pouring.

Towards the latter part of the eighteenth century a form of flagon with shaped sides, swelling out in a bulbous manner towards the bottom of the body, and a splayed, moulded foot, was occasionally seen and, later still, an urn-shaped ewer form of flagon was introduced.

BEAKERS AND CUPS. Beakers have already been defined (*v.* Drinking Vessels) as tall, tumbler-shaped vessels with sides tapering towards a flat bottom or a moulded base (Key I, 7 and the plate illustrations of the Dutch beaker by an unknown maker and the Ghiselin beaker at Christ Church, Philadelphia). For the sake of nice distinction, it seems desirable to make the following differentiation between beakers and cups, as set forth by Miss Paull, of the Boston Museum:—While the beaker had a flat bottom or else a moulded base, the cup had a rounded bottom (which might be either plain or gadrooned as in Key I, 9), rising from a splayed, moulded or reeded base. Both beakers and cups might be of any height and diameter compatible with convenience in handling and both might or might not have handles. There was almost invariably a perceptible outward flare at the rim.

ALMS BASONS AND COLLECTION PLATES. The chief points of distinction between these two pieces seem to be in the greater expanse and depth of the former. The plate illustration of the Hancock plate, with its engraved cherub heads, is sufficiently representative to render further minute description unnecessary.

BAPTISMAL BOWLS AND BASONS were of various sizes and patterns. The baptismal bason at Christ Church, Philadelphia, by Philip Syng the elder (*v.* plate illustration) is 14¾ inches in diameter and correspondingly deep and was made to be set in the font.   On the other hand, some of the old Dutch New York baptismal bowls are comparatively shallow with broad rims, while still another type, sometimes to be met with in New England, stood on a moulded pedestal or stem (*v.* baptismal bowl of the old church at Cohasset, mentioned in chapter on Pewter).   There was no prevailing standard of type, either chronological or local.

DECORATIVE PROCESSES

The decorative processes that were commonly employed for the embellishment of American silver made between the date of colonisation and the end of the first quarter of the nineteenth century were ENGRAVING, CHASING, FLAT-CHASING, MOULDING, GADROONING, EMBOSSING, FILLETING, and STAMPING.

ENGRAVING was the decorative process most frequently used.   It gave more latitude of design than other processes, yielded more variety of application, and was peculiarly adapted to the material as a medium of surface embellishment.   It was performed with the ordinary graving tools, and the proficiency of the early silversmiths, displayed in this method of ornamentation, found its echoing manifestation in their achievements on copper and wood.   One of the essential characteristics of engraving, indeed, it might be called the distinguishing characteristic, was the removal of a part of the metal by the gouging of the shaving tool, no matter how small the quantity removed might be.

The three usual channels in which the smith could show his skill in engraving were *lettering,* the execution of *armorial bearings,* and the tracing of *decorative* or *symbolic devices.*   To these must be added the "bright-cut'' engraving which was extensively practised in the latter part of the eighteenth century and early nineteenth for the ''dog-toothed'' decorative bands, ovals, and other *motifs* so freely used in the application of patterns of Adam provenance, and consisted of a succession of broad, shallow side cuts of the tool, much on the principle used in executing the ''wriggled work'' on pewter surfaces, which produced numerous small facets at a slight angle. Examples of this, usually in conjunction with the direct line process, may be seen in Fig. 1, A; Key III, 16; Key V, 15, the Revere tea-pot of the plate illustration, and the other pieces shown herewith. The difference in method may readily be seen by comparison with such a piece of work as the small section of surface showing armorial bearings in large detail, in one of the plate illustrations.

CHASING differed essentially from engraving in that the design was effected with punches, none of the metal being removed and a slight burr being sometimes raised which was afterwards burnished off.

FLAT-CHASING had reference to the depth or rather shallowness of punch marks as distinguished from deep punched lines.

MOULDING consisted of casting in moulds such parts as it was not convenient or suitable to work up with hammer or fashion over shaped anvils, such, for instance, as the pineapple finials on sugar bowls and tea-pots, some of the masque, fruit, and flower ornaments on tankard handles, the cherub heads on tips or plates, legs of salts, and cream pitchers (Fig. 6, A), the scroll work of sugar scissors or tongs and their shell tips (*v*. plate illustration), porringer handles (Fig. 2, A), and the like.

FILLETING consisted in the application of bands, rims, and the members of decorative mouldings.

GADROONING consisted in producing a series of convex gadroons or nulling by working up the sheet of metal or piece of hollow-ware over a shaping anvil or over a mould shaped for the purpose (Key I, 8 and 9; plate illustration, base of sugar bowl by Dowig).

EMBOSSING or REPOUSSE work is really an amplification of the previous process and its application to the production of more than one *motif*. The design had to be worked up by the agency of beak irons (*v. supra*) *inside* the vessel and hammering from the *outside* over the beak irons' horns, thus raising the design in relief. One of the most beautiful examples of decoration produced by this process is the beaker by Samuel Drowne (1728–1774) with an acanthus base which is also chased.

STAMPING, besides being applied to spoon bowls and like shallow objects, was resorted to for making decorative bands and repeats, such as the acanthus leaves about the base of the tankard in Key III, 11. When stamped by dies in a strip, these decorations were soldered in place.

TYPES OF DECORATIVE MOTIFS

LETTERING was the simplest form of engraved decoration, and was executed in all manners, from Roman capitals to numerous variations of flowing script. In nearly all cases the lettering is well spaced and the letters themselves are well proportioned and graceful (Key I, 2; Fig. 1, B and E, the rim of the Christ Church baptismal bowl by Philip Syng, the back of the "Margaret Tresse, spinstor" plate by Cesar Ghiselin, the rim of the Hancock plate, and the flagon of the Brattle Street Church).

When lettering was done it was customarily engraved on the fronts of tankards, mugs, cups, and cans, on the rims or bottoms of plates, the handles of porringers, and the handles of spoons and forks. It is interesting to note that, during the 1st chronological division and part of the 2d, while it was customary to turn the end of the spoon *up* in front, initials and crests were modestly engraved on the back (Fig. 1, B and C; Key I, 2, and Key II, 3). After that time, when the ends were turned *down*, crests and initials were generally moved in *front,* and other decorations also then began to be employed on the handle (Key III, 1, 3, 5 and 7; Fig. 1, A).

HERALDIC ORNAMENT, consisting of armorial bearings and crests, was one of the most beautiful and legitimate forms of silver embellishment. Wherever there was a broad surface, the front of a tankard or urn, the side of a tea-pot or sugar bowl, the level expanse of a tray, or even a small, flat surface like the head of a spoon handle (Fig. 1, C; Key II, 3), one is likely to meet with some heraldic device—it may be merely the crest, or it may be the full arms with crest, torce, mantlings, and all. The character of the engraving was almost universally excellent, and this form of decoration was far more dignified and seemly than some of the tortured modern efforts.

STRAP-WORK was peculiarly characteristic of silver made by smiths of Dutch birth or descent, and is almost never found on a piece of American silver made outside of the New York sphere of influence. The beaker of the plate illustration shows how this interlacing strap-work was employed in conjunction with floriated and foliated scroll-work (Fig. 8), and Fig. 9 shows how strap-work decoration was further elaborated by the addition of human figures, birds, fruit, and other objects.

FIG. 8.   Detail of engraved strap work and foliation as applied by Dutch New York silversmiths.

Courtesy of R. T. Haines Halsey, Esq.   (Catalogue of New York Exhibition)

FIG. 9.   Detail of engraved fruits and figures with strap work.

Courtesy of R. T. Haines Halsey, Esq.   (Catalogue of New York Exhibition)

FOLIAGE, SCROLLS, both foliated and floriated, CHERUBS' HEADS, GARLANDS and RIBBONS and various

EARLY AMERICAN TWO HANDLED BOWL, MADE BY JACOB BOELEN,
NEW YORK, c. 1654–1729
Courtesy of Metropolitan Museum

EARLY AMERICAN TWO HANDLED BOWL, c. 1680–1710 MARKED WITH
INITIALS OF VAN SCHAICK FAMILY
Courtesy of Metropolitan Museum

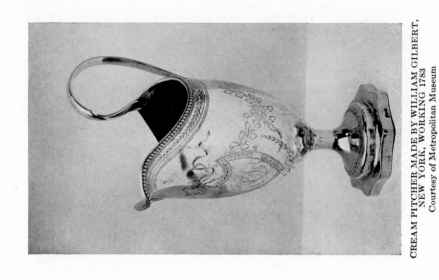

CREAM PITCHER MADE BY WILLIAM GILBERT,
NEW YORK, WORKING 1783
Courtesy of Metropolitan Museum

LATE EIGHTEENTH CENTURY CREAM
PITCHER, MADE BY A. DUBOIS,
PHILADELPHIA

other decorative *motifs,* including the Adam SWAGS AND
DROPS, PENDENT HUSKS, and PATERÆ were freely used, as
may be seen by the illustrations, for the enrichment of
surfaces.

MARKS AND MARKING

The Colonial silversmiths were not required, as in
England, to set their mark upon a piece of silver they
had fashioned, in connexion with the hall-mark and date
letter. There was no regulation requiring official assay-
ing and hall-marking, and it was not done. Neither
was a date letter or mark stamped. As there was no
regulation about marking silver, some of it is entirely
unmarked and we can only make conjectures as to
the maker.

Most of the early smiths, however, followed the
English tradition of marking their wares. They generally used their initials placed within rectangles, ovals,
shields, circles, and the like (Fig. 10), and either with
or without some device such as a fleur-de-lis, a crown, a
pellet, or a star in conjunction (Fig. 10; bottom of
Cesar Ghiselin plate, in plate illustration). The name
of the place of manufacture is not given. In some
instances, where the surname was short, the full surname was given.

Makers did not confine themselves to one mark, but
used several indiscriminately from time to time. John
Hull and Robert Sanderson, John Potwine, Jacob Burt,
and various others had a succession of marks, while
the Reveres, father and son, had a bewildering array.

About the first quarter of the eighteenth century it
became common to use the surname, with or without an

initial, and occasionally the full name appeared. Plenty of instances occur, however, up to about 1770, where only the initials are used. The employment of devices along with the makers' initials gradually fell into disuse towards the middle of the eighteenth century.

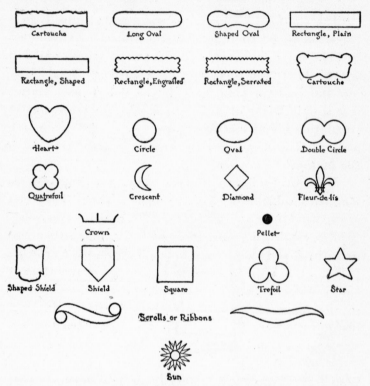

FIG. 10.   Makers' devices and enclosures for names

The various enclosures for makers' names or initials and the more usual devices employed in conjunction with them are shown in Fig. 10, which, along with the list of makers' names and references to their marks, will supply a method of ready identification to be applied by the reader.[4]

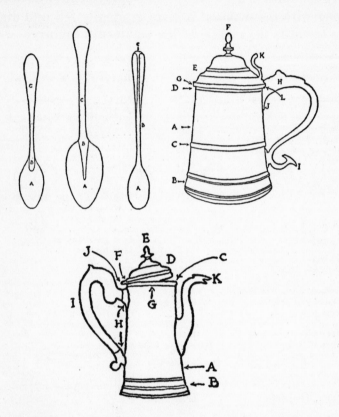

FIG. 11. SPOONS: A, *bowl*; B, *moulded drop or rat tail*; C, *handle*. TANKARD: A, *body*; B, *base*; C, *mid-band*; D, *lip*; E, *cover*; F, *finial*; G, *rim*; H, *handle*; I, *tip*; J, *body drop*; K, *purchase*; L, *hinge*. COFFEE POT: A, *body*; B, *base*; C, *lip*; D, *cover*; E, *finial*; F, *rim*; H, *handle sockets*; I, *handle*; J, *hinge*; K, *spout*.

---

[4] This list is not complete, and the authors will be grateful for any additional names or marks that readers may be able to supply; also any data, biographical or otherwise, respecting makers listed or unlisted that they may be able to furnish.

LIST OF MAKERS AND THEIR MARKS PRIOR TO 1830.

BOSTON:

Allen, John	1671–1760	I A (in inverted heart)
Allen, Thomas	1758	....
Andrews, H.	c. 1830	....
Austin, Nathaniel	1731–1818	Austin (script, small, in rectangle); N·A (in rectangle)
Bailey, Benjamin	c. 1800	....
Bailey, Henry	1808	....
Baker	1765	....
Baldwin & Jones	c. 1815	BALDWIN & JONES (in scroll)
Ball, John (Boston ?)	c. 1770	J.BALL (in rectangle) JOHN BALL }(in cartouche)
Ball, S. S.	1838	....
Ball, True M.	1815	....
Barnes, Abraham	1716	....
Belknap, Samuel	1751–1821	....
Bentley, Thomas	c. 1762–c. 1800	....
Bingham, John	1678	
Blowers, John	1710–1748	BLOWERS (in long oval); Blowers (script, in rectangle)
Boyer, Daniel	c. 1725–1779	BOYER (in rectangle) D B (in rectangle) D B (in two ovals)
Boyer, James	c. 1700–1741	....
Bridge, John	1723–c. 1794	BRIDGE I·BRIDGE (in a cartouche)
Brinton, Gordon & Quirk	1780	....
Brown, Ebenezer	1773–1816	....
Burnett, C. A.	......	C-A-BURNETT (in rectangle)
Burrill, Joseph	1823	....
Burrill, S.	c. 1680–c. 1733	*S.B.* (pellets above, fleur-de-lis below, heart-shaped shield) S: *Burrill* (in cartouche) S.B. (in rectangle)
Burt, Benjamin	1728–1803	*BENJAMIN* (in cartouche) *BURT* BURT (in rectangle) B-BURT (in rectangle)
Burt, John	1690(?)–1745	*JOHN BURT* (in oval) (also in cartouche) I. BURT (in cartouche) I B (crown above, pellet below, in shaped shield)
Burt, Samuel	1724–1754	SAMUEL BURT (in cartouche)
Burt, William	1726–1752	W.BURT (in rectangle)

Butler, James	1713–1776	J.BUTLER (in rectangle)
		I B (in rectangle)
Carpenter, Charles	1807	. . . .
Cary, Lewis	1820	L· CARY (in engrailed scroll ending in rosettes)
Chasley, ...	1764	. . . .
Churchill, Jesse	1773–1819	I . CHURCHILL (in rectangle)
		CHURCHILL (in rectangle)
Churchill & Treadwell	1815	. . . .
Clark, Samuel	c. 1681	. . . .
Clark, Thomas (Boston?)	–1783	. . . .
Cobb, E.	c. 1710–c. 1762	E. Cobb (in rectangle)
Coburn, John	1725–1803	J. COBURN (in rectangle)
Codner, John	1754–1782	. . . .
Cole, John	1686	. . . .
Cony, John (Coney)	1655–1722	I C (in a shaped heart, fleur-de-lis below)
		I C (crowned, in a shaped shield, coney below)
		I C (in rectangle)
Conyers, Joseph	c. 1708	. . . .
Conyers, Richard	–1708	. . . .
Coolidge, Joseph, Jr.	1770	
Cowell, William	1682–1736	W Cowell (in a cartouche)
		W C (in a shaped shield, star and two pellets above, pellet below)
		W C (in oval)
		W· Cowell (script, in a cartouche)
Cowell, William, Jr.	1713–1761	. . . .
Crosby, Jonathan	c. 1743–	. . . .
Cross, ...	1695	. . . .
Crouckeshanks, Alexander	1768	
Dane, Thomas	c. 1724–c. 1796	T· DANE (in long oval)
Davis, Joshua	1796	I DAVIS (in serrated rectangle)
Davis, T. A.	1824	. . . .
Davis, William	1823	. . . .
Davis, Watson & Co.	c. 1820	. . . .
Dawes, William	1719–1802	. . . .
Demmock, John	1798	. . . .
Deverell, John	c. 1764–1813	. . . .
Dixwell, Basil	1711–1746	
Dixwell, John	1680–1725	I D (in oval)
Doler, Daniel	1765	. . . .
Donaldson, John W.	1823	. . . .
Drowne, Shem	1728–1774	. . . .
Dummer, Jeremiah	1645–1718	I D (in heart, fleur-de-lis below)
Dunkerly, Joseph ?	1787	. . . .
Dwight, Timothy	1654–1691	T D (in heart, six pellets below)

Eames, Joshua	–1722	....
Eayres, Thomas Stevens	c. 1760–c. 1803	....
Edwards, Andrew	1763–1798	....
Edwards, John	c. 1670–1746	I E (in quatrefoil)
		I E (crowned, in shaped shield, fleur-de-lis below)
		I E (in lobed shield); I E (in cartouche)
Edwards, Joseph	1707–1777	I Edwards (script, in rectangle)
		I · E (in rectangle) ?
Edwards, Joseph, Jr.	1737–1783	....
Edwards, Samuel	1705–1762	S · E (crowned, in shaped shield, fleur-de-lis below)
Edwards, Thomas	1701–1755	T Edwards (script, in rectangle) and
		T E (in rectangle)
		T E (crowned, in shield) and T E (in rectangle)
Emery, Stephen	c. 1752–1801	S. Emery (in cartouche)
		S E (in rectangle)
		Emery (in cartouche)
Emery, Thomas Knox	c. 1781–1815	T - K - EMERY. (large, in rectangle)
Emery & Co.	1798	....
Epps, Ellery	–1808	....
Evans, Robert	c. 1768–1812	EVANS (in engrailed rectangle)
Faris, Charles (Boston ?)	c. 1790	C's Faris (script, in oblong oval); Chas. Faris (script, in oblong oval)
Farnam, Henry	1773–	H. FARNAM (in rectangle)
Farnam, Rufus (Farnham)	c. 1771–	R. FARNHAM (in rectangle)
Farnam, R. & H.	1807	R & H FARNAM (in rectangle)
Flagg, Josiah (Jeweller)	c. 1713–1741	....
Flagg, Josiah, Jr. (Jeweller)	1738	....
Fletcher, Thomas	c. 1810	....
Fletcher & Gardiner	c. 1810	....
Foster, Joseph	1789	FOSTER (in rectangle); I. FOSTER (in rectangle)
Foster, Samuel	1676–1702	....
Frothingham, Ebenezer	1756–1814	....
Gardner, Sidney	c. 1810	....
Gay, Nathaniel	1680	....
Gibbs, Daniel	1716	....
Glidden, Joseph ?	c. 1697–c. 1780	I G (crowned, fleur-de-lis below in shield)
Goodwin, Benjamin	1756	B : Goodwin (in rectangle)
Gray, John	1692–1720	....
Gray, Samuel	1684–1713	GRAY (in rectangle)
Gray, Samuel	1710	S : GRAY (in rectangle)
Green, Benjamin	1712–1748	B : GREEN (in rectangle)

Greene, Rufus   1707–1777   R · GREENE (in shaped rec-
                                          tangle)
                                      R · G (in shaped rectangle)
                                      R G (small in rectangle)

Griffith, David   –1789   ....
Grignon, Benjamine   1685   ....
Guille, Noah   1701   ....
Haddock, Henry   1830   ....
Hanners, George   c. 1696–1740   G . HANNERS (in rectangle)
                                      G H (crowned, pellet below,
                                      in shield)

Hanners, George, Jr.   1721–1760   ....
Hansell, Robert   1823   ....
Harding, Newell   1799–1862   ....
Haugh, Samuel   1675–1717   S H (in rectangle)
Healy, ...   –1773   ....
Henchman, Daniel   1730–1775   Henchman (in rectangle)
                                      D H (in rectangle)

Hewes, Abram   1823   ....
Hiller, Benjamin   1687–   B H (two crescents below, in
                                      a shaped shield)
                                      B H (in cartouche)

Hiller, Joseph   1721–1758   ....
Hitchborn, Samuel   1752–1828   ....
Holyoke, Edward   1817   ....
Homes, William   1717–1783   W · Homes (in rectangle)
                                      HOMES (in rectangle)
                                      HOMES and W. H (both in
                                      rectangles)
                                      W H (in rectangle)

Homes, William, Jr.   1742–1825   ....
How, David   c. 1745–   ....
Howard, William   –1823   ....
Howe, Otis   1788–1825   ....
Hull, John   1624–1683   I H (in heart, fleur-de-lis
                                      below)
                                      I H (in shaped shield, rose
                                      above)

Hull & Sanderson   1652–1683   I H ⎫ (in heart, fleur-de-lis
                                      ⎬ below)
                                  R S ⎰ (in shaped shield, rose
                                         above)
                                  I H ⎱ (in shaped shield, rose
                                         above)
                                  R S ⎰ (in shaped shield, sun
                                         above)
                                  I H ⎱ (in heart, fleur-de-lis
                                         below)
                                  R S ⎰ (in shaped shield, sun
                                         above)
                                  R S ⎱ (in shaped shield, sun
                                         above)
                                  I H ⎰ (heart-shaped shield,
                                         rose below)

Hull & Sanderson	1652–1683	I H (in square with rounded top, four pellets above) R S (in shaped shield, rose above) I H (in square with rounded top, four pellets above) R S (in shaped shield, sun above)
Hurd, Jacob	1702–1758	I HURD (in cartouche) Jacob Hurd (in cartouche) Hurd (in oval) Jacob Hurd (in cartouche) I Hurd (in shaped oval) I H (in rectangle) HURD (small in rectangle) Hurd (in shaped oval)
Hurd, Nathaniel	1729–1777	N · Hurd (in rectangle) N. Hurd (small in cartouche)
Hurst, Henry	c. 1665–1717	H H (in shield)
Jesse, David	1670–1708	D I (circle above, pellet below, in a circle)
Jones, John	c. 1810	. . . .
Jones, J. B.	1782–1854	J. B. JONES (in rectangle) PURE COIN (in rectangle)
Jones & Ward	c. 1815	. . . .
Kelly, Grael	1823	. . . .
Kneeland, Joseph	1698–1760	I : Kneeland (script in a cartouche)
Leach, Charles	c. 1765–1814	. . . .
Leach, Nathaniel	–1789	. . . .
Legare, Daniel	1688–1724	. . . .
Legare, Francis	1636–1711	. . . .
Leverett, Knight	1703–1753	K · Leverett (script, in a cartouche) K L (in shield) K L (in rectangle)
Loring, Henry	1773–1818	. . . .
Loring, Joseph	1776	v. Hull, Mass.
Low, Francis	1806–1855	. . . .
Low, John J. & Co.	1828	. . . .
Luscomb, John G.	1823	. . . .
Manning, Daniel	1823	. . . .
McFarlane, John	c. 1796	J . M$_c$ F (in rectangle) and eagle
Mecum, George	1830	. . . .
Millner, Thomas	c. 1690–c. 1745	T M (in shaped rectangle)
Minott, Samuel	1732–1803	S·M (in rectangle); Minott (script, in rectangle); Minott (script, in rectangle) and M (script, in square)
Mitchell, Phineas	1812	. . . .
Morse, David	–1798	. . . .

Morse, Hazen	1813	. . . .
Morse, Moses	1816	M. MORSE (in rectangle)
Morse, Nathaniel	c. 1685–1748	N M (crowned, bird? below, in a shaped shield); N M (in rectangle); N M (crowned, flower below; shaped shield); N M (in rectangle)
Morse, Stephen	1796	v. Newbury, Mass.
Moseley, David	1753–1812	D Moseley (script, in rectangle); D M (in rectangle)
Moulton, Ebenezer	1796	. . . .
Neuill, Richard	–1674	. . . .
Norcross, Nehemiah	1796	N N (in a cartouche)
Norton, Benjamin	1810	. . . .
Noyes, John	1674–1749	I N (cross below, in shaped shield); I N (fleur-de-lis below, in a shield); I N (in an oval)
Oliver, Andrew	c. 1722	. . . .
Oliver, Peter	1682–1712	P O (in a heart)
Paddy, Samuel	c. 1659	. . . .
Parker, Daniel	1727–1786	D · PARKER (in rectangle); D·P (in a rectangle); D:P (in oval)
Parkman, John	1716–1748	. . . .
Perkins, Isaac	c. 1707–1737	. . . .
Phillips, Samuel	1658–c. 1722	. . . .
Pierce, John	c. 1810	. . . .
Pollard, William	c. 1690	W. P (in an oval)
Pons, Thomas	1757–c. 1817	PONS (large, in an engrailed rectangle); *PONS* (in rectangle)
Poor, Nathaniel C.	1808–1895	. . . .
Potwine, John	1698–1792	I : Potwine (script, in cartouche); I—P (in oval); I P (crowned, in shaped shield); PO (in heart-shaped shield)
Prince, Job	1680–1708	. . . .
Putnam & Son	1822	. . . .
Revere, Edward	1767–1845	. . . .
Revere, J. W.	1798	. . . .
Revere, Paul, Sr.	1702–1754	P. REVERE (in rectangle); P · Revere (italic script, in rectangle); P R (in crowned shield); P R (crowned, in shaped shield); P. REVERE (in rectangle). P. REVERE (in shaped oval)
Revere, Paul	1735–1818	· REVERE (in rectangle); · REVERE and P. R. (script, in rectangles); REVERE (in a rectangle);

12

Revere, Paul	1735–1818	P. R (script, in rectangle); P R (in rectangle); P R (incised)
Revere, Paul	1760–1813	. . . .
Revere, Thomas	1765–1817	T R (in rectangle)
Revere & Son	1796	. . . .
Ridgway, James	–1789	. . . .
Ridgway, John	1807	. . . .
Roberts, Frederick	1770	. . . .
Rouse, Michael	1687–	M R (in rectangle); M R (in a shield)
Rouse, William	1639–1704	W. R. (star and two pellets above, pellet below, in a shaped shield); W R (fleur-de-lis above and below, in a circle)
Royalston, John	1770	I R (crowned, shaped shield)
Sanderson, Robert	c. 1610–1693	R S (rose above, in a shaped shield); R S (sun above, in shaped shield)
Sargeant & Ensign	1823	. . . .
Savage, Thomas	1664–1749	T S (star below, in a heart)
Sawin, Silas	1823	. . . .
Shreve, Benjamin	1813–1896	. . . .
Simpkins, Thomas Barton	1728–1804	. . . .
Simpkins, William	1704–1780	W. SIMPKINS (in cartouche); W. SIMPKINS and Simpkins (script, in rectangle); W. Simpkins (script, in rectangle); W Simpkins (script, in rectangle) and W S (in rectangle); W S (in rectangle)
Smith, Joseph	1789	I. SMITH (in a rectangle)
Somerby, Robert	1794–1821	. . . .
Stacy, P.	1819	. . . .
Stanwood, Henry B.	1818–1869	. . . .
Stodder & Frobisher	1817	. . . .
Sutherland, George	1810	. . . .
Swan, Caleb	1754–1816	. . . .
Symmes, John	1766	. . . .
Thomson, Peter	1817	. . . .
Trott, George	c. 1765	. . . .
Trott, Jonathan	1730–1815	J. TROTT (in cartouche, or shaped oval)
Turner, James	1744	I T (in shaped shield)
Tyler, Andrew	1692–1741	A T (fleur-de-lis below, in a heart); A T (fleur-de-lis, below in a heart), A T (crowned, cat ? below, in a shaped shield); A T (crowned, cat below, in a shaped shield); A. TYLER (in rectangle)

Tyler, David	c. 1760–1804	D T (in a rectangle)
Tyler, George	1740–	G . T (in a rectangle)
Vinton, David	. . . . . .	. . . .
Ward, Richard	c. 1815	. . . .
Waters, Samuel	1804	S. WATERS (in rectangle)
Watson, Edward	1821	. . . .
Webb, Barnabas	c. 1729	. . . .
Welch, John	1730–1812	. . . .
Welles, George	1784–1827	. . . .
Welles & Co.	c. 1800	. . . .
West, B.	1770	. . . .
West, Charles	c. 1830	. . . .
Whiton, Ebed	1826	. . . .
Willis, Stillman	1823	. . . .
Winslow, Edward	1669–1753	E W (fleur-de-lis below, in a shaped shield); E W (in a double circle); E W (in rectangle)

NEW YORK CITY:

Alstyne, Jeronimus	1787	. . . .
Anderson, William	1746	W A (in rectangle)
Archie, John	1759	I A [John Archie?] (in oval)
Backus, Delurine	1796	. . . .
Bancker, Adrian	1703–c. 1761	A B (in oval); A B (pellet below, in a heart)
Bayley, Simeon A.	1790	BAYLEY (in shaped rectangle)
Bayley & Douglas	1798	. . . .
Benjamin, Barzillai	1774–1844	. . . .
Bennett, James	1769	. . . .
Besley, Thauvet	1727	T B (monogram, crown above)
Boelen, Hendrik	–1755	H B (monogram, in shaped shield)
Boelen, Jacob	–1705	I B (rose below, in shield); I B (with crown above, in cartouche); I B (in shaped shield)
Bogardus, Everardus	1698	. . . .
Bogert, Albert	1816	. . . .
Bolton, James	1790	. . . .
Bourdet, Stephen	1730	. . . .
Bowne, Samuel	1805	S . BOWNE (in rectangle)
Boyce, G.	1829	. . . .
Brasher, Ephraim	1786	E B (in oval)
Brevoort, John	1742	. . . .
Brinckley, William	1804	. . . .
Broadhurst, Samuel	1725	. . . .
Bruff, Charles Oliver	1763	. . . .
Burger, John	1786	Burger (script, in rectangle), N. York (script in rectangle)
Byrne, James	1790	. . . .
Cady, Samuel	1796	. . . .
Cady & Backus	1796	. . . .

180   EARLY AMERICAN ARTS AND CRAFTS

Cant, Godfrey	1796	....
Caralin, Pierce	1804	....
Caston, Francois	1804	....
Chat, Le Sieur	1790	....
Chene, Daniel	1786	....
Chitry, P.	1816	P. Chitry (in long oval)
Clapp & Ricker	1805	....
Coen, Daniel	1787	....
Coley, Simeon	1767	....
Coley, Wm.	1816	....
Cooke, John	1804	....
Cornelison, Cornelius	1712	....
Crawford, John	1815	....
Dally & Halsey	1787	....
Dawson, John	1767	....
Denise, John & Tunis	1798	J & T. D (in rectangle), phœnix's head (in rectangle), sheaf of wheat (in rectangle)
DePeyster, Wm.	1733	....
De Remier, Peter	1769	....
Dobbs	1788	....
DuBois, Joseph	1790	J. DUBOIS (in rectangle)
Duche, René Rock	1804	....
Dunn, Cary	1765	C·DUNN (in rectangle)
Edmechat, Claude	1790	....
Edwards, Thomas	1731	....
Elleson, Peter	1796	....
Eoff, Garrett	c. 1785–1850	G. EOFF (in rectangle); G. Eoff (in rectangle)
Etting, Benjamin	1769	....
Evans, John	1816	....
Feurt, Peter	–1737	....
Fielding, George	1731	....
Forbes, Abraham G.	1769	....
Forbes, Colin V. G.	1816	....
Forbes, G.	1816	....
Forbes, I. W.	1805–1820	I. W. FORBES (in rectangie, sheaf of wheat below); I W FORBES (in rectangle, sheaf of wheat); I. W. FORBES (in rectangle)
Forbes, W. G.	1773	W G FORBES (in rectangle); W FORBES (in rectangle); W G FORBES (in rectangle; eagle's head in oval, sheaf of wheat in rectangle); W G Forbes (in oblong), eagle's head (in oval), sheaf of wheat (in rectangle); W G FORBES (script, in rectangle), eagle's head (in oval).

Fournequet, Lewis	1796	....
Francis, N.	1805	N FRANCIS (in oblong, eagle (in square with serrated top)
Fueter, Daniel Christian	1754	....
Fueter, David	1789	....
Fueter, Lewis	1770	....
Gale, John	1816	v. Heyer
Gale, Wm.	1821	....
Gardiner, B.	1829	....
Gilbert, Wm.	1783	....
Goelet, Philip	1701–1747(?)	P G (in oval)
Gordon, Andrew	1796	
Gordon, A. & J.	1798	....
Gordon, James	1796	....
Grigg, William	1765	Grigg (script, in shaped rectangle)
Hall, Drew	1789	....
Halsey, Benjamin	1764	....
Halsey, Jabez	1762–1820	I · HALSEY (in rectangle)
Halsted, Benjamin	1764	v. Philadelphia
Hamersley, Thos.	1756	T H (in rectangle)
Hastier, John	1726	I H (in heart); J-H (in rectangle)
Hastier, Margueritte	1771	....
Hays, Andrew	1769	....
Heath, John	1761	....
Hendrickse, Ahasuerus	1698	A - I (in oval)
Heron, Isaac	1768	....
Heurtin, Wm.	1731 (d. 1771)	W. H (in oval)
Heyer, W. B.	1798	W. B. HEYER (in rectangle), H & N (in rectangle); W. B. HEYER (in rectangle), J. GALE (in rectangle)
Hinsdale, Epaphras	1796	....
Hutton, John	1720	I H (in rectangle)
Hutton, John S.	1684–1792	v. Philadelphia
Jackson, John	1731	....
Johnson, Samuel	1783	....
Judah	1774	....
Kendal, Charles	1787	....
Kierstead, Cornelius	c. 1675–c. 1753	C K (in rectangle); C K (a diamond and two pellets below, in a shield)
Kingston, John	1775	....
Kip, Benjamin	1702	....
Leddel, Joseph	1752	....
Lent, John	1787	....
LeRoux, Bartholomew	1739	....
LeRoux, Charles	1725	C L
LeRoux, John	1723	I. L. (in oblong); I L (in oval)
Lintot	1762	....
Luzerder, Benj.	1796	....
Lyell, David	1699	....

Lyng, John Burt	1761	LYNG (in rectangle), N. YORK (in rectangle)
Malrid & Co.	1787	. . . .
Martin, P.	1756	. . . .
Maverick, Peter R.	1755–1811	. . . .
McClymon, J. C.	1805	. . . .
Mecom, John	–1770	
Merick, J. B.	. . . .	J. B. Merick (in rectangle)
Merkler, John H.	1788	. . . .
Morris, John	1796	. . . .
Morris, Sylvester	1759	. . . .
Mott, John & Wm.	1789	. . . .
Moulinar, John	1744	I M (in rectangle)
Myers, Myer	1746	Myers (script in shaped rectangle)
Newkirke, Joseph	1716	I. N (in oval)
Onclebagh, Garrett	1698	G^{BO} (in trefoil)
Overin, Rich.	1702	. . . .
Parisien, Otto	1769	. . . .
Parisien, O & Son	1789	. . . .
Pattit, Thomas	1796	. . . .
Pearce, Samuel	1783	. . . .
Pearson, John	1796	. . . .
Pelletreau, Elias	1750	E P (in rectangle)
Petit, Thomas	1796	. . . .
Pinto, Joseph	1758	. . . .
Pontran, Abraham	1727	A P (in heart)?
Quintard, Peter	1731	P ꟼ (in square); P Q (in square)
Reeves, Stephen	1776	v. Burlington, N. J.
Richard, S.	1828	. . . .
Richardson, Thos.	1769	. . . .
Ridout, Geo.	1745	G R (in square)
Riker, P.	1801	. . . .
Riker & Alexander	1798	. . . .
Ritter, Michael	1786	. . . .
Robbs	1788	. . . .
Robert, Christopher	1731	. . . .
Roberts, Michael	1786	. . . .
Romney, John	1770	. . . .
Roosevelt, Nicholas	1735	N R V (in rectangle)
Roshore, John	1796	. . . .
Russel, John H.	1796	. . . .
Sayre, Joel	1778–1818	I SAYRE (in rectangle); I. Sayre (script, in shaped rectangle)
Schaats, Bartholomew	1670–1758	B S (in square); B.S. (in heart, with fleur-de-lis below)
Schenck, John	1796	. . . .
Sexnine, Simon	1722	. . . .
Skinner, Abraham	1756	. . . .
Slidel, Joshua	1765	. . . .

Smith, James	1797	....
Smith, Wm.	1770	....
Soumaine, Simeon	1719	S S (in square); S S (in circle)
Staples, John J. Jr.	1788	....
Stephens, Geo.	1790	....
Stone & Osburn	1796	....
Stoutenburgh, Tobias	1731	
Targee, John & Peter	1798	I & PT (in rectangle), eagle's head (in oval); I & PT (in rectangle) leopard's head.
TenEyck, Koenraet	1716	K TE (in rectangle)
Thomas, Walter	1769	....
Thomson, W.	1830	....
Tingley, Sam'l.	1767	....
Underhill, Andrew	1788	A UNDERHILL (in rectangle), A U (in oval)
Underhill, Thomas	1787	....
Underhill & Vernon	1786	....
Van Beuren, P.	1790	....
Van Beuren, Wm.	1797	
Van der Spiegel, Jacobus	1685	I V S (in trefoil); Io^{S}V (in trefoil)
Van der Spiegel, Johannes	1666–1716	I V S (in serrated rectangle)
Van Dyck, Peter	1684–1750	P-V-D (in oval); PVD (in oval) P. V. D. (in rectangle P^{V}D (in trefoil)
Van Dyck, Rich.	1750	R V D (in rectangle)
Van Voorhis, Daniel	1787	D. V. V. (in rectangle), eagle (in diamond); D V (in rectangle), eagle (in diamond); D. V. V. (in oval)
Van Voorhis & Cooly	1786	....
Van Voorhis & Son	1798	....
Vergereau, Peter	1721	....
Vernon, John	1789	....
Vernon, J. & Co.	1796	....
Wenman, Barnard	1786	....
Whitlock, Thos.	1796	....
Wilson, R.	1805	....
Windover, John	c. 1672–1727	J. W (in cartouche)
Wishart, Hugh	1789	H. WISHART (in rectangle), spread eagle (in oval); H. WISHART (in rectangle); H. WISHART (in rectangle), eagle (in oval), imitation English Hall Marks; WISHART (in rectangle)
Woods, Freeman	1790	Woods (script, in shaped oval)
Wool, Jeremiah Ward	1791	....
Wynkoop, Cornelius	1701–1740(?)	....
Wynkoop (Wyncoope), Benj.	1675–1741(?)	W$_B$K (in a heart); B W (in long oval)

Philadelphia:

Aitken, John	1796	....
Alexander, Saml.	1797	....
Alexander, S. & Simmons, A.	1800	....
Alford, Samuel	1759	....
Alford, Thos.	1762	....
Allen, James	1720	....
Allen, Robert	1796	....
Andrews (?), Jr.	1746	....
Andrews, Henry	1796	....
Anthony, Joseph	1762–1814	J. Anthony (script, in rectangle)
Anthony, Joseph & Son	1811	....
Armstrong, John	1811	....
Ashmead, Wm.	1797	....
Atherton, Nathan, Jr.	1824	....
Baily, John	1762	....
Ball, Wm.	1752	....
Bartram, Wm.	1769	....
Berard, Andrew	1797	....
Best, Joseph	1723	....
Black, John	1819	....
Blondell, Anthony	1797	....
Boudinot, Elias	1747	....
Bright, Anthony	1740	....
Brown, John	1796	....
Bruff, Joseph	1767	....
Bumm & Shepper	1819	....
Burdock, Nicholas	1797	....
Camoin	1797	....
Campbell, Wm.	1765	....
Cario, Michael	1736	....
Cario, W.	c. 1740	W. CARIO (in shaped rectangle)
Carnan, John	1771	....
Cooke, Joseph	1789	....
Cumming, David B.	1811	....
Curry & Preston	1830	....
David, John	1736–1798	J D (in oval, small); I· DAVID (in oblong); I· DAVID (in rectangle)
David, Peter	1738	....
Davy, Adam	1796	....
Dickerson, John	1797	....
Dorsey, Joshua	1797	....
Dowig, George	1765	....
Drewry, George	1763	....
DuBois, A.	1797	....
DuMorte, John	1796	....
Dumoutet, I. B.	1797	....
Dunlevey, Robt.	1787	....
Dupuy, Daniel	1719–1807	D D (in rectangle)
Dupuy, Dan'l, Jr.	1796	....
England, Wm.	1718	....
Fletcher, Thomas	c. 1830	....

Fletcher & Gardiner	1819	....
Fling, George	1749	....
Ford, Samuel	1797	....
Fraser, Wm.	1738	....
Garret, P.	1811	....
Gee, Joseph	1788	....
Georgeon, Bernard	1797	....
Germon, G. D.	1819	....
Germon, John	1788	....
Ghiselin, Cesar	c. 1670–1733	C G (in square, with star); C G (in heart-shaped shield)
Ghiselin, Wm.	1751	....
Gilley, Peter	1797	....
Grant, Wm.	1796	....
Guirna, Anthony	1796	....
Hackle, Wm.	1766	W H (in rectangle)?
Hall, David	1765	....
Halsted, Benj.	1783	Halsted (script, in shaped rectangle)
Hollingshead, Wm.	1762	....
Houlton, John	1797	....
Howell, James	1811	....
Howell, G. W. (Phila.?)	c. 1790	G W Howell (script, in rectangle)
Humphrey, Rich.	1771	R. Humphrey (script, in rectangle)
Humphrey, Thos.	1814	....
Hunt, Edward	1718	....
Hurlbeart, Philip	–1764	....
Husband, John	1796	....
Hutton, John S.	1684–1792	....
Jenkins, John	1796	....
Kucher, Jacob	1811	I KUCHER (in rectangle)
Lamar, Matthias	1796	....
Leacock, John	1751	I. LEACOCK (in rectangle), I · L (in rectangle)
Letelier, John	1770	....
Lewis & Smith	1811	Lewis & Smith (script, in irregular oval)
Lewis, Harvey	1819	....
Lownes, Edward	1819	....
Lownes, Joseph	1796	J. LOWNES (in rectangle)
Lownes, J. & J. H.	1819	....
Lyng, John	1734	....
Marshall, Joseph	1819	....
McFee, John	1797	....
McMullin, John	1796	I. McMullin (in rectangle), I. M., on each side of it; I. McMullin (in rectangle)
McMullin & Black	1811	....
Miles, John	1796	....
Milne, Edward	1761	....
Musgrave, James	1797	? (in rectangle)
Myers, John	1796	....
Olivier, Peter	1797	....

Pepper, H. J.	c. 1795	H. I. PEPPER (in rectangle)
Perkins, Jacob	1766–	....
Perraux, Peter	1797	....
Pinchin, Wm.	1784	....
Pitts, Rich.	1741	Pitts (script, in long oblong)
Poincignon, Francis	1796	....
Poissonnier, F.	1797	....
Polgrain, Quom	1797	....
Poupard, James	1772	....
Price, Benj.	1767	....
Rasch, Anthony	1815	ANTY RASCH (in rectangle)
Rasch & Willig	1819	....
Reeder, Abner	1797	....
Rich, Joseph	1790	....
Richards, Samuel	1796	S. RICHARDS (in rectangle)
Richards, T (Phila.?)	c. 1790	T. RICHARDS (rectangle)
Richards & Williamson	1797	....
Richardson, Francis	1718	....
Richardson, Joseph	1730	....
Richardson, Joseph	1796	J.RICHARDSON(rectangle)
Riggs, ...	1819	....
Robinson & Harwood	1819	....
Sacheverell, John	1732	....
Saint Martin, Anthony	1796	....
Seal, Wm.	1819	....
Shepper, John D.	1819	....
Shields, Thos.	1765	....
Shoemaker, Joseph	1796	....
Simmonds, Andrew	1796	....
Simmons, Anthony	1796	....
Skerret, Joseph	1797	....
Soumaine, Saml.	1765	....
Syng, Phil.	1676–1739	P S (in square)
Syng, Phil.	1703–1789	P S (in shield), with leaf
Taylor, Wm.	1772	....
Thibarult & Co.	1797	....
Tingley, Saml.	1767	....
Turner, James	1759	I T (in shaped shield)
Tuthill, Christopher	1730	....
Vanderhaul	1740	
VanVoorhis, Daniel	1782	D. V. V. (in rectangle), eagle (in diamond); D V (in rectangle), eagle (in diamond)
Vilant, Wm.	1725	W V (in heart-shaped shield) with fleur-de-lis below
Walker, Geo.	1796	....
Walker, Wm.	1796	....
Ward, John	1811	WARD, 67 Market St.
Ward & Cox	1811	....
Warner, Joseph	1811	....
Warner, Samuel	1797	....
Westphal, C.	1800	C. WESTPHAL (irregular rectangle)
Whartenby, Thom.	1811	....

Williams, Samuel	1796	. . . .
Williamson, Samuel	1796	. . . .
Willig, Geo.	1819	. . . .
Wilson, Robt.	1819	. . . .
Wiltberger, Christian	1793	C. Wiltberger (in shaped rectangle)
Wyatt, Jos.	1797	. . . .
Yettons, Randal	1739	. . . .
Young, Wm.	1761	. . . .

MASSACHUSETTS (outside of Boston):

Andrew, John	1747-1791	Salem. I·ANDREW (in rectangle)
Austin, Ebenezer	1733-1788(?)	Charlestown
Austin, James	1750-	. . . .
Austin, Josiah	1719-1780	Charlestown. J. AUSTIN; I·A; I·A (in oval)
Bailey, Loring	1740-1814	{Hull {Hingham
Baldwin, Jabez	c. 1810	Salem. BALDWIN (incised)
Barrett, S.	c. 1760	Nantucket
Bartlett, Samuel	c. 1750-1821	Concord. S. BARTLETT (in rectangle); S. BART-LETT (in rectangle), S. B. (script, in rectangle); S. B. (script, in rectangle)
Beal, Caleb	1746-1801	Hingham
Boutelle, James	1783	Worcester
Boylston, E.	1789	Stockbridge
Bradbury, Theophilus	c. 1815	Newburyport
Bradbury & Bro.	c. 1810	Newburyport
Brigden, Z. (Charlestown)	1734-1787	Z·Brigden (in a cartouche) Z-B (in a rectangle)
Cleveland, William	c. 1790	Salem
Coverly, Thomas	c. 1730-1800	Newburyport. T. COV-ERLY (in rectangle)
Davenport, Samuel	1720-1793	Milton
Davis, E.	1775	Newburyport. E DAVIS (in rectangle), rampant lion (in cartouche); E D (in rectangle) lion passant; E D (in rectangle)
Davis, Samuel	1801	Plymouth
Delano, Jabez	1763-1848	New Bedford
Dexter, John	1735-1800	Dedham
Easton, James	1828	Marlboro
Edwards, Abraham	1763	Ashby
Edwards, Calvin	1763	Ashby
Edwards, Samuel	1726-1783	Natick
Farley, Charles	1791-1877	Ipswich
Geffroy, N.	c. 1750	Mass (?); N. GEFFROY (in engrailed rectangle); GEF-FROY (in serrated rectangle)
Gill, Caleb	c. 1790	Hingham

Gill, Leavitt	c. 1790	Hingham
Goodhue, John	c. 1760?	Salem. J. GOODHUE (in rectangle)
Gowen, William	1749–c. 1803	{Charlestown}{Medford} W. GOWEN (in rectangle); W G (in rectangle)
Grant, Thomas	1731–1804	Marblehead. T. GRANT (in rectangle)
Grant, William	1766–1809	Marblehead
Greenleaf, David	1737–1800	Bolton
Hadwen, William	1820	Nantucket
Hancock, John	1732–	Charlestown. J. HANCOCK (in rectangle)
Harding, Newell	1799–1862	Haverhill
Howard, Abram	1810	Salem
Hurd, Benjamin	1739–1781	Roxbury. B H (arrow? between, in a rectangle)
Lamson, J.	c. 1790	Mass.(?) J. LAMSON (in rectangle); J. L. (in rectangle)
Lincoln, Elijah	1818–1833	Hingham. E. Lincoln (in rectangle)
Little, William	1775	Newburyport
Loring, Joseph	1743–1815	Hull. J. LORING (in cartouche); J. Loring (script, in rectangle)
Low, John J.	c. 1800–1876	Salem
Lynde, Thomas	1748–1812	Worcester. T. LYNDE (in rectangle)
Mansfield, John	1674	Charlestown, 1634
Morse, Stephen	1743–	Newbury
Moulton, Abel	1815	Newburyport
Moulton, Joseph, 1	1680–1756	Newburyport. J. M (in engrailed rectangle); I M (script, in rectangle); I M (script monogram, in oval); I M (in rectangle); I. MOULTON (in rectangle)
Moulton, Joseph, 2	c. 1740–1818	Newburyport
Moulton, Joseph, 3	1814–1903	Newburyport
Moulton, William, 1	1710	Newburyport. W. MOULTON (in rectangle); MOULTON (in rectangle); MOULTON (incised)
Moulton, William, 2	1720–1793	Newburyport
Moulton, William, 3	1772–1861	Newburyport
Munroe, John	1824	Barnstable. I. MUNROE (in serrated rectangle)
Newhall, Dudley	c. 1730	Salem
Nickerson, Baty	c. 1825	Harwich
Northey, Abijah	c. 1760 (?)	Salem. A N (in rectangle)
Norton, Samuel	c. 1790	Hingham

EARLY NINETEENTH CENTURY AMERICAN TEA SERVICE, MADE BY CRAWFORD

Courtesy of Metropolitan Museum

EARLY NINETEENTH CENTURY GADROONED TEA SERVICE, MADE BY BOYER & JONES,
NEW YORK
Courtesy of Metropolitan Museum

Osgood, J.	1817 (?)	Salem
Parker, Isaac	1780	Deerfield
Perkins, Houghton	1735–c. 1777	Taunton
Perkins, Isaac	c. 1707–1737	Charlestown
Perkins, Jacob	1766–	Newburyport
Phillips, Samuel	1658–c. 1722	Salem
Pierpont, Benjamin	1730–1797	Roxbury. PIERPONT (in shaped oval); B·P (in rectangle); B PIERPONT (in shaped oval)
Prince, Job	1680–1708	Hull
Putnam, Edward	c. 1810	Salem
Quincy, Daniel	1651–	Braintree
Sanderson, Robert, Jr.	1652–1714	Watertown
Shreve, Benjamin	1813–1896	Salem
Stevens & Lakeman	1825	Salem
Stickney, Jonathan	c. 1796	Newburyport
Swan, Caleb	1754–1816	Charlestown
Swan, Robert	1775	Worcester. R SWAN (in rectangle)
Swan, William	1715–1774	
Titcomb, Francis	1813	Newburyport
Touzell, John	c. 1726–1785	Salem

CONNECTICUT AND RHODE ISLAND:

Adams, Pygan	1712–1776	New London, Conn. P. A. (crowned, in rectangle); P. A. (in rectangle).
Adgate, Wm.	1744–1779	Norwich
Allen, Joel	......	Middletown, Conn.
Arnold, Thomas	1750	Newport, R. I. T·A (in rectangle); ARNOLD and T· A (script, in rectangle); ARNOLD (in rectangle)
Atterbury, J.	1799	New Haven, Conn.
Austin, John	c. 1770	Hartford, Conn.
Austin, Joseph	1719–	Hartford, Conn.
Avery, John	1732–1794	Preston, Conn.
Avery, Robert Staunton	1771–1846	Preston, Conn.
Baldwin & Baker	c. 1817	Providence, R. I.
Barrett, S.	c. 1760	Providence, R. I.
Bartholomew, Roswell	c. 1780–1830	Hartford, Conn.
Beach, Miles	1742–1828	Goshen
	1771	Litchfield
	1785	Hartford
Beach & Sanford	1785	Hartford
Beach & Ward	1789–1797	Hartford
Beebe, Stanton	1818	Providence, R. I.
Beecher, Clement	1801	Berlin, Conn.
Benjamin, Barzillai	1774–1844	Milford, Conn. Bridgeport, Conn. New Haven, Conn.
Benjamin, John	c. 1750	Stratford, Conn. I.B (in oval)
Benjamin, Samuel C.	1819	New Haven, Conn.
Billings, Daniel	1795	Preston, Conn.

Bontecou, Timothy	1693–1784	New Haven, Conn.
Bontecou, Timothy, Jr.	1723–1789	New Haven, Conn.
Botsford, Gideon B.	1776–1866	Woodbury, Conn.
Bradford, Charles H.	. . . . . .	Westerly, R. I.
Bradley, Aner	1753–1824	New Haven, Conn.
Bradley, Luther	1798	New Haven, Conn.
Bradley, Phineas	1745–1797	New Haven, Conn.
Bradley, Richard	1825	. . . .
Bradley, Zebul	1806	New Haven, Conn.
Brainard, Charles	1809	Hartford, Conn.
Breed, John	1776	Colchester, Conn.
Breed, W.	c. 1755(?)	Conn.(?) W. Breed (script) and W.B (in rectangles)
Brewer, Charles	1803	Middletown, Conn. C. BREWER (script, in cartouche)
Brewer & Mann	1804	Middletown, Conn.
Brewster, Abel	{1797 {1804	Canterbury, Conn. Norwich, Conn.
Brown, Elnathan C.	. . . . . .	Westerly, R. I.
Buel, Abel	1742–1825	New Haven, Conn.
Buel, John	1783	New Haven, Conn.
Buel, Samuel	{1777 {1779	Middletown }S. B (in rectangle) Hartford }
Bull, Caleb	1791	Hartford, Conn.
Bull, Martin	1744–1825	Farmington, Conn.
Bunker, Benjamin	1810	Providence, R. I.
Burdick, William S.	. . . . . .	New Haven, Conn.
Burnap, Daniel	1791	E. Windsor, Conn.
Burr, Christopher	1824	Providence, R. I.
Burr, Ezekiel	1764–1846	Providence, R. I.
Burr, William	1792	Providence, R. I.
Bushnell, Phineas	1775	Guilford, Conn.
Canfield, Samuel	1780–1800	Middletown, Conn. CANFIELD (in long oval)
Carpenter, Joseph	1747–1804	Norwich, Conn.
Case, George	1779	E. Hartford, Conn.
Casey, Gideon	1753	South Kingston, R. I.
Casey, Samuel	c. 1724–c. 1770	Newport, R. I. S: CASEY (in rectangle)
Champlin, John	1745–1800	New London, Conn.
Chapin, Aaron	1825	Hartford, Conn.
Chittenden, Ebenezer	1726–1812	Guilford, Conn. E C (in oval)
Church, Joseph	1794–1876	Hartford, Conn.
Church & Rogers	1828	Hartford, Conn.
Clark, Charles	1798	New Haven, Conn.
Clark, George C.	1813	Providence, R. I.
Clark, I.	c. 1757–	Conn.(?) I. CLARK (in rectangle)
Clark, Joseph	1791	Danbury, Conn.
Clark, Peter G.	1810	New Haven, Conn.
Clark, Wm.	1774	New Milford, Conn.
Clark, James	1734	Newport, R. I.
Clarke, J.	1734	Newport, R. I. I. Clarke (in large oval)
Cleveland, Wm.	1770–1837	Norwich, Conn.

Coit & Mansfield	1816	Norwich, Conn.
Collins, Arnold	1690	Newport, R. I. A C (in shield)
Copp, J.	1776	New London, Conn.
Crandall, Benjamin	1824	Providence, R. I.
Curtis, Candee & Stiles	c. 1820	Woodbury, Conn.
Curtis, Lewis	1797	Farmington, Conn.
Cutler, Richard	1736–1810	New Haven, Conn.
Cutler, Richard & Sons	1806	New Haven, Conn.
Dagget, Henry	1800	New Haven, Conn.
Davis & Babbitt	c. 1815	Providence, R. I.
Davison, Barzillai	1738–1828	Norwich, Conn.
Denis, Ebenezer	1772–1785	Hartford, Conn.
Denis, George, Jr.	1775	Norwich, Conn.
Deshon, Daniel	1697–1781	New London, Conn.
Dodge, Ezra	1766–1798	New London, Conn.
Dodge, Nehemiah	1794	Providence, R. I.
Dodge, Seril	1795	Providence, R. I., S. DODGE (serrated rectangle) star incised each side
Doolittle, Amos	1754–1832	New Haven, Conn.
Doolittle, Enos	1781	Hartford, Conn.
Douglas, Robert	1769	New London, Conn.
Elderkin, Alfred	1792	Windham, Conn.
Elderkin, Elisha	{1753–1822 / 1777	Killingworth, Conn. / New Haven, Conn.
Elliot, John A.	1815	Sharon, Conn.
Ellsworth, David	1742–1821	Windsor, Conn.
Fairchild, Joseph	1824	New Haven, Conn.
Fairchild, Robert	1703–1794	Stratford, Conn.
Fifield, John S.	......	Westerly, R. I.
Fitch, Allen	1808	New Haven, Conn.
Fitch & Hobart	1812	New Haven, Conn.
Foot, William	1796	East Haddam, Conn.
Frost & Mumford	c. 1810	Providence, R. I.
Gardner, John	1734–1776	New London, Conn. J. GARDNER (in rectangle)
Gibbs, John	c. 1815	Providence, R. I. J. GIBBS (in rectangle)
Gilbert, Samuel	1798	Hebron, Conn.
Goodwin, Horace	1828	Hartford, Conn.
Goodwin, H. & A.	1825	Hartford, Conn.
Goodwin, Ralph	1828	Hartford, Conn.
Goodwin & Dodd	1812	Hartford, Conn.
Gorham, Jabez	1792–	Providence, R. I.
Gorham, John	1820–	Providence, R. I.
Gorham, Miles	1757–1847	New Haven, Conn.
Graham, Daniel	1789	West Suffield, Conn.
Gray, John	1692–1720	New London, Conn.
Gray, Samuel	1684–1713	New London, Conn.
Greene, Williams & Co.	c. 1815	Providence, R. I.
Greenleaf, David	1737–1800	{Norwich, Conn. / Hartford, Conn.
Greenleaf, Joseph	1778–1798	New London, Conn.
Grignon, Rene	1708	Norwich, Conn.

Gurley, Wm.	1804	Norwich, Conn.
Hallam, John	1773	New London, Conn.
Hamlin, Wm.	1772–	{ Providence, R. I. / Middletown, Conn.
Hancock, John	1772	Providence, R. I.
Hanks, Benjamin	1779	Windham, Conn.
Harland, Thomas	1735–1807	Norwich, Conn.
Harland, Thomas, Jr.	1806	Norwich, Conn.
Hart, Eliphaz	1812	Norwich, Conn.
Hart, Judah	1777	Berlin, Conn.
Hart & Brewer	1803	Middletown, Conn.
Hart & Wilcox	1805	Norwich, Conn.
Hilldrup, Thomas	1772–	Hartford, Conn.
Hitchcock, Eliakim	1766–	New Haven, Conn.
Hobart, Joshua	1813	New Haven, Conn.
Hookey, Wm.	c. 1750	Newport, R. I.
Hopkins, Jesse	1766–	Waterbury, Conn.
Hopkins, Joseph	1730–1801	Waterbury, Conn.
Hopkins, Stephen	1721–1796	Waterbury, Conn.
Hotchkiss, Hezekiah	–1761	New Haven, Conn.
Hughes, Edward	1804	Hampton, Conn.
Huntington, Philip	1770–1825	Norwich, Conn.
Huntington, Roswell	1763	Norwich, Conn.
Jenckes, John C.	1785	Providence, R. I. J JENCKES (incised)
Johonnot, Wm.	1766–1849	Middletown, Conn.
Kelley, Allen	c. 1810	Providence, R. I.
Kelley, E. G. & J. H.	c. 1820	Providence, R. I.
King, Joseph	1770	Middletown, Conn.
Kinney, Thomas	c. 1825	Norwich, Conn.
Kippen, George	1790	Middletown, Conn.
Kirtland, Joseph P.	1796	Middletown, Conn.
Lathrop, Rufus	–1805	Norwich, Conn.
Lewis, Isaac	1815	Ridgefield, Conn.
Mann, Alexander	1804	Middletown, Conn.
Mansfield, Elisha H.	1816	Norwich, Conn.
Marble, Simeon	1806	New Haven, Conn.
Merriman, Marcus	1767–1820	Cheshire, Conn. M M (in rectangle)
Merriman, Marcus & Co.	1806	New Haven, Conn. M: M: & CO (serrated rectangle)
Merriman, Reuben	1783–1866	Litchfield, Conn.
Merriman, Samuel	1794	New Haven, Conn.
Merriman, Silas	1734–1805	New Haven, Conn.
Merriman & Bradley	1817	New Haven, Conn.
Merriman & Tuttle	1802	New Haven, Conn.
Merrow, Nathan	1783	East Hartford, Conn.
Mumford, Henry G.	1813	Providence, R. I.
Munson, Amos	1776	New Haven, Conn.
Munson, Cornelius	1742–	Wallingford, Conn.
Newberry, Edwin C.	1828	{ Mansfield, Conn. / Brooklyn, Conn.
Nichols, Bassett	c. 1815	Providence, R. I.
Nichols, Wm. S.	1785–1871	Newport, R. I.
Norton, Andrew	1765–1838	Goshen, Conn.

Norton, Thomas	1796	Farmington, Conn.
Noyes, Samuel	1747–	Norwich, Conn.
Oaks, Frederick	1825	Hartford, Conn.
Oaks & Spencer	1814	Hartford, Conn.
Olmstead, Nathaniel	1826	New Haven, Conn.
Otis, Jonathan	⎰1750	Newport, R. I. J. Otis (large script in rectangle) and Otis (small script in rectangle); OTIS (large, in rectangle); J. Otis (script, in oval)
	⎱1766–1791	Middletown, Conn.
Parmele, Samuel	1737–1807	Guilford, Conn. S. Parmele (in shaped rectangle)
Parmelee, James	1763–1828	Durham, Conn.
Peabody, John	1779	Enfield, Conn.
Peck, Timothy	1791	Middletown, Conn.
Perry, Thomas	......	Westerly, R. I.
Pitkin, Henry	1811	Hartford, Conn.
Pitkin, John O.	1803	Hartford, Conn.
Pitkin, Walter	1808	Hartford, Conn.
Pitkins, James F.	1812	Hartford, Conn.
Pitman, Saunders	1732–1804	Providence, R. I. PITMAN (in rectangle); Pitman (script in rectangle)
Pitman, John K.	1805	Providence, R. I.
Pitman & Darrance	1795	Providence, R. I.
Post, Samuel	⎰1736	Norwich, Conn.
	⎱1783	New London, Conn.
Potter, Niles	......	Westerly, R. I.
Potwine & Whiting	1735	Hartford, Conn.
Pratt, Phineas	1772	Lynne, Conn.
Prince, Job	1680–1708	Milford, Conn.
Quintard, Peter	1737	Norwalk, Conn. P. Ꝑ (in square); P Q (in square)
Richmond, G. & A.	c. 1815	Providence, R. I.
Roath, Roswell Walston	1805	Norwich, Conn.
Rogers, Daniel	1750	Newport, R. I. D R (in cartouche); D. ROGERS (in rectangle); D R (in shaped shield)
Rogers, Wm.	1825	Hartford, Conn.
Russell, Jonathan	1804	Ashford, Conn.
Sackett & Willard	c. 1815	Providence, R. I.
Sadd, Hervey	1776–1840	New Hartford, Conn.
Sanford, Isaac	1793	Hartford, Conn.
Sargeant, Jacob	⎰1761–1843	Mansfield, Conn.
	⎱1795	Hartford, Conn.
Shethar, Samuel	1795	Litchfield, Conn.
Shethar & Thompson	1798	Litchfield, Conn.
Shipman, Nathaniel	1764–1853	Norwich, Conn.
Sibley & Marble	1802	New Haven, Conn.
Staniford, John	1790	Windham, Conn.
Stanton, Enoch	1745–1781	Stonington, Conn.
Stanton, Daniel	1755–1781	Stonington, Conn.

13

Stanton, Zebulon	1753–1828	Stonington, Conn.
Stillman, Barton	....	Westerly, R. I.
Stillman, Paul	....	Westerly, R. I.
Stillman, William	1767–1858	Hopkinton, R. I.
Sutton, Robert	1825	New Haven, Conn.
Tanner, John	1750	Newport, R. I.
Terry, Geer	1814	Enfield, Conn.
Thompson, Isaac	1798	Litchfield, Conn.
Tilley, James	1740–1792	Hartford, Conn.
Tompkins, Edmund	1757–	Waterbury, Conn.
Tracy, Erastus	1768–1798	Norwich, Conn.
Tracy, Gurdon	1767–1792	Norwich, Conn.
Trott, Jonathan	1734–1815	New London, Conn. J. TROTT (in cartouche)
Trott, Jonathan, Jr.	1771–1803	New London, Conn.
Trott, John Proctor	1769–1852	New London, Conn. J:P. TROTT (in long oval); J. P. T. (in serrated rectangle)
Trott & Brooks	1798	New London, Conn.
Trott & Cleveland	1792	New London, Conn.
Tuttle, Bethuel	1806	New Haven, Conn.
Ufford & Burdick	1814	New Haven, Conn.
Veazie, Joseph	1815	Providence, R. I.
Vernon, Samuel	1683–1737	Newport, R. I. S V (in heart-shaped shield, trefoil below); S V (in heart, fleur-de-lis below); S V (in heart-shaped shield, cross below)
Vinton, David	1792	Providence, R. I.
Wallace, Wm. F.	......	Westerly, R. I.
Walworth, Daniel	1785	Middletown, Conn.
Ward, Billious	1729–1777	Guilford, Conn. B W (in rectangle)
Ward, James	1768–1856	Guilford, Conn.
Ward, William	1736–1829	Litchfield, Conn.
Ward & Bartholomew	1804	Hartford, Conn.
Ward, Bartholomew & Brainard	1809	Hartford, Conn.
Wardin, Daniel	1811	Bridgeport, Conn.
Weeden, Peleg	c. 1803	North Kingston, R. I.
Welles, George	1784–1827	Hebron, Conn.
Wheaton, Caleb	1784–1827	Providence, R. I.
Wheaton, Calvin	1790	Providence, R. I.
Whipple, Arnold	1825	Providence, R. I.
Whitaker & Greene	c. 1825	Providence, R. I.
White, Amos	1773	Haddam Landing, Conn.
Whitting, Charles	1725–1765	Norwich, Conn.
Wilcox, Alvan	1816	Norwich, Conn.
Wilcox, Cyprian	1827	New Haven, Conn.
Williams, Deodat	1775	Hartford, Conn.
Williams, Stephen	1799	Providence, R. I.
Wilmot, Samuel, Jr.	1808	New Haven, Conn.
Wilmot & Stillman	1800	New Haven, Conn.

Woodward, Antipas	1791	Middletown, Conn.
Woodward, Eli	1812	Hartford, Conn.
Yeomans, Elijah	1794	Hartford, Conn.
Young, Ebenezer	1778	Hebron, Conn.

OTHER PLACES:

Adam, J.	......	Alexandria, D. C.
Addison, George M.	1804	Baltimore, Md.
Aitkins, W.	1802	Baltimore, Md.
Austin, Benjamin	1775	Portsmouth, N. H.
Baielle, Lewis	1799	Baltimore, Md.
Balch & Fryer	1784	Albany, N. Y.
Baldwin, Jedediah	c. 1790	Hanover, N. H.
Ball, W.	1802	Baltimore, Md.
Barry, Standish	1790	Baltimore, Md.
Becker, Philip	1764	Lancaster, Pa.
Bedford, John	c. 1785	Fishkill, N. Y. I Bedford (script, in rectangle)
Benjamin, Solomon	1817	Baltimore, Md.
Bevan, Richard	1804	Baltimore, Md.
Blanchard, A.	c. 1800	Lexington, Ky. A. BLAN-CHARD (in long oval)
Boehme, Charles L.	1804	Baltimore, Md.
Boyd, William	1810	Albany, N. Y.
Brigden, Timothy	1813	Albany, N. Y.
Brown & Houlton	c. 1799	Baltimore, Md.
Burot, Andrew	1824	Baltimore, Md.
Bussey, Thomas	1799	Baltimore, Md.
Butler, John	1763	Falmouth (Portland), Me.
Butler, N.	1803	Utica, N. Y.
Campbell, R.	1824	Baltimore, Md.
Carson, Thomas	1813	Albany, N. Y.
Carson & Hall	1813	Albany, N. Y.
Coleman, Nathaniel	1790	Burlington, N. J.
Daverne, John	1799	Baltimore, Md.
Dickerson, John	1778	Morristown, N. J.
Douglas, Cantwell	1799	Baltimore, Md.
Drowne, Benjamin	1800	Portsmouth, N. H.
Drowne, Samuel	1749–1815	Portsmouth, N. H. S x Drowne (in rectangle); S x D (in rectangle)
Drown, T. P.	c. 1805	Portsmouth (?) T. P. DROWN (in rectangle)
Erwin, John	1817	Baltimore, Md.
Evertson, John	1813	Albany, N. Y.
Farley, Charles	1812	Portland, Me.
Flott, Lewis	1817	Baltimore, Md.
Folsom, John	1781	Albany, N. Y.
Forman, B. B.	1813	Albany, N. Y.
Franciscus, George	1817	Baltimore, Md.
Gerrish, Timothy	1753–1813	Portsmouth, N. H.
Hall, Abijah	1813	Albany, N. Y.
Hall, Charles	1765	Lancaster, Pa.
Hall, Joseph	1781	Albany, N. Y.
Ham, George	1810	Portsmouth, N. H.

Hamilton, James	1766	Annapolis, Md.
Holland, Littleton	c. 1804	Baltimore, Md.
Holton, David	1804	Baltimore, Md.
How, David	1805	Castine, Me.
Howard, Thomas	1620	Jamestown, Va.
Howe, Otis	1817	Portsmouth, N. H.
Huges, Christopher & Co.	1773	Baltimore, Md.
Hull, John	1624–1683	England
Hurtin & Burgi	1766	Bound Brook, N. J.
Huston, James	1799	Baltimore, Md.
Hutton, Isaac	1767–1855	Albany, N. Y. HUTTON (in rectangle, eagle in circle); HUTTON (in rectangle, eagle's head in oval)
Hyde & Goodrich	1830	New Orleans, La.
Jackson, James	c. 1775	Maryland
Jackson, Joseph	1804	Baltimore, Md.
Jacobs, George	1802	Baltimore, Md.
Johonnot, William	1766–1849	Windsor, Vt.
Johnson, M. W.	1815	Albany, N. Y.
Kenrick, Anwill	c. 1775	Maryland
Kirk, Samuel	c. 1815	Baltimore, Md.
Kirk, Samuel & Sons	1817	Baltimore, Md.
Le Ret, Peter	c. 1799	Baltimore, Md.
Lewin, Gabriel	1771	Baltimore, Md.
Mix, James	1817	Albany, N. Y.
Moore, Robert	c. 1775	Maryland,
Moulton, Enoch	1780	Portland, Me.
Ogier, John	1799	Baltimore, Md.
Parker, George	1804	Baltimore, Md.
Phelps, Jedediah	1781	Great Barrington, Vt.
Poncet, Lewis	......	Baltimore, Md.
Reeves, Stephen	1767	Burlington, N. J.
Roe, W.	1803	Kingston-on-Hudson
Sadtler, Philip	1824	Baltimore, Md.
Sardo, Michael	1817	Baltimore, Md.
Scofield, Solomon	1815	Albany, N. Y.
Shepherd, Robert	c. 1800	Albany, N. Y.
Simes, William	1800	Portsmouth, N. H.
Sheets	1697	Henrico, Va.
Smith, John and Thomas	1817	Baltimore, Md.
Stall, Joseph	1804	Baltimore, Md.
Stone, Adam	1804	Baltimore, Md.
TenEyck, John	c. 1730	Albany, N. Y. I T (in oval)?
Truax, Henry R.	1815	Albany, N. Y.
Van Bergen, John	1813	Albany, N. Y.
Vincent, Richard	1799	Baltimore, Md.
Warner, Andrew E.	1811	Baltimore, Md. A. E. WARNER (in rectangle)
Warner, A. E. & T. H.	1805	Baltimore, Md.
Warner, Thomas H.	1814	Baltimore, Md.
Webb, Barnabas	c. 1729–c. 1786	Thomaston, Me.
Wedge, S.	1804	Baltimore, Md.
Wilson, Hosea	1817	Baltimore, Md.
Wright, Alexander	c. 1775	Maryland

A supplementary List of Silversmiths brought up to date is given at page 355.

EARLY NINETEENTH CENTURY PEWTER COFFEE POT
Courtesy of Pennsylvania Museum and School of Industrial Art

EIGHTEENTH CENTURY PEWTER SUGAR BOWL AND CREAM PITCHER
Courtesy of John C. Nippes, Esq., Haddonfield, New Jersey

LATE EIGHTEENTH CENTURY PEWTER TEAPOT
In possession of Harold D. Eberlein, Esq.

PEWTER PLATTER AND PEWTER BASON, EIGHTEENTH CENTURY
Courtesy of Pennsylvania Museum and School of Industrial Art

CHAPTER VII

EARLY AMERICAN PEWTER

PEWTER is coming into its own again. It is winning its new place in our esteem not merely as the object of a passing fad, but through a rational recognition of its many estimable qualities. Down the centuries from Roman days—in the East from a much earlier period, probably—it has enjoyed a measure of popularity in proportion to the varied scope of its employment. Its vogue has waxed and waned and waxed again, from time to time, with the passing whims of fashion, but its genuinely useful qualities always preserved for it a sure place among the resources of domestic equipment until our unfortunate forebears, whose lot it was to pass through the deadly doldrums of smug Victorian artificiality and ugly dulness, learned to look on it with contempt, along with some other things that had previously, and have since, been rated for their intrinsic worth or beauty rather than by ''how much they cost,'' and relegated it to the garret or cellar or to any base use that chance might suggest.

With a return to more rational standards of judgment, we have once more begun to heed the claims of pewter to our consideration, and, though we are apt to regard it chiefly as a decorative asset, its utilitarian aspect has not been wholly overlooked. While directing our admiration pewterward, it is gratifying to find that our own early American pewter was possessed of no mean merit and, in many instances, was not behind the product of the British pewterers in point of design, quality of the metal, or excellence of workmanship.

197

Some of the early American pewter has furnished patterns for modern emulation, and the suspicion is not wanting that the reproducer occasionally sends forth a crop of brand-new antiques. A survey of the chief characteristics of early American pewter, therefore, will be of use both to the professional collector and to the amateur, who may delight now and then in picking up a choice piece in the course of travel or in poking about in provincial second-hand or antique shops, where many a rich find is often made. It will be of use, also, to the reviver of crafts to know exactly what the old American pewter was like and wherein its points of excellence consisted.

Pewter was in great demand in the Colonies all through the seventeenth and eighteenth centuries and also during the early part of the nineteenth. In nearly every household it took the place that was afterwards filled by either silver or porcelain, and, even in the houses of the wealthier colonists, where both silver and china in considerable quantities were possessed and treasured for use upon state occasions, pewter occupied an important place in ordinary daily use.

Although much of the pewter used in the earlier part of the Colonial period, and indeed during a good part of the eighteenth century, was brought from England, a great deal was made by enterprising craftsmen among the colonists. When we find that silversmiths began to ply their calling with success before 1650, it is not to be wondered at that pewterers should have done the same, especially as they had a far more universal demand to supply with their wares, and accordingly we learn of at least one pewterer at work in Boston as early as 1639.

Boston, during the first part of the Colonial period, was the chief distributing centre of British pewter, as well as the chief seat of pewter manufacture. New York and Philadelphia soon followed in both respects, and a great deal of pewter ware, excellent in design and in the quality of metal, was produced in each of those cities, although the variety in design was not as great, perhaps, as in the pieces sent from England. The specimens illustrated are chiefly of Boston, New York, and Philadelphia make. Good pewter ware was made in other places, to be sure, but the characteristic types are to be judged from the products of those three places, which are thoroughly representative. The local and distinctive peculiarities of American pewter are better learned by sight than by description, and for this purpose the collections in museums are invaluable, as they afford opportunities for minute comparison and study.

The making of pewter ware was not wholly confined to craftsmen whose time was altogether given up to this occupation. Not a little of the small moulded ware, such as spoons and other objects that soon wore out with constant use, was cast by amateurs, and this home-made aspect of the subject lends an additional note of interest. The possessor of a mould would lend it to his neighbours all through the village or countryside as they had occasion to use it, and the comparative ease with which the alloy was prepared and managed made it a simple matter for them to replenish their stock as it became unfit for further use. This practice was quite in accord with the Colonial spirit of self-helping resourcefulness. It was also a common practice, at a time when so many things that we now buy in shops were made by travelling craftsmen and artisans at the farmstead, for tinkers who owned pewter moulds to make a yearly round of visits and cast, on the spot, what was needed by their customers.

NATURE AND VARIETIES OF PEWTER

Definitions are always helpful in enabling us to know exactly where we stand, and, before going into further considerations, it will be well to state that pewter is an alloy of which the preponderating component is tin. The other elements entering into the composition are various and, at different times and places, have been used in varying proportions, but, ordinarily speaking, lead is the principal secondary substance. Sometimes, however, in preparing the alloy, lead has been altogether omitted and its place has been taken by copper. A broad definition, by Mr. Starkie Gardner, of the character of the alloy observes that "The proportions are so variable that it is scarcely possible to exclude any in which tin forms the bulk, where the result is a darkish silvery, soft metal, fusible at a low temperature, and eminently adapted to a variety of household and artistic purposes."

In American-made pewter, lead, for the most part, was the secondary element. The relative proportions of tin and lead, however, varied considerably. The finer the pewter and the higher the percentage of tin, occasionally with a slight admixture of brass entering into the composition, the whiter, harder and more silvery the surface. On the other hand, a large percentage of lead gave the surface of the pewter a dark or bluish tone lacking the brilliance and lustre of that of superior quality. The proportion of tin sometimes ran as high as ninety per centum, or even more. At the other end of the scale, lead in excess of twenty-five per centum was now and again employed.

As may be readily imagined, this variation caused the widest diversity in quality and appearance of different pieces of old pewter. A surplus of lead in the alloy will account for the dull, dark surface, often badly scarred and eroded, of many pieces that turn up in antique shops. It is useless to try to make these take on the same soft, mellow sheen, the same satiny surface of polished silver as seen on pewter ware made from a superior quality of alloy. It is only really good pewter, with a high percentage of tin and a low percentage of other components, that can be expected to exhibit the delightful patina somewhat comparable to that of old hand-wrought silver.

In England a high standard of pewter metal and pewter workmanship was maintained by the Pewterers' Company in London and by other similar organisations in different parts of the kingdom. The members were required to observe certain regulations and preserve an alloy of approved proportions. It was also customary to apply touch-marks, analogous to the hall-marks upon silver plate, and the name of the maker. Although the regulations of the pewterers' guilds were not so rigorously enforced by legislation and penalties as were the regulations governing silversmiths, and although many pieces were debased in recasting through the agency of unscrupulous itinerant tinkers and pedlars, public opinion and the moral force of the authorised craft guilds served to keep the average purity of the metal and the average quality of workmanship up to a fairly satisfactory level.

In America there was no compulsory standard of

excellence to be observed as a gauge, as there usually was on the other side of the Atlantic, and the only restraining influence for preserving a high quality of metal came from respect for tradition and the pewterer's sense of common honesty, along with shrewd discrimination on the part of the buyer, and the seller's knowledge that his wares were made in competition with the imported pewter and that an obvious disparity in metal or workmanship must inevitably damage his trade. So far as statutory restrictions were concerned, any tinker who had the necessary moulds was free to mix his alloy and make his wares as he chose, without regard to fixed and compelling regulations. Under the circumstances, it is not to be wondered at that the metal in some of the home-made pewter was of poor quality.

ARTICLES MADE

Articles of pewter may in general be classified under the heads of "sad ware" and "hollow-ware." Sad ware included such flat or slightly concave pieces as were wrought into the required shape by hammering them from a flat sheet of metal. The word "sad" in this connexion probably refers to the quality of the metal used, which was what was technically known as "fine pewter," an alloy of tin "satiated" or "saturated" with as much copper as "of its own nature it will take." The alloy of tin and copper was especially ductile and readily lent itself to the process of shaping with the hammer. Under the head of flat ware or sad ware are numbered platters, chargers, large plates, trenchers, trays, or such dishes as could be fashioned without casting in a mould.

"Hollow-ware" is a term sufficiently obvious as

designating bowls, tankards, mugs (Fig. 1, B), pitchers, and all other concaved or hollow pieces. Hollow-ware articles and many small plates were cast in moulds, sometimes in as many as three or four pieces, which had to be built up and soldered together.

The articles made in pewter embraced a long list, comprising numerous items of domestic equipment that have been made of silver, glass, porcelain, pottery, or some other material since pewter making declined in the early years of the nineteenth century. Besides the

FIG. 1. A, Tankard by William Wills, Philadelphia, early nineteenth century. Frishmuth Collection, Pennsylvania Museum and School of Industrial Art. B, Ale Mug by Parks Boyd, Philadelphia, 1800–1812.

Courtesy of Pennsylvania Museum and School of Industrial Art.

pewter for domestic use, there were pewter vessels for ecclesiastical purposes. Church vessels included chalices, patens, beakers, flagons or tankards, alms dishes, and baptismal bowls. Some of the pewter church sets, and also the later Britannia sets, may still be found in use in remote rural churches, or, if their place has been taken by more recently acquired silver vessels, they are usually preserved for association's sake, although this is not invariably the case. The writers remember some years ago to have picked up in a Massachusetts coast town what purported to be the baptismal bowl of the old First Church of Cohasset. It was a bowl of singularly graceful contour, raised on a pedestal, and closely resembled a fruit dish.

The pieces of domestic pewter most usually found in America are articles of table-ware and include salt cellars, which are for the most part early and follow the old English pattern of the circular or trencher salt; mugs or cans; tankards (Fig. 1, A) or flagons; pitchers and jugs; porringers; plates, platters, and chargers; dishes; bowls; teapots and coffee pots (Fig. 2, A and B);

FIG. 2.—A, Coffee Pot by Boardman & Co., New York, c. 1830.   B, Teapot by Boardman & Hall, Philadelphia, c. 1825.
Courtesy of Pennsylvania Museum and School of Industrial Art.

creamers and sugar bowls and butter dishes. The writers understand that forks were sometimes made of pewter, but they have never seen any. Spoons, both large and small, are of common occurrence. Besides all these, which may be found in considerable numbers, there were other pieces of table-ware that seem not to have been manufactured quite so extensively, or, at any rate, they have not so numerously survived the ravages of time. Among them may be mentioned soup tureens, chocolate pots, saucers, sifters, hot-water dishes, egg cups, pepper shakers, mustard pots, and tea-caddies.

The miscellaneous articles not to be included in table-ware are ladles, canisters, boxes for spices, powder, and the like, tobacco boxes, trays and salvers, buckles, ink pots, measures (Fig. 3, B), vases and ewers and basons. Some of these, such as measures and basons, are frequently to be met with; others, such as buckles and spice boxes, are to be found only occasionally. One old pewter bason, known to the writers, was used until almost the end of the nineteenth century for the ablutions of guests' hands at the pump in the garden of a distinguished old country house in the neighbourhood of Philadelphia where primitive Colonial customs were maintained unchanged by the march of modern fashion. Candlesticks are fairly numerous, and lamps, with one or more burners, are of quite common occurrence. The latter are distinctively American pieces (Fig. 4, A and B; Fig. 3, A).

PROCESSES AND ALLOYS

Pewter ware was fashioned by (1) hammering, (2) by casting in moulds, or (3) by a combination of both processes. It was finished either (1) by hand or else (2) by turning and burnishing on a lathe.

The equipment of tools and appliances required was comparatively simple. It included moulds, a lathe, a swage, hammer, burnishers, gouges, chisels, hooks, point tools, a spear grater, and a spear burnisher.

The qualities of pewter employed were designated by three names: fine pewter, or the best quality, which "consisted of tin, with the addition of as much brass or copper as the tin could take up." Of this were generally made platters, chargers, and articles that were square, ribbed, or fluted. The second quality "consisted of tin and lead in the ratio of 112:26 and was used for articles more or less round in shape." The third quality was called *trifle,* much used for common tankards and mugs, and was "sometimes made with nearly forty per centum of lead." Ley-metal, lea, or lay was common pewter, or pewter below the prescribed standard of purity.

When antimony was used instead of lead, the alloy was harder and more brittle. More than twenty per centum of lead darkened the alloy and produced a bluish tinge. Good Britannia metal, consisting of a high percentage of tin with a small quantity of antimony and a

FIG. 3. A, Fluid Lamp with single wick.   B, Measure, Philadelphia made, early nineteenth century.   Frishmuth Collection, Pennsylvania Museum and School of Industrial Art.

still smaller quantity of copper, is really pewter of excellent quality.

The most expensive part of the pewterer's outfit and the most troublesome to make was the set of moulds. The most durable and generally satisfactory were made of gun-metal. They would last indefinitely, and there are some still in use after more than a century of service. They are in good condition, just as are the old wood blocks made in the seventeenth century for printing fabrics, some of which are now being used again for the stamping of modern linens. Moulds could also be made of plaster of Paris, although they were not very durable; of lithographic stone or, finally, fashioned in sand. As mentioned, the more elaborate moulds were often made in three or four separate pieces, and the articles moulded in them were moulded in separate parts. In England a set of moulds would often be the common property of a pewterers' guild, and they were either lent or hired to the members as they needed them.

Fig 4. A, Fluid Lamp on stock. B, Fluid Lamp with handle. Frishmuth Collection, Pennsylvania Museum and School of Industrial Art.

Before casting, the moulds were prepared inside with white of egg and red ochre or with finely powdered pumice. After removal, the roughened surface of the article cast was smoothed by turning and finishing on a lathe.

If it was possible to do so, each article was cast in a single piece. This was an easy enough matter in the case of small objects of simple shape; where the shape was complicated, however, it was necessary to cast the piece in sections and then build it up. For example, a jug with a wide belly and narrowing top would have to be cast in two or three pieces, which would be built up by soldering, and then the handle would also be soldered on.

Large dishes, chargers, and platters were made by hammering from a piece of metal, previously rolled into a sheet, and fashioned on a swage. The hammering process firmed and stiffened the body of the metal and gave it an exceedingly smooth surface.

In addition to the two processes of hammering and casting in moulds, by which latter most articles were made, spinning on a lathe was also practised in some instances, and the final treatment was given on an anvil. Many of the best plates were thus cast and turned, and the hammer marks of the finishing process are plainly visible on the underneath side of the curve. These hammer marks are in concentric circles, just as are the hammer marks on the outside curve of the bowls.

Burnishing was done while the article was revolving rapidly on the lathe.

TOUCH-MARKS AND MARKING

The practice of marking pewter with the maker's touch or mark was observed in England from a very early date. In addition to the touch or mark—a distinctive device to be used by only one person—the maker at times stamped his initials or even his whole name. The Pewterers' Company of London made various regulations about the name of the individual pewterer, so that sometimes it was allowable to stamp it and sometimes not. The mark X was used to denote metal of especially fine quality. In addition, the corporate mark of the Pewterers' Company appeared.

In America there was no corporation to regulate the making of pewter, and the business conduct and practices of the pewterers, and the placing of touch-marks upon American pewter was, therefore, merely a transference of an English custom without any particular significance in this country beyond attesting a respect for tradition. American pewter, like American silver, is often unmarked, and thus, at times, occasions embarrassment in identification. A great deal of the pewter, however, bears the touch-mark of the maker, with his name or initials and, sometimes, the place of manufacture. The touch-mark is usually applied outside, on the bottom of the piece, though sometimes it is to be seen inside. A favourite device with the American pewterers was the eagle. The later makers very generally forsook the device and merely stamped their name and, perhaps, the place of manufacture. As an example of pewter marking may be mentioned the device of Thomas Badger, of Boston, who wrought in the latter part of the eighteenth century. His mark consisted of an eagle with ''Thomas'' above and ''Badger'' below. ''Boston'' in a rectangle with scroll design was stamped separately.

Not all English pewter was marked, for the itinerant tinkers omitted marks, and the artisans not affiliated with any of the pewter guilds frequently left off any mark of identification. It is not safe to assume, therefore, that any unmarked piece of pewter is necessarily of American origin, although a great quantity of American ware is devoid of marks by which the maker may be identified.

The list of American pewterers and their marks, so far as they can be gathered, printed at the end of the

14

chapter, is not by any means complete. It will serve to show, however, over what a range of time some of the best known among the craft worked. We still await a full and exhaustive list.

PATTERN AND DECORATION

To the unalterable necessity for simplicity in the ordinary moulds we must attribute, at least in part, the prevalent simplicity of form in pewter. Pewter that is obviously moulded in imitation of silver forms is far less felicitious in appearance than ware whose expression is suited to the medium in which it is executed. The chief beauty of pewter must always lie in truthfulness of proportion and contour and the surface of the metal, and not in overly refined lines or intricate surface decoration. The very nature of the metal presupposes staunch and robust structure with bold, vigorous, and simple lines, and the occasional attempts to emulate the work of the silversmiths make pewter look finicky and foolish.

The seventeenth- and eighteenth-century American pewter is of robust aspect and generally pleasing design, very similar to the English pieces of the Stuart period in many instances. Towards the end of the eighteenth century, however, a state of decadence set in, and from thence onward shapes were often attenuated and meagre. The early pewter, therefore, is usually the best.

In England, and on the Continent far more than in England, various elaborate types of pewter decoration were, from time to time, indulged in by the pewterers. With these, however, we have no concern, because they do not, fortunately, appear in pewter of American make. The only three methods of orna-

mentation that we have to take into account are the
distribution of lines and decorative but simple mouldings; engraving, and, finally, "wriggling" or "joggling," an exceedingly effective but little-used method
of embellishment, so far as it was practised by American
pewterers.

Mouldings and rims that had to be cast in a mould
necessarily drew their charm from simplicity and a
restrained convexity of proportion rather than from
multiplicity of members and concavity or undercutting.
As a matter of fact, the mouldings and rims of the best
pewter were exceedingly simple, but they were well
placed and effective, and their unobtrusive and oftentimes flattened contour did not interrupt the beauty of
the metal's surface as seen in the plain portions of the
plate or vessel.

Engraving was little used for tracing decorative designs on American pewter, and was chiefly confined to
lettering or to tracing one or more lines on the surface
of flat-ware or about the body of hollow-ware near rims
or mouldings. Even lettering was rarely employed, and
that sparingly and in the simplest manner possible.
In its absolutely free surfaces pewter offered a contrast to silver, which, though of plain surface, was often
adorned with armorial bearings and ornamentally lettered inscriptions. English pewter was occasionally
embellished with engraving, and Continental pewter
often displayed elaborate embossing, as well as intricate
engraved designs. By nature pewter was not particularly suitable as a medium for engraving. Deep-cut
lines tended to weaken the work, and thin, delicate
lines soon became wholly or partially effaced.

"Wriggling" or "joggling" was a form of surface

ornamentation in broken or wavy lines or what some-times at first sight appeared to be disconnected gouges, done by forcing a flat-bladed tool forward, breadth-wise, with a rocking or wriggling motion, and holding it, the while, at an angle of about 45 or 50 degrees. Some idea of the method of applying this process may be gained by pushing a carving chisel forward over a piece of sheet lead. The character of the wriggled line pro-

FIG. 5. Sugar Bowl with "wriggled" ornament, eighteenth century, Bucks, Pennsylvania.
Courtesy of Pennsylvania Museum and School of Industrial Art.

duced was governed by the speed and regularity of the forward wriggling motion and the width of blade of the tool used. The blade of the tool was usually about one thirty-second of an inch wide. Scrolls, foliated designs, lettering, and various decorative devices could thus be executed and made to cover the whole surface if desired. The pear-shaped sugar bowl illustrated (Fig. 5) shows a good example of wriggled decoration. It was made in Pennsylvania, either in Bucks or Berks County, about the middle of the eighteenth century, and its contour approximates that of some contemporary silver sugar bowls.

Other forms of decoration, such as pearling, tracing, and punch-work, to be seen on foreign pewter, were not practised by American pewterers, or only in such exceptional cases that they cannot be considered as in any sense representative.

THE CARE AND CLEANING OF PEWTER

Much of the old pewter that one picks up in antique shops and at country sales has been so abused or neglected that its surface is not prepossessing. Pewter, as well as any other metal, in its normal condition should be kept clean and at least reasonably bright. There are those that profess to admire it more when it has a dull and ancient look, but, in the days when it was made and habitually used and prized, housewives took a pride in keeping it immaculately polished, and it is only when polished that the beautiful sheen, which constitutes a great part of its charm, can be seen. By proper treatment, old pewter pieces with dull, disfigured, and corroded surfaces—if the metal be of at all a good quality—can be restored to their pristine beauty, or, at any rate, to some degree of it.

If pewter is to be left for long periods without an occasional rubbing, it is well to wipe it with a woollen rag and a touch of vaseline, leaving a very thin and virtually invisible coat of vaseline on it.

The black oxide often found on pewter that has been neglected for a long time may be removed in either one of two ways. The first is to apply hydrochloric acid with a brush or with a rag held between the cleft ends of a stick. When the oxide scales soften, wipe off the acid with a wet sponge. The second and slower way is to use paraffin oil, either as an application or as a bath. Several treatments may be necessary where the pewter is badly oxidised.

Do not scrape pewter to remove scratches. Rub first with fine emery cloth or emery paper and then apply a burnisher. A jeweller's polishing lathe or buffing wheel is the best thing to use for polishing pewter.

To clean pewter, one of the following formulæ may be used: Rub with rotten-stone and oil and finish with dry rotten-stone on a soft cloth or piece of chamois skin. A paste of rotten-stone and soft soap mixed with turpentine may also be used, polishing off with dry rotten-stone and a chamois skin as before. Dry putty powder or oxide of tin, rubbed on with a cloth or chamois skin; oxalic acid dissolved in water with sifted rotten-stone, or, finally, almost any of the commercial polishing pastes may be used with satisfactory results.

The making of pewter began to decline in the latter part of the eighteenth century and continued on a downward course until 1835 or 1840, when the practice of the craft almost ceased. It was commercially displaced either by china, glass, and silver-plated ware, or else by some of the alloys that resembled it. These later wares are often mistaken for pewter, and, in many instances, the articles made in them followed pewter forms. Frequently they were made by the same individuals or concerns that had previously made pewter, and they may be reckoned, in a way, as belonging under the classification of pewter, since they are to some degree evolutionised pewter. They all, however, lack the subtle charm of the earlier and genuine pewter, and their colour and surface are generally hard and unsympathetic in aspect. One who has seen and handled good pewter cannot fail to detect the difference without much difficulty.

The collector of old American pewter is blessed with numerous opportunities for making acquisitions, as there is scarcely a place in the Atlantic States and the States immediately to the west of them where good pieces may not be picked up. In some places one must be on the lookout for faked antiques, but the evidences of age and wear are too unmistakable for a person with a keen collecting instinct and a keen collecting eye to be very easily deceived.

Pewter making is not to be regarded as necessarily a dead craft. Rather is it to be considered as quiescent and susceptible of revival in the proper hands. The *art nouveau* attempts in some quarters cannot be looked upon as a proper employment of the metal. The inspiration for a healthy pewter revival must come from a thorough acquaintance with the old forms and methods of work. Like methods will produce approximately like results. Given the taste and proper feeling on the part of the craftsman and a sympathetic knowledge of, and respect for, the qualities of the medium in which he is working, there is no good reason why pewter making should not again assume an honourable place in the list of American handicrafts.

The collections of American pewter in the Boston Museum of Art, the Pennsylvania Museum and School of Industrial Art and the Metropolitan Museum of Art are especially worthy of study.

Besides these, collections in other museums are assuming considerable proportions and excellence of quality, and a number of private collections from time to time are opened to the examination of an appreciative public.

A full list of American Pewterers known to date (January, 1927) is given in the Supplement, page 350.

CHAPTER VIII

EARLY AMERICAN SLIP-DECORATED POTTERY

THE making of slip-decorated pottery is one of the long-forgotten early American crafts brought to light within comparatively recent years by intelligent collecting and searching enquiry. The characteristics and markings of these interesting pieces are described in the latter part of this chapter. The manufacture and decoration of this species of earthenware constituted an industry whose existence was unsuspected by collectors and connoisseurs until, in 1891, Dr. Edward AtLee Barber, of the Pennsylvania Museum and School of Industrial Art, in Philadelphia, made a discovery that soon led to a wealth of finds and opened up a mine of engaging information. To Dr. Barber's efforts, indeed, we owe substantially all we know of the origin and practice of this phase of American ceramic development, from the initial attempts of a few eighteenth century potters to the ultimate abandonment of the kilns, about the middle of the nineteenth century.

The incident that led to Dr. Barber's discovery was the chance purchase, in a junk-shop, of a red earthenware pie plate, decorated with a device of flowers and birds, done in *sgraffito,* and bearing an inscription in a peculiar German dialect. The plate was thought, at first, to be of European workmanship, but careful scrutiny of the inscription showed that some of the words were not German, but "Pennsylvania Dutch."

This fact, and the enquiries set on foot regarding the source whence this particular plate had fallen into the junk dealer's hands, furnished a clew that led to the discovery that the art of making this decorated pottery had been brought from Germany and "was flourishing in Eastern Pennsylvania before the middle of the eighteenth century."

Subsequent investigations showed that slip-decorated earthenware was potted in several other parts of the country, also, in the latter years of the eighteenth century and early in the nineteenth. Outside of the German settlements in Pennsylvania, the small potteries that produced ware of this description were located in Philadelphia; in West Whiteland and Uwchlan townships of Chester County, Pennsylvania; at Morgantown, in West Virginia; in Connecticut, and possibly in the upper part of New York State and one or two other places. The slip ware made in all the potteries, other than those in the German district of Pennsylvania, lacked the ornate decoration which the colonists from the Palatinate lavished upon their work, and, although it displayed some degree of ornamentation, the embellishment was nearly always of the simplest type. It is not at all improbable that the making of slip-decorated pottery in the non-German parts of the country represented a survival of the art as practised by the old English potters, and that the American potters were merely perpetuating traditions that they had brought from their old environment, just as the Germans were perpetuating their peculiar hereditary methods of manufacture and adornment.

The Germans of Pennsylvania, or the "Pennsylvania Dutch," as they are commonly called, began to

emigrate from their fatherland in 1683, and continued
to come to America in ever-increasing numbers until, by
1727, they composed a very considerable portion of the
population of the Province.   After 1727 their immigra-
tion was still more rapid, but, by the year just mentioned, they had indelibly impressed with their characteristics the counties where they were chiefly settled—
Bucks, Berks, Montgomery, Lancaster, Lehigh, and
Northampton.   These immigrants hailed from various
German principalities, but most of them came from the
Rhenish Palatinate and adjacent provinces, and the
local peculiarities of those same provinces, in dialect
and customs, are said to predominate to this day in
the German sections of Pennsylvania.

By far the great majority of these people were from
the humbler walks of life; simple, sturdy, industrious
folk who devoted themselves to agriculture with all
their might and main, staying on the land they tilled
and carefully avoiding the political entanglements of
their neighbour colonists.   They were good farmers,
thrifty in their habits, moderate in their wants, resourceful and capable of raising in their fields, or
making at home, nearly everything they needed—in a
word, they were sufficient unto themselves and quite
content to let the world outside their own small sphere
wag as it might, without troubling their heads seriously
about it.

It is easy to understand how people of such tendencies, keeping to themselves, preserved their local
manners and customs quite distinct from those of the
surrounding communities.   It is also easy to understand how, under such conditions, people of their
strongly conservative temperament would faithfully

perpetuate all the traditions they had brought with them from their old home. The making of slip-decorated pottery was extensively practised in the parts of Germany from which they came, and when occasion arose for them to engage in potting, what more natural than that they should stick to methods of manufacture and types of decoration with which they were thoroughly familiar? As stated before, these people were, first and foremost, farmers, and, in nearly every instance, potting was a side issue, to be pursued in off seasons when farm duties were not urgent. Most of the potteries, therefore, were small concerns, operated by one man, with such occasional assistance as he might require, so that it is plain to be seen why there is often such a marked individuality discernible in the pieces coming from one kiln and such a difference between them and the output of another kiln, perhaps hard by.

VARIETIES OF SLIP-DECORATED WARE

The Pennsylvania German slip-decorated ware was the first decorated pottery [1] to be made by white settlers within the present limits of the United States, and presents two distinct varieties, which are the converse of each other. On one the design is *traced in slip,* while on the other the entire surface of the article to be decorated is covered with an *engobe* or coating of slip

---

[1] It is a matter of history that a pottery was established and worked at Burlington, New Jersey, in the latter part of the seventeenth century. Pottery with a white glaze is said to have been made. One or two fragments of such pottery have been found in the vicinity and show a simple relief ornamentation. Presumably they are from this source. The refuse heap of the old pottery is now covered by a lawn, whose owner, we are informed, refuses to permit excavation, so that it is impossible to identify the fragments as unmistakably of Burlington origin.

THREE EARLY AMERICAN PEWTER PORRINGERS
Courtesy of Metropolitan Museum

SGRAFFITO SLIP WARE PIE PLATE; "MISCHIANZA"
DEVICE, 1786
John T. Morris Collection, Pennsylvania Museum and School of
Industrial Art

SGRAFFITO SLIP WARE MEAT DISH; CREAM GROUND:
TULIP AND PEACOCK. DECORATION GREEN AND
RED, 1789
John T. Morris Collection, Pennsylvania Museum and School of
Industrial Art

and the design is then done in *sgraffito* or by an incised
scratching away of the slip coat from the underlying
surface.

MATERIALS

The materials required for the manufacture of slip
ware were simple and few in number. The common
yellowish clay, from which the ordinary commercial red
earthenware is made, formed the body or base of the
articles to be decorated. The *slip* or liquid clay, with
which the design was applied or from which the *engobe,*
in the case of *sgraffito* decoration, was made, was usually
of a cream colour and was composed of light-hued clay,
mixed with water. At first this clay was imported from
overseas, but was afterwards fetched from Jersey.
The glaze was made from either red lead or galena.
Various colouring substances, such as manganese and
verdigris, were used for the more elaborate pieces.
Water was added to the lead to make a thin mixture,
and then ordinary clay, worked fine and smooth, was
used as a thickening factor of the preparation.

IMPLEMENTS

The implements employed by the potters (Fig. 1)
were the *potter's wheel;* the *smoother* or *rib* (Fig. 1,
H), a "small piece of wood, leather, or calabash,
of square or rounded form, usually having a hole in the
centre for the thumb and finger," used to smooth the
outside surface of hollow-ware while still revolving on
the wheel; the *finishing brush,* made of hog bristles,
for touching up parts that could not be reached conveniently by the smoother; the *cutting wire,* about a
foot long, with wooden handles at the ends, with which
vessels were loosened from the wheel; the *pounder* or

batter (Fig. 1, D), a wooden tool, "flat on one side and rounded on the other, with a handle at one end," for beating out the clay into flat form; the *rolling pin* (Fig. 1, F), shaped like a wooden dough-rolling pin, but with separate handle, like a stick, passing through

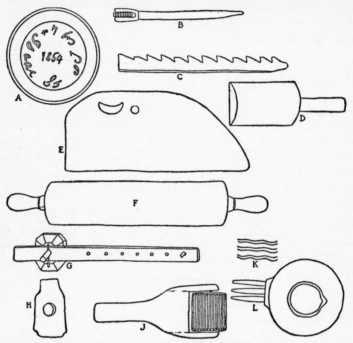

Fig. 1.—A, Plate. B, Coggle. C, Rule for gauging height of vessels on potter's wheel. D, Batter. E, Palette. F, Two-handled Roller. G, Disc Cutter. H, Rib for smoothing surface of ware on wheel. J, Coggle. K, Lines traced by slip cup. L, Three-quilled Slip Cup.

Courtesy of Pennsylvania Museum and School of Industrial Art.

the cylinder body, for completing and evening the work begun by the batter; the *disc cutter* (Fig. 1, G), consisting of a "wooden arm supported on one end by a small foot or block of wood, of circular or octagonal form, in which the arm revolved, and, in the other end,

set at right angles, a metal point'' adjustable in a series
of holes along the length of the arm; the *slip cup* (Fig.
1, L) or *quill box,* with one to seven quills, as occasion
required, from which the slip was applied to the piece
to be decorated; the *mould* for shaping bowls and concave dishes from flat clay discs, and, last of all, the
decorating wheel or *coggle* (Fig. 1, B and J), for notching or indenting the edges of pie plates.

PROCESSES

After the clay was ground, mixed, kneaded, and
worked to the proper consistency, it was divided into
balls or lumps, each of which contained enough material to make a vessel or dish. For making hollow-
ware, a lump was thrown on the potter's wheel and
worked to the desired shape in the manner ordinarily
pursued by potters. For flat-ware and moulded pieces,
the clay lump was beaten and then rolled to the proper
thickness, cut with the disc cutter, if it was of circular
form, and then shaped over the mould and the edge
notched with the coggle, if notching was to be done.
The pieces were then set away to dry. When the drying
process was sufficiently advanced the decoration was
applied.

In the *slip-traced* or *slip-painted* ware, the *slip* or
liquid clay of about the consistency of batter or thick
cream was trickled from the slip cup or quill box
through one or more quills over the surface of the un-
burned ware when it had partially dried. When the
slip itself had become dry enough to get set it was sometimes pressed or beaten into the still plastic surface of
the plate or platter. At other times the design was
allowed to stand out in low relief. The slip was gen-

erally of a lighter colour than the coarse clay underlying it.   Indeed, the slip was almost always cream coloured or nearly white, while the body of the pottery was a dark orange or red.   Occasionally the scheme was reversed and a design in red slip was traced on a cream-coloured ground.

In making the *sgraffito* ware, the red body of the pottery was entirely covered with a coating or *engobe* of the cream-coloured slip and, when this had sufficiently dried, the decorative designs were incised or etched upon it with a sharp-pointed stick.   This method of decoration admitted of greater elaboration of design and far more accuracy and nicety of execution than the former method by which the design had to be applied by tracing lines with a thick, flowing liquid that required no little dexterity to regulate.

Ordinarily the slip-decorated ware, whether *slip traced* or done by the *sgraffito* process, was subjected to only one firing.   In the case of the more elaborate pieces, however, two firings were sometimes given.

The glazing mixture was poured into hollow-ware that was to be glazed only on the inside; the vessel was then whirled rapidly round and round until the entire inner surface was thoroughly covered and the residue of the glaze was emptied out.   Vessels to be glazed both inside and outside were dipped in the glazing mixture. The glaze was painted upon the upper surface of pie plates, platters, dishes, and other flat or semi-concave articles with a brush.

In the process of firing, the glazing mixture "became a yellowish, translucent glass."   To darken the glaze, manganese was added in various quantities, according to the depth of tone desired, a black being

ultimately attainable by using enough manganese.
When a greenish tinge was required, verdigris was
added to the ordinary glazing mixture, previously described, instead of manganese. To produce a mottled
effect, verdigris was occasionally dabbed on the glaze
in spots and allowed to melt into the glaze in the heat
of the kiln. In a few instances, glaze of a chocolate-
brown hue has been found. This variety, however, is
very unusual and was obtained by the use of manganese.
On some of the more elaborate pieces one occasionally
finds either slips or glazes coloured blue, dark red, dark
brown, olive, yellow, and other hues, so that it is plain
that the chromatic possibilities were not necessarily
restricted to narrow limits, though, as a rule, the potters
stuck to the simpler schemes, and it was only the more
ambitious who strove, and that in exceptional instances,
to achieve a more varied polychrome effect. Confining
themselves to their red, white, and green, or simply red
and white, it is remarkable how much variety they succeeded in getting. From the nature of conditions, a
greater variety of colour was possible in *sgraffito* ware
than in *slip-traced* pottery.

After the glaze was put on, the pieces were set away
to dry and wait until there were enough to fill the kiln.
The firing process generally took about a day and a
half. The kiln was then sealed and allowed to remain
so for about a week, by the end of which time it had
cooled off sufficiently so that the ware could be removed.

ARTICLES MADE

Although platters, pie plates, jars or crocks, and
cooking pots seem to have been the most numerous
articles manufactured by the Pennsylvania German

15

potters, many other pieces also were produced by these farmer craftsmen. The common commercial form of pie plate was a concave, shallow disc with a notched or coggled edge, and the decoration usually consisted of parallel waving lines (Fig. 1, K). More elaborately decorated pie plates, however, were by no means uncommon. The plates and the platters were generally round, either with or without a broad rim, but oblong

FIG. 2. Green Glaze Jar, Vickers' Pottery, Downingtown, Pennsylvania.
John T. Morris Collection, Pennsylvania Museum and School of Industrial Art.

and oval shapes also occurred, and sometimes fluted ovals. Jars or crocks and cooking pots were of various shapes and sizes, but, in most cases, followed the ordinary familiar type still to be seen in the farmhouse kitchens of the Middle States. The cooking pots were made both with and without lids.

Besides the articles of most common manufacture just enumerated, there were also deep vegetable dishes, sometimes circular, sometimes octagonal or hexagonal:

meat dishes; fancy dishes or trays; cake plates; soup plates; shaving basons, like soup plates, with a curved piece cut out of the rim to fit the neck; shaving cups; spherical or cylindrical jars, usually with lids and either with (Fig. 2) or without handles; honey jars; tobacco jars (Fig. 3, B); apple-butter pots; bowls; cake and jelly moulds; decorative flower-pots; jugs for vinegar and molasses; mugs or measures, either straight sided with one handle (Fig. 3, A) or else

FIG. 3. A, Sgraffito Mug, Eastern Pennsylvania. John T. Morris Collection, Pennsylvania Museum and School of Industrial Art. B, Tobacco Jar, red ground with cream-coloured and black slip decoration; c. 1830.

Courtesy of Dr. Edwin AtLee Barber.

tumbler shaped, flaring towards the top, without handle; flower holders or vases of different shapes more or less fanciful; pitchers large and small; tea canisters; coffee-pots; sugar bowls; cream pitchers; ink stands; sand shakers and toys in the form of birds, animals, whistles, and miniature eating and drinking vessels. These pieces of domestic utility were made by the farmer potters from about 1720 to about 1850.

The slip-ware was of two sorts, commercial or common, which was produced in large quantities; and the finer articles, elaborately decorated, that were made in fulfillment of special orders or for presentation pieces, and, for that reason, cannot be said to have ever had any strictly commercial value. In the distinctly decorative *slip-traced* ware, not intended for constant hard usage, the design was often allowed to remain in slight relief. On the *slip-traced* ware of simpler design, meant for regular daily wear and tear, the figure was beaten or pressed into the surface of the plate or platter, or whatever the article might be, while it was still "green," or not thoroughly dry before glazing and firing, so that when glazed there might be no roughness to chip or wear through. The *sgraffito* ware almost always bore more or less elaborate decoration, but, as the glaze filled all depressions, there were no conspicuously uneven places to wear through.

DECORATIVE METHODS AND *MOTIFS*

Besides the processes of slip tracing and *sgraffito* decorating ordinarily employed by the potters, there were several other methods of ornamentation to which they now and then resorted. One of these was a transfer process; the other was a kind of embossing or relief work obtained by moulding. In the transfer process a leaf was laid on the body to be decorated, an *engobe* of white slip was spread over the rest of the surface, and then the leaf was removed, leaving its shape silhouetted in the surrounding coat of slip. For the embossed or raised decoration, the design to be reproduced was cut into the surface of the mould over which the dish was shaped. The mould being withdrawn, the raised decoration was left standing out from the surface in strong relief. The whole was then glazed and fired.

SGRAFFITO SLIP WARE DISH; UNITED DOVE AND TULIP.
DECORATIONS GREEN AND RED, 1786
John T. Morris Collection, Pennsylvania Museum and School of
Industrial Art

LARGE SLIP DECORATED VEGETABLE OR MEAT DISH,
CREAM-COLOURED SLIP ON RED GROUND, 1769
John T. Morris Collection, Pennsylvania Museum and School of
Industrial Art

OCTAGONAL DISH WITH MOULDED RELIEF DECORATION.
PENNSYLVANIA GERMAN, 1794
John T. Morris Collection, Pennsylvania Museum and School of Industrial Art

SLIP DECORATED PIE PLATES, FROM THE VICKERS POTTERY, CHESTER
COUNTY, PENNSYLVANIA. DISH MOULD
Courtesy of Pennsylvania Museum and School of Industrial Art

The *motifs* chosen for the decorative treatment of the slip-ware were of the most varied description, ranging from extremely simple conventional floral subjects to the human figure. Indeed, on the cheaper sort of pottery which was turned out in large quantities, the decoration often consisted of merely a succession of wavy parallel lines, as previously noted, traced with a slip cup that had from two to seven quills side by side. In the embellishment of the more ambitious pieces, it is often quite possible to recognise easily the flowers and fruits and leaves or the birds and animals with which the old potters wrought their decorative schemes; then, again, the subjects have been so conventionalised or so crudely treated that identification is altogether out of the question. A bird, it may be, is "no particular kind of a bird," but just a nondescript fowl that might equally well be taken for a parrot, a hen, or a peacock. Sometimes the birds or animals are strongly suggestive of the composite and impossible creatures one encounters in heraldry or ancient mythology. In almost all cases, however, let the treatment be as crude as it may, the decorative effect is distinctly interesting, if not really good. For the sake of convenience it will be well to classify the most frequently used *motifs* under the general heads of *Flowers, Fruits, Birds, Animals, Human Figures, Miscellaneous Devices* and *Inscriptions,* or *Initials* and *Dates.*

Flowers.—THE TULIP. Among the flowers chosen by the Pennsylvania German potters for the decoration of their ware, the tulip was easily first in point of popularity. It was so universal a favourite and its employment was so prevalent, during the whole period of manufacture, apparently being esteemed beyond all other *motifs* taken together, that the pottery made by the German colonists is often spoken of as "Tulip Ware." So beloved was the tulip by these early German settlers in America, indeed, that they habitually pourtrayed it in every conceivable place and under every conceivable form, either natural or conventionalised. They cast it in their iron stove plates, they painted it on the dower chests of their brides, they worked it on their samplers, they illuminated it on their *Vorschriften,* they carved it on the date-stones of their houses along with the initials of the goodman and his spouse, and, finally, they chiselled it on the headstones of their graves when they were gathered to their fathers. Besides all this, the early colonists cultivated the bulb most extensively. It could scarcely have had greater veneration in Holland in the days of Tulipomania. Some mystic symbolism seems to have attached to this prevalent use of the tulip *motif*—perhaps, like the old Persians, the "Pennsylvania Dutch" associated it with the ideas of life, love, and immortality. At any rate, it lent itself admirably to decorative treatment in the hands of unskilled draughtsmen, and is by far the most successful of all the subjects they attempted. Indeed, the plates, platters, jars, and other articles decorated with the tulip design often possess much genuine artistic merit and charm, whereas many of the other designs appeal to us merely by their rugged vigour in both conception and execution or by their naïve grotesquerie.

THE FUCHSIA. Next to the tulip in popular favour as a *motif* for decoration came the fuchsia. Like the tulip, it lent itself conveniently to conventional treatment or, if preferred, to a semi-naturalistic representation. "One of the striking characteristics of the German people in Pennsylvania, which has clung to them through all the years that have elapsed since their ancestors left the fatherland, is their love for flowers." Historians tell us that the people in the Rhine country take an especial delight in flowers, and that "nowhere is this trait so universal as in the Palatinate, along the left side of the river," the district from which so many of the Pennsylvania German colonists migrated. The fuchsia was a familiar and much-esteemed flower in the gardens of the farmhouses, and its almost invariable presence there is probably to be accounted for in part by the fact that "the fuchsia in Germany has long been regarded as sacred, since it is one of the first signs of the returning life of spring."

THE FORGET-ME-NOT. Sometimes in connexion with roses, sometimes by itself, the forget-me-not appears as a decoration on slip-traced or sgraffito pottery. Its clearly defined outline invited depiction. Sentiment, also, dictated its use, especially on pieces intended for presentation. It was a traditional subject, too, and often appears as a *motif* on some of the old pottery made in Germany.

OTHER FLOWERS. The rose, the lily of the valley, the Persian pink, and other blossoms also were used by the potters to embellish their handiwork. While, in some instances, it is quite impossible to tell what the botanic affinities of the blossom represented may be, the indications are usually plain enough for identification. In the selection of floral *motifs,* the craftsmen were guided not only by personal preference or the readiness with which certain species lent themselves to adaptation for decorative purposes, but also by a regard for the symbolism expressed in the language of flowers—the accom-

panying inscriptions on many pieces prove this—and
by the promptings of traditional attachment, for these
simple colonists, under an oftentimes uncouth exterior,
were, after all, tender sentimentalists, rigorous con-
servatives, and mystics in their own somewhat clumsy
and bucolic way (Fig. 4).

FRUITS. Apples and grapes seem to have been the
favourite fruits chosen for representation on the slip-
decorated ware, although other fruits also may now

FIG. 4. A, Dish, cream, green and black slip decoration. By John Leidy, Pennsylvania, 1796. B, Sgraffito Dish, polychrome glaze, Eastern Pennsylvania, c. 1790.
John T. Morris Collection, Pennsylvania Museum and School of Industrial Art.

and then be found. Fruit *motifs*, apparently, were not
nearly so popular as some other subjects.

Birds.—THE TURTLEDOVE. Among birds, the turtledove held a place comparable in favour to that of the
tulip among floral *motifs*. It was the emblem of love
and conjugal felicity, and its recurrence is frequent not
only on the sgraffito decorated plates, platters, and jugs,
but also in other decorative work wrought by the Pennsylvania Germans.

THE EAGLE. The eagle appears both in its natural
shape and in the traditional double-headed form proper

PAINTED LEATHER FIRE BUCKET AND FIRE HAT
Courtesy of Pennsylvania Historical Society

PENNSYLVANIA-GERMAN PAINTED "BRIDE BOX," EIGHTEENTH
CENTURY
Frishmuth Collection, Pennsylvania Museum and School of Industrial Art

PAINTED METAL TRAY WITH BUFF GROUND AND DARK BORDER,
FLOWERED AND HATCHED; EARLY NINETEENTH CENTURY
In possession of Abbot McClure, Esq.

EIGHTEENTH AND EARLY NINETEENTH CENTURY TOLEWARE OR TIN
WITH DECORATIVE PAINTING
Courtesy of John C. Nippes, Esq., Haddonfield, New Jersey

to heraldic representation. As a natural bird it was, perhaps, indicative of patriotism on the part of the potters who potted after the king of birds had become a national emblem. As a double-headed creature it was reminiscent of the devices they had so often seen blasoned in the land of their origin or of the design on some treasured heirloom they had brought with them to a new land.

THE PEACOCK. The decorative possibilities suggested by the peacock could not fail to impress a craftsman considering a subject of design. Furthermore, the peacock was a familiar fowl in the farmhouse dooryards, as it "was raised quite extensively in the Pennsylvania German settlements, as elsewhere in the Eastern States, and in some of the rural districts it was looked upon as a weather prophet, its discordant cry being supposed to indicate the approach of rain. Its gorgeous plumage was used for mantel decoration, sometimes being placed in an earthen jar, and was also made into pliant brooms to be waved across the dining table in fly time. For ordinary purposes brushes made of fringed paper were in common use, but the peacock broom was always brought forth on state occasions."

OTHER BIRDS. In addition to the birds just named, the potters made more or less use of the following in their decoration: the duck, the drake, the swan, the oriole, the parrot, the domestic cock (Fig. 5, B) and hen, and the pelican (Fig. 5, A), the last being regarded as emblematic of maternal devotion.

ANIMALS. Besides the deer, the horse, and the rabbit, which seem to have been looked upon with special favour among the representatives of the animal kingdom, lions, dogs, and other four-footed creatures made their appearance from time to time. Although the drawing of animals was never so successful as the delineation of certain flowers and a few of the birds, the representation was not infrequently vigorous and spirited.

HUMAN FIGURES. When it came to tracing the "human form divine," the "Pennsylvania Dutch" potter can scarcely be reckoned a skillful limner. Most of his efforts in that direction are frankly grotesque, but refreshing, nevertheless, if we take them simply for what they are worth and do not expect too much. On

FIG. 5. A, Deep flaring Dish, red ground with slip decoration. Eastern Pennsylvania c. 1830. B, Deep Dish with flaring rim. Decorations in cream slip with touches of green glaze. Probably by John Leidy, Eastern Pennsylvania, c. 1796.
John T. Morris Collection. Pennsylvania Museum and School of Industrial Art.

a plate showing a wedding scene the bride and groom are evidently people of very positive mould. If physiognomy be any criterion, one might reasonably suspect the lady of having a truculent disposition and a shrewish temper. The wasp-like waists of the damsels on the Mischianza plate excite our pity, but, notwithstanding the physical limitations of their tenuity, they seem to be having such an agreeable time treading the minuet with their gallant British partners that perhaps our compassion is not needed. At any rate, whatever their defects from an artistic point of view, they are interesting from historical considerations, for they throw many a valuable sidelight on the dress and manners of the time.

MISCELLANEOUS DEVICES. The slip-ware decorators now and again had recourse to miscellaneous devices not included in any of the foregoing classifications. Among these may be found houses, trees, hearts, swords, stars, fish, serpents, herring-bone patterns, and serpentine scrolls.

INSCRIPTIONS. For marginal use or incorporation in the body of the decoration, inscriptions, dates, names, and initial letters were of frequent occurrence. Moral admonitions, mottoes, proverbs, expressions of affectionate regard, and indications of ownership are all to be found, and sometimes the name of the maker occupies a conspicuous place. The snatches of verse and the couplets thus employed are often exceedingly quaint, and, by this means, one occasionally finds an allusion to some peculiar local custom or gets an insight into an interesting bit of folk-lore. The general tone may be judged by the following specimens:

> To paint flowers is common,
> But God alone is able to give fragrance.

> Rather would I single live
> Than the wife the breeches give.

> A pipe of tobacco does a man as much good
> As though he spends his money with the girls.

> I cook what I can,
> If my sow will not eat, my husband will.

The last was probably in allusion to an old German saying that "He is a poor farmer because he eats all the good things himself and does not give his pig any."

Nearly all of these inscriptions are in the "Pennsylvania Dutch" dialect. The lettering is generally vigorous and possessed of a certain rude grace which accords well with the *naïveté* of the sentiments expressed. Sometimes the marginal inscriptions on plates were in the nature of a grace, and filled a useful purpose in supplying occasional reminders of moral principles and food for reflection while the plate itself supplied food for the body. It must be remembered, too, that among these people there was little popular reading matter, so that the inscriptions, therefore, ministered to another want.

The potters, in some cases, put small marks or devices on their work to indicate authorship, instead of signing the pieces with their names.

In forming our estimate of the intrinsic merits of Pennsylvania German slip-decorated pottery it is not, of course, fair to apply the tests that we should ordinarily apply to work of a more finished character. It was a spontaneous expression of folk-art among a crude people, and we must consider all the attendant circumstances of its production. The conception is full of vitality, and the depiction energetic and straightforward. The artists were not skillful, but they were sincere, and their honest efforts should command our respect, because they were evidently doing the best they knew how. Above all, it was appropriate, for it suited the conditions of the people by whom and for whom it was made. Notwithstanding all the imperfections in drawing, notwithstanding the frequent crudity of colour, notwithstanding the general bizarrerie of many of the pieces, they all possess a decorative charm that compels our interest, if not our admiration. Indeed, in the light of recent post-Impressionistic inspiration, it seems hard to deny the old potters some artistic rating. Surely the habitual deficiency of drawing, the painfully jimp waists of the women, the misshapen anatomy of the men, the exaggerations and distortions in the pourtrayal of birds, beasts, and flowers, are all very like the earmarks of draughtsmanship that receive the approval of our most modern art mentors. There is this difference, however. None of the old potters were posing, and all of them were unquestionably sincere.

The old potteries are now all idle or have fallen into ruin. They have not been operated since about 1850. We cannot help feeling some regret that this craft is no longer practised, and it is quite possible to understand the inspiration that prompted English Colonial potters living near the Germans to imitate their ware. Apart from the purposes of the collector, the present value of the pottery is twofold. By its own visible evidence we can learn much of the people who made it, and, more important still, it is capable of supplying a stimulus to the craftsman of to-day. It can never be exactly duplicated, nor is it desirable that it should be, but the processes by which it was made can be used again and with as great success.

The collector never knows when or where he may chance upon a piece of slip-ware and, incidentally, a discovery regarding manners and methods. If one really wishes to find novel pieces he must be constantly on the lookout in every imaginable place, just as he would for any other kind of pottery or porcelain, and he must be willing to poke into all sorts of unpromising nooks and corners. One can never tell where the treasure may lie. The rural districts of Pennsylvania,

however, and the cities not too far removed from the
eastern portion of the State are likely to be the most
fruitful hunting ground. In any of these places it is
worth while to nose about any antique shop or the
habitat of any junk dealer.

The finest collection of slip-ware in any one place is
to be seen at Memorial Hall, in Fairmount Park, Philadelphia, a part of the Pennsylvania Museum and School
of Industrial Art. There is also a collection at Manheim, Pennsylvania.

STONEWARE

It would be unjust to the eighteenth century craftsmen to conclude a chapter on early pottery without some
allusion to the grey or grey-brown stoneware with
blue decorations. Such ware, consisting chiefly of
pitchers, mugs, butter crocks and pickle jars, was made
in several places and, in one or two instances—notably
at Haddonfield in West Jersey—has been manufactured
without interruption to the present day, the same forms
and methods of decoration being employed without
change.

The shapes of these vessels were good and the
colour scheme—deep blue decorations in a grey or
grey-brown ground—pleasing. Simple floral devices
were either painted on a flat surface or else blue colouring was run into shallow incised patterns, after which
the glaze was applied. Sometimes the whole surface
was covered with incised ornament and not coloured.

CHAPTER IX

DECORATIVE PAINTING ON HOUSEHOLD GEAR

EARLY American decorative painting has far more than a purely antiquarian interest for us to-day. The various decorative objects wrought by the craftsmen and craftswomen of Colonial and post-Colonial periods, and the articles of common household utility, to which they applied some sort of painted ornamentation, have aroused in recent years a lively interest on the part of both collectors and professional decorators and have supplied abundant inspiration and patterns for modern emulation. Collectors esteem them for their intrinsic merits, for the gratification of some individual fancy, for some peculiarity of historical consideration attaching to them or the like. Decorators have recognised their value for purposes of a kind of embellishment, especially effective in certain appropriate settings, and when they cannot come by originals they are not slow to demand reproductions, so that the craftsworker has found much employment in this fruitful traditional field. The private purchaser, too, has not been slow to see the merits of this old work and turn it to good account.

Although the decorative painting representing the handiwork of long-past generations has not been made the definite object of the collector's energies in a comprehensive way, so far as the writers are aware—it really spreads over almost too wide a range to fit conveniently into the collecting scheme of any one individual—its appeal has proved so compelling, and we find the application of the decorative resources it offers made in such various and ingenious ways, either by the use of original "finds" made at antique shops or at the junk dealer's, by reproductions or by adaptations that adhere pretty faithfully to the spirit of their prototypes in colour and design, that it deserves systematic and extended attention from those who would be fully cognisant of the wealth of our decorative heritage.

Abundant examples of early decorative painting are to be found on the usual pieces of household furniture, especially chests, cupboards, chairs, and tables, and also upon mirror tops, clock faces, the doors of bracket and hanging clocks, trays, small boxes, bellows, snuff-boxes and band-boxes, and many other small odds and ends. First in order we shall consider the larger pieces of furniture.

FURNITURE

We are altogether too apt to take it for granted that our Colonial forebears depended wholly upon the Old World for such things as were thence sent overseas to them for the gratification of any taste for the amenities of existence that they might have leisure and means to entertain or cultivate. As a matter of fact, they were not so busy subduing the wilderness and battling with adverse conditions that they had no time to devote to anything not savouring of severely practical utility.

One of the things for which the desire seized them was some sort of decoration for their simpler and often home-made furniture, much of it constructed of cheap, common, and easily worked wood of whatever kind chance brought readiest to hand. With characteristic resourcefulness, they supplied the want themselves, depending for inspiration upon the traditions they had brought with them, as a part of their heritage, from the lands whence they were sprung. The form of decoration they applied to their plainer furniture was painting, and we find furniture painting practised from New England to the Southern Colonies. Its character differed widely in different localities and was determined in the several regions by the several types of tradition to which those who practised it had fallen heir. Hence we find one style, derived from English tradition, in New England; another style, derived from Dutch tradition, in New York and the Dutch parts of Long Island and Northern New Jersey; while, in Pennsylvania, there flourished among the Pennsylvania Germans still a third style, derived from the peasant traditions of Bavaria and the neighbouring German principalities. Pennsylvania also exhibited examples of English tradition among the English colonists, and the same may be said of the Southern Colonies.

The want of some sort of decoration was perfectly natural. Of necessity, the home-made furniture, chest, cupboard, or what you will, was severely simple in form and line and evidenced the need of something to relieve its austerity and baldness of aspect. Paint afforded the easiest means of supplying the obvious need, and paint was the first to suggest itself. It ministered to native love of colour. Besides, paint was the logical preservative of the wood. But, even at the very beginning, paint was not regarded from the merely utilitarian point of view, for in some of the earliest instances it was applied to only a part of the surface and in a decorative design. This method of embellish-

16

ment was customarily employed where the object to be decorated was made of oak or some other wood whose grain and colour had a decorative value in themselves.

NEW ENGLAND.   The first examples of American Colonial furniture painting are to be found, of course, in New England.   There chests, hutches, small boxes, and the like were not infrequently adorned with simple floriated or foliated designs, more or less conventional, applied on a background of colour or upon the natural wood.   Sometimes the decoration consisted merely of scrolls and waving lines.   Nearly all the painting of this sort is of very early date, and most of the pieces in which it is found belong to the seventeenth century.

The mouldings on many seventeenth- and some early eighteenth-century New England-made chests and cupboards were of pine or some other soft wood, although the rest of the piece may have been of oak.   One of the commonest forms of colour decoration was to paint or stain these mouldings red, in imitation of cedar or rosetta-wood.   Likewise, the turned and applied ornaments for seventeenth-century New England oak cabinet work,[1] such as round or oval bosses and split balusters, spindles, or maces, were frequently made of pine, or of some soft wood that could be easily worked, and then painted black to look like ebony.   Sometimes, however, even hardwood mouldings were painted or stained.

It was a common practice to stain parts of cabinet work instead of using paint, but, as the chromatic effect was obtained in practically the same way, the process is to be included under the head of painting.   A more

[1] v. "The Practical Book of Period Furniture"; Eberlein and McClure.

extensive use of staining than that already alluded to, in the case of mouldings, is to be found on some of the "Hadley" chests—so called from the peculiar form of carved decoration found on many chests and boxes made in the vicinity of Hadley, Massachusetts—where rails, stiles, and panels are all given the adornment of colour, in addition to carving, and considerable variety is attained by the use of two or three hues, such as red, mulberry, and black or red, brown, and black. Oftentimes, also, on pieces of furniture other than chests, or on pieces with a device quite different from the Hadley pattern, where the ornament consisted of flat carving in low relief, the design was strongly accentuated by the application of colour to the background.

Occasionally panels were painted with stripes. Then, again, the flat surfaces of panels or stiles of chests, or other articles of cabinet work, are sometimes found ornamented with painted line or dot designs in geometrical or floral patterns, and, in some cases, the tulip *motif* appears in this form, which circumstance would seem to point to a strain of Dutch or German influence and occasions some surprise, as one scarcely expects to find this flower *painted*—although its occurrence elsewhere on *carving* is common enough—outside of the Pennsylvania German sphere of inspiration. The least worthy form of painted decoration was where it merely simulated panelling or some other decorative process.

After the period of profuse carving had passed, the flat drawer fronts of chests of drawers and highboys were now and again enlivened with painted patterns of flowers and leaves. Doubtless the inspiration for some of this species of ornament came from the japanned or lacquered pieces, so popular in England in the latter part of the seventeenth century and the early part of the eighteenth. Some of them, of course, found their way to America, and examples are not wanting of fairly sucessful attempts, on the part of American craftsmen, to emulate the lacquer work of contemporary British manufacture. In England, the art of lacquering was extensively practised by amateurs, with varying degrees of success, and no doubt the same was true in America, for London fashions found a very prompt echo on our side of the Atlantic, and, in all probability, a copy or two of Stalker and Parker's "Treatise on Japanning and Varnishing," published in 1688, reached Colonial readers. The execution of lacquer work, however, was not extensively undertaken, and outside of New England few, if any, serious attempts were made in that direction. Thus, with the conclusion of the lacquer episode, we reach the limit of furniture painting phases peculiar to New England. Other types of painted decoration practised there were shared with other parts of the Colonies. Before quitting the consideration of forms of decorative furniture painting peculiar to New England, however, a word must be added anent court cupboards, press cupboards or wainscot cupboards, and their various mobiliary kin and descendants, which seem always to have been especially favourite subjects for painted decoration. The taste and precedent for such decoration are, in all likelihood, to be traced through England, Flanders and Holland, and finally to Germany, where, in the early seventeenth century, the cabinet makers, inspired by the elaborate and multi-coloured inlay of woods, metals, and stones or mosaic, wrought by Italian and Spanish artisans, seem to have achieved brilliant results with paint, which offered a means of attaining, at little expense, little skill and infinitely less labour, some approximation to the interest and relief of design and colour produced by more complex decorative processes. In this connexion, in his book on the furniture of Colonial America, Mr. Lockwood calls attention to the frequent use of paint to enliven the mouldings, cornices, and turned ornaments of early New England cupboards, and the occasional presence of stain or paint as a background to set off carving. It must also be remembered that not a few of the early cupboards or buffets were painted wholly white, or in some colour, and picked out or lined with gold enrichments. This was particularly apt to be the case when the cupboards were built into the walls or when they partook of architectural features in their form or method of ornamentation. The insides were usually adorned with paint and gilding, while the coved scallop shells that generally formed the arch at the top especially invited such decoration.

NEW YORK, LONG ISLAND, NORTHERN NEW JERSEY. In Dutch New York, and the Dutch parts of Long Island and Northern New Jersey, the painting of chests, chairs, stools, cupboards, and other articles of furniture was commonly practised. Chests in the Hudson Valley were rarely made of oak, as in New England, but were customarily constructed of pine or some other cheap wood and painted. Many pieces were painted a solid colour all over, while the grace of design was added here and there as a relief. The great *kasses* or cupboards were sometimes made of black walnut, but, for the most part, were of pine and painted, not seldom with elaborate and ample decorative bunches of fruits, flowers, and ribbons.

PENNSYLVANIA GERMAN WORK. One of the most interesting and strongly individual manifestations of furniture painting in Colonial America was that practised by the Germans of Pennsylvania, to whose singularly fertile perpetuation of traditions, transplanted from their fatherland, allusion has previously been made. A comparison of the painted chests and boxes to be found by roaming about in out-of-the-way corners of the counties where the "Pennsylvania Dutch" chiefly settled — Bucks, Berks, Montgomery, Lancaster, Lehigh, and Northampton—discloses a striking resemblance to the painted furniture of Bavaria, characteristic specimens of which are preserved in the National Museum of Munich. While the colouring of the Pennsylvania chests is sometimes more subdued, it is not universally so, and there is a close likeness shown in the method of combining the colours. There is also a remarkable similarity in the decorative *motifs* employed—stiff, crudely drawn flowers and fruits, birds, and decorative bands. Of course, in the choice of designs, the "Pennsylvania Dutch" showed a local predilection for the tulip, which they never failed to introduce in every possible place, from tombstones to iron stove-plates or illuminated baptismal certificates. Other *motifs,* specifically mentioned in the chapter on slip-decorated pottery, were also employed in their furniture painting.

Besides the conventional decorative panels and bands separating them, inscriptions were almost invariably used as an additional embellishment. Sometimes merely the initials of the owner or owners and the date would appear. Then, again, some homely motto in German text, expressing an aspiration, a religious sentiment, or a practical bit of advice in proverb form, would be employed in addition.

The articles chosen for this kind of chromatic decoration were chests, especially the so-called dower chests, which the bride took with her, filled with ample store of household linen, to her new home, and the small wooden boxes, often of oval shape, which the groom customarily gave to the bride at or a little before the time of the wedding. These "bride-boxes," as they are sometimes called, were filled with linen, laces, ribbons, and other small finery dear to the feminine heart, for the personal use and adornment of the bride. Whether oval or round in shape—both forms were common—the boxes are made of four pieces of wood—two in the box itself and two in the cover. The bottom and top are made of thin pieces of white pine of the required shape. The sides of the box and the rim of the top are made of single thin and pliable strips of the same wood, long enough to cover slightly more than the circumference of the bottom and top pieces and allow enough to lap over. Where the ends lap, they are pierced and strongly sewed together with split willow withes or rattan, in much the same way that the caning of a chair seat is bound. The top and bottom pieces are fastened inside these bands with tacks or small nails. The inside is left unpainted, and the outside is coated with a solid ground colour—green, red, blue, yellow, or brown, as taste dictated. Upon this solid colour fanciful decorations in bright hues and flat treatment were lavished. Floral designs and birds were the favourite *motifs*, although representations of the human figure and inscriptions were by no means unusual. The human figures sometimes present a valuable commentary on the costumes of the day. As in most of the German peasant work, tulips, pinks, fuchsias, doves, and parrots supply the chief themes for ornamentation, although other flowers, birds, and animals frequently appear as well. The execution is crude and the colouring oftentimes exceedingly bizarre, but the effect, nevertheless, is, in the main, agreeable and harmonious after its fashion, and the perpetuation of transplanted folk traditions—practically all of this work was home-made and may be said to have been home-decorated—is made perfectly obvious.

Other pieces of household equipment besides chests and boxes were also painted, although the greatest efforts seem to have been lavished in the direction just indicated. The vivid colours of these painted articles—bright greens, reds, blues, and yellows were the favourites—added a note of life and point of interest in any room where they were placed, and it is needless to say that they were cherished with a good deal of pride and satisfaction, not to mention sentiment. It is really remarkable to see how much variety the painters sometimes achieved by the ingenious combination of comparatively few colours.

A comparison of several of the dower chests will show how closely the Pennsylvania furniture painters followed the spirit and tradition of the Old World in their work. One chest, to which we shall refer for this purpose, is an exact replica of a bride chest in the National Museum at Munich, the other was picked up at a country sale in Bucks. The Bavarian dower chest has a cream-coloured ground in which the bright-hued

METAL CLOCK DIAL WITH PAINTED DEC-
ORATION, EIGHTEENTH CENTURY
Courtesy of Mr. James Curran, Philadelphia

BANJO CLOCK. GLASS
PANELS PAINTED IN
REVERSE. Early Nine-
teenth Century.
Courtesy of Mr. Richard
W. Lehne, Philadelphia

EARLY NINETEENTH CENTURY MIRROR TOP WITH HEAD
PANEL PAINTED IN REVERSE ON GLASS
Courtesy of Mr. Richard W. Lehne, Philadelphia

PENNSYLVANIA-GERMAN PAINTED DOWER CHEST
Courtesy of Mrs. Spencer Roberts, Philadelphia

flowers, figures, and bands stand out in strong relief. The front of the chest is divided into three panels by wide yellow, decorative bands. The stiff sprays of flowers and leaves in the side panels, springing primly from graceful little vases, are painted in strong tones of red, green, blue, and yellow, while the bunch of four plums with leaves, in the central panel, is done in plum colour and green. The chequered diaper-work in blue and yellow, at the bottom of the plum panel, is exceedingly effective. The letters J. V. C. A., in the lower corners of the two side panels, are presumably the initials of the contracting pair, and the figures 1705 doubtless show the date of the marriage. The panels at the ends are likewise fully decorated. One shows a quaint little man, fancifully arrayed in mediæval costume, leaning on a staff and an equally quaint little woman, in gown of the same period, presenting him with a nosegay. The other end has simply a floral design.

The Pennsylvania chest is likewise divided into three panels in front. The body of the chest is a dull blue. That the decoration was ''home made'' may be inferred from the ruled scratchings and carpenter's compass marks on the wood, made in laying off the spaces for the painted embellishment. The groundwork of the panels is cream coloured, and the flowers, lettering, and figures are done in reds, greens, and yellows that were once brilliant and glowing, but are now dulled by age and perhaps a degree of neglect and exposure. The panels at the ends are much marred, and the design is incoherent and almost obliterated. Quite enough is visible, however, in the decoration of the old Pennsylvania chest to show the general type of

painting in vogue and demonstrate the oneness of tradition that supplied the humble painters on different sides
of the Atlantic, and at an interval of eighty years, with
inspiration to guide them in their task of adornment.

ENGLISH WORK. The English settlers in Pennsylvania did not practise this style of furniture painting,
but occasionally their work was slightly influenced by
contact with their German neighbours. An instance of
this is to be seen on an iron-bound strong-box, once
the property of Robert Morris and now in the collection
of the Pennsylvania Historical Society. The decoration
was, in all probability, done either by a German colonist,
working in Philadelphia, or else by an English colonist
who had seen somewhat of the decoration done by the
German settlers and recognised its intrinsic value.
Tulips and birds of gay plumage are the *motifs* of
ornament and are painted in the little squares between
the heavy iron bands or straps.

Windsor chairs and settees were almost invariably
painted, dark green being a favourite body colour,
although other colours also were used, and the decoration generally consisted of neat lining and banding in
some contrasting colour or gilt.

Towards the end of the eighteenth century and in
the fore part of the nineteenth, wooden chairs and
settees, with wide top rails and vertical slats in the
back, of a common farmhouse type that is probably to
be attributed, in the first place, to a Dutch origin, were
painted with great care. A body colour was first
applied—green, red, yellow, blue, brown, or grey—and
lined and banded with black, and then the decoration,
consisting of conventional designs, flowers in baskets
or sprays of flowers, was painted on the wide, flat space

of the top rail. This decoration was sometimes painted in black from a stencil pattern and sometimes in colours, with a touch of gilding added. Not a few of the top rails and cross rails of chairs and settees were decorated by the application of transfer designs, laid on in the same manner as decalcomanias. The metallic colours and the *exact* repetition of the same design in hundreds of cases prove this beyond peradventure. The painting of chairs and settees of both this type and the Windsor pattern was common throughout the country. Chairs of a late Sheraton type also came in for a share of decorative painting.

During the early nineteenth century—the American Empire period in furniture—the practice was prevalent of applying a stencilled decoration to furniture with gilt. Colours, too, were frequently included in the scheme of embellishment. The ornament was bestowed upon the top rails and cross-bars of chairs and settees, the top rails, seat rails, and rolled-over arms of sofas and couches, and the fronts of drawers. Lining was used wherever it might show to advantage. This liberal use of gilt was obviously a substitute for the elaborate brass mounts so characteristic of French Empire furniture, but the craftsmen managed to put a good deal of life and individuality into what, at first, was a mere cheap imitation, so that it came to have a distinct and legitimate decorative value. The gilding was sometimes applied directly to the mahogany, but was more commonly used for the embellishment of cheaper furniture that had been first painted with a body colour—oftentimes drab, olive green, or brown—and appropriately lined. The gilded or painted and gilded pattern of decoration, stencilled, free-hand, or transfer, was generally elaborate and embraced the *motifs* that were characteristic of the carving of the period— acanthus leaves, cornucopias, fruit, flowers, cords and tassels, drapery, swags and drops, the anthemion, and other designs that may be readily identified. When the work was done free-hand or stencilled, shading was accomplished by applying umber, sienna, or even black in the required places.

MISCELLANEOUS OBJECTS

The wider general field of domestic decorative painting, comprehending numerous small objects of miscellaneous purpose and varied form, but of a decorative value equal to, or even greater than, that of the larger articles of furniture, has been little heeded except in a fugitive sort of manner and more by way of allusion than by direct reference. We have, as a rule, failed to grasp the real character and full significance of these lesser furnishings, either because, as units of the residuary *milieu* of heirlooms constantly surrounding us, we have taken them as a matter of course, without particularly noting their details—for most people see least what is right under their very noses—or else because they have only recently been rescued from the oblivion of garrets and junk-shops and paid new honours of appreciation by antique dealer and purchaser alike, both of whom, until a few days ago, were usually too much occupied with the bulkier and more substantial pieces of furniture to bother with "small rubbish" that was only one degree better, to their then way of thinking, than the stuff sold in penny lots at country sales.

CLOCK FACES. In the household gear of our forefathers the clock was a point of central interest for its utilitarian value. It was but natural, therefore, that they should try to make an object towards which, of necessity, their eyes turned many times a day a point of decorative interest as well. Accordingly, they added the embellishment of painting to tall case, bracket, or hanging clocks, as circumstances permitted. The spot most available for ornamentation in the tall case clocks was the face, and there we find a variety of treatments, elaborate or simple, as fancy or skill dictated. In the eight-day clocks with the astronomical attachment, showing the lunar phases, there was always an excellent opportunity for painting jolly-faced, ruddy-cheeked, round-eyed moons, the rotundity of whose optics carries the beholder back to the Iliad and makes one think of the "Ox-eyed Juno." Then there were the star-spangled spaces of dark-blue sky between the moon faces, and, occasionally, square-rigged ships that sailed majestically by on heraldically waved seas, as the disc revolved with the passing days of each month. In the spandrels, at the upper and lower corners of the dial, Father Time, hour-glasses, scythes, gay-plumaged birds, stiff little bunches of flowers or baskets of vari-coloured fruits oftentimes lent an additional touch of decorative attraction. Judged from a purely natural-istic and pictorial point of view, the painting was fre-quently villainously bad, but the decorative effect, nevertheless, was good, even when there was no attempt at conventionalisation and the canons of perspective or proprieties of anatomy were cast to the winds, and so the object really aimed at was fully accomplished.

Clocks without the astronomical movement, but with a lunette or round arch at the top of the dial, especially invited the labours of the decorative painter. In the semicircle or lunette of one old clock face an ambitious country artist—probably one of the German colonists— has had the temerity to attempt a reproduction of Leonardo da Vinci's "Last Supper." Viewed seriously, it is, of course, a caricature. The drawing is grotesque, and the colouring, done purely from imagination, is startlingly crude and garish. Nevertheless, it satisfied the decorative cravings and the piety of its simple maker and owners, and it must be admitted that, when seen from a distance, it is not wholly ineffective as a piece of decoration. The stiff little bunches of flowers at the corners of the dial, however, are much more successful and convince one that it would have been far better if the decorator, for his main embellishment, had stuck to the birds or fruit or some such unpretentious subject, as most of the faces display. The faces are made of either wood or metal. Oftentimes the dials bear the name of the clock maker, so that the place of authorship is thus established, although, in some instances, the dial makers' names appear to the exclusion of the clock makers' names. It is not difficult to identify unsigned faces of native American origin, for the decoration is cruder than that found on imported dials painted in England or on the Continent.

PAINTINGS ON GLASS. Another sort of painting that challenges attention by numerous examples is executed in reverse on the under side of glass, so that the picture shows through. These glass paintings are found chiefly in panels in the heads of mirrors and on the doors of clocks of both the Willard banjo and Eli Terry bracket types. The finest painted or painted and gilt mirror heads are of English or French make, but a great many of the American efforts in that direction possess considerable merit, while others are crude and sometimes frankly ugly and clumsy. Notwithstanding their faults, however, they all have a genuine decorative value. The panels that are only painted are apt to be heavy and blotchy in colour, with a marked preference for strong greens, insistent reds, and staring whites. The drawing is generally poor and often childish, and the subjects are most frequently bits of local landscape, familiar to the painter, or merely isolated houses, trees, or fences that might be labelled "a house," "a tree," "a fence," and so on, and serve admirably for illustrations of the old-fashioned spelling-books, to which, as well as to the examples of pictorial art seen on many of the samplers of the period, they bear a close resemblance. At times, also, we find various historico-patriotic subjects depicted, or perhaps a front view of Mount Vernon, and now and again the heads of Washington, La Fayette, and other Revolutionary heroes, surrounded with laurel wreaths, flags, and other emblems of military glory.

The mirror-head panels in which gold decoration occurs are, in the main, somewhat better in execution than those that are merely painted. In such panels the design was first laid in with black paint, the drawing, of course, being done in reverse. Gold size was then applied to all the surface intended to display a gold backing. Gold leaf was next applied. This adhered firmly to the sizing and made it possible to wipe off easily whatever portions were not intended to remain. The next step was to run in the background of white or grey. The effect of such panels is often exceedingly chaste and refined. The best were made in England and France and displayed high artistic merit, but a great many of real excellence were executed in America. It was the period at which classic feeling was para-

mount in artistic expression, partly owing to the influence of the Brothers Adam and their emulators,
partly to the more recent influence of the Empire style
as set forth by David, Percier, Fontaine, and their contemporaries. It is not unusual to find mythological
subjects executed with Flaxman-like spirit, simplicity,
and delicacy. These gold bases and black-line pictures
stood out in strong relief against the background of
grey or white and were exceedingly effective. In some
of these mirror-head panels the greater part of the
ground was taken up by a cross-hatched diaper pattern
in black or black with gold rosettes, while a medallion
or cartouche in the centre was reserved for more
elaborate embellishment.

American makers eagerly copied the decorations of
the imported mirrors and produced work of all grades
of excellence, some of it rivalling the performances of
the British or French glass painters and some of it
sinking to the level of puerile crudity. In the absence
of accurate historical knowledge of the authorship of
an individual piece, it is often possible to establish its
American origin by the subject illustrated, and occasionally reliable tradition and internal evidence unite
to confirm the attribution. A case of this kind is ex-
emplified in one mirror-head whose frame is known to
have come from Baltimore. The work on the frame is
unquestionably American and is precisely similar to
that on other frames known to have been made in Baltimore about the beginning of the nineteenth century.
Added to this, the scene in the middle of the panel,
pourtrayed in black lines with gold backing on a white
ground, is, with the exception of a fanciful mountain
across the water, exactly like what one might encounter
in a thousand places along the shores of the Chesa-

peake. The style of boat, the low, bluff-like headland, and the little house of a Colonial type now fast disappearing, but still to be met with in out-of-the-way places, all contribute their share of cumulative evidence.

On the doors of bracket or shelf clocks of the Eli Terry type the painting on the under side of the glass closely resembles in general character that of the panels in the heads of the numerous small mahogany-framed, upright mirrors of the early part of the nineteenth century. These clock doors are usually made in two sections, the upper containing the clear glass in front of the dial, and the lower displaying the painting. The banjo clocks usually had two painted panels, a large one on the shank between the base and the face and another on the square or oblong base. These panels were decorated sometimes with paint only, sometimes with vari-coloured paint and gold. The battle between the *Constitution* and the *Guerrière* and other equally stirring historical events supplied a favourite set of subjects for the adornment of these clocks and held their own in popularity with the imaginary landscapes. It is worth noting that these decorations painted to show through glass are being excellently reproduced in large numbers, and it is even more worth noting that the method is susceptible of extensive and successful adaptation for decorative purposes. The small paintings on the glass sides of the hexagonal hall lanthorns should not be forgotten.

Paintings on glass of a distinctly pictorial nature—portraits, still-life, landscapes, and the like—enjoyed much vogue in England in the latter part of the eighteenth century, and there were, here and there, attempts at the same form of artistic expression on our own side of the Atlantic. Occasionally one meets with examples

17

of this more ambitious style of glass painting, and now and then a small portrait turns up that seems to bear internal evidence of American origin.

METAL, LEATHER AND SMALL WOODEN OBJECTS. Decorative painting of the same general description as that previously noted, running largely to fruits, flowers, birds, and stiff little bits of landscape, was constantly employed for the embellishment of trays, bellows, canisters, tin tea- and coffee-pots, and other small objects of household utility. Some of the most interesting and

FIG. 1.   Painted Tin Box, red ground, yellow decorations. Late eighteenth century Pennsylvania German work.   Property of Abbot McClure, Esq.

agreeable examples are to be found on the trays, both large and small, which played a conspicuous part in dining-room garniture. The usual ground colours were black, coral red, green, or straw colour, and the decoration was generally gold, black, or polychrome. Besides the trays, there were tea-caddies and small tin boxes designed for various odd purposes. All were regarded as fit subjects for painted decoration.

Decorative painting on leather was chiefly to be seen on the water buckets belonging to the members of the old volunteer fire companies. Two or three of these buckets, now highly prized as heirlooms, generally hung in a convenient and sometimes conspicuous place in the houses of the members, and, as almost every man of substance belonged to one or another organisation, they were familiar objects of household equipment.

Curtains of glazed muslin were used as a subject for painted decoration, some of which was good, while other was but indifferent. It is interesting to note the present recurrence to landscape and other painted decoration for this same purpose.

Bellows and sundry little boxes were the small wooden objects upon which the dignity of painted decoration was ordinarily bestowed.

The study of these curious manifestations of early American decorative painting is leading to a growing and wholesome appreciation of the daily intimate environment of our forebears and to the modern emulation of what was really good in their handiwork. Under all this painted decoration we can detect a sturdy spirit of self-reliance and honesty of purpose, and it is because the old fireside art had so much vigorous decorative value that it is still fresh and potent to influence us. Primitive and even grotesque it may be at times, but it all appeals to us with new force and living interest when we realise in a connected way what it really expressed, and it also possesses the charm of stimulating inquiry into its varied sources of inspiration.

Excellent examples of one sort or another are to be found in nearly every museum, and there is scarcely an antique shop that does not offer one or more specimens for purchase. The value of this old decorative painting as an inspiration to the modern crafts worker is too fully recognised to require any comment.

CHAPTER X

EARLY PORTRAITURE AND ALLEGORICAL PAINTING IN THE COLONIES

UPON first thought, it may seem to be stretching a point to include portraiture and allegorical painting among the decorative arts, but a closer acquaintance with both, as commonly practised in the Colonies, will justify the classification. With the exception of the work produced by a very few men, the pictorial attempts of the Colonial painters are scarcely to be ranked in the realm of art, and if they are not considered in their decorative capacity they would have to pass unnoticed, which would be a pity, for they represent much honest creative effort, and by ignoring them we should be deprived of a source of considerable amusement.

The modern schoolboy, the old Roman street gamin, and the early American painter all display one quality in common. The modern school lad, armed with a piece of chalk or crayon, defaces the sides of houses or fences with his crude but oftentimes vigorous pictorial fancy, for which inchoate expression of a deeply implanted human instinct he is chided by his law-abiding elders and roundly cursed by the owner of the disfigured walls. In precisely the same way did his youthful Roman prototype, two thousand years ago or more, give vent to his untutored artistic promptings in *sgraffiti,* to which we now attach importance for their historic value. In like manner did the early American painter, with no mean degree of perception, seize upon

260

the salient characteristics of the subject he was minded to depict and proceed to put it on canvas as best he might with his limited technical equipment, producing results frequently full of vitality, however lacking in accuracy or elegance. The common quality alluded to, in which Colonial limner, Roman street urchin, and the schoolboy of to-day all alike share, is vigour of conception combined with crude expression. The modern cartoonist, comic illustrator, and designer of pictorial advertisements are fully alive to the striking effectiveness of this primitive crudity and exaggeration and its appeal to popular imagination, and have assiduously employed it for their several ends at the risk of overdoing its commercial and comic usefulness.

As an episode of pictorial utterance, this aping of juvenile crudity is not devoid of interest. While we are amused, our attention is also focussed on what one might call aboriginal pictorial principles. We derive much the same sort of amusement from an examination of the early American essays in the fields of portraiture and allegorical or biblical painting, and, again, we perceive the bared workings of first principles in untutored hands. The gaucheries perpetrated attract us, of course, by their very *naïveté* and quaintness, but the chief import attaching to a scrutiny of the first Colonial efforts lies in the ground it gives us for making comparisons between the results of primitive endeavour among European colonists in the direction of pictorial art and the products of recent achievement. At the same time, an inspection of the infancy of American painting and the contrast it presents with subsequent developments is essential to a thorough and appreciative understanding of our present art status.

There is no need to dwell upon Benjamin West—at least the mature West whose labours won recognition and patronage on both sides of the Atlantic—nor to survey the work of Copley, Gilbert Stuart, Charles Willson Peale, Rembrandt Peale, Sully, and sundry others whom one naturally associates with a period when American painting had reached a point where it was entitled to serious consideration on the score of inherent artistic merit. The names of these men are household words, and their pictures are familiar to all. Our present concern is with the pioneers who represent the incipient stages of painting in America when the course of pictorial art, like the course of true love, ran none too smoothly and there were all manner of obstacles to be overcome, a time of rugged, struggling, and not altogether promising infancy. Only a few of them can be mentioned here by name, but they will serve to indicate the general types that existed.

Starting at the very beginning, there is the portrait of the pietist, Magister Johannes Kelpius, painted by Dr. Christopher Witt, in 1705. This was the first portrait in oils executed in America, and is now preserved in the collection of the Pennsylvania Historical Society. It is painted on heavy linen and pasted, like a flyleaf, at the beginning of a manuscript volume of hymns and other mystical religious effusions composed by the artist. Both subject and painter were quaint characters of unusual interest, and what the portrait lacks in technical excellence or artistic charm is made up in the remarkable associations attaching to it. Kelpius was the master or prior of the strange Rosicrucian community, composed of German mystics or pietists, which, in 1694, founded its monastery on the wild banks of the

Wissahickon Creek, upon a tract of land within the present limits of Philadelphia. The arrival of these peculiar people on St. John's Eve and their kindling of the Beltane Fire, with its mystic rites, made a suitable and spectacular introduction for the curious touch of transplanted mediævalism grafted upon the life of the Colony so long as the brotherhood continued to flourish. The head of this extraordinary society, Johannes Kelpius, wasted by the practice of a too strict asceticism with its rigid fasts and long vigils in a damp cave, whither he was wont to withdraw for meditation and prayer, died in 1706, at the age of thirty-three.

Less than a year before the death of Kelpius, the portrait was painted by Dr. Witt, who had just joined the brotherhood upon his arrival from England. In many places the paint has flaked off from the linen back and the hues are dimmed and not a little discoloured, so that it is now virtually a study in bluish greens and browns, but there is a vigour about the drawing that compels attention. Neither composition nor drawing is beyond criticism, the colour is muddy and depressing, and, even when fresh, could have had but little interest; regarded as a work of art, the painting is clumsy and crude, but, nevertheless, there is such a quality of a rough-hewn boldness and honesty about it that one feels constrained to pay it more than merely passing heed. It is, to say the least, unpretty, but it is interesting and, if tradition may be trusted, is a tolerably faithful likeness of the emaciated mystic whom we see clothed in a long, monkish gown or cassock and seated in a contemplative attitude in an armchair beside a lecturn. There are doubtless other pictures by Dr. Christopher Witt—chance may bring them to light at any time—

for he was a most versatile and productive person. Besides practising as a physician and ministering to many patients, he found time to cultivate a garden of simples, paint pictures, as we have seen, make clocks— possibly the first of native manufacture in America— play upon the virginals and organ, the latter instrument being of his own construction, pursue the study both of the occult sciences and practical astronomy, and cast horoscopes for the children of the colonists.

Another early painter who, as well as Christopher Witt, was also an organ builder was the Swede, Gustavus Hesselius, who arrived at Christiana, now Wilmington, Delaware, on May 1, 1711. A few weeks later he took up his residence in Philadelphia. In 1719 or early in 1720 he removed to Prince George County, Maryland, and received from the parish church of St. Barnabas "the first commission on record for a work of art for a public building in America," the vestry engaging him in June (1720) to paint the church, "and in August following, 'to paint ye Altar piece and Communion Table, and write such sentences of Scripture as shall be thought proper thereon.' " That the execution of this commission was satisfactory may be inferred from the fact that "on Tuesday, September 5, 1721, 'the Vestry agrees with Mr. Gustavus Hesselius to draw ye History of our Blessed Saviour and ye Twelve Apostles at ye last supper . . . proportional to ye space over the Altar piece, to find ye cloth and all other necessaries for ye same (the frame and gold leafe excepted wch. Mr. Henderson engages to procure and bestow on ye Church) Mr. Hesselius to paint ye frame for all wch. ye Vestry is to pay him wn. finished £17. currt. money.' " In writing of Hesselius,

STRONG BOX OF IRON WITH PAINTED DECORATION.   FORMERLY THE PROPERTY
OF ROBERT MORRIS

Courtesy of Pennsylvania Historical Society

SANDWICH GLASS CUP PLATES, MADE BY BOSTON AND SANDWICH GLASS CO., 1835–1850

1 and 4. American Eagle. 2. Beehive. 3. Oak Leaf and Acorn Wreath. 5. The Wedding Day and Three Weeks After.
6. Early Side Wheel Steamship.

Courtesy of Metropolitan Museum

Charles Henry Hart observes that it "surely marks an epoch to receive more than passing consideration," "that more than seven years prior to the arrival in this country of John Smibert, who is commonly regarded as the father of painting in the Colonies, an elaborate altar-piece of the 'Last Supper,' with thirteen figures—Christ and the twelve disciples—should have been commissioned to be drawn by a resident artist for a public building."

Hesselius was a limner of no mean ability, as the paintings that may with certainty be attributed to him show, and he is not included among the pioneers of American pictorial painting to be pointed out as the producer of crude or grotesque canvases, but rather to show the difficult and precarious conditions by which the path of the early painter in Colonial America was beset and how he had to resort to divers expedients to hold soul and body together. By 1735 he was back again in Philadelphia, and in the columns of the *Pennsylvania Gazette* for December 11, 1740, appears the following advertisement: "Painting done in the best manner by Gustavus Hesselius from Stockholm and John Winter from London. Vig. Coat of Arms drawn on Coaches, Chaises, &c., or any kind of Ornaments, Landskips Sign Show-boards, Ship and House painting, Guilding of all sorts, Writing in Gold or Color, old Pictures cleaned and mended &c." This advertisement simply meant that Hesselius had to come down to common sign painting to make a living. It was, however, exactly what others had to do at a time when only a small portion of the public was sufficiently discriminating in taste to distinguish between art and paint by the square foot and only a limited number of patrons could afford to employ an artist or to compensate him adequately. In England, too, it must be remembered, more than one great painter has been obliged to do signs for pot-boilers to tide over some struggling portion of his career.

The only compensating feature of the situation, so far as artistic expression is concerned, was that coach and sign painting in the eighteenth century offered a far more varied and interesting opportunity to the painter than it has at any time since. Indeed, we are only beginning to appreciate the possibilities for doing fine work on the signs of hostelries and tea-rooms, and it is only within the last few years that several eminent artists have executed such signs for places in which they felt some particular interest. Hesselius and his contemporaries did such painting not from sentiment, but of necessity, and it is mightily to their credit that they closed their eyes somewhat to the purely commercial aspect of the transaction and threw themselves into the spirit of the thing, producing many really fine pieces of work, as the weather-beaten remains of old sign-boards still occasionally testify. It may readily be imagined how wide a field of design was open to the versatile painter when not only hostelries and ale-houses, but a great percentage of the shops also, displayed signs to attract notice and give individuality at a time when street numbers were not much in use and it was customary for a tradesman to designate his place of business, when advertising, as located at the sign of the Blue Boar over against St. Paul's Church or the sign of the Three Loggerheads hard by the Pewter Platter. Besides the variety afforded by the execution of signs, there were coach doors to be blasoned heraldically and armorial bearings to be painted on hatchments or in some other form to be hung up in the churches, and, if we may believe old records, the display of such badges of family pride was often imposing in edifices like Christ Church, Philadelphia, King's Chapel, Boston, and several of the other important Colonial places of worship.

While not despising these jobs, Hesselius also found other occupation for his brush, and seems to have travelled about from time to time to execute commissions, and doubtless there are many anonymous canvasses in the Middle Atlantic States that might be ascribed to him, were all the facts known. In the hallway of the Manor House at Croton-on-Hudson hang three full-length portraits that family records show to have been painted somewhere about 1715. Certain features of internal evidence indicate that they were painted on the spot and not done at some distant place. The name of the artist, however, has long since been forgotten and cannot now be discovered. The paintings were executed by a limner of some ability, and it is not impossible that Hesselius may have been their author in the period between his arrival in America and his removal to Maryland.

While such men as Hesselius, who had the advantage of European training before their migration to America, displayed far more capability in their profession than did our own native Americans prior to their crossing the Atlantic to study under competent masters, we must remember that not a few of the local forgotten and nameless painters whose crude and clumsy portrait efforts are to be found from New England to Georgia were practically self-taught and probably had as much latent ability as their more fortunate and better tutored contemporaries who achieved eminence after a sojourn abroad. A comparison of their work with the early essays of our more celebrated Colonial artists of American birth tends to this conviction. Despite discouragement from Quaker parents and relatives, who regarded the "vanity of likenesses" with high disfavour, Benjamin West persevered in his ambitions—all honour to him for so doing!—and finally succeeded in going to England to study, with what results we well know, but many of the performances of his youthful period are sadly lacking in the qualities one might expect to find in the juvenile attempts of one who afterwards rose to such fame. As a case in point may be mentioned a little picture, painted in oils, on a piece of board, by West at an early age. In nearly every respect it is puerile. Of its authenticity there can be no doubt. Its pedigree, pasted on the back of the shingle, speaks for itself: "Painted by Benjamin West before he left America for England. Obtained by Horace W. Smith from Mrs. Pennypacker (æt. 90), in whose house, near Phœnixville, Pa., this daub had remained from the time it was painted. West was intimate in this house. Given by H. W. Smith to Dr. John H. Brinton, 1872." The picture is evidently one of West's very youthful performances and is correctly described as a "daub."

John Valentine Haidt was another painter who is almost unknown, but his crude portraits and curious allegorical pieces are fairly representative of the work produced by the generality of Colonial limners. He was born in Dantzig in 1700. His father was court jeweller in Berlin, whither the family removed in 1702. Being designed to follow his father's trade, he was instructed in drawing at the Academy. Although compelled to work as a jeweller, he longed to be a painter, and in 1714 went to study in Dresden, in 1716 in Prague and Augsburg, in 1718 in Venice and Rome, afterwards visiting Florence, Paris, and London, in which latter city he established himself in 1724 and married. He later joined the Moravians and came to Pennsylvania on the church transport vessel *Irene,* landing in New York in 1754, whence he went to Bethlehem. While there he painted in oils biblical scenes, allegorical pieces, and the portraits of prominent Moravians. A great number of his canvasses may be seen lining the walls of the archive room of the Moravian Church, where their crudity seems singularly in keeping with the quaint surroundings and piles of musty, yellow documents. Anywhere else they would be out of place and some of them almost ludicrous. Judging from their abundance, one might fancy that Haidt had been under contract to paint by the dozen the portraits of these solemn old gentlemen and their placid visaged wives, with preternaturally narrow and high corsage and tight white caps. Notwithstanding their crudity and their overpoweringly brown and sombre tone, there are occasional refreshing dashes of rich and vigorous colour and a certainty suavity of brushwork that show that Haidt imbibed and retained some of the elements of his previous instruction.

In the allegorical and heroic field we come to Edward Hicks, a cousin of the famous Elias Hicks, of Jericho, Long Island. Born in 1780, in Bucks, Pennsylvania, in which county he passed most of his life, Hicks presents the incongruous spectacle of a Quaker painter. West surmounted the obstacles of his Quaker

birth and training, but Hicks remained a rigid Friend
deeply concerned in the affairs of meeting, till his
dying day. He seems, nevertheless, to have been able
to reconcile his occupation with the principles of his
sect, whose stricter members were generally averse
to the frivolity of art. Perhaps Hicks's failure to
achieve anything worthy the name of art may account
for Friendly leniency in his case. He died in 1849,
and painted prolifically up to the time of his demise.
Although his labours spread over the first half of the
nineteenth century, their spirit of conception and execution belong rather to the immediately post-Colonial
period, when the exodus or financial ruin of large
numbers of erstwhile affluent Loyalists deprived artists
of much patronage and encouragement that they would
otherwise have had.

Although Hicks painted prolifically, he painted but
three or four subjects, which he reproduced again and
again in unending succession, sometimes on boards to be
used as fire-boards, sometimes in smaller size on canvas
to be hung on the walls as adornments—Heaven save
the mark! The most favoured subjects were "Washington Crossing the Delaware," "The Signing of the
Declaration of Independence," and "The Peaceable
Kingdom." "The Peaceable Kingdom," here reproduced in its fire-board form, is really a *chef d'œuvre* of
grotesquerie. The ruddy-faced infant in pantalets
leading the lion with an insufferably bored expression,
while a phlegmatic fatling scratches his chin on the
back of the king of beasts; the truculent wolf looking
daggers at the lamb and the spotty leopard; William
Penn and the red Indians in the distance, making a
treaty and quite oblivious of the menagerie in the

opposite corner—all these features are delightfully incongruous. Incongruous, also, is the picture of the "Signing of the Declaration of Independence," in which one of the august signers usually has three legs, while one of his less fortunate compatriots can muster but one, and another sits evenly balanced in a chair two of whose legs rest in space beyond the edge of a platform.

Frankly hideous, clumsy, and grotesque as are so many of the efforts of pictorial art done by the lesser painters of Colonial and post-Colonial times, there is at least a sincerity of purpose about them that commands our respect, and, though we may not desire to possess them or to study them, hoping to find any great intrinsic merit, an examination of their shortcomings, at any rate, is calculated to increase our appreciation of conditions existing in our own day.

CHAPTER XI

EARLY AMERICAN DECORATIVE WEAVING

THE old fireside crafts of the loom have a glamour all their own. By the very simplicity and dignity of their homely products they compel a far more general and sympathetic appreciation than many a higher type of art utterance. They afford a sincere expression of folk-spirit and indicate an inherent love of beauty that effected a happy union, wherever it could, between art and common household objects of daily utility. Furthermore, a knowledge of the old fireside loom crafts, as they have been appropriately called, throws an interesting and valuable sidelight on the intimate domestic life of the people during the early formative period of Colonial existence, a period we are somewhat too prone to associate with only the sterner and more strenuous side of nation building.

Among all those "homespun" crafts, none was of more universal practice than the decorative weaving of coverlets for the imposing bedsteads in which the eighteenth-century housewife took such vast pride. In the seventeenth, eighteenth, and early nineteenth centuries the bedstead was a far more conspicuous and important article of furniture than nowadays, when our modern notions of sanatory propriety prompt us to have the equipment of our sleeping-places as simple as possible. In the days of the Stuarts and during the reigns of William and Mary and Queen Anne, the magnificence of the pillared and canopied bedstead and its trappings was indicative of the rank or affluence of the owner,

272

while the truckle or trundle bed served for the children and domestics of the household. The elaborate embroidered or brocaded hangings of the state bedsteads and the costly coverlets belonging to them were the objects of great care and esteem, and were so highly prized that they were especially mentioned in inventories of household gear and bequeathed in wills.

During the whole of the eighteenth century, the heyday of the four-poster, bedsteads were regarded with special pride by our foremothers, and their fitting equipment was a matter of much housewifely concern. In England the bedchamber not infrequently did duty as a reception room, while, in the Colonies, plenty of instances are on record where a great bedstead, fully garnished with valances, curtains, and coverlet, formed a part of the parlour furniture. Under the circumstances, the mistress of the house, quite naturally, wished her coverlets to present the best appearance they might, and lavished a degree of pains upon them of which the modern housekeeper never dreams.

To the average woman in the Colonies, the rich silks and damasks, employed by her more affluent sisters in England, were out of the question, but, with her characteristic resourcefulness and self-sufficiency, she set to work with the materials she had at hand and wrought fabrics that compel our admiration, both for beauty of colour and grace of design. These hand-woven coverlets, which collectors and antique dealers eagerly search for to-day, were either entirely of home manufacture, the materials being spun, dyed, and woven by the women of the family, or else the threads, spun and dyed ready for weaving, were given to a professional weaver, who sometimes plied an itinerant trade, sometimes main-

18

tained a stationary loom. It is safe to say, however, that, while the textures produced by the men who followed weaving as their regular business often excel in elaboration of pattern those made at home, the latter almost invariably possess a superior charm of colour

FIG. 1. "Draft" for Coverlet from "Draft" Book of John Landes.
Frishmuth Collection, Pennsylvania Museum and School of Industrial Art.

and individuality, eloquent of the loving pride woven into warp and woof by their makers.

Coverlet weaving was not a local craft, confined to one or two sections of the country, but was universally practised from north to south, from New Hampshire to Georgia, and the patterns used seem to have been the common property of the women from one end of the Colonies to the other. While certain well-known de-, signs appear to have originated or to have enjoyed unusual popularity in certain localities, at the same time one is just as likely as not to find absolute identity of patterns in coverlets woven at the opposite ends of the land, and oftentimes the identity extends to colour as well as pattern. Doubtless patterns or "drafts," as they were called, were passed on from one woman to another, and styles in coverlet designs travelled in much the same way as fashions in clothes.

A knowledge of the decorative weaving employed in making coverlets was more or less general in European countries, and the wives and daughters of the American colonists preserved the traditions. Thus we may account for the general similarity in the character of the coverlets, no matter whether they were made by colonists of English, French, Swedish, Dutch, or German extraction. In minor details of colour and pattern the influence of the maker's nationality is occasionally visible, but in major features a remarkable uniformity prevails.

These coverlets were woven throughout the eighteenth century and continued to be made in considerable numbers till about the middle of the nineteenth. Since that time their manufacture has been practically restricted to the mountain regions of the South, where so many old customs and forms of speech have lingered unchanged. The continuous vitality of craft traditions among the southern mountaineers may be understood when we remember that it is no uncommon thing to find

them speaking idiomatically and verbally and phoneti-
cally pure Elizabethan English.

The sterling craftsmanship value of these hand-
woven coverlets has won modern recognition, and they

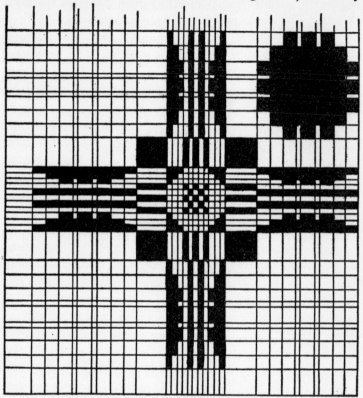

FIG. 2.   "Draft" for Coverlet from "Draft" Book of John Landes.
Frishmuth Collection, Pennsylvania Museum and School of Industrial Art.

are now made by the Department of Fireside Industries
of Berea College, in the southern mountains, and at
Asheville, North Carolina, so that the tradition of their
fabrication is sure of being conscientiously perpetuated.

Thanks to Eliza Calvert Hall's entertaining book,* published several years ago, closer interest and wider attention have been directed to the old woven coverlet handicraft and the decorative and historic value attaching to the coloured spreads that once adorned the beds of nearly every house in bygone generations.

The hand-woven coverlets consisted of a " foundation of cotton or linen overshot with wool." In a vast number of cases the flax was spun, the linen woven, the yarn made and dyed, and the coverlet woven by one woman, carrying out each successive process at her own fireside and using only such materials as the home farm supplied, for not a few of the eighteenth-century housewives were as expert with the loom as they were with the spinning-wheel, and they were likewise adepts in the mysteries of the dye-pot and knew how to make strong and durable vegetable colours whose freshness time has been powerless to dim.

A great many of the nineteenth century coverlets were woven by itinerant weavers who carried their looms with them from farmstead to farmstead and did the year's stint of weaving, just as the itinerant cobbler paid his annual visit and made the year's supply of shoes for all the household, from master and mistress down to swineherd and dairy-maid, but even till the time of the Civil War probably the majority of the women in the southern mountains and in remote districts of other parts of the country did their own weaving, and on many of the plantations in the South there was a room where an experienced slave spent most of the time weaving. Since so much of the coverlet weaving was done in this thoroughly individual manner, it

---

*Hand Woven Coverlets: Little, Brown & Company.

would be strange indeed if the products of the isolated domestic looms did not show evidence of the weaver's originality in colour arrangement and combination of patterns, although the methods of work and the limitations of design formation necessarily produced a generic similarity between the chief features of the spreads. The very act of decorative creation has always appealed to woman's imaginative faculty, from the time of Helen of Troy with her handmaidens, deftly plying the silken threads, or Queen Matilda and her tire-women, picturing on the Bayeux tapestry the story of the Norman Conquest, down to the day when the work-hardened hand of the Colonial farmer's wife drove the shuttle to and fro as she wove the coverings to adorn her beds. The individual sense of colour or harmony of design prompted many a housewife to act upon her own initiative and depart from the plan or "draft" before her in the selection of her hues or the marshalling of her figures, thus, by the exercise of her inventive ingenuity, originating new patterns, to be handed on in due time to her neighbours and by them, in turn, transmitted to others, until, in time, they passed through the length and breadth of the land.

The later coverlets, woven by professional weavers whose greater skill enabled them to deviate from the rigidity of geometrical devices and conventional repeats, display patterns of great intricacy and elaboration, including human figures, birds, and beasts, as well as flowers, fruits, and foliage in profusion.

It was customary to name the simpler geometrical designs such as were used from the earliest times by the housewives who did their own weaving or the more conservative itinerant weavers of the old school. Some-

times one design was known by two or three, or even
more, different names in different parts of the country,
and, *vice versa,* the same name was occasionally applied
to different designs in different localities. Now and
again these names were descriptive of the character of
the designs, but more frequently they were purely
fanciful and dipped into the realms of poetry, politics,
history, or geography. We hear of "Sunrise,"
"Checkers," "Stripes and Squares," "Maid of
Orleans," "Rose in the Valley," "Washington's
Victory," "Missouri Trouble," "New Jersey Dream,"
and scores of others. It is worth noting, while speaking
of these old patterns and their endless variety of colour
combination and design, that the weaves and, in many
instances, the colour schemes have been adapted by
some modern craftsworkers to the manufacture of both
silk and mercerised cotton textures.

The "drafts" or patterns which served as guides for
both the housewife at her home-made loom and the
itinerant weaver were sometimes fully worked out, so
that a modern textile worker could follow them with
comparative ease after a little study, and, on the other
hand, sometimes they were merely indicated by cryptic
signs and figures, somewhat resembling ancient musical
notation, on narrow strips of paper or parchment, that
to the uninitiated are as baffling and unintelligible as
Egyptian hieroglyphics or the Runic inscriptions of
the Norsemen. Occasionally the colours as well as the
pattern were indicated, but the chromatic choice was
usually left to the discretion and taste of the individual
weaver. The "draft" book shown in the illustration
is in the Frishmuth Collection in the Pennsylvania
Museum of Industrial Art, Philadelphia, and from the

internal evidence supplied by the paper used, the binding, the ink, and the handwriting of the compiler or owner, it seems to date from the latter part of the eighteenth century. It is not unlikely that John Landes, whose name appears in the front of the book, was an itinerant Pennsylvania weaver, and it is quite possible that he took the pains to collect a large number of acceptable patterns and transcribe them in this convenient form to carry about with him and show to his patrons, who could pick out "drafts" to their taste.

The colours most commonly used in these coverlets were blue, red, and white, but we also find a good deal of green, pink, yellow, and saffron, and sometimes other colours, too, make their appearance. The dyes employed, as previously stated, were of home manufacture and were derived from vegetable substances, so that the colours are still fresh and vivid. The renewal of interest in vegetable dyes of native manufacture, now being successfully employed by numerous craftworkers, owes not a little to the inspiration supplied by the chromatic beauty of the old coverlets.

The Colonial American woman showed herself quite as resourceful in the skillful preparation of a wide range of fast dyes as she did in other particulars, and knew how to make cochineal, madder, Brazil wood, turmeric wood, indigo, peach-leaves, barks, roots, gums, and blossoms yield all their varied hues. When there was one of them she could not obtain, she always had a satisfactory substitute.

The collecting and study of the old hand-woven coverlets is well worth while, both because of their intrinsic beauty of colour and pattern and because of the light they throw on an important domestic craft of

QUILTED AND PATCHWORK BEDSPREAD.   PIECED BEDSPREAD.   EARLY NINE-
TEENTH CENTURY
Courtesy of John C. Nippes, Esq., Haddonfield, New Jersey

QUILTED AND PATCHWORK BEDSPREADS.   EARLY NINETEENTH CENTURY
Courtesy of John C. Nippes, Esq., Haddonfield, New Jersey

bygone days which never quite died out and which has been successfully revived, a craft susceptible of numerous applications to our present-day requirements.

HOME-SPUN LINENS. Vast quantities of the linen thread, spun on the wheels that whirled busily in every well-ordered household, were woven into sheets, tablecloths and bolts that could be cut as needed for clothing requirements. The quality of this linen varied according to the notions of the individual maker, but even the coarsest was a fabric of admirable character. The weaving was, in many cases, done at home either by members of the household or by itinerant weavers who went from farmstead to farmstead at stated times, set up their looms and stopped in the house until they had finished all there was for them to do. When the weaving was not done at home, the spun thread was sent out to be woven.

Most of the linen was perfectly plain, but decorative effects in weave and colour were not wanting. In some instances a chequered pattern of blue and white was woven, the threads being dyed prior to the weaving operation (*v.* plate illustration). The writers have never met with other than a blue and white chequer pattern, but there is no reason that other colours could not have been used as, in all probability, they were.

A woven pattern was also occasionally essayed with good results (*v.* plate illustration) in linen intended for table use.

WOOLLENS

Woollens of excellent quality were also produced by the Colonial weavers for blankets (*v.* plate illustration) and dress goods.

RUGS AND CARPETS

Under the head of Colonial decorative weaving we
shall include rugs and carpets for want of a better
place to consider them, although they were not, strictly
speaking, wholly woven products.

So soon as the first strenuous phases of home-making
were past and there was the least opportunity to think
of something more than the barest necessities, the early
American colonists shewed a measure of attention to
the matter of floor covering in both its utilitarian and
decorative aspects. Bare boards were much in evidence
for a great many years, but in some of the rooms at
least there were attempts to mitigate the bareness by
one means or another.

For a long time the custom of sanding floors remained in favour and late into the eighteenth century
we find records of sanded floors upon which decorative
designs were carefully traced in the freshly strewn
and brushed sand, but such decorations were necessarily
short-lived and the process of strewing, brushing and
tracing patterns had to be repeated at frequent intervals. At best, the drawings on sand could give but
ephemeral satisfaction to the eye and nothing at all of
physical comfort, so that we can readily understand the
craving for something more permanent and comfortable in the form of rugs and carpets.

Such rugs and carpets made their appearance at a
very early date, although woven or hand-worked rugs
large enough to cover the greater part of a floor, and
fulfil the modern notion of a *carpet* in their extent, did
not appear until much later and even then were of comparatively rare occurrence. For the most part a great
portion of the floor boarding remained visible and the

rugs, though they might be fairly numerous, were generally of limited dimensions.

Hooked rugs are treated in the Supplement, page 385.

DYES

Reference has already been made to the skill of the Colonial housewife in making the dyes she needed and attention has been called to their variety, their beauty and freshness and the permanent qualities they exhibit, even after years of exposure and wear. There can be no more fitting place than right here to mention a compendious volume that must have been invaluable to housewives in the day of its publication for it is a veritable treasure-house of weaving and dyeing lore. The title, somewhat formidable in extent, is as follows:

THE
DOMESTIC MANUFACTURER'S ASSISTANT
AND
FAMILY DIRECTORY,
IN THE ARTS
OF
WEAVING AND DYEING
COMPREHENDING
A PLAIN SYSTEM OF DIRECTIONS,
APPLYING TO THOSE ARTS AND OTHER BRANCHES
NEARLY CONNECTED WITH
THEM IN THE MANUFACTURE OF
COTTON AND WOOLLEN GOODS,
INCLUDING MANY USEFUL
TABLES AND DRAFTS
IN CALCULATING AND FORMING VARIOUS KINDS
AND PATTERNS OF GOODS
DESIGNED FOR THE IMPROVEMENT OF DOMESTIC
MANUFACTURES.
BY J. & R. BRONSON.
UTICA.
PRINTED BY WILLIAM WILLIAMS,
NO. 60, GENESEE STREET.

The following list of colours and the ingredients that entered into their composition is not altogether exhaustive of the possibilities open to the woman bent upon brewing her dyes but it will sufficiently indicate resources and methods. If one substance was not obtainable, our resourceful foremothers could always make shift with some other.

RED (Scarlet and Crimson):

Cochineal	Brazil Wood
Madder	Camwood
Nicaragua wood	Pokeberry root (solferino)

BLUE:

Woad	Wax myrtle
Indigo	Knot grass
Larkspur flowers	Spiderwort flowers
Garden purslane	

YELLOW:

Fustic	Walnut bark
Wold	Hickory bark
Turmeric	Yellow oak bark
Anetta	Lombardy poplar bark
Sedge grass (with alum)	Sumac stalks
Peach leaves	Yellow locust
Smartweed leaves	Osage orange
Alder bark	Clematis
Birch bark	

GREEN:

Green, of course, could be produced in almost innumerable ways by combining blues and yellows in proper proportion, but the following also yielded desirable green dyes:

Black oak bark	Turmein or gold seal (with indigo)
Meadow garlic (with lime)	
Orange or yellow root (with indigo)	

BLACK:	BROWN:
Logwood	Butternut
Nutgalls	Hemlock
Bugle weed	Maple

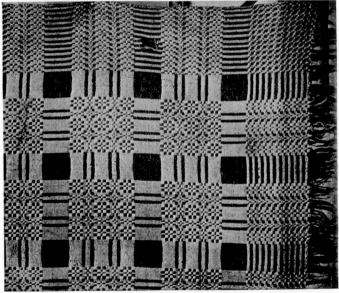

BLUE AND WHITE HANDWOVEN COVERLETS, EARLY NINETEENTH
AND EIGHTEENTH CENTURIES
Courtesy of John C. Nippes, Esq., Haddonfield, New Jersey

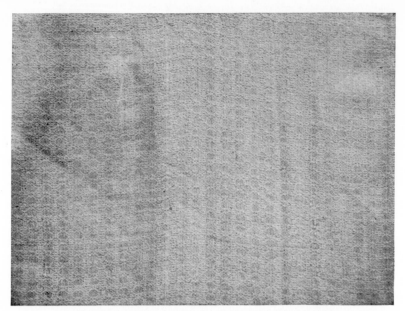

LINEN TABLE COVER WITH WOVEN PATTERN, EIGHTEENTH CENTURY
Courtesy of John C. Nippes, Esq., Haddonfield, New Jersey

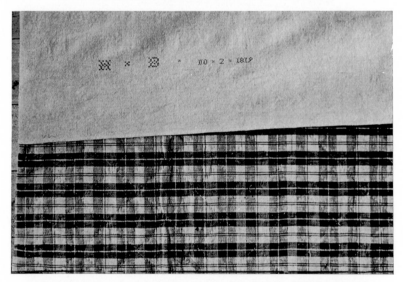

HANDWOVEN WOOLLEN BLANKET; BLUE AND WHITE CHEQUERED HAND-
WOVEN LINEN. EIGHTEENTH AND EARLY NINETEENTH CENTURIES
Courtesy of John C. Nippes. Esq., Haddonfield, New Jersey

With black and the three primary colours within their reach, it was a comparatively simple matter for the Colonial dyer to arrive at almost any hue she desired merely by the process of combination. The weaver, also, knew how to attain excellent and varied colour effects and gradations of weaving a warp of one colour with a woof of another.

MORDANTS were, of course, necessary to fix the colours and for this purpose alum was, perhaps, the most universally useful. Although the average woman of the Colonial period was quite as ignorant of chemistry, in a theoretical way, as is her granddaughter or great-granddaughter of to-day, she was, nevertheless, often able to extract three or four colours from the same substance by combining it with various chemical agents. This she had learned by experience or by oral tradition from her elders. Besides alum, sal-ammoniac, copper-as, veridigris and cream of tartar were servants ever ready to her hand.

NOTE: For some of the homely recipes, giving minute directions for distilling and using the vegetable dyes extracted from common plants, the reader is referred to the Hand-Woven Coverlet book, previously noted.

CHAPTER XII
THE ART OF "FRACTUR" OR PEN-AND-BRUSH ILLUMINATION

HEREDITY and tradition are two of the most potent forces to be reckoned in the shaping of human tendencies and actions. Deny the one and decry the other as we may, their influence, nevertheless, is very real and shows its power in every phase of creative activity. By no means the least conspicuous workings of heredity and tradition are observable in matters of art. No more apt illustration of the vitality and long persistence of hereditary art traditions could be found than the endurance of a mediæval illuminating process found among the Pennsylvania German colonists and perpetuated by their descendants, till quite the middle of the nineteenth century. This illuminating process was called *"fractur"* painting.

In a previous chapter, devoted to a consideration of slip-decorated pottery, attention was called to the origin of these same people, their dominant characteristics, and their peculiar isolation from the other colonists by whom they were surrounded, an isolation that has continued, in large measure, to the present day and made possible the vigorous survival of many customs and traditions which otherwise must inevitably have vanished long since.

However little we Americans of English descent and tradition may know of the Pennsylvania Germans, and however slightly we may understand the ways and ideals of this "people apart" who, nevertheless, have been our neighbours for centuries, we cannot fail to be strongly impressed by the various manifestations of

286

their art that come to our notice from time to time. Crude, very crude, it unquestionably is, but, all the same, there is a certain virility inherent in it and a fresh fertility of decorative sense that, despite all rudeness of form and execution, convince us that here is the genuine expression of a folk tradition transplanted from the Old World principalities whence these early settlers migrated to Penn's land of promise. This particular instance of the perpetuation of old German craft traditions that forms the subject of the present chapter, cherished for many years with an almost religious veneration among the descendants of the early settlers from the Rhine countries, shows that the history of these folk is deserving of close study, and we cannot but feel regret at its discontinuance and the discontinuance of the various other crafts about the middle of the nineteenth century, when there began a process of assimilation to the ways of the outside world, a process now well on its way to completion, with the result that the manifestation of picturesque originality has been replaced by an all too evident and commercial vulgarity. Now and again, in examining the decorative craftsmanship of the old Pennsylvania German colonists, we detect the recurrence of *motifs* and methods of expression that unmistakably evidence a close relationship with the peasant art of Bavaria and some of the neighbouring provinces.

The art of *"fractur,"* or pen-and-brush illumination, a form of painting once practised among the Germans of Pennsylvania and, in a modified form, adopted to a slight degree by some of the neighbouring English colonists, affords an intensely interesting revelation of folk-art about which next to nothing was known, outside of a limited local sphere, until comparatively recent years. This manner of painting is of deep interest, because it embodied the survival on American soil of a mediæval art tradition that had virtually disappeared in Europe by the middle of the eighteenth century, in other words, the art of illumination practised by the monks of the Middle Ages; because some knowledge of it explains many curious things that turn up from time to time in junk-shops and the purlieus haunted by collectors; because the quaint *naïveté* in the colour and design of the specimens most frequently met with is fascinating; because, finally, it reveals the vigorous but wholly untutored decorative sense of a primitive people. It may seem a far cry from the mediæval monastery to the woods of Colonial Pennsylvania, from the cell of the monkish illuminator, patiently toiling over the embellishment of a missal or breviary, to the little schoolhouse or the cloister of the Pietist, where mystic and country schoolmaster alike adorned the pages of psalm-books or painted gorgeously coloured and fancifully designed birth and baptismal certificates, but the line of descent is clear and unbroken to prove that *"fractur"* was a survival of the ancient art of illumination, and the tradition cannot be denied.

Besides being replete with the marks of a derivation from Continental sources, the pen-and-brush illuminations are engaging and varied in scope and application, as may be readily seen from the collections of such zealous collectors and antiquaries as the Honourable Samuel W. Pennypacker, sometime Governour of Pennsylvania, or Henry Chapman Mercer, Esq., of Font Hill, Doylestown, Bucks, whose valuable monograph, entitled "The Survival of the Mediæval Art of Illuminative Writing Among Pennsylvania Germans," read before the American Philosophical Society in September, 1897, contains a graphic account of the practice of the art and a classification of the several ways in which it was applied. Mr. Mercer has done more than anyone else to rescue the remaining vestiges of this folk-art from oblivion or utter destruction.

MATERIALS. A number of years ago, among a "penny-lot" of miscellaneous trash that had come from a country sale, part of the contents of a garret in Bedminster, Bucks, Mr. Mercer discovered a roughly made, lidless paint-box, about a foot long and six inches broad, with several compartments containing glass bottles. For a long time the "find" baffled all attempts at identification, but it finally turned out to be the colour-box of a teacher in one of the German schools that had been maintained in Bucks till about 1840. The longest compartment was used to contain "goose-quill pens and brushes made of the hairs of the domestic cat. The caked colours in the small bottles had been the home-mixed inks and paints of the schoolmaster, once liquefied in whiskey, and the varnish was composed of the gum of the cherry tree diluted in water." With this outfit the German schoolmasters were wont to instruct their pupils in the art of *"fractur,"* or illuminated handwriting on paper or parchment.

PURPOSE AND SORTS

During the latter part of the eighteenth century and the early part of the nineteenth this art flourished vigorously in the counties inhabited by the Pennsylvania Germans, and illuminated hymns and ornate title-pages of religious books were produced in great numbers. Although *"fractur"* painting may be said to

19

have been of two sorts, the religious and the secular or semi-religious, for even the pieces that were not of an ostensibly religious character rarely escaped altogether from some trace of religious symbolic allusion, the art was undoubtedly derived from religious sources, was first practised in America with exclusively religious intent, and seems not to have been used "for the decoration of secular themes, such as songs, ballads, or rimes." Whatever instances of its entire secularisation do occur are comparatively rare. *"Fractur"* found expression in illuminated song-books, such as those made in the religious community at Ephrata; in the title-pages of small, plain manuscript song-books, often with the owner's name inscribed in a surrounding border composed of "overhanging tulips or lotus, or birds and trumpet-blowing angels"; in rewards of merit on loose leaflets; in book-marks; in baptismal certificates, marriage and death registers in family Bibles or on separate sheets of heavy paper, and, finally, in the less common essays at pictorial adornment to be framed and hung upon otherwise bare walls.

The noticeable difference in the character and quality of these illuminations is to be explained by their difference of origin. Those that came from the religious community at Ephrata, for instance, are characterised by a certain refinement of design and dexterity of touch—they were evidently the objects of loving care and pride, and time was freely spent upon them—while some of those that emanated from the desks of country schoolmasters or were produced by their pupils were *gauche* and grotesque in form and colour to the last degree. In between the two extremes came all shades of excellence. Both sorts are shown in the accompanying illustrations.

RELIGIOUS "FRACTUR" WORK.—THE EPHRATA PAINT-INGS. A number of the designs illustrated are taken from books of psalm-tunes made by members of, or belonging to, the community in the cloister at Ephrata, in Lancaster County. They occur on title-pages, as single-page embellishments, interspersed here and there throughout the volume, and, above all, as decorations to fill the spaces between the ends of tunes and the margin. Double bars in the music were adorned with smaller illuminations of the same general character, and occasionally the tops and bottoms of the pages came in for a share of coloured enrichment. As stated before, coloured inks were used and were applied with quill pens and fine cat-hair brushes. The colours were vivid and often employed in great variety. Then, again, in some specimens, only two or three colours were used, and not a few of these simple schemed pieces are among the most artistic and effective to be found. In all the Ephrata illuminations we see the same marvellously minute pen-work that reminds one of the fine lines in old Persian miniatures.

As an example of simple colouring, the dove design may be cited. It is executed entirely in green and blue of a subdued tone, so combined, however, that there is no lack of variety and interest. The big heart with the doves from "Andenken am Schwester Martha" is effectively executed in black, vivid green, and carmine, while the lotus-like tulip, from the same volume, is done in black, green, brown, and red. This book also con-tains numerous examples of the diversity of intricate pen-work often employed. There are, for instance, many stippled or etched backgrounds edged with a fine line of bright green or red, while the bold lettering in German text is cross-hatched or left in white.

The illumination from the manuscript music-book is a full-page illustration in olive, mauve, and green, skillfully combined to give great variety of colour effect. An illumination from the Ephrata Choral Book is exceedingly interesting, because of the simplicity of colouring and delicacy of drawing. The alternate petals of the pinks are of deep blue, while the lighter petals between them are of green, delicately dotted or stippled on the white ground of the paper. The doves are of a lighter blue, as are also some of the upper leaves. The black ink has become a mellow brown from age.

Another small design is taken from a leather-bound blank receipt book which was turned into a hymn-book with characteristic thrift. There is no title-page, but a note on the flyleaf states that the owner, probably a member of the Ephrata community, bought it in 1817, and another note at the end states that it was finished in 1820. During this space of three years the one hundred and ninety-nine pages of closely written notation were transcribed and embellished with a large number of illuminations. The mere manual labour involved must have kept the scribe and illuminator busy a great portion of the time. The design is wrought chiefly in blue, red, and black. The alternate petals of the flowers are made of fine dots of blue and bright red, which, with plenty of white background showing, give the effect of pink. The dark petals are solid blue. The shank is diapered in red, black and white. Olive brown, a deeper brown, dark green, black, and bright green are observable in the leaves. The chequer border at the bottom is made of green, black, red, and white ingeniously combined.

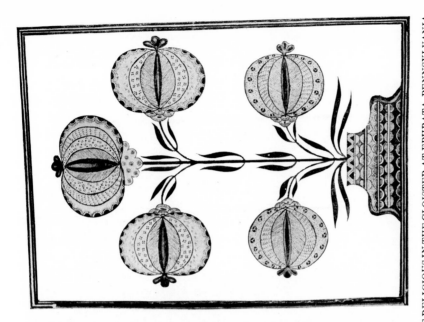

POLYCHROME *FRACTUR* PAINTINGS DONE BY THE RELIGIOUS IN THE CLOISTER AT EPHRATA, PENNSYLVANIA
EIGHTEENTH CENTURY
Courtesy of the Pennsylvania Historical Society

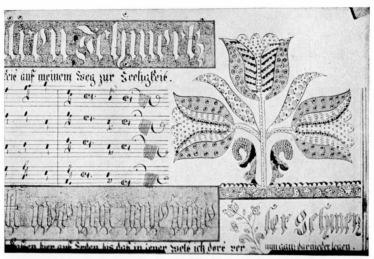

FRACTUR PAINTINGS EXECUTED BY THE RELIGIOUS AT EPHRATA,
PENNSYLVANIA, EIGHTEENTH CENTURY
Courtesy of Pennsylvania Historical Society

THE SCHOOLMASTERS' PAINTINGS. Of quite different stamp and far inferior merit is the *Taufschein,* or baptismal certificate. In design it is involved and *gauche,* the execution is grotesque, and the plenitude of clamorous reds and yellows is blatantly rampant. The lady angels at the top, loudly clad in alternate red and yellow stripes, are truly fearsome creatures. The central portion is filled with text giving the date of the baptism and also the date of the child's birth, most accurately recording the exact hour and minute. This punctilious solicitude about the hour and minute of birth is found in all these old records, and the entries were thus made for reference for astrological purposes; in other words, so that the local astrologer might have accurate data for casting the child's horoscope. White magic—witch doctoring it is called—and the casting of horoscopes are still practised in rural Pennsylvania German communities.

The baptismal certificate, just discussed, represents the opposite extreme of *fractur* expression to that executed by the religious at Ephrata. It is evidently the indifferent work of a country schoolmaster or one of his pupils. In between this extreme and the delicate, finished illuminations from the Ephrata cloister were paintings of all grades of excellence wrought by clever pupils and their instructors. There is little doubt that some of the potters who decorated the slip-traced and sgraffito plates and platters produced in the field potteries also tried their hand at illuminating baptismal and birth certificates, marriage records and death memorials, book-marks, testimonials, and pictorial devices for wall embellishment with *fractur* painting. It is also highly probable that these same potters received

their first training in draughtsmanship and the principles of design, which they afterwards applied to the
decoration of pottery, through their lessons in *fractur*
painting as children or youths at the hands of village
schoolmasters, for a course in *fractur* was reckoned one
of the finishing touches in the curriculum.

After the middle of the nineteenth century, when
illumination or *fractur* was no longer taught in the German country schools and the art was rapidly dying
out, substitutes for the hand-painted certificates were
printed in coloured inks, and were so dreadful that the
kindest thing is to let them pass without further notice.

Although the semi-secular application of *fractur*
painting was reminiscent of religious inspiration, and
the baptismal and birth certificates had their distinctly
religious significance, they also served a purely secular
purpose by being used as wall adornments.

SECULAR "FRACTUR" WORK. Other *fractur* paintings there were, too, although few in number by comparison, that were devised altogether for ornament and
had no religious inspiration whatever. Both sorts supplied a need in the homes of their possessors, who had
practically nothing else in the shape of pictorial garniture. Human nature is the same the world over, and
has not changed from the earliest times in its deeply
implanted love of ornament. We see this innate fondness for decoration equally in the bone scratchings of
the cave-men and the *fractur* paintings of the German
colonists. The resources for wall adornment in Colonial
days were not abundant, and in the houses of the majority they were decidedly scant. The English colonists, besides samplers and little pieces of simple
framed embroidery, had a few paintings on glass and

such edifying and gruesomely moral prints as "Death and the Lady." The German settlers, with a child-like devotion to bright colours, rebelled against the unbroken austerity of whitewashed walls, and had their *fractur* paintings, which were certainly more worth while than the ghastly chromos and appalling crayons that have now taken their place in the houses of simple farmer folk.

Of the secular pieces of *fractur* work, one of the most amusing is the apocalyptic fantasy, which exhibits in the lower part a behemoth with a murderous mouth, a blandly idiotic simper, and a pointed tail. His forelegs are black and his hind legs are red, and his claws are fearsomely sharp. His body is of a whitish yellow mottled with black spots, with red veinings running between the markings, and he is evidently a long-suffering and patient creature, or else quite pachydermatous, for he seems not in the least to mind acting as a stage for the antics of the two slim and jaunty green-bodied, red-legged beasts, although the needle-like claws of one are jabbing his nose, which might supposedly be tender.

Just what may be the full significance of these strange animals with pallid faces and rouge-spotted cheeks, furred or crocketed tails waving gracefully aloft, and towering crowns set on their heads at a rakish angle, it would be hard to say. It would be equally difficult to determine the meaning of the heart-bearing vine growing from the behemoth's back, of the red and black rhapsodic birds fluttering above the beasts, or of the vixenish little parrot trying to pluck the tail feathers from one of the aforesaid birds. Surely there is no passage in the Apocalypse by which this pictorial caprice could have been inspired. It has been suggested that the theme might have been derived from one of the "Lives of the Saints," but it is scarcely possible that the artist even knew of the *Vitæ Sanctorum*. It might, perhaps, be explained by some old legend preserved in the heritage of folk-lore.

Quite as vigorous and quite as ungraceful is the picture, about sixteen inches by twenty in size, of two women. This "masterpiece" is executed entirely in ink and is altogether devoid of bright colour, even in the nondescript tree at the left, with its top divided like the antennæ of a beetle and its fruits and flowers alternating with extreme regularity. Judging from the peering, inquisitive expression of the younger woman and the didactic attitude of the elder, a lesson in botany seems to be going forward, based upon the portions of a plant which each holds in her hands. The lower portion of the picture has nothing to do with the upper.

"Fractur" Work by English Colonists. The birth certificates of the three Shinn children and of Caleb Lippincott are particularly interesting as showing the development of *fractur* painting when it got into the hands of English colonists. The Lippincott painting is still further interesting because it depicts one of the local sports, and the fox-hunters apparently wear the coats and caps of the old Gloucester Fox Hunting Club, which started a few years before the date of the certificate and afterward became the nucleus of Philadelphia's First City Troop.

For the Collector. Now and again these paintings may be picked up in the most unexpected places, and are always worth examining as specimens of an amusing and instructive art episode and for the light they occasionally throw upon Colonial history or the manners of the colonists. In his monograph Mr. Mercer

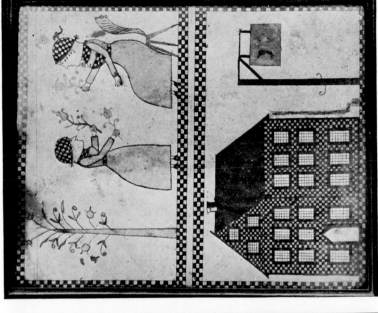

PENNSYLVANIA GERMAN SECULAR *FRACTUR* PAINTING,
EIGHTEENTH CENTURY

Frishmuth Collection, Pennsylvania Museum and School of Industrial
Art

PENNSYLVANIA GERMAN SECULAR *FRACTUR*
PAINTING, EIGHTEENTH CENTURY

Frishmuth Collection, Pennsylvania Museum and School of
Industrial Art

PENNSYLVANIA GERMAN BAPTISMAL CERTIFICATE OR *TAUFSCHEIN*,
EIGHTEENTH CENTURY
Courtesy of Pennsylvania Historical Society

BIRTH RECORD, *FRACTUR* PAINTING, EXECUTED BY ENGLISH COLONISTS
Frishmuth Collection, Pennsylvania Museum and School of Industrial Art

observes that previously the existence of these illuminations had been "little more than casually alluded to by
any writer." With the exception of Mr. Mercer's account, the same is still true, and comparatively few
people have seen or know anything about them,
although, in the counties where they were once made,
it is by no means unusual to happen upon them in
second-hand shops and at the country sales of household
effects. Sometimes these specimens are of the sort once
traced at Ephrata, but more often they are either semi-
secular (birth and marriage certificates and the like) or
else the secular wall embellishments. They are especially numerous in the Mennonite and Dunkard communities along the Perkiomen and the Skippack Creeks
and in Berks and Bucks. Besides the *fractur* paintings
in the collections previously mentioned, there are some
excellent specimens in the Frishmuth Collection in the
Pennsylvania Museum (Memorial Hall) and School of
Industrial Art, Philadelphia, and also in the collection
of William Springer, of Kulpsville, Montgomery
County.

The old art of *fractur* painting contains the seed of
suggestion for a modern development utilising the same
processes and methods. No one, of course, would wish
to emulate the grotesque and childish performances of
many of the specimens, but a study of the Ephrata work
reveals many points of substantial merit and a general
character quite different, in conception and technique,
from that of the small amount of ecclesiastical illumination now being performed. A resumption of this delicate pen-and-brush work with coloured inks might be
suitably carried out in the execution of such things
as book-plates, place cards, and certain types of
illustration.

CHAPTER XIII
HAND-BLOCK PRINTING ON FABRICS AND PAPER

"HE likewise cuts neatly in Wood and Printeth Calicoes.'' So ran the end of an advertisement that appeared in a Boston paper, in 1715, setting forth the occupations of one Francis Dewing, lately come into the Colonies from London. Of this same Francis Dewing we shall hear more in a later chapter. What concerns us here and now is the end of his advertisement, stating that he "printeth calicoes," a statement plainly indicating that the craft of printing designs upon fabrics with hand-blocks made of pearwood, or of some other wood, such as box, holly, or maple, was certainly practised at this date to a sufficient extent to make commercial mention of it worth while. Had not the good housewives of Boston Town been familiar with hand-block printing, Dewing's announcement that "he cuts neatly in Wood and Printeth Calicoes" would have been without point. It is not at all impossible, in view of the other activities he also practised, that he may occasionally have cut blocks and sold them for the women to do their own printing from. A competent housekeeper would have sufficient knowledge of making the dyes it would be necessary to use.

Whether hand-block printing was done upon fabrics or wall-paper, substantially the same method was employed. Printing on fabrics was a household craft and might be successfully pursued, as occasion demanded, by any woman who owned or could borrow the blocks.

298

No doubt blocks were lent from one neighbour to another throughout whole communities, just as were the moulds for pewter spoons and platters.

Hand-block printing on paper for walls was necessarily somewhat restricted in extent and specialised in the hands of a few craftsmen. In the majority of cases, when wall-paper was used, it was of imported origin, and the attempts at home manufacture in the hands of a country craftsman were primitive in the extreme, both as regards colour and pattern. Attempts at hand-block printing in colours on paper for wall decoration were not made in America until very late in the eighteenth century or early in the nineteenth, and, as the demand was so limited, owing to the presence of good imported papers and the fact that not nearly so much of it would be required as of printed fabrics, the hand-block printing of wall-paper in the Colonial and post-Colonial periods is practically a negligible matter, so far as any great results were concerned. Nevertheless, the specimens that have come down to us are amusing and show a decided spirit of independence and enterprise on the part of American craftsmen which ought to afford encouragement to the present craftsworker, endowed with infinitely superior facilities.

FABRICS

MATERIALS USED. As we have seen from Dewing's advertisement, calico was a favourite material for block printing. Besides this, linen, muslin, and any kind of cotton cloth could be used. Most of the fragments that have been preserved are either of linen or calico.

The colours were made from vegetable dyes, blues and reds being the usual favourites.

The blocks were generally about an inch thick and of any size and shape the design to be printed called for. A fine, close-grained wood had to be used so that the design could be cleanly cut: pear, maple, box, holly, bass, or gum was suitable for this purpose. The design was carved in bold relief with a smooth surface (Fig. 1),

Fig. 1. Pearwood Handblock with design carved in sharp relief. Frishmuth Collection, Pennsylvania Museum and School of Industrial Art.

or else reversed so that the design was incised. The effect of the first was to print the design in colour on the fabric; the effect of the second was to colour the background and reserve the design in white or whatever was the natural colour of the fabric before the dye was applied. Specimens of both are shown in the plate illustrations.

PROCESSES. The design was first drawn upon the

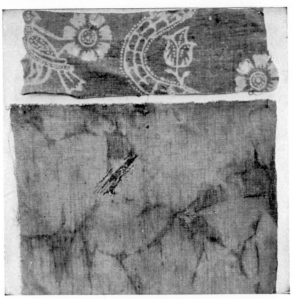

EIGHTEENTH CENTURY PENNSYLVANIA BLUE AND
WHITE HANDBLOCK PRINTED LINEN; DESIGN RE-
SERVED IN WHITE (UPPER); DESIGN PRINTED
IN BLUE (LOWER)
Frishmuth Collection, Pennsylvania Museum and School
of Industrial Art

BOXES COVERED WITH PRINTED PAPER
Frishmuth Collection, Pennsylvania Museum and School of Industrial Art

SPECIMENS OF HAND-BLOCK PRINTED BORDERS FOR WALL
PAPER; EARLY NINETEENTH CENTURY
Frishmuth Collection, Pennsylvania Museum and School of Industrial Art

uncut surface of the block or traced upon paper and pasted on. With a sharp knife it was then cut out and the background gouged out to a depth sufficient to insure a clear impression. Some of the blocks were large (Fig. 1), while others were very small (Fig. 2) and often of irregular shape (Fig. 1; Fig. 2, A and B). Simple figures, geometrical patterns, and flower-and-leaf designs were ordinarily employed. If more than one colour was used, there had to be an additional plate

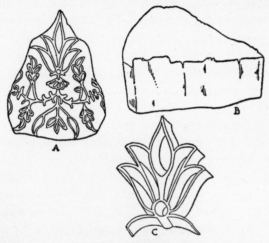

FIG. 2. A, Obverse of small Handblock. B, Section of same showing irregular shape and comparative thickness. C, Detail of same.

Frishmuth Collection, Pennsylvania Museum and School of Industrial Art.

for each colour. As a matter of fact, in the home-done block printing more than one colour was very rarely used.

Besides the block, there was a pad on which the block was charged before making the impression, and this pad was saturated with the dye, which had been mixed to about the consistency of cream and spread on the pad with a brush. A little mucilage or glue was sometimes added to keep the colour from spreading, and a mordant was occasionally needed to set or fix the colour. The material to be printed was laid flat and fastened down, and then the impressions were made, moving the block along as the impressions covered the fabric.

PAPER

The processes in use for printing coloured paper were, as previously noted, substantially the same as those employed for fabrics. The main difference was that the paper was, for the sake of its decorative effect, printed in several colours and therefore required more blocks in the process. It was printed in very small sections, no larger than could be conveniently covered by one block, or by several adjacent impressions from one block, and these small and gaily coloured pieces were used for borders. Festoons of drapery and floral patterns were executed with more concern for trenchant hues than for refinement. The illustrations will give a fair notion of the wall-paper block printer's efforts. Printing paper in several colours in this way with small blocks necessarily consumed much time, to say nothing of the time required to put small pieces on the wall. It is not surprising, therefore, that it was used chiefly for borders only. The introduction of rollers or cylinders, with the repeat adjusted to one revolution, of course wrought a complete change in methods.

It is worth noting that the old wall-paper, both of domestic and imported origin, was habitually used to cover hat-boxes, cap-boxes, band-boxes, and numerous small boxes, which were extremely decorative in their effect of colour and pattern.

CHAPTER XIV

EARLY AMERICAN WOOD AND STONE CARVING

CARVING is the outward manifestation of a natural impulse. It is an impulse partly destructive, partly creative, and partly decorative. The boy with a new jack-knife affords an epitomised evidence of the result of innate promptings, too strong to be resisted, to whittle and shape if the means and material be at hand. Wood first, and then stone, have always invited the craftsman to prove his prowess in the decorative manipulation of their surfaces.

Examples of the early American carver's handiwork in both wood and stone are more numerous and varied than most of us, at first thought, realise. For specimens of wood carving, some of it of considerable excellence, we must look to the furniture made by the colonists from the seventeenth century onward; to various small articles of household utility that were deemed worthy of ornamentation; to the figureheads of American-built ships and, lastly, to such portions of architectural woodwork as required or permitted carved embellishment. Specimens of the last-named sort of carving are abundant in both exterior and interior application. For examples of early American stone carving we must turn to date-stones, inscriptions, and simple mural devices on old houses; window and door trims and capitals of pillars; old milestones with heraldic devices, and last of all, tombstones and monuments.

The interest attaching to these evidences of the Colonial craftsman's handiwork in wood and stone is necessarily, to a great degree, historical and antiquarian, in the first place, because in no other field of decorative activity do we find more convincing testimony to the continuity and perpetuation of Old-World craft traditions on this side of the Atlantic, and, in the second place, because they show the extent of Colonial achievement and stimulate our appreciation of a native craftsmanship whose best accomplishments we are too ready to attribute to an overseas origin, without taking the pains to inform ourselves of the real facts concerning them. Despite the comparatively limited scope of any modern application that can be made of these Colonial precedents and patterns, there are, nevertheless, not a few points in which they are pregnant with suggestions that we shall do well to study and ponder, both in the matter of technique of execution and in the uses to which carved embellishment was put. They also show, in most cases, notwithstanding certain minor crudities that occasionally appear, the strong innate sense of refined proportion so eminently characteristic of much of the work done in the seventeenth and eighteenth centuries, particularly the latter. Furthermore, they materially increase our esteem for the average ability of the Colonial artisan, and no account of the early arts and crafts would be complete if it did not include some notice of the labours of both wood and stone carvers.

WOOD CARVING

PROCESSES. Before specifically directing attention to the several fields in which carved ornamentation was customarily employed, it is desirable to explain the varieties of carving methods and their points of difference.

"MODELLED" carving exhibits the design standing out in well-moulded relief from a surrounding background that has been lowered by gouge and chisel (Fig. 1, A and B; Fig. 2, A and B).

Close akin to MODELLED carving—indeed, it is only a further development of it—is "CARVING IN THE ROUND"; that is to say, carving in which the figures, cleanly undercut, stand well forth from their ground (Fig. 3)

FIG. 1. A, Side view, Wooden Handle of Pennsylvania German Pie Edge Cutter in "Modelled" carving. B, Reverse Side of same.

Frishmuth Collection, Pennsylvania Museum and School of Industrial Art.

or else stand altogether clear of it, being supported by some suitable projection from the rear, from below or from above. Excellent examples of CARVING IN THE ROUND are ships' figureheads and carved finials or pendants of any description.

"FLAT" carving shows a design whose surface is flush with the uncarved surface of the piece of wood (Fig. 4) on which it is wrought. The relief is secured by a "sunk" or sharply gouged-out groundwork, and the edges of the figures composing the design are not rounded off or modified in any way, but are left sharp and rectangular.

20

"Scratch" carving is just the reverse of the forms of carving more commonly practised, in that the design, usually of simple character, is vigorously and sharply incised (Fig. 4).

Kinds of Wood Used. *White pine, poplar, oak, mahogany,* and *walnut* were the woods most used by the American craftsmen for carving purposes.

White pine was the wood used almost exclusively for purposes of architectural carving, and it was usually

Fig. 2.   A and B, Carved Details from the John Penn Instrument Cupboard or Press in the Philadelphia Library, 1739.
Courtesy of the Library Company of Philadelphia.

protected afterwards by a coat of paint. In a few instances poplar was used for the same purpose.

Oak was used by the seventeenth-century carvers for both furniture and architectural embellishment. Examples of both are shown.

Walnut was used in the eighteenth century almost exclusively for furniture, but occasional instances of its

architectural use may be found. It was also used for
small objects of household utility (Fig. 1, A and B).

Mahogany was used solely for furniture; with **rare**
exceptions for other purposes.

Other woods than the four mentioned were sometimes met with, but not sufficiently often to merit special
notice.

FURNITURE. So far as carved furniture is concerned,
the best seventeenth-century examples are to be found
in the oaken pieces of New England origin, which **are**,

FIG. 3.   Carved Pine Capital of Pilaster, undercut or carved in the round, Eighteenth
Century.   Collection of Pennsylvania Historical Society.

to all intents, the same as the articles of contemporary
English manufacture, save that, in the English work,
there is, as a rule, greater nicety of finish. In the Bolles
Collection, in the Metropolitan Museum of Art, New
York City; in the Boston Museum, and also in several
smaller and private collections may be seen excellent
specimens of this seventeenth-century American carving in oak. It should be added that the Bolles Collection
is especially comprehensive in this respect and affords
typical examples of *modelled, flat,* and *scratch* carving.

The execution of some of the carving is so exactly
similar to that of English pieces, both in point of
technique and pattern, that its American authorship can
be determined only by the fact that it is wrought on
American oak. It is but natural that semi-mediæval
(Fig. 4) and Renaissance traditions of wood carving
should be thus faithfully perpetuated on American soil,
for the craftsmen who did the work were English to the
core, no matter on which side of the Atlantic they happen to have been born. Indeed, not only in the case of
wood carving, but also in most of the other crafts practised in the Colonies, the obvious continuity of traditional methods and processes forcibly brings home the

FIG. 4. *Motif* from Hadley Chest showing "flat" carving with tendrils wrought in
"scratch" carving. New England, late Seventeenth Century.
Bolles Collection, Metropolitan Museum of Art, New York City.

realisation that, after all, we, through our *American*
English forefathers—Washington and Adams, though
the staunchest Americans, considered themselves also
Englishmen to their dying day—have quite as ample
and honourable a traditional background as our contemporary *British* English cousins, even though we may
sometimes have been oblivious of it and withheld our
appreciation.

The designs employed were, to all intents, identically
the same on both sides of the Atlantic, although certain
local preferences for one pattern or another are observable in the New England work, just as they were

CARVED WOODEN PORTRAIT BUST OF GENERAL
WASHINGTON BY SAMUEL McINTIRE
Courtesy of Essex Institute, Salem, Massachusetts

CARVED OAK FIREPLACE BEAM FROM HOUSE BUILT BY PHINEAS
PEMBERTON, BOLTEN FARM, FALLSINGTON ROAD, BUCKS,
PENNSYLVANIA
Courtesy of Pennsylvania Historical Society

CARVED WOOD BUTTER MOULD
Frishmuth Collection, Pennsylvania Museum and School of Industrial Art

CARVED WOODEN BUTTER MOULDS USED BY THE DUTCH COLONISTS OF THE HUDSON VALLEY

Courtesy of the Senate House, Kingston-on-Hudson.

in different parts of England, and occasionally we meet
with a design that has no exact counterpart in English
work, albeit the manner of execution does not differ
from the customary processes. A notable instance of
such a local peculiarity of design (Fig. 4) is found on
the "Hadley chests." These chests are so called
because a number of them seem to have been made in
the vicinity of the town of Hadley, in Massachusetts.
The device used for the decoration consists of a crudely
drawn leaf and flower, carried out in the requisite
number of repeats, wrought in flat carving, while
numerous small scrolls or tendrils, the veining of leaves,
and the divisions of petals appear in scratch carving
(Fig. 4). This seventeenth-century method of carving,
characteristic of the Stuart period in mobiliary par-
lance, continued to be practised during the fore part
of the eighteenth century.

The other early American manifestation of carving
on furniture is to be found on the walnut, cherry, bilsted,
and mahogany articles in the Chippendale, Hepplewhite,
Sheraton, Phyfe, and Empire styles, the best of which
were made in New England, Philadelphia, and New
York, where the most expert chair and cabinet makers
and carvers seem to have been established. In these
cases the carving is chiefly of the modelled or moulded
variety, sometimes in the round, and rivals in excellence
the work done by the English carvers of the same period.
Those who wish to investigate the subject of furniture
in detail are referred to "The Practical Book of Period
Furniture," by the present authors, and issued by the
same house as this volume.

SMALL ARTICLES OF DOMESTIC UTILITY. Small wooden
objects of household use were now and again dignified

with carved adornment. Such articles are more likely
to be met with among the domestic effects of the Dutch
and German colonists than among the goods of colonists of English or Welsh extraction. Good examples
of these ornate minor domestic accessories are to be
found among such articles as the carved hanging spoon
racks or *lepel-borties* of the Dutch housewives, the
brush-and-comb holders that hung beside the pumps in
the wash-sheds or out-kitchens of farmhouses among
the Germans in Pennsylvania, the razor boxes and shaving boxes, and the kitchen implements of both Dutch
and Germans, such as butter moulds, tankards for cider,
and the handles of pie markers. An excellent specimen of this German peasant domestic wood carving
appears on the handle of the pie marker (Fig. 1, A
and B), from the Frishmuth Collection in the Pennsylvania Museum of Industrial Art, Fairmount Park,
Philadelphia. The design is characteristically German,
and the carving is carefully executed and probably
represents the winter evening industry of a farmer with
a jack-knife, sitting in the light of a roaring wood
kitchen fire.

SHIPWRIGHTS' CARVING. It was a matter of no small
pride among seafaring men and merchants in Colonial
times and in the early days of our national existence—
in fact, until the advent of steam put an end to the
picturesque side of maritime life—to have their ships,
barques, and smaller sailing craft adorned with elaborately carved, painted, and gilt figureheads. The
figurehead gave a stamp of individuality and, as a thing
almost alive, seemed to personify the character of the
hull and rigging behind and above it. Both pains and
expense were lavished upon the carving of these pieces,

and they were boldly wrought in the round with a refreshing degree of lively spirit. Their design and execution alike do credit to their nameless and forgotten
carvers, to whom we cannot help feeling that we owe a
debt of gratitude whenever, in old seaport towns of our
Atlantic coast or in the neighbourhood of ancient ship-
yards, we come upon one of these relics of a bygone day,
removed from its former place of honour and doing
duty as an adornment in some unfrequented corner.
The least we can do is to remember with thankfulness
the men who made them and the wholesome spirit in
which they wrought. Somewhat akin to the work on
the figureheads, though not so fine and executed for a
purely commercial and land-lubber purpose, was the
carving of Indians and other figures to stand by way of
advertisement before the doors of tobacconists' shops.
These figures belong to the nineteenth century. Some
of them display considerable excellence of craftsmanship in their execution.

ARCHITECTURAL CARVING. Architectural opportunities for wood carving were abundant and were not
neglected. In the earliest Colonial period the oaken
beams, posts, and studs of the half-timbered New England houses (the same that were afterwards encased in
clapboard coats) (see "The Architecture of Colonial
America," H. D. Eberlein, 1915, p. —) were embellished
with stopped chamfer edges and hand-wrought moulds
executed in a bold and virile manner that clearly be-
spoke the persistence of the mediæval wood-worker's
methods. Brackets and corbels and the pendants or
drops from the corners of overhangs were decorated in
the same lusty fashion.

Nor was the architectural application of the wood-

carver's art in seventeenth-century America confined to
New England. In some of the old houses in the other
Colonies were to be found creditable examples of craftsmanship in this direction. One of them—and there were
others—is shown in a plate illustration. It is a piece of
oak and is wrought in the modelled type of bold relief,
displaying such characteristics of technique as one is
accustomed to find on the Jacobean cupboards, panelled
chests, and wainscot chairs of English make. It bears
the initials of Phineas Pemberton and the date of the
house he built for himself in 1683 at Bolton Farm, near
Bristol, in Bucks, Pennsylvania.

With the increasing popularity of Georgian architectural amenities during the eighteenth century, however, the wood-carver's art was called more frequently
into play for purposes of both exterior and interior
ornamentation, and, at the same time, was given a wider
scope for displaying the niceties of craftsmanship. It
has, unfortunately, been the custom of a great many
people either to assert or assume that most of the finely
wrought woodwork in our more ornate Georgian houses
came from England, because they have heard, perhaps,
that such was the case in some one particular instance.
Nothing could be more unjust to the reputation and
memory of our own Colonial craftsmen. An interesting
bit of tangible and eloquent evidence of the American
wood-carver's ability is the instrument cupboard or
press made, in 1739, to hold the air-pump and other
scientific apparatus presented, in 1738, to the Library
Company of Philadelphia by the Honourable John Penn.

Although a piece of movable furniture, this press
is of such distinctly architectural character that it is
to be ranked in the category of "architects' furni-

CARVED MULBERRY; OVER-
DOOR DEVICE FROM MUL-
BERRY CASTLE, SOUTH
CAROLINA, 1715
Courtesy of Charles Brendon,
Esq., New York City

CARVING IN STONE UNDER WINDOW, BARTRAM HOUSE, KINGSESSING,
PHILADELPHIA. WROUGHT BY JOHN BARTRAM, 1770

EARLY EIGHTEENTH CENTURY "SCRATCH"
CARVED TOMBSTONE, ST. THOMAS'S
CHURCHYARD, WHITEMARSH VALLEY,
PENNSYLVANIA

EIGHTEENTH CENTURY CARVED TOMBSTONE, NEWPORT,
RHODE ISLAND
Courtesy of Henry Oothout Milliken, Esq.

ture,''[1] an important division of mobiliary equipment in the Queen Anne-Early Georgian period, and
it is, therefore, appropriate that it should be discussed
in this connexion. It was wholly designed and made in
Philadelphia, and all the circumstances anent its construction are duly recorded in the minutes of the
Library Company. The carving of this press is an enduring tribute to the skill of the artisan or artisans
who executed it, and any man who could accomplish
such a piece of work could, beyond all question, have
done any of the architectural wood-carving in the State
House or in any other of our Georgian buildings, public
or private, no matter how elaborate it is. With this
incontrovertible proof of the ability of at least one
wood-carver—there were doubtless other wood-carvers
in the Colonies every whit as apt as he—there is a
strong presumption in favour of the American craftsman that the beautiful carved architectural woodwork
of our Georgian houses and public edifices was the
product of his hands, except in cases where the records
show that the carvings were fetched from England.
Certain it is that the examples of architectural carving
of undoubted American origin compare very favourably with the work we know to have been brought over
from the Mother-Country.

In the latter part of the eighteenth century and the
early part of the nineteenth, one wood-carver who ably
upheld the traditions and maintained the reputation of
the American craftsman was Samuel McIntire, of
Salem, master carpenter, wood-carver, and architect.
Not only did his work compare more than favourably
with any that was executed in either England or

_____
[1] v. "Practical Book of Period Furniture": Eberlein and McClure.

America in his own day, but it has stood the test of time and has never had to yield the palm for excellence to any work executed since. Though ranked as one of the foremost architects of his generation, and though his work had far more than a local influence on our domestic architecture,[2] wood-carving seems always to have been his first love, and the fame of his houses rests on the beauty of their embellishments—"their doorways, window frames, cornices, gate posts, and their incomparable interior woodwork"—rather than on any other quality. In summing up his work, Mr. Dyer says of McIntire: "He was the artistic descendant of Inigo Jones, Sir Christopher Wren, Grinling Gibbon, and the Brothers Adam; he was also their peer in originality as well as in fidelity to the best classic traditions. More chaste and severe than Wren and Gibbon, he was more fanciful than Adam. Perhaps it was his very freedom from the schools that gave him faith in his own genius to do the thing that best suited given conditions, and this faith seldom led him astray."

McIntire also tried his hand at sculpture to some extent, and executed in wood several medallion likenesses of General Washington and a bust of Governour Winthrop. The Washington medallion was first designed and carved in 1805 as a decoration for the western gateway of Washington Square, in Salem, Massachusetts, and was fashioned "after drawings from life made by McIntire during Washington's visit to Salem in 1789."

Another carver of signal ability was William Rush, of Philadelphia, born July 4, 1756. He was apprenticed to Edward Cutbush, "the then best carver of his

---

[2] See "The Architecture of Colonial America," H. D. Eberlein, 1915.

day," in Philadelphia. He specialised in carving figureheads for ships and his work elicited such universal admiration both in British and in foreign parts that he received orders from England. His best known and, perhaps, his finest piece of wooden sculpture is the statue of Washington in the State House in Philadelphia.

The *motifs* employed in the Georgian architectural wood-carving were chiefly of classic provenance or else of Renaissance or Baroque inspiration, tempered by a classic spirit of interpretation. They included roses, rosettes, foliated scrolls, acanthus leaves (Fig. 3), egg and dart courses, urns with flame or cover tops, swags and drops of flowers or drapery, cockle-shells, pineapples, masques, and, towards the end of the period, some of the more delicate Pompeian devices imported into English usage by the Brothers Adam. Nor are attempts wanting to emulate occasionally the more florid conceptions of the Grinling Gibbon school. We must also include in our chronicle of wood-carving the chubby-cheeked cherubs whose heads and wings often figured in the embellishment of Colonial churches and were usually placed somewhere near the pulpit or the organ loft. In nearly every case the old American wood-carver's work is executed with a refreshing boldness and freedom of sweep. Heraldic carving, too, was practised to some degree, and in more than one place the royal arms of England, carved and displayed during our Colonial period, are still carefully treasured.

The objects upon which this architectural wood-carving was bestowed by way of enrichment were the brackets beneath stair treads, mantels and overmantels, pediments and overdoor adornments in general, door and window trims, cornices, the capitals of pillars and pilasters (Fig. 3), and whatever architectural features or details were fitting subjects for ornamentation. Carving on the exteriors of buildings was, of course, not as abundant as carving for interior adornment, but it was by no means uncommon. Many old cornices, capitals, finial urns on the posts of balustrades and masques still compel our sincere admiration. In reckoning the achievements of the wood-carver we must remember to make a distinction between carving in wood and modelling in compo when we come to examine some of the very elaborate mantels of the late Georgian period. Not a few of these mantels displaying exquisite Pompeian *motifs* of adornment which at first appear to be carved are, in reality, moulded in compo and painted after being set in place.

STONE CARVING

PROCESSES. The processes used in stone carving were virtually analogous to those employed in the carving of wood, or sufficiently so, at any rate, to make the same set of definitions answer in indicating the treatment of both substances.

KINDS OF STONE USED. The kinds of stone used by the Colonial and early post-Colonial stone-carvers were *marble, sandstone, limestone, slate, 'soapstone,* and, occasionally, *granite* and *mica stone.*

Marble served both for architectural work, especially in the later period, and for carved tombstones and mural tablets.

Sandstone and limestone were employed for both architectural and mortuary work, but chiefly for the latter.

Soapstone and slate were mainly used for tomb-stones. Slate could be used only for scratch carving and inscriptions.

Granite was but slightly used, and that for archi-tectural purposes.

Mica stone was occasionally used in Pennsylvania, both for rude architectural work and for tombstones, but it was not a kindly medium for carving.

ARCHITECTURAL CARVING. Two things militated against any extensive architectural development of the stone-carver's art among the craftsmen of the Colonial and post-Colonial periods. The first was the common lack of, or at least the difficulty of obtaining, suitable stone as a medium in which the sculptor might conveni-ently express his cunning. The second was the fact that, in the majority of our Georgian buildings, wood was ordinarily substituted for the stone or marble that was often used in England, so that there was little opportunity for the stone-carver to develop his craft in its application to the exterior embellishment of build-ings, and little encouragement for him to attempt to do so.

In New England the native granite did not offer a kindly medium for the art of the stone-carver, and it is not surprising, therefore, that there are few examples of this sort of craftsmanship to be found upon any of the New England structures dating from the Colonial period.

In New York and the Middle Colonies the presence of sandstone was occasionally taken advantage of, and a few keystones and capitals were executed.

In Pennsylvania, also, one now and then finds ex-amples of attempts at carving the native mica stone.

The most notable instance of this crude work, necessarily crude owing to the intractability of the material, is to be seen on the Bartram house, at Bartram's Gardens, Kingsessing, Philadelphia. There a date-stone in the western gable bears the inscription " $\Theta EO\Sigma \Sigma\Omega Z$ [God save] John and Ann Bartram, 1731" (the year in which John Bartram added to the structure originally standing on the site). On the river front of the house are roughly wrought Ionic capitals to the pillars of the portico (a later addition), and carved window trims with an interesting inscription beneath one of the windows:

> It is God alone
> Almyty Lord
> The Holy One
> By me ador'd
>   John Bartram 1770

Quaint little scrolls fill in the otherwise vacant spaces, as they also do on the earlier date-stone in the gable.

Other specimens of carving in this native mica stone are to be found in the milestones set out in 1703 along the Lancaster Pike bearing Penn's arms in bold relief on a sunk ground, and on date-stones and wall devices, such as the tulip and heart or other mystic emblems, among the Pennsylvania Germans.

Late in the Colonial period and in the early post-Colonial period, architectural carving in marble came more and more into fashion, and was wrought in the manner in which we of to-day are accustomed to seeing it treated. It was at this time, too, that some of the exquisite marble mantels of Adam pattern were carved. Others, also, were wrought in Empire designs at a slightly later date.

TOMBSTONE CARVING. If the early American stone-carver was limited in his architectural scope, he made up for his lack of opportunity in that field when he was turned loose on tombstones and mural tablets. Every old churchyard and burial ground in the country is full of the evidences of his prowess with the mallet and chisel. The choice of subjects, to be sure, was somewhat circumscribed—cherubs, death's heads, skulls and crossbones, and hour-glasses, with and without wings, seem to have been the universal favourites—but he managed to inject not a little variety into his interpretations of these lugubrious emblems of mortality. There were dolorous cherubs and merry cherubs; lean cherubs and fat, mumpy-cheeked celestial youngsters joyously fluttering their robust little wings; cherubs with curly hair and cherubs with head dresses, and, now and again, cherubs with their ambrosial locks done up in puffs that would have put the most proficient Parisian *friseur* to unending and envious shame. Occasionally the cherubs were dour of visage, and there is one creature, done in scratch or incised carving, on a mica stone in St. Thomas's Churchyard, Whitemarsh, Pennsylvania, with a frilled head dress and three-cornered ears, whose aspect is positively devilish. No wonder Lord Howe's soldiers, when they were encamped on St. Thomas's Hill, used this vixenish object as a target for pistol practice. The majority of cherubs, however, were apt to be phlegmatic and stupid looking.

In some cases tombstones were bordered with decorative bands of fruit, flowers, leaves, and, now and then, other *motifs*. The tulip was a favourite flower, and its use was not restricted to the Pennsylvania Germans, for instances of its employment have been found in parts of New England for tombstone enrichment.

In a great number of cases the lettering on tombstones was of rare excellence, and the letters were shaped with such delicacy and beauty of proportion that they are carefully copied to-day by architects. Of course, the lettering was not universally good and sometimes it was exceedingly poor, but, as a rule, it was at least creditable; and, indeed, it had need to be, for when soapstone or slate were used, materials that did not readily lend themselves to sculpture, the lettering was the only decoration.

As an agreeable change from cherubs and death's heads, numerous old tombstones exhibit armorial bearings, which it was comparatively easy to execute creditably when the material of the monument was either marble or sandstone. Urns also enjoyed considerable vogue as *motifs* of adornment.

Mural tablets in churches usually displayed a far greater nicety of finish than the stones that stood in the open. The devices employed for their embellishment were of the same general character as those already mentioned—heraldic devices, urns, cherubs, and hourglasses.

CHAPTER XV

EARLY AMERICAN LACE

CONTRIBUTED BY MABEL FOSTER BAINBRIDGE

IPSWICH, situated on the Massachusetts coast, some thirty miles north of Boston, is the one place in the territory of the present United States where, in the early days, bobbin or pillow lace makers settled. That they came from the Midland Counties, north of London, is proved both by the town records and by the kind of lace that they made, a lace peculiar to the middle shires of England. The term "pillow lace" is applied to the particular kind of lace that was made on a peculiarly shaped cushion or pillow which, along with the other implements used in the craft of lace making, is described below.

The settlers' hands were empty of implements to ply their craft when they came to America, but were skilled as are only the hands of generations of lace makers. Nothing thwarted, they made pillows, a sort known as a bolster pillow, about twenty-five inches in circumference and twelve inches long. These cylindrical pillows they stuffed with hay, pounded very hard, using a heavy, hand-woven linen as a covering. A stocking leg was slipped over the pillow to keep it clean. The homespun and the stocking were gathered at the ends, but a hole was always left so that the fingers could be inserted to turn the pillow. Into these holes the fastidious pressed lemon verbena, lavender, and other sweet-scented herbs. The pillow, when not in use, rested in a basket that kept it from rolling. The pillow

21

in the illustration is in an old Malay measuring basket. This pillow was used by Lydia Lord Lakeman, who was born in 1781. On it lie some of the old parchment patterns, and the pins are rusted in with age. A little bag was pinned on the back to hold the lace as it was finished. This little bag, and a cover that was always thrown over all, were of bright printed India cotton.

In the Midland Counties of England, the previous home of our Ipswich settlers, the bobbins were distinctive and decorative in character. They were made of bone or wood, deftly carved and often inlaid with silver or pewter, and they had one feature absolutely unique—bright beads hung from their ends. Ardent youths carved them for their sweethearts, and the history of the bobbins on a single pillow might well fill a small volume. Apparently the Ipswich settlers did not bring any bobbins with them and, in making new bobbins, adhered to the Puritan principles that had guided them to the shores of New England, for they fashioned for themselves new, simple bobbins of bamboo. These were of varying sizes, cut about five inches long, with a wide groove whittled out below the head to hold the thread. The bobbins make a fascinating clicking sound as they are "thrown," for, being hollow and of different sizes, they give forth different notes. Nowhere else in the world, to my knowledge, is another bamboo bobbin to be found. If we recall that Ipswich was an important Colonial seaport, and that the old town is full of Oriental treasures brought back by sea captains, we can understand how our lace makers were able to get bamboo. It doubtless came along with the exquisite china, embroideries, carved ivories, and other precious articles that husbands and lovers fetched home

to their dear ones on return voyages from India or
Cathay in the stately square-rigged craft that have now,
unfortunately, all but disappeared from our coasts.

The original patterns or "prickings," as they were
called, I have reason to believe, came from England.
They are of sheepskin parchment, such as is used for
drum-heads. Sometimes a "pricking" is made from a
single strip of parchment, and again it is pieced every
few inches. I have seen writing and figures on patterns, showing that old deeds and other documents were
pressed into service by the pattern designer or copier.
The holes indicate the placing of the pins that make the
pattern. The two rows of pinholes in the "pricking"
of the illustration show that that pattern was made in
two widths. Note, also, that there were no pins to hold
the mesh; making the mesh without some such means
of mechanical assistance seems to the modern lace
maker a feat almost impossible of achievement. The
pins used were fine lace makers' pins; at first they were
all hand headed.

The method of procedure was this—which is equally
true of all bobbin lace, whether made in our Colonial
wilderness or in the doorway of Oxfordshire's most
ancient cottage: the pillow having been stuffed and
pounded, a parchment "pricking" was pinned around
the centre. If possible, the pattern joined so that it
could be worked continuously. The bobbins were generally wound by hand, although there were reels in
which a bobbin could be inserted and a handle turned to
facilitate a tedious process. A slip-knot was tied in the
threads so that they would not unwind as they hung
from the pillow, but could be lengthened by pulling the
bobbin. The required number were tied to a few pins

and the weaving began. The stitch was simply an over-
and under-weaving, with extra twists to form the
meshes. After every stitch a pin was set, the position
of the pin, as stated before, determining the pattern.
An edge about half an inch wide required from thirty
to fifty bobbins.

The heavy outline thread, which is characteristic
of Buckinghamshire lace, the kind that was made in
Ipswich, is a loosely twisted flax. We have some that
was never used, and it shows plainly the irregularity
of a softly hand-spun thread. The early settlers were
obliged to spin. In 1656, the records tell us, ''The selectmen are to divide their towns into classes of five, six,
and ten and appoint a class leader, for the purpose of
spinning. Each family which can furnish one spinner
shall spin thirty weeks in a year, three pounds of linen,
cotton, and woollen, monthly. . . . The commons
are to be cleared for sheep. The seed of hemp and flax
is to be saved.'' This proves beyond doubt that they
made their own thread.

The lace was always made in strips, never in set
figures. Although there are some wide pieces in existence, most of it was narrow. It was extensively used
on baby clothes and was known to our grandmothers as
''English thread lace.'' If you are fortunate enough
to possess a garret, seek out the little linen shirts which
your grandmother made for her babies, and more than
likely the hand-made lace which trims them, if not
made in Ipswich, is the same type of lace, exquisite,
dainty, and yet durable. The christening dress is surely
ornamented with lace, and caps, both for babies and the
grandmothers, were finished with more or less elaborate
edges.

The pins were used over and over again. As the

worker progressed, she took out the first set of pins, and the lace held by these pins fell finished into the little India cotton bag. Bobbin lace used commonly to be known in England as "bone lace," and, although the reason has never been definitely ascertained, it has been suggested that the use of small fish-bones to hold the pattern, in the days when pins were very dear and almost unprocurable, may account for the name.

Aunt Mollie Caldwell collected the Ipswich workers' lace once a week and took it to Boston by stage coach; in exchange she brought back French calico, sugar, tea, coffee, and sometimes, surreptitiously, little packages of much-desired snuff. It was not alone the lace makers who were not paid in currency, for the town records, as far back as 1640, read that "no persons are compelled to pay future debts in cash, but in cord, cattle, fish, and other articles." Goody Caldwell not only disposed of the workers' lace, but was clever enough to buy a bit from a peddler, prick off a pattern from it and give it to one of the workers to reproduce.

Felt's History, published in 1834, states that "Lace of thread and silk was made in large quantities, and for a long period by girls and women. . . . Black as well as white lace was manufactured of various widths, qualities, and prices. The females of almost every family would pass their leisure hours in such employment. In 1790 no less than 41,979 yards were made here [Ipswich] annually."

Bobbin or pillow lace making is a most interesting and beautiful craft, and, although distinctly feminine, at the time of Queen Victoria's marriage, the peasants in the Midlands, both men and women, found it so much more profitable than tilling the fields that the plough was neglected for the pillow. Travellers often notice the small hands of the Midland County people; small they are, due to the fact that, for generations, they have made lace and not done hard manual labour. From these people came our American lace makers. As children, they learned the craft at four or five years of age; when they were too old to do much else, they were still able to work at their pillows. Most of the hand-made lace produced was either made by girls between childhood and the time they married, when their lives became too full of other duties, or else it was woven by women who had brought up their families and found again a lull in their heretofore strenuous lives. An old lace maker actually loved her pillow; the bobbins were as full of associations for her as were the patterns she wove. Contrary to the general belief, the making of pillow lace is not hard on the eyes. I have some excellent pieces of work done by women over eighty years of age.

Let us go back a little that we may understand the sudden appearance of an entirely different sort of lace in Ipswich at a somewhat later date. In England, about 1809, a Mr. Heathcoat perfected a machine that made a good hexagonal mesh, so that a yard of yard-wide net could be woven in the time it took to make six inches of inch-wide net on a pillow. The pillow lace makers naturally resented this innovation keenly. Indeed, they banded themselves together and took drastic measures to destroy these machines. So much damage was actually done that many operators were driven out of employment and, between 1818 and 1822, a number of them emigrated to Ipswich, in Massachusetts, to be relieved of the constant annoyance they suffered in Nottingham and several other towns in England. The English government, realising the danger to British textile industries should these skilled emigrating workmen get machines, put an excessive export duty on the machinery, together with a £500 fine or a long term of imprisonment for the offender. Despite all this, the important parts of the machinery reached our shores, hidden, I have read, in tubs of Yorkshire butter!

In a short time an excellent quality of net, both black and white, was being produced in Ipswich. This net was the foundation or background for the second and later kind of lace, a lace made by darning the pattern in. The factory or headquarters for the lace makers was in one of the old houses on High Street, where many girls and women spent their working days. More, however, did the work in their own homes.

The bobbin or pillow lace making was a distinctly local industry, but the "point net lace" ("point," because the size of the mesh varied according to the size of the points on the machine) or Ipswich lace, as it was called, was also done in many neighbouring towns.

The net was stretched on a large frame; the pattern darned in with a glass-like thread, and the centres of the flowers and many other *motifs* filled in with fancy stitches. The first patterns were taken from the bobbin laces, and they were very good copies, too; later a new style was developed with more attenuated designs. The work is similar to that done in Ireland under the name of Limerick. The same sort is made in large quantities in Italy and called Sicilian lace.

Our bobbin lace makers, with their well-trained hands, were at once pressed into service on this new work and seemed quite ready to drop their pillows for the needle. Large quantities of net were darned, and to-day there is hardly an old family in Ipswich that cannot show some of their ancestors' work. The net adapted itself to a variety of shapes, and, besides the edges of every known width and style, there are exquisite caps both for babies and old ladies, kerchiefs, collars and cuffs, and wedding veils and gowns. A straight veil that hung from the brim of the hat must have been fashionable, for I have been shown a number of these, both in black and white lace. The gowns were divided into breadths and, even then, were a long, tedious task to make. The finishing of a large order was considered ample excuse for a village festival; bedspreads were hung from the windows and the lace makers made merry.

The darned net lace is really beautiful, but incomparable, in a craftsman's eyes, with the earlier work of the bobbins; the machine-made net gives it a somewhat commonplace aspect that an entirely hand-made article has not. That infinite skill and patience are required to make the bobbin lace, one feels as wells as knows.

At the present time no net is darned in Ipswich, that industry having succumbed to the entirely machine-made lace that one may buy so cheaply. The pillows, however, have never been totally relegated to the past. Fifteen years ago I found several women who still loved their pillows, even though the work they were able to do was very inferior to what had been done a hundred years before. We formed a little industry and interested other workers who attempted more elaborate designs. It is to be feared, however, that the old lace requires too much patience to gain a strong foothold in our busy American lives. There are, nevertheless, many kinds of bobbin lace that can be made and used in this everyday world that do not demand either endless time or patience and that are still very much worth while.

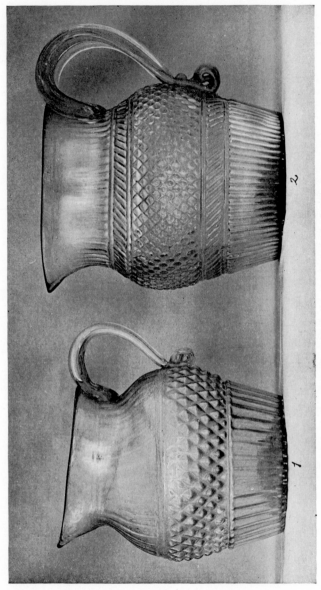

EARLY NINETEENTH CENTURY AMERICAN PRESSED GLASS JUGS

Courtesy of Metropolitan Museum

EARLY NINETEENTH CENTURY AMERICAN GLASS
1. Etched Flip on Toddy Glass. 2. Mug
Courtesy of Metropolitan Museum

INDEX

A

Accomplishments, feminine, 15
Adam and Eve, needlework, 91
Adam, influence, 133, 149, 154, 156, 256; *motifs*, 128; pattern, 318
Adams, John, 308; Pygan, 155
Albany, N. Y., 17, 32, 117, 118
Albarelli, 26
Allegorical, pictures, 15; painting, 17, 260–271
Alloways, Creek, 36; Town, N. J., 31, 32, 35
Alloys, pewter, 200; and processes, pewter, 205–208
Alms basons, 163
Altar, frontal, 81; piece, painted, 264
American, glass, 16, 28–54; origins of dec. objects, 55; pewterers' list, 216; Philosophical Society, 289; silversmiths' list, 172–196
Americana, 14, 18
Ancient and Honourable Artillery Company, Boston, 109
Animals, samplers, 93; slip-ware, 229, 233, 234
Annapolis, 119
Anthony, Joseph, 119
Apparel, wearing, 15
Apple corers, 140
Application, of paint, 241
Appliqué patchwork, 98
Apprentice system, 121
Architectural, amenities, Georgian, 312; carving, stone, 317, 318; carving, wood, 311–316; features, samplers, 91–93; ironwork, 57–61; woodwork, 303
Architects' furniture, 312
Architecture, 127
Armorial bearings, 320; coaches, 265; hatchments, 267; silver, 164, 167
Arts, decorative, 14; conditions favourable to, 15; industrial, 14
Ashby, Mass., 113
Asheville, N. C., 276
Astrologers, Colonial, 293
Aztecs, 20

B

Badger, Thomas, 209
Badges, insurance, 72
Ball feet, 150
Baltimore, 17, 32, 119, 256
Balusters, 242
Balustrades, 316
Bamper, Loderwick, 31
Bancker, Adrian, 149
Band-boxes, 240, 302
Banding, 250
Baptismal, bowls, 163, 203; certificates, 293
Barber, Dr. L. A., 19, 107, 217
Baroque, inspiration, 315
Bartram, Ann, 318; Gardens, 318, House, 318; John, 318
Basons, alms, 163; baptismal, 163
Bavarian dower chest, 248
Bayeux tapestry, 91, 278
Beach, Col. Miles, 114
Beads, 32
Beaker, 145, 146, 150, 163, 203
Beasts, samplers, 93
Bed, coverings, 98, 99; hangings, 83; spreads, 15
Bedstead, canopied, 272; pillared, 272
Bedminster, Bucks, Pa., 289
Bellows, 258
Berea College, 276
Berlin wool, 96
"Betty" lamps, 62
Birds, glass, 29; samplers, 93; slip-ware, 229, 232, 233
Blacksmith, silvermaker, 115; skill, 56
Bleeding cups, 136
Blocks, printing, 298–301
Bloodletting, 136
Bobbin, 322; lace, 323–327
Boelen, Hendrik, 116; Jacob, 116
Bolles Collection, 307
Bolster pillow, for lace, 321
"Bone lace," 325, 327
Bolting monopoly, 117
Bolton, Farm, 312; Mass., 113
Book-covers, embroidered, 100

329

22

W

Wafer irons, 62
Waistcoats, embroidered, 100
Wald-Hilspach, 35
Wall devices, 318; paper, 298, 302
Walnut, 306
Warming pans, 70, 71
Warren, Sir Peter, 31
Warwick Furnace, Pa., 66
Washington, 33, 93, 129, 255, 308, 314, 315
Water-buckets, 258, 259
Waterbury, Conn., 114
Weather vanes, 60–61
Weavers, itinerant, 273, 277, 279
Weaving, coverlet and decorative, 272–285
Welsh Colonists, 310
West, Benjamin, 262, 268
West Indian trade, 42
West Jersey, 35, 54
Whistles, 159
Whitemarsh Valley, 319

Willard, clocks, 254
Willet, Helena, 138; Thomas, 138
Williamson, 119
Windham, Conn., 114
Window glass, 30, 33, 38, 39
Windsor chairs, 250
Wine, labels, 159; tasters, 136, 146
Winslow, Edward, 112
Winter, John, 265
Winthrop, Governour, 314
Wistar, Caspar, 16, 31, 32, 35, 36, 39, 70; Richard, 36, 39, 40, 70; glass, 35–41; where to be found, 54; Wistarberg, 35–41
Witt, Dr. Christopher, 262, 263, 264
Wood carving, 16, 304–316; architectural, 311–316; processes, 304–306; shipwrights, 310; small domestic articles, 309, 310
Wren, Sir Christopher, 314
"Wriggling," pewter, 211, 212
Wyck, 36

SUPPLEMENT

SANDWICH GLASS AND SOME OTHER PRESSED GLASS

BY LENORE WHEELER WILLIAMS

ANY ONE who has looked into a grandmother's china closet that has remained for many years undisturbed by death or invasion by the " collector " has seen on the top shelf, or perhaps, on the shelf next below, pieces of pressed glass—fruit dishes, deep dishes for berries or desserts, sugar bowls, and cream pitchers, sauce dishes neatly stacked in piles, and back in a corner of the shelf a small stack of cup plates—reminders of the days when it was the fashion to drink tea from the saucer while the cup rested in a " cup plate." Much of this glass came into use less than a hundred years ago, then replacing the more expensive china brought from abroad. It was much esteemed for the intricate patterns impressed on the outer surface of each piece, the many facets brightly reflecting the light and supplying a welcome contrast to the dark blues of the English ware, the browns of the New England potteries, the "block-tin" teapot, or the few remaining pieces of pewter. Before that time table glass of the heavier sort—tumblers, cruets, salts, and plain decanters—had been mainly imported from Germany by the earthenware trade, though some flint glass had been made at South Boston and nearly every old family owned a piece or two of the glass made in Pennsylvania, just before the Revolution, by Stiegel, and brought to Boston by the coasting vessels sailing to and from Philadelphia.

Nearly all of this early pressed glass was made in

the town of Sandwich on the south shore of Massachusetts Bay. The company was organised in 1825 and commenced making glass on Independence Day, July 4, 1825. At first all the glass was "blown," but in 1827 a workman in the New England Glass Company at East Cambridge invented a machine for pressing molten glass into iron moulds which was adopted and perfected at the Sandwich works and thereafter practically its entire product was pressed glass until the eighties when machine-blowing was introduced. It is puzzling, sometimes, to find early examples of "pressed glass" whereon appears a pontil mark made when the piece was broken off from the glass-blower's pipe. This is because the earlier specimens were actually blown against and into the moulds before the invention of mechanical pressure.

Blown glass was one of the first manufactures of European settlers in America. Glass beads for the Indian trade were made at Jamestown, Va., as early as 1608. Between 1639 and 1659 glass bottles and hollow ware were being blown at the glass house in Salem, Mass. In 1753 a company of German glass blowers settled in Braintree, Mass., and made bottles and other heavy ware until 1759 when the glass house was destroyed by fire. New Haven, Conn., was making blown glass in 1789 and Temple, N. H., was doing the like about 1780. A works for making crown window glass was established in Boston in 1787, but led a precarious existence until 1803 when an experienced workman from abroad arrived and took charge, and twenty years later "Boston Window Glass" was a quality of glass known everywhere in the New England States.

The oldest, and for a long time the most successful glass works, was the New England Glass Company

SANDWICH GLASS OCTAGONAL FLAT DISH
"Constitution"—issued to arouse sentiment against
contemplated destruction
Courtesy of Lenore Wheeler Williams

EARLY NINETEENTH CENTURY AMERICAN PRESSED GLASS DISH
Courtesy of Metropolitan Museum

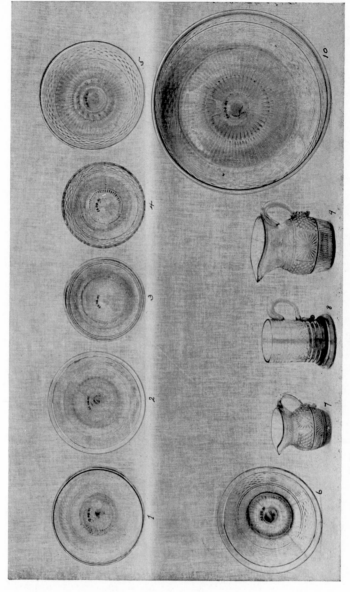

EARLY NINETEENTH CENTURY PRESSED AND MOULDED GLASSWARE
Courtesy of Metropolitan Museum

located at East Cambridge in November, 1817, at that time succeeding the Porcelain and Glass Manufacturing Company formed in 1811. The New England Glass Company began operations with a six-pot furnace having a capacity of seven hundred pounds to each pot and a working force of forty men. In 1853 the business had increased to five furnaces with ten pots of two thousand pounds each and five hundred workmen. In the same year, 1853, the Boston and Sandwich Glass Company employed an equal number of workmen and produced yearly $600,000 worth of lamps, dishes, cup plates, salt cellars, etc.

In order to understand the process by which glassware is produced it should be borne in mind that previous to 1827 table glass as well as hollow ware—bottles and the like—was made by the pressure of the breath of the glass worker blowing through a long tube. In the first instance, the bubble of molten glass was blown to the desired size, worked into shape and cut off where required. By reheating and attaching to other shapes it was possible to reproduce almost anything in glass.

Another process was moulded glass. Here the workman by means of his breath forced the molten glass into a two-part hollow mould, made of cast iron, frequently cut on the inside with an incised design into which the glass was forced, thereby repeating the design on the sides of the bottle or other utensil. When the glass was sufficiently cool, the two-part mould would be opened and the piece taken out.

By the process of pressing glass the machine holds the mould of the dish, salt cellar, or other object to be made, and a man cuts off and drops into it a lump of red-hot glass while another man pulls the lever that forces the plunger into the mould and so shapes the object. Moulded glass preserves the form of the design on the mould on its interior as well as on its exterior surface. In pressed glass the exterior surface is modelled by the mould, while the interior surface is smooth and is modelled by the plunger. Pressed glass as soon as taken from the mould is exposed to heat so as to melt a thin surface layer and so remove the slightly roughened surface produced by the mould. This was called "fire polishing" and left a smooth, bright surface. In pressed glass the facets being cast instead of cut, the angles are always slightly rounded and the lustre is less. Sometimes, however, the pressed surfaces are heightened by the sharpness of the mould and by cutting them over and polishing by hand so that only the expert can distinguish the article from hand-cut ware. Pressed glass always lacks the "fire polish" of blown glass, but this is partially restored by reheating. The secret of the bright surface on the old Sandwich pressed glass was the use of barytes or "heavy earth" which gave the beautiful silvery tint found in old pressed glass. The New England Glass Company did not use barytes and its glass is dull in comparison with Sandwich glass. Its patterns also were heavy, lacking the lacey quality of early Sandwich.

In the early days of the works the life of a glass blower was short, due to the overheated glass house. It was the invention of the mould machine that made the occupation more healthful. The fuel for the furnace also had to be carefully controlled. Until the development of the Virginia coal mines wood was used. This was split in equal lengths, with an average diameter of two inches, kiln-dried, and then fed into the furnace, a stick at a time, through a "fire hole." The working spaces above the furnaces were called by the workmen "glory holes." Glass blowers became itinerant and whole "factories" sometimes moved for lack of fuel.

The rapid increase in the production of Sandwich glass has been mentioned. While large quantities were sold in the stores in Boston and in the large towns, a dependable outlet and manner of distribution was the tin peddler's cart—an institution found everywhere about New England. In effect, a huge packing case, usually painted a dark red or yellow and mounted on wheels, with a seat in front for the driver. Long doors lifted on either side and others opened at the back, while piled on top and fastened everywhere on either side, were tubs, pails, clothes baskets, washboards, brooms, mop handles, and wooden ware of all descriptions. Large bags of rags hung behind and filled available space on top. Inside the cart were closely packed all manner of tin and iron ware for the varied use of the countryside and with it a stock of common pottery and pressed glass, the latter usually kept in a capacious box under the driver's seat.

For some time unusual pieces of Sandwich glass have been turning up in Pennsylvania, a puzzling problem until it appeared that this glass had been carried there before 1855 by Quakers who had come to Massachusetts to attend Yearly Meetings and on returning home had carried with them choice examples of glass as presents for their wives.

Probably the best-known form of Sandwich glass at the present time is the cup plate. Previous to about 1830 the dinner sets made in England for the American market included cup plates in accordance with the requirements of the fashion of the time, but the pressed glass cup plates made by the Sandwich Glass Works soon gained such popularity due both to their beauty and their fitness with any china, that soon cup plates were omitted when shipments were made from England. People who could not afford entire dinner sets had previously done without cup plates and the glass cup plate was an inexpensive innovation that became very popular. Some were made in blue, green, amber, and other colours, but the clear glass and opalescent tones were more popular and considered in better taste.

Glass candlesticks are always attractive. Old glass candlesticks are moulded in two sections and fused together. This fusing section varies from one-sixteenth to one-quarter of an inch in thickness and is irregular on different sides of the same candlestick. The mould seams along the side of the candlestick where the sections are joined will be found not to be in continuous perpendicular line. The seam may be in line on one side, but never on both. The side lines on modern moulded candlesticks will be found to be continuous from top to bottom. This test should be applied to all the coloured glass candlesticks of the hollow base type that are now appearing in the market.

Another product of the Sandwich Glass Works was the whale oil or lard oil lamp which, by a change of burner at a later date, could be used for camphine or "burning fluid." The brass burner for the camphine lamp always has an extinguisher hanging from a chain fastened to the collar of the burner. Wick picking was not required with the camphine burner, but "burning fluid," made of alcohol and turpentine, was danger-

EARLY HOOKED RUGS, WROUGHT IN GEOMETRICAL OR "TILE"
PATTERNS, SHEWING EARLIEST TYPE OF DESIGN
Courtesy of Messrs. Lord & Taylor

HOOKED RUGS, WROUGHT IN GEOMETRICAL OR "TILE" PATTERNS,
WITH THE ADDITION OF FLOWERS OR SPRIGS IN THE DIVISIONS,
SHEWING SECOND TYPE OF DESIGN
Courtesy of Messrs. Lord & Taylor

ously explosive and many accidents occurred. Then came kerosene with a round wick, later the flat wick and a deluge of commonplace lamps in great variety.

All pieces of pressed glass with a star (sunburst) in the bottom are decidedly late. The star was invented in England to cover the ground-off pontil on cut glass and was imitated in this country in machine-made pressed glass. As to rarity of colours in Sandwich glass the following are important to collectors: opalescent should not be confused with opaque; amethyst is rarer than dark purple; peacock blue is rarer than dark purple in early types and the reverse in later types; then comes dark amber and rarest of all, opaque jade green.

About twenty years ago there were made in Belgium some little opaque white and coloured glass butter plates resembling cup-plates. A few of these have come into the present market. The design in every instance is a rather weak, conventional pattern embossed instead of impressed on the reverse side of the plate. The design does not shew at all unless the plate is inverted.

There is no royal road to a certain knowledge of Sandwich glass, but there is a sharpness to the edges, a resonance when struck, an unevenness of surface never found in modern pressed glass. There need be no undue excitement over reproductions appearing on the market from time to time as the necessity of commercialising such products make them easily distinguishable from the old. All this modern glass is lime glass while the old was lead glass. The former is lifeless and its mould seams are regular and edges smooth; its surface entirely lacking the "molasses-like" quality of old Sandwich.

LIST OF EARLY AMERICAN PEWTERERS

SEVENTEENTH CENTURY

Bumpsteed, Thomas (Bumsteed) (Bumstead)	1654	Boston, Mass.
Clarke, Thomas	1687	Boston, Mass.
Comer, John	1678	Boston, Mass.
Graves, Richard	1642	Salem, Mass.
Shrimpton, Henry	1660–1665	Boston, Mass.

EIGHTEENTH CENTURY

Austin, Richard	1796–1810	Boston, Mass. R-A BOSTON
Austin, Nathaniel	b. 1741 d. 1816	Boston, Mass.
Badger, Thomas	1789–1810	Boston, Mass. Name in full, with eagle and BOSTON
Bancks, C.	....	Chelmsford? Mass. Name
Bassett, Francis	1750–1799	New York. F-B, fleur-de-lys above and below (in a circle)
Bassett, Frederick	1792–1798	New York. F B, dot above and below in a roped circle; full name with crowned rose and N Y; F. BASSETT, NEW YORK (in a leaf-shaped punch)
Belcher, J.	Late 18th Cent.	JO-BELCHER, and lion? (in oval)
Boyle, Robert	1745–1780	New York
Bradford, Cornelius	Before 1776	Philadelphia
Bradford, William	1750–1780	New York
Bush & Perkins	c. 1740	Name and seated figure in a circle
Coldwell, George	1792–1808	New York
Danforth, Thomas	b. 1708 d. circa 1786	Taunton, Mass., and Norwich, Conn. T D large (in rectangle lion rampant)
Danforth, Thomas	1778–1807–1813	Rocky Hill, Conn., and Philadelphia. T. DANFORTH, PHILAD'a in rectangle; T.D. with eagle holding shield
Danforth, Thomas	b. 1792 d. 1836	Rocky Hill, Conn., Philadelphia and Augusta, Ga. Rampant lion and T D, four small hall marks
Edgell, Simon	1717–1718	Philadelphia
Elsworth, William I.	1792	New York
Everet, James	1717–1718	Philadelphia
Fields, Philip	1799	New York

350

Green, Andrew	1789–1798	Boston, Mass.
Green, Samuel	1798–1825	Boston, Mass.
Green, Thomas	1789	Boston, Mass.
Grilley, Henry	1790	Waterbury, Conn.
Hamlin, William?	b. 1772 d. 1869	Providence, R. I. HAMLIN with spread eagle
Hera (Hero) Charlotte, widow	1796	....
Holden, John	1743	New York
Jones, G.	Late 18th Cent.	Providence, R. I. Name and four hall marks
Kirkby, William (Kirby)	1786–1792	New York
Lafetra & Allaire	1744–1780	New York
Leddell, James	c. 1770	Taunton, Mass.
M'Ewen, Malcolm & Son	1794	New York
Michel, André	1796	New York
Pearse, Robert	1792	New York
Revere, Paul	1770	Boston, Mass.
Roby, Joseph	1789	Boston, Mass.
Skinner, John	1789–1796	Boston, Mass.
Trask, Israel	b. 1786 d. 1867	Beverly, Mass. I T R A S K (in rectangle)
Ward, James	1795	Hartford, Conn.
Welch, John	1796	Boston, Mass.
Whitehouse, E.	Late 18th Cent.	....
Will, Henry	1765–1786	New York. Name, address, crowned rose, four hall marks
Youle, George	1798–1821	New York

NINETEENTH CENTURY

Babbitt & Crossman	1824	Taunton, Mass.
Barns, B.	1811–1819	Philadelphia. B B (in oval held by eagle) ; name and PHILAD'a, in rectangle; name on a ribbon above spread eagle
Bast, S.	19th Cent.	New York
Bird, James	1820	New York
Boardman & Co.	1824	New York. BOARDMAN and lion
Boardman & Hart	1828–1841	New York and Philadelphia. Name and PHILAD'a (in rectangles and eagle in oval)
Boardman, Henry S.	1841	Hartford, Conn.
Boardman, J. D.	1828	Hartford, Conn.
Boardman, Sherman	1828	Hartford, Conn.
Boardman, Thomas D.	After 1825	Hartford, Conn. Name in full around a spread eagle; name in full, X crowned, HARTFORD

Boardman, T. D. & S.	1854	Hartford, Conn. T. D & S B (in rectangle)
Boardman, Timothy & Co.	1824	New York. T. B. & Co. (in engrailed rectangle)
Boyd, Parkes	1800–1812	Philadelphia. P. BOYD, PHIL, with eagle and fifteen stars
Brooks, David S.	1828	Hartford, Conn.
Broadhead, Gurney & Co.	....	Hartford, Conn.
Bush, Robert	....	Name and harp (in circle)
Calder, William	1824	Providence, R. I. CALDER, PROVIDENCE and eagle; also name and address (in rectangle)
Capen & Molineaux	c. 1840	New York
Crossman, West & Leonard (britannia ware)	After 1824	Taunton, Mass.
Curtis, Edgar & Co.	....	Name in full
Curtis, D.	19th Cent.	New York?
Danforth, Samuel	Early 19th Cent.	Hartford, Conn. S D and eagle, four hall marks
Dunham, R.	Early 19th Cent.	Boston, Mass.? Name impressed
Estabrook	c. 1820	....
Fuller & Smith	19th Cent.	....
Gerhard & Co.	19th Cent.	....
Gleason, Roswell	1830	Dorchester, Mass. R. GLEASON (in rectangle; or full name incised)
Graves, Henry	1849	Middletown, Conn.
Hall & Boardman	19th Cent.	Philadelphia
Hall, Franklin	1840	Hartford, Conn.
Hall & Cotton	Early 19th Cent.	....
Hale	Early 19th Cent.	New York
Hamlin, Samuel (E.?)	c. 1824	Providence, R. I. Name and X crowned, or HAMLIN PROVIDENCE, eagle with anchor (in oval)
Hart, Lucius	1828	New York. HART, N. York
Heave, Christian	Early 19th Cent.	Philadelphia. Name (in a cartouche)
Hera, C. and L. (Hero)	1810	Philadelphia. Name and address, shield
Homans & Co. (Homan)	c. 1830	Cincinnati, O.
Hopper, H.	1841	Hartford, Conn.
House, Edwin	1844	Hartford, Conn.
Jagger, Daniel H.	1843	Hartford, Conn.
Jagger, James H.	1839	Hartford, Conn.
Jagger, Walter W.	Early 19th Cent.	Boston, Mass.
Jackson, Mary	....	....
Knight, W. W.	1812–1816	New York
Lafetra, Moses	1815–1816	New York

Lee, Richard,	Est. 1835	Taunton, Mass. Name incised
Leonard, Reed & Barton		New York. Name, NEW York (in rectangle)
	After 1825	
Lock (e?) D.	After 1825	New York?
Locke, J. B.	c. 1830	New York
Manning, Thaddeus	1849	Middletown, Conn.
Maton, Marcus	1828	Hartford, Conn.
Morey & Ober	Early 19th Cent.	Boston
Moore, S	c. 1820–1830	Kensington, Conn.
Palethorp, Robert, Jr.	Early 19th Cent.	Philadelphia
Parker, C.	Early 19th Cent.	New York?
Pierce, Samuel	....	....
Porter, A.	....	Southington, Conn. Name (in rectangle)
Porter, Edmund	c. 1800	Taunton, Mass.
Porter, Edmund	c. 1847	Taunton, Mass.
Porter, F.	After 1825	Westbrook, Conn. Name and address
Porter, Lincoln	c. 1800	Taunton, Mass.
Porter, Samuel	c. 1800	Taunton, Mass.
Putnam	....	Name (in engrailed rectangle)
Quilkin	....	Philadelphia
Reed & Barton	Est. 1845	Taunton, Mass. Name incised
Richardson, C. or G.	Early 19th Cent.	Cranston, R. I. Name, address and eagle
Richardson, George	1825	Boston, Mass.
Rigden, Thomas	Early 19th Cent.	Philadelphia
Rush, S.	19th Cent.	New York
Savage	....	....
Sellers & Co.		Cincinnati, O.
Strange, Jireh	c. 1800	Taunton, Mass.
Strange, Joseph	c. 1800	Taunton, Mass.
Smith & Co.	c. 1830	Philadelphia. Name (in semi-circle); axe? (in serrated square)
Smith & Feltman	....	Albany, N. Y. Name and place incised
Stedman, S.	....	....
Starr, W. H.	....	New York
Taunton Britannia Mfg. Co.	Est. 1830	Taunton, Mass.
Trask, John	1825–1842	Boston, Mass.
Trask, Oliver	b. 1792 d. 1874	Beverly, Mass.
Vose & Co.	....	Albany, N. Y. Name and address
Wadsworth, Lester	1838	Hartford, Conn.
Ward, H. B.	1820	Guilford, Conn.
Wallace, R.	....	....
Wildes, Thomas	1832–1840	New York
Will, George W.	Early 19th Cent.	Philadelphia

23

Will, William	c. 1800	Philadelphia. Wm. W. (in rectangle)
Williams, L. L.	....	Philadelphia
Yale, H. & Co.	....	Wallingford, Conn. Name and address
Yale, W. & S.	Early 19th Cent.	Wallingford, Conn. Name, eagle and stars
Yale & Curtis	....	New York
Youle, Thomas	1815–1821	New York
Youle, Thomas & Co.	1811	New York
Youle, Widow of Thomas	1820–1821	New York

SUPPLEMENTARY LIST OF EARLY
AMERICAN SILVERSMITHS

BOSTON:

[Ball, John] *add*	d. 1808	....
Bell & Co.	c. 1825	(S. Bell) Name in capitals (in rectangle, with rosettes flanking)
[Bentley, Thomas] *add*	....	T B (Roman capitals in long oval with bird's head flanking)
Brackett, Jeffrey R.	1815–1876	Full name, or surname, in capitals (in rectangle)
Brackett, Crosby & Brown	1850	....
Breed, W. (Boston?)	1750	W. Breed (script in rectangle)
		W. B. (Roman capitals in rectangle)
Brigden, Zachariah	1734–1787	Z. Brigden (script in cartouche)
		Z. B. (Roman capitals in rectangle)
Brigham, John	1678	....
[Burrell, Samuel] *add*	....	S B (with diamond below, in a heart)
Burrill, Theophilus	d. 1739	....
Callender, Benjamin	1784	....
[Churchill & Treadwell] *add*	....	Name in capitals in rectangle
Clark, C. & G.	1833	....
Clark, I. (Boston or Salem)	1754	I CLARK (with or without pellet, in rectangle); CLARK (in rectangle)
Clark, Metcalf	1835	....
[Clark, Samuel] *add*	1659–1705	....
Clemmons, Isaac	c. 1775	....
[Cobb, E.] *add*	1708–1775	E C (in rectangle)
Cogswell, H.	c. 1750	H. COGSWELL (in rectangle)
[Crosby, Jonathan] *add*	1796	J C (in double circle)
Crosby, Samuel T.	1850	....
Cutler, A.	c. 1820	A. CUTLER (in rectangle)
[Davis, T. A.] *add*	....	T. A. DAVIS (in rectangle)
Davis, Palmer & Co.	c. 1841	Name in Roman capitals in rectangle
[Deverell, John] *add*	....	DEVERELL (in small Roman letters in rectangle)
Dewing, Francis	c. 1716	....
Doane, John	1733–1801	....

355

Farrington, John	1833	....
Farrington & Hunnewell	1835	F & H (in rectangle)
[Foster, Joseph] *add*	1760–1839	....
Foster, George B.	1838	Full name in capitals in rectangle, with "Coin" in Gothic
Frobisher, Benjamin C.	1792–1862	B. C. FROBISHER (shaded, in rectangle).
Garden, Francis	1745	....
[Gay, Nathaniel] *add*	1643–1713	....
Gelston, George P.	1830	....
Gelston, Henry	1828	....
Gelston, Hugh	1816	....
Gelston, Maltby	d. 1828	....
Goldthwaite, Joseph	1706–1780	I G (crude capitals crowned, fleur-de-lys below, in shield; same also in quatrefoil)
Gooding, Henry	1833	GOODING (small shaded, in rectangle)
Gooding, Josiah	c. 1810	JOSIAH GOODING (small, in rectangle)
Gookin, Daniel	1682	....
Gordon & Co.	1849	....
Green, Bartholomew	1697	....
Haddock & Andrews	1838	....
Halstrick, Joseph	1815–1886	....
[Harding, Newell] *add*	....	Name in small Italic letters in scroll; also name in small Roman letters in rectangle
Harris & Stanwood	1845	Name in capitals in rectangle
Haskell, Barnabas	1833	....
[Healy] *add* Samuel	....	....
Hearn, R.	....	R. HEARN (in rectangle)
[Henchman, Daniel] *add*	....	Name in shaded Roman capitals, pellet between, in rectangle
Hews, A., Jr	c. 1850	Name in capitals incised
[Hiller, Benjamin] *add*	1687–c. 1739	....
Hobbs, Nathan	1792–1868	HOBBS (small, in rectangle)
[Holyoke, Edward] *add*	....	Name in capitals, in rectangle
Horn, E. B.	1847	....
Johnson, William	1799	....
Jones, George B.	c. 1815–1875	....
[Jones, John] *add*	....	J. JONES (in rectangle)
Jones, John B. & Co.	1838	....
Jones, Ball & Poor	1846	Firm name in capitals, incised
Jones, Low & Bell	1839	Firm name in capitals, in rectangle
Kay, Am.	c. 1725	A K (crudely formed, in rectangle)

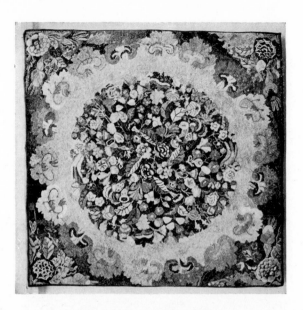

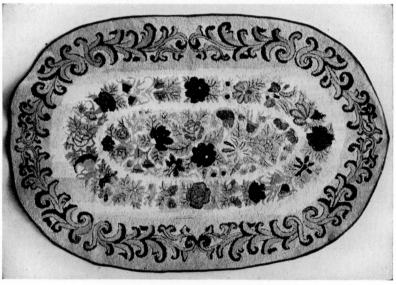

HOOKED RUGS WITH MULTI-COLOURED SCROLL, LEAF AND FLOWER
PATTERNS IN THE MANNER OF THE MID-EIGHTEENTH CENTURY,
SHEWING THIRD STAGE OF DESIGN

Courtesy of Metropolitan Museum

HOOKED RUG OF CHEVRON ON SCROLL STRIPES, SHEWING SURVIVAL
OF EARLY PATTERN TYPES

HOOKED RUG WITH MULTI-COLOURED BIRD AND LEAF PATTERN
IN EARLY NINETEENTH CENTURY MANNER
Courtesy of Messrs. Lord & Taylor

Keith, Timothy	c. 1800	T–KEITH (in rectangle)
Kind, Jane	1624–1710	....
Laforme, F. J.	1835	....
Laforme, Vincent	1850	V. LAFORME (incised)
[Leach, Charles] *add*	....	C · L (shaded, in scalloped rectangle)
Libby, J. G. L.	c. 1830	J. G. L. LIBBY (very small, slightly shaded, in rectangle)
Lincoln & Reed	c. 1790	Firm name in rectangle
Low, Ball & Co.	1840	....
McClinch, John	1760	....
[Oliver, Andrew] *add*	....	AO (shaded Roman capitals in heart)
Parker, Caleb	1731–c. 1770	....
Pear, Edward	1833	EDWARD PEAR (in cartouche); E P (in cartouche)
[Peirce or Pierce, John] *add*	....	PEIRCE (very small, shaded in rectangle)
Perkins, Houghton	1735–1738	....
[Phillips, Samuel] *add*	....	S P (crude letters, in rectangle) ?
Phinney & Mead	c. 1825	P & M (shaded, in rectangle)
[Pons, Thomas] *add*	....	*PONS* (large, in rectangle)
Porter, H. & Co.	c. 1830	Firm name in capitals, in rectangle
[Potwine, John] *add*	....	I · P (crude, in heart-shaped shield, with pellet)
Raymond, John	d. 1775	....
Rogers, Augustus	1840	....
Russell, Eleazer	1663–1691	....
Sanderson, Benjamin	1649–1678	B S (large and crude, in rectangle)
[Sawin, Silas] *add*	....	SS (small, crude, in flat oval)
Sherman, James	c. 1770	....
Skates, John	c. 1668–1680	....
Skerry, George W.	c. 1837	....
Trott, Thomas	c. 1701–1777	T · T (large, in rectangle, with pellet); also, with letters crowned in cartouche; also, large, crowned, in rectangle
[Vinton, David] *add*	c. 1792	D . V (small, in rectangle, with pellet below)
Walcott, Henry D.	1797–1830	....
Walcott & Gelston	c. 1824	....
[Waters, Samuel] *add*	....	S · W (shaded, in rectangle, pellet between); S . W (large, shaded, in oval, pellet below)
[Watson, Edward] *add*	....	E. WATSON (in rectangle); also E. Watson (in rectangle)

Watson & Brown (?)	c. 1830	Firm name, in capitals, in rectangle
[Webb, Barnabas] *add*	c. 1729–c. 1786	B W (small, crude, in rectangle)
Welles, A. & G.	c. 1810	A. & G. Welles (in rectangle); also, A. & G. W. (in rectangle)
[Welles, George] *add*	....	WELLES–BOSTON (in separate rectangles)
[Welles & Co.] *add*	....	WELLES & CO. (in rectangle)
[West, B.] *add*	....	B. WEST (in rectangle)
West, Charles	c. 1830	....
White, Thomas Sturt	c. 1734	....
[Whiton, Ebed] *add*	....	E. Whiton (small, in rectangle and scroll)
Whittemore, Edward	d. 1772	....

NEW YORK:

Adams, William	1833	W. ADAMS—NEW YORK (shaded in serrated rectangles; rectangle separated)
Amory	....	AMORY (in rectangle)
Austin, Ebenezer	1733–c. 1818	Surname, shaded small letters in rectangle; also, initials and pellet in rectangle
Bacon & Smith	c. 1830	Names in capitals, in rectangle
Ball, Tompkins & Black	....	Firm name in small, shaded Roman capitals, in circle
Bateman, William	1774	....
[Bayley, Simeon A.] *add*	....	BAYLEY (in rectangle)
Bean, John Anthony	1770	....
Becham	c. 1740	BECHAM (in rectangle)
Bogart, N. J.	c. 1820	....
Bond, C.	c. 1840	C BOND (in rectangle)
Bond, W.	c. 1765	W BOND (shaded, in scalloped rectangle)
Boyce, Gherardus	1829	G: BOYCE (in rectangle, with four pellets and N. Y.; also, in two separate rectangles; G. B (in rectangle, with pellet between letters)
Brady, William V.	1835	....
[Brasher, Ephraim] *add*	....	E B (shaded in rectangle); BRASHER—N. YORK (shaded, in separate rectangles)
Brasier, A.	....	A. BRASIER (in rectangle)

Brevoort, John F.	1742	I B V (crude capitals in oval); I B V (crude capitals in trefoil)
Brock, John	c. 1833	. . . .
Brower & Rusher	c. 1834	B & R (in rectangle, with pseudo hall-marks)
Cann, John	c. 1836	. . . .
Chandlers, William	c. 1846	. . . .
Charters, James	c. 1844	. . . .
[Chitry, P.] *add*	. . . .	P. Chitry (in rectangle)
Coe & Upton, & H. L. Sawyer	c. 1840	COE & UPTON (in rectangle); also, N Y (in small separate rectangles) and H. L. SAWYER (in rectangle)
Cole, Albert	c. 1850	. . . .
[Coley, William] *add*	. . . .	W. Coley (in script, in shaped oval)
Cooper, F. W.	c. 1840	Woman's head, C, old English lion
Cox, J. & I.	c. 1840	J & I COX and N. YORK (in separate rectangles); also without rectangle
Dalley & Halsey	c. 1787	. . . .
David, John	c. 1736–1798	. . . .
Davison, C.	. . . .	C DAVISON (in oval)
Dawkins, Henry	c. 1754–1776	. . . .
Dawson, John	c. 1767	. . . .
[DeRemier, Peter] *add*	. . . .	PDR (in flat oval)
Duyckinck, D.	c. 1790	D. DUYCKINCK (in rectangle)
Ensign	post 1800	ENSIGN (in rectangle, with pseudo hall-marks)
Eoff & Conner	c. 1833	. . . .
Eoff & Phyfe	c. 1850	E & P (shaded, in rectangle)
[Fielding, George] *add*	. . . .	G F (in oval)?
Forbes, B. G.	c. 1833	. . . .
[Forbes, G.] *add*	. . . .	G. FORBES (shade in rectangle)
Forbes, W.	c. 1839	W. FORBES (in rectangle)
[Fourniquet, Lewis] *add*	. . . .	Fourniquet (italics, in cartouche)
Furer	c. 1759	. . . .
[Gale, John] *add*	. . . .	J. GALE (in rectangle)
[Gale, William] *add*	. . . .	W . G (with pseudo hall-marks)
Gale, William & Son	c. 1850	W. G. & S. *or* G & S (with pseudo hall-marks)
Gale & Hayden	c. 1848	G & H (with pseudo hall-marks)
Gale, Wood & Hughes	c. 1833	G . W & H (between a head and eagle, in circles)

[Gardiner, B.] *add*	c. 1829	B. GARDINER and NEW YORK (on curved band, with pseudo hall-marks)
Gelston, G. S.	c. 1833	....
Gelston & Co.	c. 1836	....
[Gilbert, William] *add*	....	W. Gilbert (semi-script in rectangle); W G (in rectangle)
Gilbert & Cunningham	c. 1839	....
Guide, Thomas	1751–c. 1774	....
[Gordon, Andrew] *add*	....	GORDON (shaded, in serrated rectangle)
Gurnee, B. & S.	c. 1833	....
[Hammersley, Thomas] *add*	....	TH (script, in oval)
Hamill, J.	c. 1810	J. HAMILL, N. Y. (in rectangle)
Harmon, Reuben	c. 1787	....
Hays & Myers	c. 1765	H & M (shaded, in rectangle)
[Heath, John] *add*	....	I · HEATH (in flat oval)
Hebberd, H.	1847	....
Heming, Thomas (N. Y. ?)	c. 1764	....
[Hendrickse, Ahasuerus] *correction*	....	A–I (in oval)
[Heyer, W. B.] *add*	1827	....
Hinsdale, H.	c. 1831	....
[Huertin, or Heurtin, William] *add*	....	W H (in rectangle)
Hutt, John	c. 1774	....
Hyde & Nevins	c. 1798	Hyde & Nevins (shaded, in rectangle)
[Jackson, John] *add*	1632–1736	IACKSON (crude, in rectangle)
Jacobs, A.	c. 1800	Name in capitals, in rectangle; name in capitals incised
[Johnson, Samuel] *add*	....	S · J (?) (crude, in rectangle, with pellet)
Lamb, Anthony	c. 1760	....
Lamb, John	c. 1756	....
[Le Roux, Bartholomew] *correction*	d. 1713	....
Lockwood, F.	1845	....
[Lyng, John Burt] *add*	....	J L (in rectangle, with pellet)
Marquand, Frederick	c. 1800	F. MARQUAND (in rectangle, with pseudo hall-marks)
Marquand & Co.	c. 1820–1840	Firm name, with pseudo hall-marks
Maverick, D.	....	D MV (shaded, in cartouche) ?
Moore, E. C.	c. 1850	....
Moore, J. C.	c. 1836	....

Moore & Brown	c. 1833	....
Mott, John	1789	J. MOTT (in flat oval)
Murray, John	c. 1776	....
[Myers, Myer] *correct*		
and *add*	....	Myers (shaded italics, in rectangle; also, shaded script in cartouche); M.M (small shaded script in oval); M M (crude, in cartouche)
Parisien, David	w. 1789–1817	....
[Parisien, O. & Son] *add*	....	OPDP (in rectangle)
Polhamus, J.	c. 1839	....
[Poutran, Abraham]		
correction	....	A P (shaded, in heart, emblem below)
Pursell, Henry	c. 1775	....
[Quintard, Peter]		
correction	1699–1762	....
[Richard, S.] *add*	....	S. RICHARD (in rectangle); RICHARD (in rectangle)
[Riker, P.] *add*	....	P. RIKER
[Robert, Christopher] *add*	....	C R (in circle or oval)
Rollinson, William	1762–1842	....
[Roosevelt, Nicholas]		
correction	....	N · R (monogram, in oval, with pellet between N and R); VR (in monogram, in wedge)
Salisbury & Co.	c. 1835	Name in rectangle
Savage, Edward	1761–1817	....
Sawyer, H. L.	c. 1840	H. L. SAWYER (in rectangle)
[Schanck, J. (Schenck)]		
add	....	J. SCHANCK (shaded, in rectangle, with spread eagle and false date letter); SCHANCK (shaded in rectangle)
[Sexnine, Simon] *add*	....	S S (crude, in square)?
[Skinner, Abraham] *add*	....	Skinner (crude, in rectangle)
Squire & Bros.	c. 1846	....
Stebbins, E. & Co.	c. 1841	E. STEBBINS & CO. (in rectangle)
[Stephens, George] *add*	....	G . S (in cartouche with serrated ends)
[Stoutenburgh, Tobias] *add*	....	T. S. (in rectangle)
[Ten Eyck, Koenract]		
correction	....	K E (crude, monogram in square)
Thomson, James	c. 1839	....
[Thomson, William] *add*	....	Wm. Thomson (script, in shaped rectangle)

362   SUPPLEMENT

Tiebout, Cornelius	1770–1830	....
[Underhill, Thomas] *add*	....	T–U (shaded, with hyphen, in rectangle)
[Underhill & Vernon] *add*	....	T–U (in rectangle) and I–V (in cartouche)
[Van Beuren, P.] *add*	....	V B (shaded, in oval with decorated top)
[Van Beuren, Wm.] *add*	....	W. V. B. (shaded, in cartouche)
[Van Der Spiegel, Johannes] *correction*	....	I V S (shaded, in engrailed rectangle)
Van Ness & Waterman, N. Y.?	....	V & W (in rectangle)
[Van Voorhis & Son] *add*	....	V. V. & S (shaded, in rectangle)
[Vernon, John] *add*	....	I · V (shaded, in cartouche) ; I V (shaded, in oval, with sheaf of wheat [?] in rectangle)
[Wenman, Bernard] *add*	....	B WENMAN (shaded, in rectangle)
Wood, Benjamin, N. Y. (?)	1794	B. WOOD (with pseudo hall-marks)
Wood, J. E.	c. 1845	....
Wood & Hughes	w. 1845	W & H (in rectangle, with W eagle and head) ; & (in H lozenge, with eagle and head)
[Woods, Freeman] *add*	....	Woods (script in cartouche)
[Wynkoop, Cornelius] *add*	....	W K }(crude, in heart) C

PHILADELPHIA:

Adams, Dunlap	1764	....
Adams, Henry B.	1848	....
Adams, Jonathan	1783	....
Aitken, William	1825	....
[Alexander, Samuel] *add*	....	S. ALEXANDER (small, in rectangle)
Allen, John	1814	....
Allen, Richard	1816	....
Andrews, Abraham	1795	....
[Anthony, Joseph] *add*	....	J A (small, in rectangle); J A (small, in double circle)
[Anthony, Joseph & Son] *add*	....	J . A }(one above the other & } in square, pellet be-I . A } tween initials)
Anthony, Michael H.	1814	....
Anthony, Michael and Thomas	1816	....

Armstrong, Allen	1814	Name and Philadelphia in separate rectangles, Roman letters
Atkinson, Isaac	1825–1833	....
Atlee, Charles	1837	....
Austen, David	1837	....
Bailey & Kitchen	1846	....
[Ball, William] *add*	....	WILLIAM BALL (in rectangle); BALL (very small, in rectangle); W. B. (crude capitals in rectangle); W. Ball (in shaped rectangle)
Barbier, P.	1823	....
Bard, Conrad	1825	....
Bardick, John	1805	....
Bardur, Connard	1830	....
Bard & Lamont	1841	....
Bard & Hoffman	1837	....
Barrington & Davenport	1806	....
Bartholomew, Joseph	1833	....
Bayly, John	1793	....
Beam, Jacob	1821	....
Beam, Jacob C.	1818	....
Bean, Jacob	1819	....
Belin, Lewis	1818	....
Bentson (Bentzon), Peter	1817	....
Berard, Andrew	1797	....
Berselievre, Thomas	1829	....
Best, Joseph	1723	....
Binneau, Theodore	1820	....
Black, James	1795	....
[Black, John] *add*	....	J · B (in rectangle, pellet between)
Bond, C. & Son	1850	....
Boone, Jeremiah	1791	....
[Boudinot, Elias] *add*	1706–1770	BOUDINOT (in shaped rectangle); E B (in rectangle)
Boullieu, ——	1811	....
Bouwer, C.	1828	....
Bray, Henry	1799–1813	....
Britton, Isaac	1811	....
Britton, Jacob	1807	....
Brown, D.	c. 1811	D. BROWN (shaded, in rectangle)
Brown, Henry	1777	....
Brown, James	1785	....
Brown, Jesse	1813	....
[Brown, John] *add*	....	J · B (in rectangle, with pellet between) ?
Browne, Liberty	1801	....
Browne & Seal	c. 1819	Firm name in capitals, on scroll with PHILAD'a in rectangle

Bryan, Philip	1802	....
Buckley, J. B	1807	....
Buddy, Daniel	1769	....
Bumm, Peter	1814–1833	....
Burdock, George	1791	....
[Burdock, Nicholas] *add*	....	N · B (in rectangle, with pellet between letters)
Burns, Anthony	1795	....
Burrows, William	1829–1837	....
Burton, Jacob	1839	....
Butler, Henry	1837–1845	....
Butler & McCarthy	c. 1850	....
Carlisle, Abraham	1791	A Carlile (script, in rectangle)
Carnan, John	1771	....
Chadwick, Thomas	1809	....
Chat, Claudius	1793–1798	....
Chaudron's & Rasch, Philadelphia?	c. 1820	CHAUDRON'S & RASCH (shaded, in scroll)
Cherry, James	1824	....
Childs, George K.	c. 1837	....
Chittery, Peter	1814	....
Churchwell, Charles	adv. 1781	....
Clark, Henry	d. 1813–1814	....
Cline, Charles	d. 1824–1837	....
Cole, Jacob	d. 1785	....
Connell, M., Philadelphia (?)	c. 1800	M: CONNELL (shaded, in rectangle)
Conning, J., Philadelphia (?)	c. 1800	J. CONNING (in rectangle)
Cooper	d. 1816	....
Cornelius, Christian	d. 1810–1819	....
Corrin, Josiah	d. 1823–1824	....
Cowen, William D.	d. 1811–1814	....
Cox, John,	d. 1818	....
Crawford, John	d. 1837	....
Currin, Joseph	d. 1829–1833	....
Curry, John	c. 1831	....
[Curry & Preston] *add*	....	CURRY & PRESTON (in serrated rectangle)
Dallon, John	d. 1791	....
Dauce, Simon	d. 1798–1809	....
Daubayson, Victoire	d. 1820–1822	....
[David, John] *add*	....	I D (crude, in oval); I David (in long oval); I David (Roman, in rectangle)
David, Lewis A.	c. 1837	....
Dawkins, Henry	c. 1754–1776	....
Dawson, William	d. 1793	....
Deas, David	d. 1829–1833	....
Delagrow, Andrew	d. 1795	....

Descuret, Lewis	d. 1799–1801	....
Dobleman, Fredrick	d. 1813–1818	....
Donovan	adv. 1784–1785	....
Dontremei, G	d. 1805	....
Dorgy, Peter	d. 1816–1817	....
[Dorsey, Joshua] *add*	....	I · DORSEY (shaded, in rectangle, with pellet)
Dorsey, Samuel	d. 1804	....
Dorsey, Simon	d. 1820–1822	....
Douglass, Jeremott Wm.	d. 1791–1793	....
Doutiemer, Gille	d. 1791	....
[Dowig, George] *add*	....	G D? (in oval)
Downes, J.	c. 1770	J. Downes (in shaped rectangle)
Drewrey, George	adv. 1763	....
[Dubois, A.] *add*	....	A DUBOIS (in rectangle); A D (capitals in oval)
Duche & Donnand	d. 1820–1822	....
Duffield, Edward	c. 1756	....
[Dumoutet, I. B.] *add*	....	DUMOUTET (in scroll)
Dumourier, Joseph	d. 1814–1816	....
Eaton, Timothy	d. 1793–1794	....
Ellis, Lewis W.	d. 1837	....
Erwin, Henry	d. 1817–1829	H. Erwin (in engraved rectangle)
Faber, William	c. 1831	....
Faber & Hoover	c. 1837	....
Fairman, Gideon	1774–1827	....
Ferguson, John	d. 1803–1810	....
Fisher, Thomas	d. 1797	....
[Fletcher, Thomas] *add*	....	T. FLETCHER and PHILAD. (in rectangles)
Fletcher & Bennett	d. 1837–1839	....
[Fletcher & Gardiner] *add*	....	F & G (in rectangle)
Fortune, Anthony	adv. 1767	....
Foster, Abraham	d. 1816	....
Foster, Hiram	d. 1817–1818	....
Franks, Jacob	d. 1785–1794	....
Garren, Anthony	d. 1811–1814	....
[Garret, P. (Garrett)] *add*	....	P. GARRETT (in rectangle)
Geley	d. 1793–1814	....
Gero, Francis	d. 1818	....
Gethen, John	d. 1811–1818	....
Gethen, William	d. 1797–1798	....
Girard, Frances	d. 1817	....
Girreaun, Stephen	d. 1785	....
Goforth, Jeremiah	1700	....
Gomback, John	d. 1802	....
Govett, James	d. 1805–1813	....
Griscom, George	d. 1791	....
[Hall, David] *add*	....	D H (in shaped rectangle); D. Hall (in rectangle)
[Halsted, Benjamin] *add*	1764–1783	....
Harper, Alexander	d. 1819	....

Harper, David	adv. 1755–1756	....
Harper, Thomas W.	d. 1813–1817	....
Hart, William	d. 1818–1824	....
Hartford, George	d. 1794	....
Hartley, Samuel	d. 1818–1819	....
Hartman, Philip	d. 1813–1814	....
Harwood, John	d. 1816–1821	....
Haverstick, Wm.	d. 1791–1793	....
Head, Joseph	d. 1798	....
Hemphill, Alexander	1741	....
Herbert, Lawrence	w. 1748	....
Herils, Francis	d. 1804–1833	....
Hiams, Moses	b. 1751 w. 1775	....
Hilton, William	d. 1814	....
Hollingshead, John	adv. 1768	....
Holton, John	d. 1794	....
Hopper, Samuel	d. 1835	....
Howard, John	d. 1819–1822	....
[Howell, James] *add*	....	J. Howell (semi-script in shaped rectangle); J. Howell and Co. (script, in shaped rectangle); Howell (script, in shaped rectangle)
Hulbeart, Philip	adv. 1761–1763	....
[Humphreys, Richard] *add*	....	(Script in shaped oval); |R.H.|—(capitals in rectangle); R H (script, in cartouche); R. Humphreys (script, in cartouche)
Hunlock, Baumann	1752	....
Inman, Benjamin	d. 1814–1819	....
Jacobs, Moses	b. 1753 w. 1775	....
Jones, James	d. 1815	....
Jones, John	d. 1768	....
Joubert, Peter	d. 1807–1830	....
Jourdon	d. 1823–1824	....
Kennedy, Nathan	d. 1825	....
Kline, B. & Co.	w. 1837	....
Krider, P. L.	w. 1850	P. L. K.
Kucher, Jacob	d. 1806–1817	....
[Lamar, Mathias] *add*	....	ML (monogram in rectangle)?
Lamesiere, Peter	1811	....
Langer, Joseph	d. 1811	....
Lawrence, Josiah	d. 1817	....
Lawrie, Robert D.	w. 1841	....
Leach, Samuel	w. 1741	....
[Leacock, John] *add*	....	I · L (emblem above, pellet between, in cartouche); I L (in small oval)
Le Blanc, Lewis	d. 1818	....
Le Dorc	d. 1797	....
Lefevre, F.	d. 1818	....

Lefevre, J. F	d. 1806–1813	. . . .
Lefevre & Gravelle	d. 1811	. . . .
Lemaire, Baptiste	d. 1804	. . . .
Lemaire, Benjamin	d. 1785	B L (Roman capitals, in oval)
Le Merre, Matthew	1781	. . . .
Lent, John	w. 1751	
[Letelier, John] *add*	. . . .	I · L T (shaded, with pellet, in rectangle); LeTeLier (Roman, in rectangle)
Levis, William	d. 1810–1814	. . . .
[Lewis, Harvey] *add*	. . . .	H. Lewis (in rectangle); H. Lewis (script, in shaped rectangle); Harvey Lewis (Roman, in rectangle)
[Lewis and Smith] *add*	. . . .	Lewis and Smith (script, in shaped rectangle)
Link, Peter	1817–1822	. . . .
Lofland, Purnel	d. 1825	. . . .
Logan, James	adv. 1764	. . . .
Long, William	d. 1807–1822	. . . .
Lord, Joseph	adv. d. 1795	. . . .
[Lownes, Edward] *add*	. . . .	E. LOWNES (in rectangle)
[Lownes, Joseph] *add*	. . . .	J. Lownes (script in regular shaped oval); J. Lownes (script, in shaped rectangle); J. Lownes (in shaped rectangle, with eagle displayed, preceding and following maker's mark)
[Lyng, John] *add*	. . . .	I · L (in rectangle, pellet between letters)
Lyng, Philip	d. 1785 adv. 1778	. . . .
McConnel, Hugh	d. 1811–1813	. . . .
McConnelly, H.	d. 1811	. . . .
McCrea, Robert	d. 1785	. . . .
McDonough, John	1775	. . . .
McFee & Reeder	d. 1793–1796	. . . .
McFee, M.	adv. 1769	. . . .
McMahon, John	d. 1803–1804	. . . .
McMaster, John	d. 1805	. . . .
McMullen, James	d. 1814	. . . .
[McMullin, J.] *add*	w. 1765–1843	I. McMullin (italics, in rectangle; *sometimes* with eagle, in shaped shield)
McMullin and Black	1811–1813	McMullin and Black (in long rectangle)
McPherson, Robert	d. 1828–1841	. . . .
Mansfield, Thomas	d. 1804	. . . .
Marcelou, Isaac	adv. 1735	. . . .
Matlack, William	d. 1828–1833	. . . .
Meyrick, Richard	w. 1729	. . . .
Millard, George	d. 1816	. . . .

Miller & Sons	d. 1833–1835	....
Millondon, Phillipe	d. 1811	....
Mills, Edmund	d. 1785	....
Mills, Edward	d. 1794	....
Mills, John	d. 1811–1819	....
[Milne, Edmund] *add*	....	E M (Roman capitals, in shaped rectangle) ; E. M. (in oval)
Moore, Charles	d. 1803–1804	....
Moore, J. L.	c. 1810	J. L. MOORE (shaded in rectangle)
Moore, Thomas	d. 1805	....
Moore & Ferguson	d. 1801–1805	....
Morin, John	d. 1808–1831	....
Mormagea, Michael	d. 1817	....
Morrison, Israel	d. 1823–1824	....
Murdoch, John	d. 1785	I. M. (in rectangle; three points directed toward middle of rectangle)
[Musgrave, James] *add*	1797–1811	Musgrave (italics, in shaped rectangle) ; Musgrave (script, in rectangle)
[Myers, John] *add*	....	I · MYERS (shaded, initials larger, in rectangle) ; Myers (script, in shaped rectangle)
Naglee, John	1748–1755	....
Neuss, Jan	1698–d. 1719	....
Nixon, Richard	d. 1820–1835	....
Norman, John	1748–1817	....
Norris, George	b. 1752 w. 1775	....
Norris, George	adv. 1776	....
Owen, Jesse	d. 1794	....
Owen, John	d. 1804–1831	....
Pancoast, Samuel	d. 1785–1794	....
Parasel, William	d. 1811	....
Parham, William	d. 1785–1791	....
Parker, Charles H.	1793–1819	....
Parker, Richard	d. 1785	....
Parry, Rowland	d. 1795–1797	....
Parry and Musgrave	d. 1793–1796	....
Paschall, William	d. 1696	....
Patton, Thomas	d. 1824	....
Paxson, John A.	d. 1810–1811	....
Peale, Charles Willson	1741–1827	....
Peck, Lawrence M.	d. 1837	....
Pedosy, S.	d. 1810	....
Perpignan, Peter	d. 1809–1825	....
Perpignan, S. & Varnier	d. 1800–1801	....
Perraux, Peter	d. 1797	....
[Perraux, Peter] *add*	....	P R (in rectangle)
Pervi, Joseph	d. 1811	....
Peters	d. 1813	....

Peters, James	d. 1821–1856	....
Peters, R.	d. 1807–1809	....
Peterson, Henry	w. 1783	H. P. (in square, with pseudo hall-marks) ?
Philip Ranard Guyeon & Yver	d. 1796	....
Pickering, Charles	1683–d. 1749	....
Pinchon, William	d. 1785–1802	....
Pitkin, J. O. & W.	w. 1811–1831	J. O. & W. PITKIN (in rectangle)
Pitts, Richard	adv. 1741–1745	....
Poincy, Peter	d. 1813–1814	....
Pointe & Tanguay	d. 1811	....
Poessenot, N. J.	d. 1806	....
[Poupard, James] add	–1814	....
Pratt	b. 1709 d. 1749	....
Rasch, A. & Co.	c. 1815	Firm name and city, in capitals, in rectangles
Ravee, Xavier	d. 1796–1797	....
Reed, Osmon	w. 1843	....
Reynolds, Theodore	d. 1830–1833	....
[Richards, Samuel] add	....	S. Richards (script, in shaped rectangle); S R (in rectangle)
Richardson, Francis	1681–1729	F R (crude Roman capitals in heart)
[Richardson, Joseph] add	w. 1730 d. 1770	I R (crude, in oval); I R (crude, in rectangle); I R (in square); J R (in square or in oval)
Richardson, Joseph & Nathaniel	1780–1790	I : NR (in rectangle)
[Riggs] add	....	Riggs (unshaded italics, in cartouche)
Roberts, Thomas	b. 1744 w. 1774	....
Robertson, Alexander	d. 1751	....
Robinson, Benjamin	d. 1818–1844	....
Robinson & Harwood	d. 1819–1822	....
Russell, George	w. 1831	....
Saint-Martin, Anthony	d. 1794–1796	....
Saint-Maurice, James	adv. 1748	....
Savage, Edward	1761–1817	....
Schaffield, Jeremiah	d. 1785	....
Scott, John B.	c. 1850	Name incised, pseudo hall-marks
Segn, George	d. 1820–1822	....
Sénémand, John B.	d. 1798–1800	....
Sharp, W. & G.	w. 1850	....
Shaw, Edward G.	d. 1825–1830	....
[Shields, Thomas] add	....	T S (?) (in rectangle)
Shiviny	adv. 1779	....
[Shoemaker, Joseph] add	....	J. SHOEMAKER (Roman, in rectangle)

24

[Simmons, Anthony] *add*	....	A. S. (pellet between and after, in oval); A SIM-MONS (shaded, in rectangle)
Simmons, J.	c. 1810	J. Simmons (script, in rectangle)
Simmons, J. & A.	c. 1810	J. & A. S. (in rectangle)
Simmons, S.	c. 1797	S. SIMMONS
Smith, Christian	d. 1820–1822	....
Smith, Jacob	d. 1809–1822	....
Smith, James	d. 1807–1808	....
Smith, John	d. 1819–1822	....
Smith, Joseph	d. 1804–1810	....
Smith, Robert	d. 1820–1831	....
Smith, William	d. 1837	....
Smither, James	w. 1768–1777	....
Snyder, George	d. 1816–1818	....
Sonnier, Joseph	d. 1818	....
[Soumaine, Samuel] *add*	....	SS (?) (small, in rectangle)
Sowerlt, Anthony	d. 1811	....
Sowerwall, Anthony	d. 1823–1824	....
Sparrow, Henry	d. 1811	....
Stedman, Alexander	d. 1793–1814	....
Stillman, Alexander	d. 1806	....
Stockerman & Pepper	c. 1840	Firm name in oval
Strong, William	d. 1807–1811	....
Stuckert, Isaac	d. 1809	....
Supplee, Jacob	d. 1791	....
Swan, Robert	1739–1791	R. Swan (in rectangle)
Swan, Robert	d. 1799–1831	
Tanguay, John	1801–1822	I. Tanguay (in rectangle); I. T. (in rectangle)
Taylor & Lawrie	w. 1841	....
Towson, Obadiah	d. 1819–1824	....
Trall, William	d. 1810–1811	....
[Turner, James] *add*	w. 1744 d. 1759	I T (?) (small, in rectangle)
Ubelin, Frederick	adv. 1773	
Vanhorn, David	d. 1801	....
Waglin, Thomas	d. 1818–1819	....
[Walker, William] *add*	....	W. WALKER (in rectangle)
Walton, Daniel	d. 1816–1817	....
Ward, Jehu	1808–1848	J. Ward (in rectangle)
[Warner, Joseph] *add*	....	J. Warner (Roman, in rectangle)
Watts, J. & W.	w. 1841	....
West, Joseph	adv. 1776	....
Westphall, Charles	d. 1801	....
Westphall, Charles William	d. 1802–1822	....
Whartenby, John	w. 1831	
Whartenby, Thomas & Co.	w. 1850	....
White, Alfred	d. 1807–1809	....
White, William	d. 1805–1806	....

[Williamson, Samuel] *add*	....	WILLIAMSON (small, shaded, in rectangle)
Wilson, R. & W.	w. 1831	R & W W (in rectangle)
Wilson, William	w. 1850	....
Wriggins, Thomas	w. 1841	....

MASSACHUSETTS, outside of Boston:

Anthony, Isaac	1690–1773	Swansea
[Austin, Josiah] *add*	....	L. Austin (crude, in rectangle)
[Bailey, Loring] *add*	....	L B (?) (shaded, Roman, in rectangle)
[Barrett, S.] *add*	....	S. BARRETT (in rectangle)
Bassett, Francis	1678–1715	Charlestown
[Bradbury, Theophilus] *add*	....	Surname, Roman capitals (in rectangle)
Brahmhall, S.	c. 1800	Plymouth (?) S. BRAM-HALL (shaded, in rectangle)
Brookhouse, Robert	1779–1866	Salem. R B (intertwined script, in oval)
Bussey, Benjamin	1757–1842	Deham
[Cleveland, William] *add*	....	Cleveland (Roman, in rectangle); W C (Roman, in rectangle)
Easten, J. 2nd	w. 1847	Nantucket. J. Easten, 2d and Nantucket Pure Coin (in rectangles)
Easton & Sanford	w. 1837	Nantucket. Easton & Sanford (in rectangle)
[Farley, Charles] *add*	....	C. FARLEY (shaded, Roman, in rectangle, spread eagle in oval at each end); FARLEY (shaded, Roman, in rectangle, with spread eagles in ovals)
[Greenleaf, David] *add*	1737–1800	Bolton. D. Greenleaf (Roman, in rectangle)
[Harding, Newell] *add*	....	N. Harding (small italics in scroll); N. HARDING (very small, unshaded, in rectangle)
Higgins, Abraham	1738–1763	....
Hiller, Joseph	1748–1814	....
Jones, William	1694–1730	Marblehead. W : I (crude, in rectangle)
Kettel, Thomas	w. 1784	Charlestown. T · K (?) (pellet between)
Lakeman, E. K.	c. 1830	Salem. E. K. LAKEMAN (small, shaded, in rectangle)
Lang, Edward	1742–1830	Salem. LANG (in rectangle); E L (in rectangle)

Lang, Jeffrey	1707–1758	I · LANG (small, shaded, in long oval) ; LANG (small, shaded, in long oval)
Lang, Richard,	1733–1820	Salem. R · LANG (in rectangle)
Loring, Eliphalet	b. 1740 w. 1764	Barnstable. E : Loring (large, shaded italics, in cartouche)
[Loring, Joseph] *correction*	....	J. Loring (small, shaded italics, in cartouche) ; same in rectangle ; J · L (small, shaded, with pellet, in rectangle) ; J. Loring (italics in shaped rectangle)
[Moulton, Abel] *add*	....	A. MOULTON (shaded, Roman, in rectangle)
[Moulton, Joseph, 3rd] *add*	....	J. MOULTON (shaded, Roman, in rectangle) ; J. MOULTON (very small, Roman, incised)
[Moulton, William, 1st] ? *correction*	b. 1602 c. 1638	....
[Moulton, William, 2nd] *correction*	b. 1640	....
[Moulton, William, 3rd] *correction*	b. 1710	....
[Moulton, William, 4th] *correction*	1720–1793	....
[Moulton, William, 5th] *correction*	1772–1861	W. MOULTON (shaded, Roman, in rectangle) ; MOULTON (shaded, Roman, in rectangle) ; MOULTON (shaded, Roman, incised)
Moulton & Bradbury	c. 1830	Newburyport. MOULTON (small, shaded, in rectangle) with B (in square) and two pseudo hall-marks
Moulton & Lunt	late 19th Cent.	Newburyport
Munroe, D.	....	Barnstable? D. MUNROE (in serrated rectangle)
[Munroe, John] *correction*	1784–1879	....
Newman, Timothy H.	1778–1812	Groton. Newman (fine script, in rectangle)
Northee, David L.	d. 1778	Salem. D. L. NORTHEE (shaded, Roman, in rectangle) ; D N (crude, shaded, in rectangle)
[Osgood, John] *correction*	w. 1795–1817	Haverhill. J: OSGOOD (in rectangle)
Parker, Charles H.	1793–1819	Salem
[Parker, Isaac] *add*	....	I · PARKER (shaded, Roman, in rectangle)

Phelps, Jedediah   w. 1781   Great Barrington

[Phillips, Samuel] *add*   ....   S P (?) (crude, in rectangle)

[Pierpont, Benjamin] *add*   ....   B P (Roman, in oval)

[Putnam, Edward] *add*   ....   E · P (?) (crude, in rectangle, pellet between)

Russell, Moody   1694–1761   Barnstable. M R (small, Roman, in rectangle); M R (large, Roman, in shaped shield)

Sanborn, A.   w. 1850   Lowell. Name in scroll, with city in rectangle

Sanford, F. S.   w. 1830   Nantucket

[Stevens & Lakeman] *add*   ....   STEVENS & LAKEMAN (small, Roman, in rectangle)

[Stickney, Jonathan] *add*   ....   I · STICKNEY (crude, shaded, in rectangle; occasionally flanked by lions passant, in rectangles)

Stowell, A., Jr.   Charlestown. Name in capitals, in rectangle; town in small letters in long oval

[Swan, William] *add*   Worcester. W SWAN (crude, in cartouche); Swan (script, in cartouche); W S (?) (in cartouche)

Terry, Geer   1775–1858   Worcester. G. TERRY (Roman, in rectangle); TERRY (Roman, in rectangle)

Thaxter, Joseph Blake   1791–1863   Hingham

[Titcomb, Francis] *add*   ....   F. TITCOMB (small, shaded, Roman, in rectangle)

Toppan, Benjamin   c. 1760   Northampton

[Touzell or Towzell, John] *add*   ....   J. Towzell and I T

Warner, Caleb   1784–1861   Salem. C. Warner (Roman, in rectangle); Pure Silver Coin (Roman, in shaped rectangle)

Warner, D.   c. 1810   Ipswich (?). D. WARNER (small, Roman, in scalloped rectangle)

Wyer, Eleazer   1752–1800   Charlestown

CONNECTICUT AND RHODE ISLAND:

Anthony, Isaac   1690–1773   Newport (also Swansea, Mass.)

[Arnold, Thomas] *add*   1739–1828   T. ARNOLD (small, shaded, Roman, in rectangle)

Austin, Ebenezer	b. 1733 w. 1818	Hartford. Austin (shaded, Roman, in rectangle); E : A (shaded, in rectangle, pellet between)
[Avery, John] *add*	....	I AVERY (shaded, Roman, in rectangle); I A (shaded, in rectangle)
Avery, John, Jr.	1755–1815	Preston
Avery, Samuel	1760–1836	Preston
Avery, William	1765–1798	Preston
Babcock, Samuel	1788–1857	Middletown and Saybrook
Baker, George	w. 1825	Providence. G. BAKER (Roman, in rectangle)
Balch, Ebenezer	1723–1808	Hartford and Wethersfield. E. BALCH (in rectangle)
Barker & Mumford	c. 1825	Newport. BARKER & MUMFORD (in cartouche)
Barrett, James	c. 1800	Norwich. J B (?) (script capitals, in rectangle)
Barrows, James M.	b. 1809 w. 1832	Tolland, Conn.
Beach, Isaac	w. 1788	New Milford
[Beach, Miles] *add*	....	BEACH (shaded, Roman, in rectangle); M B (shaded, Roman, in oval)
[Benjamin, Barzillai] *add*	....	B. BENJAMIN (Roman, in rectangle); B B (in rectangle)
Benjamin, Everard	1807–1874	New Haven
[Billings, Daniel] *add*	....	D. Billings (script, in oval)
Blackman, John Starr	1777–1851	Danbury
Blakeslee, William	1795–1879	Newton
Blakeslee, Feba	1768–1825	Newton
[Bontecon, Timothy] *add*	....	T. B. (letters incised)
[Bontecon, Timothy, Jr.] *add*	....	T B (shaded, Roman, in oval)
Bradbury, Capt. Phineas	w. 1779	New Haven
Bradford, Charles H.	....	Westerly (?)
[Bradley, Abner] *correction*	....	Abner, New Haven. A. BRADLEY (shaded, Roman, in rectangle, flanked by quadranted circles)
[Bradley, Phineas] *add*	....	P B (Roman, in rectangle)
[Bradley, Richard] *add*	1787–1867	Hartford
Bradley & Merriman	w. 1826	New Haven. B & M (Roman, in rectangle, emblem above)
Brenton, Benjamin	b. 1710	Newport. B B (small, Roman, crude, in oval)
[Brewer, Charles] *correction*	1778–1860	C. Brewer (script, in shaped rectangle); C. BREWER (shaded, Roman, in rectangle)
Babe, Stanton	c. 1805	Providence (?)

[Buel, Abel] *add*	....	BUEL (shaded, Roman, in serrated rectangle); A B (shaded, Roman, in rayed oval)
Buel & Mix	w. 1783	New Haven
Buell, Samuel	w. 1777	Middletown and Hartford. S · B (shaded, Roman, in rectangle, pellet between)
[Burdick, William S.] *add*	w. 1814	....
[Burr, Ezekiel] *add*	....	E · BURR (crude, in long oval); E B (script in double octagon); E B (Roman, in rectangle)
Candee, Lewis Burton	1806–1861	Woodbury, Conn.
Canfield & Foot	w. 1795	Middletown
[Carpenter, Joseph] *add*	....	I C (?) (shaded, Roman, in rectangle)
Carrington, Daniel Noble	w. 1793	Danbury, Conn.
[Casey, Samuel] *add*	....	S: CASEY (Roman, in long oval)
[Chittenden, Ebenezer] *add*	....	E. CHITTENDEN (Roman, in rectangle); E C (in rectangle)
[Clark, George C.] *add*	....	G. C. CLARK (large, Roman, in rectangle)
[Clark, Joseph] *add*	....	J C (Roman, in rectangle)
Clark, Levi	1801–1875	Norwalk
[Clark, William] *add*	...	W C (Roman, in rectangle)
[Clarke, J.] *add* Jonathan	....	J. Clarke (script, in long oval); I C (large, crude, in rectangle); J. CLARKE (shaded, Roman, in rectangle)
Cleveland, Aaron	w. 1820	Norwich. A C (in elongated octagon)
[Cleveland, William] *add*	....	Cleveland (Roman, in rectangle); W C (Roman, in rectangle)
Cleveland & Post	c. 1799	New London (?). C. & P (Roman, in rectangle)
Coddington, John	1690–1743	Newport. I C (crude, in leaf or flower-shaped emblem)
Coit, Thomas C.	1791–1841	Norwich
[Collins, Arnold] *add*	d. 1735	A C (in heart)
Connor, J. H.	....	Norwalk. J. H. CONNOR (Roman, in rectangle)
Cornell, Walter	c. 1800	Providence (?). CORNELL (shaded, Roman, in serrated rectangle)
Cranston, Samuel	1659–1727	Newport
Curtis, Joel	b. 1786	Wolcott, Conn.
[Curtis, Lewis] *add*	....	L. CURTIS (Roman, in rectangle)
Curtiss, Daniel	1801–1878	Woodbury, Conn.
Cutler, Richard, Jr.	1774–1811	New Haven

Cutler, William	1785–1817	New Haven
Cutler, Silliman, Ward & Co.	w. 1767	New Haven
Dexter, Minerva	b. 1785	Middletown
Dickinson, Anson	c. 1800	Litchfield, Conn.
Doane, Joshua	d. 1753	Providence. DOANE (Roman, in cartouche)
[Dodge, Nehemiah] *add*	....	N. DODGE (thin, crude, in serrated rectangle)
[Doolittle, Amos] *add*	....	A D (thin, Roman, in oval)
[Douglas, Robert] *add*	1740–1776	R D (monogram, in shield); R D (monogram, in wedge)
Eddy & Barrows	w. 1832	Tollard, Conn.
[Fairchild, Robert] *add*	....	R · FAIRCHILD (Roman in rectangle); R×F (Roman, x between, in cartouche)
Fairman, Gideon	1774–1827	New London
Fellows	c. 1800	Newport (?). FELLOWS (Roman, in long oval)
Francis, Julius C.	1785–1862	Middletown
[Gardner, John] *add*	....	I G (in rectangle)
Geffroy, Nicholas	1761–1839	Newport. N GEFFROY (Roman, in scalloped rectangle); GEFFROY (Roman, in scalloped rectangle)
[Gibbs, John] *correction*	d. 1797	....
[Gilbert, Samuel] *add*	....	S G (in rectangle)
Goodwin, Allyn	1797–1869	Hartford
Gorham, J. & Son	w. 1841	Providence
Gorham, John	w. 1814	New Haven
[Gorham, Miles] *add*	....	M.G (in rectangle); M. GORHAM (in rectangle)
Gorham, Richard	1775–1841	New Haven
Gorham & Webster	w. 1831	Providence. Script name, in rectangle or in scroll
[Gray, John] *add*	....	I . G (?) (in rectangle)
[Gray, Samuel] *add*	....	S: GRAY (Roman, in rectangle); GRAY (?) (Roman, in rectangle)
[Greenleaf, David] *add*	....	D. Greenleaf (Roman, in rectangle)
Greenleaf, David, Jr.	1765–1835	Hartford. GREENLEAF (shaded, Roman, in scalloped rectangle)
[Grignon, René] *add*	....	R G (crowned, in shield, above a stag *courant*)
Griswold, Gilbert	c. 1810	Middletown, Conn.
Gunn, Enos	b. 1770	Waterbury. E. GUNN (in rectangle)
[Gurley, William] *add*	....	W . G (in rectangle)
Hadwen, William	w. 1813–1820	Providence

[Hancock, John] *add*	....	J · HANCOCK (shaded, Roman, in rectangle)
[Hanks, Benjamin] *correction*	1738–1810	*Add* Litchfield and Ashford, Conn.
[Harland, Thomas] *add*	....	HARLAND (in rectangle or on scroll, flanked by profile and spread eagle)
[Hart, Eliphaz] *add*	....	E. HART (shaded, Roman, in rectangle); E H (shaded, Roman, in rectangle)
[Hart, Judah] *correction* *add*	1777–1824	Middletown and Norwich J. HART (Roman, in rectangle); J. Hart (script, in rectangle)
Hart & Bliss	w. 1803	Middletown
[Hart & Wilcox] *add*	....	H & W (in rectangle) preceded by pointing hand (also in rectangle)
Hayes, W.	c. 1780	Conn. (?). W. Hayes (in rectangle; W H (large, in rectangle)
Hays & Myers	c. 1765	Newport. H & M (shaded, Roman, in rectangle)
Helme	....	South Kingston, R. I. HELME (in wedge, diminishing horizontally)
Heguemburg, Charles, Jr.	1760–1851	New Haven
[Hobart, Joshua] *add*	....	J · HOBART (in rectangle)
Holmes, Israel	1768–1802	Greenwich and Waterbury
Hotchkiss & Schroeder	....	New Haven?. H & S (incised)
Hunter, Daniel	c. 1785	Newport, R. I.
[Huntington, Philip] *add*	....	P H. (in rectangle)
Hyde	c. 1730	Newport. HYDE (in rectangle)
Jarvis, Munson	1742–1825	Stamford. M · J (Roman, in rectangle, pellet between)
Jennings, Jacob	1728–1817	Norwalk
Jennings, Jacob, Jr.	b. 1779	Norwalk
Keeler, Joseph	1786–1824	Norwalk. I K (in rectangle)
[Kinney, Thomas] *add*	....	T K (in rectangle)
[Kippen, George] *add*	....	G . KIPPEN (in rectangle)
Lee, Thomas	1717–1806	Farmington
[Lewis, Isaac] *add*	....	I x LEWIS (in rectangle)
Loud, Asa	1765–1823	Hartford
Main, David	1752–1843	Stonington
[Marble, Simeon] *add*	....	S. MARBLE (in rectangle)
Merriman, Marcus, Jr.	w. 1826	New Haven
[Merriman, Samuel] *add*	....	S. Merriman (in rectangle)
[Merriman & Bradley] *add*	....	M & B (small, in rectangle, with a grapevine above)
Moss, Isaac Nichols	1760–1840	Darby, Conn.

Mygatt, Comfort Starr	1763–1823	Danbury
Mygatt, David	1777–1822	Danbury. D : MYGATT (crude, in serrated rectangle)
Mygatt, Eli	1742–1807	Danbury
North, W. B.	w. 1831	New Britain
North, W. B. & Co.	c. 1820	Firm capitals, in rectangle
[Norton, Thomas] *add*	....	T N (shaded, Roman, in rectangle)
[Oakes, Frederick] *add*	....	OAKES (shaded, Roman, in partly serrated oval)
[Oakes & Spencer] *add*	....	O & S (in rectangle, with pseudo hall-marks)
O'Neil, Charles	w. 1823	New Haven, Conn.
Parker, William	w. 1777	Newport, R. I.
[Parmele, Samuel] *add*	....	S. P. (in rectangle) ; S P. (in oval) ; S. Parmele (vertical script, in rectangle)
[Peabody, John] *add*	....	J. PEABODY (shaded, in rectangle)
Peck, B.	c. 1820	Connecticut (?). B. PECK (in rectangle)
Perkins, Joseph	b. 1749	South Kingston, R. I.
Pitkin, Horace E.	b. 1832	Hartford
Pitkin, Job Q.	w. 1780	Hartford
Pitkin, William L.	b. 1830	Hartford
Pratt, Nathan,	1772–1842	Essex. N. PRATT (shaded, in rectangle)
Pratt, Nathan, Jr.	b. 1802	Essex
Pratt, Seth	1741–1802	Lyme, Conn.
Reed, Isaac	b. 1746	Stamford
Rockwell	c. 1839	Bridgeport, Conn. (?). ROCKWELL (in rectangle)
Rockwell, Thomas	d. 1795	Norwalk
[Rogers, Daniel] *add*		D. Roger (in rectangle)
Rogers, Joseph	d. 1825	Newport, R. I. and Hartford, Conn. I R (in rectangle) ; J R (in square)
[Rogers, William] *add*	....	Wm ROGERS (in rectangle)
Russell, Daniel	c. 1750	Newport, R. I. D R (in a bell)
[Sadd, Harvey] *add*	....	H. SADD (in rectangle)
Sargeant, E.	1761–1843	Mansfield and Hartford, Conn. E. SARGEANT and HARTFORD (in separate rectangles)
[Sargeant, Jacob] *add*	....	J. SARGEANT and HARTFORD (in separate rectangles)
Sargeant, T.	c. 1810	Connecticut. T. SARGEANT (in rectangle)
Shaw, John A.	w. 1802	Newport, R. I. I·A· SHAW (crude, in scalloped rectangle)

[Shethan, Samuel] *add*	....	New Haven, Conn.
[Shipman, Nathaniel] *add*	....	N S (shaded, in rectangle)
Sibley, Clark	1778–1808	New Haven, Conn.
Silliwan, Hezekiah	b. 1738	New Haven, Conn.
Spencer, George	1787–1878	Essex, Conn.
Spencer, James	w. 1793	Hartford, Conn.
[Stanton, Daniel] *add*	....	D. Stanton (Roman, in rectangle)
[Stanton, Zebulon] *add*	....	Z S (in rectangle, with emblem)
Starr, Jasper	1709–1792	New London, Conn.
Stiles, Benjamin	c. 1825	Woodbury, Conn.
[Stillman, Barton] *add*	1767–1858	....
Stillman, E.	c. 1800–1820	Stonington (?) Conn. E. Stillman (Roman, in rectangle)
Taylor, Najah	w. 1793	Danbury, Conn.
[Terry, Geer] *add*	....	G. TERRY (Roman, in rectangle) ; TERRY (Roman, in rectangle)
[Tiley, James] *add*	....	I . TILEY (shaded, Roman, in rectangle) ; Tiley (shaded, Roman, in rectangle)
Tisdale, B. H.	c. 1825	Newport, R. I. Name and place in capitals, in rectangles
[Trott, John Proctor] *add*	....	J. P. T. (capitals, script, in oval) ; J. P. T.	& Son (Roman, in halved rectangle)
[Trott, Jonathan] *add*	....	I. TROTT (Roman, in rectangle)
[Trott, Jonathan, Jr.] *add*	....	I . T (?) (in rectangle)
[Trott & Cleveland] *add*	....	T & C (in rectangle)
Tuttle, William	1800–1849	New Haven and Suffield, Conn.
Veazia, Samuel & Jos.	c. 1820	Providence, R. I.
Vernon, Daniel	b. 1716	Newport, R. I.
[Vinton, David] *add*	....	D . V (?) (in rectangle)
Waite, John	....	Kingston, R. I. I. WAITE (in rectangle)
Waite, Jonathan	1730–1822	Wickford, R. ".
Ward, Ambrose	1735–1808	New Haven, Conn.
[Ward, Billions] *add*	....	B W (crude, in oval, one end engrailed) ; B W (crude, in oval)
[Ward, James] *add*	....	J. WARD (in rectangle) ; WARD, HARTFORD (incised)
Ward, John	w. 1805	Middletown, Conn.
Ward, Macock	b. 1705	Wallingford, Conn.
Ward, Timothy	1742–1768	Middletown, Conn.
Ward, William	1678–1767	Wallingford, Conn.

Ward, William	1705–1761	Guilford, Conn. W. WARD (in rectangle); W. W. (in rectangle); W. Ward (script, in rectangle)
[Ward & Bartholomew] *add*	....	WARD & BARTHOLOMEW HARTFORD (in rectangles); W & B HARTFORD (in rectangles); WARD & BARTHOLOMEW. HARTFORD (in the rectangle)
Webster, H. L.	w. 1831–1841	Providence, R. I.
Welles, Andrew	1783–1860	Hebron, Conn. (afterwards in Boston)
[Welles, George] *add*	....	WELLES BOSTON (in separate rectangles)
Wells, William	1766–1828	Hartford, Conn.
[Wheaton, Calvin] *add*	....	C WHEATON (in rectangle)
White, Peregrine	1747–1834	Woodstock, Conn.
White, Peter	1718–1803	Norwalk, Conn.
Wilson, S. N.	c. 1800	Connecticut. S. N. WILSON (in rectangle)
[Woodward, Antipas] *add*	....	Woodward (Roman, in rectangle); A W (in rectangle)
Young, Levi	w. 1827	Bridgeport, Conn.

OTHER PLACES:

Abbott, J.	....	Portsmouth, N. H. Name, capitals, in rectangle
Ackley, E.	c. 1800	E. ACKLEY (shaded, Roman, in rectangle)
[Adams, J.] *correction* *add*	c. 1800	Alexandria, Va. J. Adam (script, in shaped rectangle; spread eagle in circle, in addition); J A (script capitals in monogram, in rectangle)
Adam, L.	d. 1731	L A (shaded, Roman, in shield, pellet beneath)
Adriance, E.	c. 1820	St. Louis, Mo. E. ADRIANCE—ST. LOUIS (small, shaded, in separate rectangles)
Aiken, George,	c. 1815	Baltimore, M. G. Aiken (script, in rectangle)
Alcock & Allen	c. 1810	Name, capitals, in rectangle
Alexander, Philip	....	Name large, incised, block letters
Anwyl, Kenrick	b. 1748 w. 1775	Maryland
Arms, T. N.	w. 1849	Albany, N. Y.
Bailey, Edward	w. 1774	Maryland

Bailey, E. E. & S. C.	c. 1825	Portland, Me. E E & S C BAILEY (in rectangle)
Bailey, R. H.	c. 1830	Woodstock, Vt. R. H. BAILEY WOODSTOCK (in separate rectangles)
Bailey & Co., E. L.	c. 1800	Claremont, N. H. Name in Roman letters
[Barry, Standish] *add*	....	BARRY (shaded, Roman, in shaped rectangle)
Battels, A. T.	w. 1847	Utica, N. Y.
[Becker, Philip] *add*	....	P B (in rectangle)
Billings, Andrew	1743–1808	A. Billings (in rectangle; pseudo hall-marks)
Blakeslee, C.	c. 1820	Vermont (?). Name, capitals, in rectangle; Pure Coin, in separate rectangle
[Boehme, Charles L.] *add*	....	C. Boehme (script, in cartouche, with spread eagle)
Boyd & Hugh	w. 1830	Albany, N. Y.
Boyd & Mulford	w. 1840	Albany, N. Y.
Brewer, S. D.	w. 1834	Troy, N. Y.
Brown, William	w. 1849	Albany, N. Y.
Burnett, Charles A.	w. 1800	Georgetown, D. C. C · A · BURNETT (in rectangle)
Butler, John	w. 1763	Falmouth (Portland), Me.
Calder & Co.	w. 1830	Troy, N. Y.
Cameron, Alexander	w. 1813	Albany, N. Y.
Campbell, R. & A.	w. 1850	Baltimore, Md.
Canfield Bros. & Co.	w. 1850	Baltimore, Md.
Canfield, Samuel (v. Conn.)	w. 1780–1807	Lansingburg and Scanticoke, N. Y. CANFIELD (in long oval)
Carrol, James	w. 1834	Albany, N. Y.
Carson, David	w. 1849	Albany, N. Y.
Chalmers, L.	w. 1780	Annapolis, Md.
Chapman, Henry	b. 1744 w. 1774	Carolina
Clark, L. & H.	....	Portsmouth, N. H. I · & H · CLARK (in rectangle)
Clark, Joseph	w. 1800	Portsmouth, N. H.
[Coleman, Nathaniel] *add*	....	N. COLEMAN (in rectangle)
Colwell & Lawrence	w. 1850	Albany, N. Y.
Cook, J.	c. 1820	Portland, Me. (?). J. COOK (in rectangle)
Copp, Nathaniel P.	w. 1834	Troy, N. Y.
Crew, J. T.	w. 1849	Albany, N. Y.
Cutler, J. N.	w. 1849	Albany, N. Y.
Dabrall, Willson	b. 1749 w. 1774	The Carolinas
DeRemier & Mead	w. 1831	Ithaca, N. Y.
Durand, Cyrus	1787–1868	Newark, N. J.
Ewan, J.	c. 1800	Charleston, S. C. J. EWAN (in scalloped rectangle).

[Farley, Charles] v.
Ipswich, Mass., *add*   ....   C. FARLEY (in rectangle, spread eagle in oval at each end; also the same without initial)

Fellows & Green   c. 1825   Maine (?). FELLOWS & GREEN (in rectangle)

Felt, J. S.   c. 1825   Portland, Me. J. S. FELT (in rectangle)

Finch, Hiram   w. 1840   Albany, N. Y.

Finlayson, Henry   w. 1770   Savannah, Ga. (?)

Fireng, J. P.   c. 1830   Burlington, N. J.

Fisher, T.   c. 1765   Baltimore, Md. (?). *T. Fisher* (italics, in horizontal wedge)

Forrest, Alexander   w. 1802   Baltimore, Md.

Fryer, John W.   w. 1813   Albany, N. Y.

Gadley & Johnson   c. 1849   Albany, N. Y.

[Gerrish, Timothy] *add*   ....   T. Gerrish (script, in rectangle); GERRISH (in engrailed rectangle); T G (?) (in rectangle)

Getz, Peter
Lancaster, Pa.   c. 1790   P. Getz (in rectangle)

Gilman, Benj. Clark   1763–1835   Exeter, N H. B C G (in rectangle)

Gilman, John Ward   1771–1823   Exeter, N. H. I. W. G. (incised)

Given, A.   w. 1849   Albany, N. Y

Gray, Charles   b. 1749 w. 1774   Maryland

Gray, Robert   d. 1850   Portsmouth, N. H. ROBT GRAY (small, in rectangle with fine scallops); R. Gray (in rectangle)

Hall, Green   d. 1863   Albany, N. Y.

Hall & Hewson   w. 1819   Albany, N. Y.

Hall, Hewson & Brewer   w. 1845   Albany, N. Y.

Hall, Hewson & Co.   w. 1836   Albany, N. Y.

Hall, Hewson &
Merrifield   w. 1840   Albany, N. Y.

Hardy, Stephen   1781–1843   Portmouth, N. H. HARDY (in long octagon); HARDY (in rectangle)

Harris & Wilcox   w. 1844   Troy, N. Y.

Hascy, Alexander   w. 1849   Albany, N. Y.

Hascy, Nelson   w. 1849   Albany, N. Y.

Hayden & Gregg   w. 1832–1840   Charleston, S. C.

Hayes & Cotton   w. 1831   Newark, N. J.

Henghan, John   w. 1772   Schenectady, N. Y.

[Holland, Littleton] *add*   ....   HOLLAND (small, in rectangle; pseudo hall-marks)

Hood & Tobey   w. 1849   Albany, N. Y.

Howe, Otis (v. Boston)   1788–1825   Portsmouth, N. H.

Hoyt, George B.	c. 1830	Albany or Troy, N. Y. GEO. B. HOYT, and pseudo hall-marks
Hughes, Henry	b. 1756 w. 1774	Maryland
Hutton, George	w. 1796	Albany, N. Y.
[Hutton, Isaac] add	....	HUTTON ALBANY (in rectangle, horizontally halved)
Johnson, C.	w. 1825	Albany, N. Y. Name in rectangle; pseudo hall-marks
Johnson & Godley	w. 1847	Albany, N. Y.
Johnson & Reat	c. 1810	Portland, Me. (?). JOHNSON & REAT (in shaped rectangle, with eagle)
[Kirk, Samuel] add	....	S. KIRK (in scalloped rectangle); S. KIRK (in rectangle); S. K (in rectangle); KIRK (capitals incised)
Kirk & Smith	w. 1818	Baltimore, Md.
Lane, Aaron	w. 1780	Elizabethtown, N. J. A. L (?) (in cartouche)
Lansing, John G.	w. 1780	Albany, N. Y. I · L (in half oval)
Leach & Bradley	w. 1832	Utica, N. Y.
[Lewin, Gabriel] add	....	G L (in rectangle)
Long, Robert	b. 1753 w. 1774	Maryland
Lowell & Senter	c. 1830	Portland, Me. Name, capitals, incised
Lynch, John	w. 1804	Baltimore, Md.
Marsh, B.	c. 1850	Albany, N. Y. Name, place, incised capitals, pseudo hall-marks
Massi, Seraphim	w. 1832	Washington, D. C.
McDougall, Wm.	c. 1825	Meredith, N. H. WM. McDOUGALL (in rectangle)
McHarg, Alexander	w. 1849	Albany, N. Y.
Mead, Adriance & Co.	w. 1832	Ithaca, N. Y.
Mead & Adriance	c. 1820	St. Louis, Mo. MEAD & ADRIANCE ST. LOUIS (in separate rectangles, with pseudo hall-marks)
Merrifield, Thomas V. F.	w. 1840	Albany, N. Y.
Mix, Visscher	w. 1849	Albany, N. Y.
Mood, I.	c. 1800	Charleston, S. C. (?). I MOOD (in two separate rectangles)
Morris, James	b. 1754 w. 1775	Maryland
[Moulton, Enoch] add	....	E. MOULTON (in serrated rectangle)
Mulford & Wendell	w. 1842	Albany, N. Y.
Myer or Meyer	....	Norfolk, Va.
Nichols	c. 1840	Albany, N. Y. (?). Name incised, pseudo hall-marks
Nuttall, Joseph	b. 1738 w. 1774	Maryland

Parry, Martin	1756–1802	Kittery, Me. and Portsmouth, N. H. PARRY (small, in rectangle)
Pitman, I,	c. 1785	Maryland (?). I. Pitman (script, in cartouche)
[Poncet, Lewis] *add*	w. 1804	....
Poole, Henry	b. 1754 w. 1775	Maryland
Price, John	w. 1764	Lancaster, Pa.
Reeves, Enos	d. 1807	Charleston, S. C. REEVES or Reeve (in rectangle)
Rice, Joseph T.	w. 1813	Albany, N. Y.
[Roe, W.] *add*	....	W. ROE (shaded, Roman, in rectangle; indented ends)
[Sadtler, Philip] *add*	....	P. Sadtler (Roman, in rectangle)
[Shepherd, Robert] *add*	....	SHEPHERD (incised)
Shepherd & Boyd	w. 1810	Albany, N. Y. SHEPHERD & BOYD (in rectangle); S & B (in rectangle)
Shropshire, Robert	b. 1748 w. 1774	Maryland
[Simes, Wm.] *add*	....	W · SIMES (large, shaded, in rectangle); W · S (shaded, in rectangle, pellet between)
Simpson & Beckel	w. 1849	Albany, N. Y.
Skaats, Bartholomew	1784	Freeman, N. Y.
Smith, David	b. 1751 w. 1774	Virginia
Storrs, N.	c. 1800	Utica, N. Y. (?). N. STORRS (large, shaded, in rectangle)
Storrs & Cooley	w. 1832	Utica, N. Y.
Strong, John	b. 1749 w. 1774	Maryland
Templeman, John	b. 1746 w. 1774	Carolina
[Ten Eyck, John] *add*	....	I E (crude, monogram, in square)
Trezvant, Daniel	w. 1768	Charleston, S. C.
Vernon, Nathaniel	1777–1843	Charleston, S. C. N. VERNON (in rectangle); N V (in rectangle)
Walraven	w. 1796	Baltimore, Md. Name, in script
Warner, Andrew E., Jr.	w. 1837	Baltimore, Md. [For mark v. Andrew E. Warner].
Waterman, George	w. 1849	Albany, N. Y.
Webb, George W.	w. 1850	Baltimore, Md.
Webb, James	w. 1817	Baltimore, Md.
Whetcroft, William	w. 1766	Annapolis, Md.
Whittemore, William	1710–1770	Portsmouth, N. H. Whittemore (italics, in rectangle)
Whittlesey	c. 1808	Vincennes, Ind.
Woodcock, Bancroft Wilmington, Del.	1754–1772	B. Woodcock (Roman, in shaped rectangle)

Above. RUG WITH PATTERN ADAPTED FROM LATE EIGHTEENTH
CENTURY FRENCH FABRICS

Below. HOOKED RUG OF EARLY NINETEENTH CENTURY, SHEWING
LATE NATURALISTIC TENDENCY

Courtesy of Messrs. Lord & Taylor

NEEDLEWORK CARPET, WROUGHT IN WOOLLEN YARN ON CANVAS GROUND
Courtesy of the Metropolitan Museum

"DRAFT" BOOK OF JOHN LANDES, WITH PATTERNS FOR COVERLETS
Frishmuth Collection, Pennsylvania Museum and School of Industrial Art

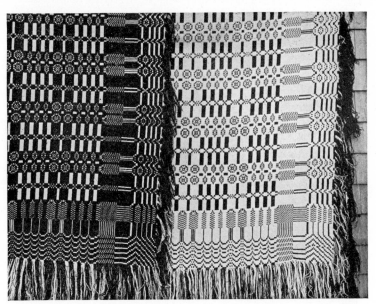

HANDWOVEN BLUE AND WHITE COVERLETS, EIGHTEENTH CENTURY
Courtesy of John C. Nippes, Esq., Haddonfield, New Jersey

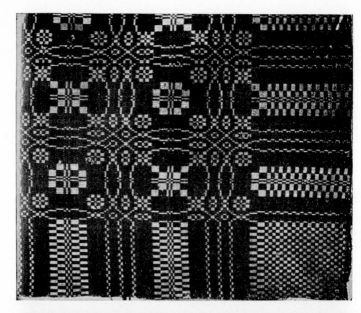

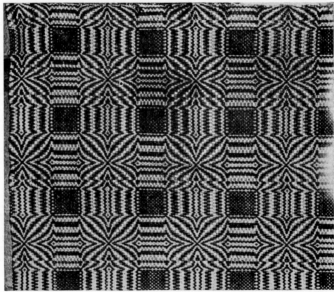

BLUE AND WHITE HANDWOVEN COVERLETS, EIGHTEENTH
CENTURY
Frishmuth Collection, Pennsylvania Museum and School of Industrial Art

HOOKED RUGS AND OTHER
FLOOR COVERINGS

IN READING early inventories of household effects the greatest care must be exercised in interpreting references to *rugs* and *carpets* for both terms were often used to designate covers for tables and settees as well as floor coverings. Nevertheless, certain of these entries unmistakably referred to floor coverings and can be accepted as such without reserve, especially when other rugs and carpets for tables and settees are expressly mentioned amongst the furnishings of the same room.

Long before the end of the seventeenth century, floor coverings of this description formed a regular part of the household equipment of colonists in comfortable circumstances, although even then they were none too large or plentiful. They were not ignored nor treated casually and were quite worth specific mention in the lists of household chattels. In the inventory of the goods of Captain George Corwin, who died in Salem in 1685, we find listed in the furnishings of the "Old Hall," "4 turky worke chaires with Backs, 1£, 12s . . . 2 Tables, 20s. . . . 1 Carpet, 15s; in the Red Chamber, 1 Red carpet, 10s; in the Glase Chamber, 1 red Ruge, 8s. and 1 linsy carpet, 10s; in the Hall Chamber, 2 Ruges, 12s; in the Hall, 1 Turky worke Carpet, 1£, 5s. and 1 old small Turky worke Carpet, 3s; in the Maides Chamber, 1 Rat eaten Carpet, 5s; and, in the Kitchen Chamber, 1 worsted Stript Ruge, 3£ and 1 Red Ruge, 10s." These entries all occur in company with other entries of rugs and carpets specified for table use or as covers for seat-ing furniture so that there can be little or no question of their reference to floor coverings. Those of doubtful interpretation have been omitted. In comparing the values attached to the rugs and carpets with the values of other important and handsome pieces of furniture, it is interesting to note that high value was set upon the floor coverings. Other inventories of the period tell precisely the same tale and shew the same store set by floor coverings.

The rugs and **carpets** (the latter rarely more than large rugs) that come within our purview were *textiles* only in the coarse canvas or sacking foundation or body upon which the decorative patterns were afterwards wrought in vari-coloured woollen yarns or rags cut into strips, the finished product being a nap of chenille-like effect. Choice of colour and design lay altogether within the discretion of the individual worker.

Of the several sorts of early American floor covering, the hooked rug was the most numerous and the most popular. For the sake of clearness we may make three classifications of American home-made rugs and carpets—(1) *hooked,* (2) *needlework* or "embroidered," and (3) *rag-woven*.

The *needlework* or "embroidered" rugs and carpets will be dealt with further on. The *rag-woven* rugs and carpets possessed little decorative value beyond the prismatic-coloured stripes often woven into them, so that they need not detain us. We may, therefore, address ourselves directly to the *hooked* rugs.

HOOKED RUGS

All rugs made by the "hook and pull through" process are to be ranked in the category of hooked rugs,

no matter whether the material, hooked and pulled
through the canvas ground into loops, be woollen yarn
or rags cut into strips and rolled. Both sorts of materials were used, sometimes separately, sometimes in
conjunction. Care must be taken not to confuse hooked
rugs in which the pattern is made by vari-coloured
woollen yarns with the needlework rugs wrought likewise with woollen yarns of different colours. The
process of their making was altogether different.

The process of hooked-rug making was as follows:
Canvas, hempen sacking or burlap was first stretched
tightly on a wooden frame. The design or pattern to
be executed was next traced or drawn upon this foundation. Then, a wooden-handled steel needle or hook,
whose end resembled the end of a crochet needle, was
inserted downward from above through the meshes of
the canvas or burlap. With this hook the pieces of
woollen yarn or strips of rag were caught and drawn
through the meshes of the canvas from the under side
to the upper, where they were pulled up evenly into
loops. These loops had to be in even rows and stand up
evenly in height from the canvas foundation.

The loops were one quarter to one half inch in length
or height if their tops were afterward to be clipped in
order to give a chenille-like effect to the surface of the
rug. If they were to be left unclipped, they were sometimes a little less in height. These loops had to be of
uniform size and thickness.

When woollen rags were used, the strips were usually one quarter to one half inch wide and the strips
were often rolled. Cotton strips could be three quarters
of an inch to an inch wide as they were of less bulk. The
ends of these strips were not sewn together as they

were for making woven-rag carpets. Woollen yarn was used in exactly the same way as the rags that had been cut or torn into thin strips.

In many rugs both rags and yarns were used in conjunction, the yarns being employed for the finer details of the pattern. Other rugs, executed wholly in yarn, had the loops in different parts of the design of different lengths in order to produce what may be called "raised work." Generally in "raised work" some of the loops were clipped and some were left unclipped. By means of "raised work," looped of graded lengths, and clipping or leaving the loops unclipped, in the case of either yarns or rags, a wide variety of textures was possible. The unclipped rugs were usually considered capable of standing harder wear than those that were clipped.

Hooked rugs were not an invention peculiar to the American Colonies, as is sometimes stated. The art of making them was a part of the handicraft heritage brought by the Colonists from England, where they had been made before either the Southern or New England settlements were established. The great development of hooked rug making, however, is to be credited to New England, although the practice was not confined to that region. Hooked rugs were made in Canada, in the Middle Colonies and in the South. They were not as numerous in the Middle Colonies, where rag-woven rugs and braided rugs enjoyed more vogue than in New England, and they were still less numerous in the South. In New England, the making of hooked rugs was often the winter's evening occupation in farmhouses and great diversity of execution was developed.

Hooked rugs were made virtually from the beginning of colonisation, continued to be made in numbers until well into the Victorian era, and the craft has now been extensively revived. Indeed, it never wholly died out.

Although the manual process never varied, the manner of expression in design and colour manifested characteristic phases coincident with the advent of fresh influences from the realm of contemporary decoration overseas.

In the earliest period the colours were not generally of great diversity, nor very brilliant, and the patterns were simple and chiefly geometrical—bands, squares, circles, octagons and sundry variations that could easily be made from a geometrical base or "tile" forms. The next development of pattern disclosed little conventional flowers and sprigs set within the circles, squares or octagons. Here the colour element became more varied.

By the middle of the eighteenth century, although the earlier fashions persisted to some extent, we find scrolls, leaves, flowers and other naturalistic features in high favour. In some of the rugs it is easily possible to trace the inspiration to contemporary fabrics—rugs, Aubusson carpets and upholstery materials—of Louis XV design or to the ribbon and medallion patterns of Louis XVI style. The colouring was brilliant and varied in many cases.

In the early nineteenth century, animals and birds became favourite *motifs,* surrounded by scrolls and foliage or reposing, perhaps, on a less elaborate background. The Victorian era brought a multitude of mottoes and sentimental legends. Other subjects, such as ships, anchors and various things connected with seafaring life were to be found originating near seaports, and besides these, there were often patriotic and historical subjects.

NEEDLEWORK RUGS

The needlework rugs, executed wholly in woollen yarns, were always the product of some sort of stitchery done by a needle in the hands of the executant and not by means of the hook and the "hook and pull through" method. The Turkey work rugs belong in this category. *Gros Point* and *petit point* stitchery played their parts in making these embroidered rugs, just as in England, and, in some cases, rugs large enough to be styled carpets were wrought in this manner. The patterns were such as were adapted to working with a needle.